Woman Battering in the United States

DATE DUE

Woman Battering in the United States
Till Death Do Us Part

Helen M. Eigenberg
University of Tennessee at Chattanooga

WAVELAND
PRESS, INC.
Long Grove, Illinois

For information about this book, contact:
Waveland Press, Inc.
4180 IL Route 83, Suite 101
Long Grove, IL 60047-9580
(847) 634-0081
info@waveland.com
www.waveland.com

Cover: *The Scream*, Edvard Munch

Copyright © 2001 by Waveland Press, Inc.

10-digit ISBN 1-57766-169-9
13-digit ISBN 978-1-57766-169-6

Printed in the United States of America

9 8 7 6 5 4 3

Dedicated to Don and Joan

ACKNOWLEDGMENTS

This book is a combination of original work and previously published articles. Each section begins with an overview that frames the issues and reviews major debates in the literature. These original chapters create the narrative of the book. Each section includes articles selected to compliment and elaborate on the issues introduced in the overviews. These readings serve several purposes. First, they allow the reader to hear a different voice—another reality if you will. Second, they allow the reader to examine other material to evaluate the strength of the narrative. Third, they discuss some issues in more depth than is provided in the introductory chapters. The combination of original text and selected articles allows the reader to examine the social construction of battering within a detailed context for the analysis. While the book is written primarily for the undergraduate audience, I believe that the central issues reviewed are sufficiently complex to make it appropriate for graduate courses as well.

This book has come to fruition in the midst of some very difficult experiences in my life, and it would never have been finished without the support of so many friends and colleagues to whom I owe so much. I would like to thank all of my students, past and present, whose probing questions taught me how to frame these issues. I am forever indebted to my former colleagues at Old Dominion University for providing a safe place for a feminist scholar to pursue areas of interest without fear of reprisal. I thank those individuals at Eastern Kentucky University who had the courage to tell the truth under difficult circumstances. I am grateful to work with wonderful colleagues and staff at The University of Tennessee at Chattanooga. They have been supportive of me and have encouraged me to finish this book. I especially want to thank Dean Galan Janeksela for allowing me to free up some time from my administrative duties to finish the project. I am grateful to Drs. Munn, Sloan, Kramer, Johnson, Lovett, and Wilson, Celeste McGrath and the hoards of wonderful medical personnel I have encountered in the past two years who have made it possible for me to be among the many survivors living with cancer. I am forever indebted to Susan Sears who is not only an outstanding attorney but a great friend. I thank all the members of the American Society of Criminology's Division on Women and Crime where I have found a place to network and share experiences with like minds. I would like to thank many other friends who have stood beside me always, but I have certainly needed them more than ever in the past few years; these include Agnes Baro, Laura Smith, Gloria Lessan, Jana and Aaron Kappeler, Debbie Harrod Owens (and the entire Harrod clan), A. Alda, Nick Parsons, Annie Schwendeman, and Jo Belknap. My gratitude is forever yours. I especially want to thank Victor Kappeler for being a good friend and for challenging me to think through things from another perspective. I also am grateful to him for introducing me to Carol and Neil Rowe, who have been wonderful to work with and the most patient folks on Earth. I also owe a special debt to Carol for her suggestions, which always improved the quality of the manuscript. I would like to thank my parents, Don and Joan Eigenberg, for their unconditional love and support. I do not know what I would have done without their assistance. Words cannot describe my feelings of gratitude. Finally, I would like to thank all the unnamed people who fight discrimination and prejudice on a daily basis and find ways to survive and even thrive despite tremendous obstacles. It is my hope that my niece and nephew, Melissa and Tyler Eigenberg, may someday live in a world where women are free from violence and where both men and women are able to realize their potential regardless of gender role expectations.

CONTENTS

CHAPTER ONE

OVERVIEW

The United States continues to arrest and imprison more of its citizens than almost any other nation. Fear of crime, especially among women, remains high despite declining crime rates. Many people are afraid to walk the streets at night or to leave the well-guarded fortresses they have built. In contrast to the national obsession with violent, random crime committed by strangers, the reality is that it occurs infrequently. When this type of victimization does occur, it is most often experienced by men. In contrast, women are more likely to be victimized by men they know—men who often profess to love the very intimates they victimize. Thus, women's experiences of victimization are virtually absent even from the very narrow, but quite popular, focus on street crime.

While criminologists often note that the emphasis on predatory street crime serves those in power by ignoring and/or minimizing corporate and white-collar crime, they less often note that our understanding of crime is profoundly affected by gender and that the concentration on street crime helps maintain a power system based on gender. Battering, like other types of violence against women, is regularly ignored when discussing crime, both in terms of the professional and academic treatment of the subject and in the arena of everyday discourse. Battering rarely is defined and/or treated as serious, violent crime because crime is socially constructed in ways that minimize and trivialize women's victimization. It is essential that male violence against women, especially intimates, be ignored because patriarchal social structures effectively use violence against women as an important means of social control.

This book concentrates on one specific type of violence against women—battering—to demonstrate how society minimizes violence by intimates in favor of definitions of crime that concentrate on violent crime committed by strangers. It asks you to think about how social definitions of crime might change if the magnitude and seriousness of woman battering were addressed. It asks you to think about how public policies might be different if violence by intimates were viewed as seriously as violence by strangers and points to the irony of trivializing

1

harm done to us by those we know and love. It examines how the conceptualization of gender and crime are related to the understanding of battering as a social problem rather than a private, family matter.

This book contends that woman battering is a pattern of coercive control whereby men use physical, sexual, and/or emotional abuse to exercise control over women. It asserts that woman battering has historically been legitimized. Society has provided domain assumptions about women, gender, and the nature of the family that allow for and even encourage violence against women in the home. Violence in the family is tolerated and has been viewed as a private matter rather than as a crime. Victims have been blamed for their victimization, and violence is trivialized by powerful stereotypes that depict battering as minor violence (slapping or shoving) provoked by nagging wives. The law and official agents of social control rarely have addressed the problem. The silence surrounding women's victimization and its relationship to our understanding of crime is not a matter of mere coincidence. A broader understanding of women's experiences of crime and victimization would require a re-definition of both the concept of crime and an acknowledgment that one of society's most sacred institutions is less than perfect. The "family" is a very dangerous place for women.

This book has three specific objectives. First, it demonstrates how a feminist, social constructionist theoretical perspective on woman battering differs from other types of perspectives. Second, it discusses the ways in which woman battering serves as a means of social control. Third, it examines the ways in which society continues to minimize the extent and magnitude of woman battering in the United States. The three objectives combined ask you to think about how definitions of crime are impacted by the invisibility and marginalization of women's victimization, which in turn distorts our understanding of crime—especially violent crime—and public policies toward it.

THEORETICAL PERSPECTIVE

This book uses a feminist perspective to examine the social construction of woman battering. A review of the fundamental concepts associated with this perspective is presented below.

Feminist Perspective

It is somewhat of a misnomer to talk of "feminism" as if it were a monolithic approach, and this statement also is true of feminist criminology (Daly & Chesney-Lind, 1988; Renzetti, 1993). Instead, there are multiple feminist perspectives (socialist, Marxist, liberal, moderate, or radical) represented in the criminological literature. Any individual, male or female, can be a feminist and do feminist research. People may consider themselves feminist activists but not "do" feminist research. Scholars may conduct feminist research but may not be involved in activist politics. Professors may teach feminist scholarship, even if they do not participate in feminist research. Thus, there are many ways to be a feminist or to do feminist work (Daly & Chesney-Lind, 1988).

To say that there is great diversity in feminist perspectives does not mean that there are no commonalities. Daly and Chesney-Lind (1988) have developed five themes that are present in most feminist literature. Each of these themes will be discussed in some detail.

- *Proposition One: Gender is not a natural fact but a complex social, historical, and cultural product; it is related to, but not simply derived from, biological sex difference and reproductive capacities.*

The reading by Lorber does an outstanding job of outlining this point. As she notes, feminist scholarship assumes that gender and gender distinctions are primarily a product of socialization and rarely are the product of biological differences. Behavior is exhibited more often by men than women or vice versa because each gender is taught to behave differently depending on the socially created categories called male and female. In contrast to this approach, most individuals never stop to question whether biology is destiny or if biological differences cause differences in behavior among men and women.

While there are some biological differences in men and women, it is not easy to link gender differences with physical variations. For example, some biological differences between men and women include variation in body size, reproductive functions, and hormone production. Most men produce sperm. Most women menstruate and have the capability to gestate a fetus. However, not all individuals with a penis produce sperm, not all women menstruate, nor do women do so throughout their entire lives. Some individuals are born with both male and female genitalia. Some people born with a penis believe that they have a female identity and may even have a sex change operation. So even these rather narrow categories of male and female fail to be mutually exclusive or exhaustive.

In addition to emphasizing the idea that there are two opposite gender categories, society also tends to identify and accentuate the idea that there are many "natural" differences between the two genders. Reverberations from the nursery rhyme prompt us to "know" that boys are full of frogs and snails and puppy dog tails and that girls are sugar and spice and everything nice. Implicit in the message, although less often discussed, is that these differences are attributed to biological differences in the sexes. In contrast, feminist analyses emphasize the power of socialization and contend that biological variations are rather limited in number and account for less variation in social behavior than does socialization. A feminist perspective contends that men are socialized (taught) to be strong, powerful, and aggressive; women are socialized to be weak, passive, and nurturing. Men are perceived to be more independent, aggressive, calm, dominant, active, competitive, and self-confident; women are perceived as more vulnerable, passive, emotional, submissive, placid, cooperative, and insecure. Sociological, not biological, influences create these attitudes.

Children are taught what it means to be male and female. The onerous (and effective) process of gender socialization begins, literally, at birth when pink blankets are placed on girls and blue blankets on boys. Adults coo at little girls and toss boys in the air. As a result of socialization, children's play is highly gendered. Little girls play house complete with miniature ovens, brooms, and shopping carts (most of which are bright pink). They play dress-up and put on make-up; they spend hours feeding their baby dolls and dressing up Barbie for dates with Ken. Little boys may dress up GI Joe but not for a date with GI Jane. Instead, little boys play soldier and practice war games. By the time children get out of grade school, most boys know how to fight, and most girls have been on a diet.

Gender role socialization is an extraordinarily complex, ongoing process. A feminist perspective explores the ways in which the social structure and cultural expectations result in differences in behavior by men and women. For example, feminists contend that women tend to act more nurturing because they have been socialized to take care of others—to mother—since birth. Women do not have a "nurturing" gene, and there is no reason to believe that this difference is attributable to genetic make-up. However, there is a tendency in society to assume that it is somehow normal for women to be more nurturing than men. When we assume that women or men are *naturally* one thing or another, it implies that the difference is biological. Many of us never stop to question this assumption. As Lorber notes, the most powerful means of maintaining gender roles is the invisible process that renders alternatives virtually unthinkable. Feminism, however, asks us to stop and analyze these assumptions—to think about gender in a different light and to think about other alternatives.

- *Proposition Two: Gender and gender relations order social life and social institutions in fundamental ways.*

The selection by Lorber also demonstrates that gender is a central organizing influence in our culture. Societies can, and do, make a variety of choices about how they are structured and organized. A variety of characteristics can organize social relations. In our culture we make distinctions based on age, race, ethnicity, social class, sexual orientation, physical ability, and gender (to name a few). Feminism points to these distinctions and draws attention to the ways in which gender, in particular, is used to order social relations and social structures.

Language is an important reflection of social arrangements. Linguists generally agree that whenever a culture uses many words to make distinctions about a subject, that subject is quite important to the society. It is clear that English designates gender in myriad ways. It assigns gender to a variety of nonhuman phenomena including buildings, ships, cars, and hurricanes (until relatively recently). Women are specifically identified as "belonging" to men through the terms of Miss and Mrs. While Ms. was created and is increasingly used more commonly, Mr. has always identified all men and revealed nothing about marital status. Language also conveys the highly gendered nature assigned to various men's and women's roles. Aggressive businesswomen are often labeled "bitches" for exhibiting behavior that is viewed as positive—"assertive"—when demonstrated by men. When one nurtures a child, this behavior is described as "mothering" not fathering. Or fathers sometimes "babysit" their own children, while mothers raise their children and "babysit" for someone else's kids.

Language also makes women invisible through the use of the generic "he." Masculine terms and pronouns that define males in our culture are supposedly inclusive of women. However, feminine terms and pronouns do not represent all of humankind. Mankind, manmade, manpower, manhole, man-hour, man-sized, manhandled are a few examples of words that minimize the very existence of women. The generic he is not a gender-free term. For example, your mental image differs considerably if I say my brother married a policeman from the image constructed if I say my brother married a female police officer. There is a sometimes a tendency to minimize the importance of gender-free language and to criticize feminists as being overly sensitive or politically correct. However, if pronouns are truly insignificant, then one might question why there often is so much resistance toward modifying language—a process that society engages in constantly. Furthermore, if such language is inconsequential, there should be little reaction if the situation is reversed by using a generic female term. It is easy to test the power of pronouns. Simply tell people that your power comes from God and you are sure that she meant for you to do well. The reactions of others will indicate that the generic he often is assumed to be male rather than representing all persons male and female.

In addition to being made invisible, women are trivialized by language that makes women appendages to men: actress, stewardess, hostess, or waitress for example. Likewise, the widespread acceptance and use of the word girl reduces adult women to the status of children and marginalizes their status as adults. It suggests that women are immature, silly, and childlike. It is not coincidental that the term boy was used as a slur to attack the masculinity and adult status of African-American men. However, it is common and socially acceptable to refer to women as girls. While women may use this expression with one another (as a term of endearment), the larger social structure promulgates this use to reinforce stereotypes that define women as childlike and powerless.

As Lorber's article demonstrates, gender is embedded in all social interactions. Gender is a social process rather than a static characteristic. While most of us assume that gender is a given—that a person is simply male or female—we often fail to recognize the role that each of us plays in categorizing other people's gender as well as the role we play in presenting ourselves as a certain gender to others. Instead of simply *being* one gender or another, gender is something we *do*—something that individuals as social actors produce on a daily basis in all social interactions (West & Zimmerman, 1987).

Each of us do gender every day. The majority of the time, we cannot visually discriminate between men and women (as we could if viewing them naked). Instead, we assign gender to other people based on a system of clues (including clothes, make-up, hair, nails, shoes, etc.). These cues are used both to decipher other people's gender and to maintain our own gendered state of being. Each of us communicates our maleness and femaleness through a complex set of social attitudes and activities.

We often forget the role that we have played in interpreting and classifying the behavior. For example, the process of doing gender is what made the character Pat on *Saturday Night Live* work. This character's body, clothing, hairstyle, and other physical attributes made it impossible to identify a gender category. The sketches focused on putting Pat in situations where gender would be important. For example, one episode required Pat to get a haircut in a place where there were two prices, one for women and one for men. The dialogue focused on which price Pat would pay for the haircut—the stylist could not determine Pat's gender. The ways in which Pat talked, walked, and dressed made it impossible to decipher the cues and assign gender to the character. These comedy sketches were humorous because they played on the discomfort that we feel when we cannot attribute gender with confidence.

- *Proposition Three: Gender relations and constructs of masculinity and femininity are not symmetrical but are based on an organizing principle of men's superiority and social and political-economic dominance over women.*

Feminists contend that gender definitions are created and maintained in order to ensure that men have social, political, and economic power over women (Edwards, 1987; Glick & Fiske, 1999; Kokepeli & Lakey, 1995; MacKinnon, 1987, 1989). Thus, gender distinctions are used as part of a hierarchy of power, as perceived differences between men and women are used to maintain women's subordination. This type of social structure represents a patriarchal system of power. A feminist analysis points to this hierarchal system of power and examines the ways in which patriarchy affects our understanding of any social act, including battering.

We live in a culture that divides people according to false dichotomies: black and white; heterosexual and homosexual; rich and poor; male and female. Different, however, rarely means equal. Instead whiteness, maleness, heterosexuality, and wealth have been used to define the "norm." The more one deviates from this norm, the more one is viewed as "the other." For example, traits that are defined as more valuable in our society are those usually associated with masculinity: e.g., independence, assertiveness, competitiveness, confidence. Likewise, traits viewed less positively and/or as weaknesses are often identified as feminine: e.g., vulnerability, passivity, emotionalism. There is nothing inherently good or bad about any of these traits. If I have extraordinarily good news, I want someone to be emotional when I tell them. I want them to share my joy. If I am in the middle of a tense crowd, I do not want someone with me who needs to appear dominant and arrogant. I do not want to be with someone who increases the level of aggression. However, we tend to think of traits in terms of opposites, and the ones defined as male are often viewed as superior.

The process of creating and maintaining gender roles identifies women as different and unequal. To maintain the hierarchy, it is essential to accentuate gender distinctions. If the line between masculine and feminine behavior becomes too blurred, it would be impossible to keep women in an inferior social status. It is difficult to justify disparate treatment unless you can point to an alleged difference. A patriarchal culture, then, uses gender to organize society in ways that benefit men at the expense of women.

This is often perceived to be a controversial assertion. Many women, especially younger women, feel they have not been disadvantaged by being female. Most feminists assert that women are affected negatively by a social structure that is designed to work against them. The key to the disparity between the two positions is to understand the complexity and diversity of what is meant by disadvantage and discrimination. For example, a wealthy female model may have the ability to exploit society's obsession with beautiful young women, but in the middle of the night she may become just another battered woman unworthy of police protection if her husband or boyfriend beats her. She may be treated like a stupid woman incapable of understanding her car by a sexist mechanic, or she may undergo an unnecessary hysterectomy because a male-dominated medical field has socialized doctors to believe that non-childbearing women do not need their uteruses. In other words, feminism contends that no woman is totally insulated from the effects of patriarchy and sexist social structures because society is organized and structured in ways that give women unequal power.

Likewise, then, all men benefit from this same structure. Obviously not all men are sexist pigs. Such an idea would be as foolish as it is simplistic. However, all men benefit from their male privilege in our culture even if they fight daily (hourly) to end patriarchy. It is something that society gives to them whether they ask for it or not. Similarly, all whites (or those perceived as "white") benefit from racism because society affords certain benefits based on skin color.

Some contend that affirmative action has created "reverse discrimination" and point to such programs as evidence that white men are a disadvantaged minority. However, any cursory examination of the status of those in power strongly contests these assertions. Even situation comedies dismiss this argument. For example, one of the white, male characters on *Spin City* was bemoaning his status in society and asked "who is looking out for the white, heterosexual males in this society?" The African-American, gay, male character quickly responded "Congress."

Most legal, social, political, and economic power is held by economically privileged white men. The vast majority of Congress and the Senate are men. After the United States Senate confirmed the appointment of Clarence Thomas to the Supreme Court, despite accusations of sexual harassment, there was an increase in the number of women elected to Congress. This increase led journalists to dub 1992 "the year of the woman" (Dolan, 1998). When looking at the data, 47 of the 435 members of the House and 6 of the 100 Senate members were women. Obviously, the representation did not match the media's designation.

Currently, 87% of Congress and 91% of the Senate are males (Feminist Majority Foundation, 1999). Men make up 71% of lawyers and judges in the United States (Bureau of Labor Statistics, 1998). Many occupations, such as policing, continue to show very little improvement in the percentage of female employees, despite 20 to 30 years of equal employment opportunity efforts (National Center for Women in Policing, 1997). Women in the United States earn approximately two-thirds as much money as men (Rotella, 1995). Much of women's labor is undervalued; if it occurs in the home, it is unpaid. Many women now work the proverbial double shift—working outside the home for salary and returning home to do the majority of the housework and childcare duties (Rotella, 1995). Notice that the woman's salary in a heterosexual relationship is often used to "help" with the bills, while some men "help" with housework.

Men, and some women, often resist acknowledging the unequal distribution of power in our society and deny patriarchy exists or that men benefit from patriarchy. However, most men, if asked, report that their lives would be less desirable if they were women. They would have to worry about maintaining their appearance, raising children, and about being raped. In contrast, women report that they would experience more freedom, could pursue different careers or do so with less harassment, would have fewer restraints put on their sexual conduct, would do less housework, and would make more money. Conduct your own sociological experiment. Ask your friends. How many men think that their quality of life would be better if they were women? How many women think that their quality of life would be better if they were men? (Note: the question is not if they would rather be the other gender—the issue is not preference but quality of life).

- *Proposition Four: Systems of knowledge reflect men's views of the natural and social world; the production of knowledge is gendered.*

Feminism asserts that everything in society is influenced by gender and gender relations, including the production of knowledge and the way we do science. Therefore, most of what we think we know about any given subject reflects a masculine view of the world—one that too frequently ignores women and their concerns. Criminologists have offered empirical documentation of the exclusion of research on and by women. Women clearly are underrepresented as scholars in the field. While precise data are difficult to obtain, current evidence suggests that only 15 to 20% of criminologists are women (Eigenberg & Baro, 1992; Gerwerth & Bachand, 1993).

Several studies (Garrison, McClelland, Dambrot, & Casey, 1992; Wonders & Caulfield, 1993) report that 1 to 8 percent of the total pages in introductory criminal justice texts and about 4% of introductory criminology texts (Wright, 1987, 1992) discuss "women and women's issues." Furthermore, all of these studies suggest there has not been an increase in the number of textbook pages devoted to women in the past twenty years (Wright, 1987). Other research (Baro & Eigenberg, 1993) shows that women lack a significant visual presence in criminology and criminal justice texts. Only 19% of the individuals portrayed in these texts include women, and they are most often portrayed as victims—not as criminal justice professionals or criminals.

These studies indicate that women are ignored as subjects of inquiry and excluded from research studies. However, women also are excluded as the "knowers" or as those who produce knowledge. In other words, the discipline ignores women in general and feminist scholarship in particular. Feminist criminology is viewed as an "alternate" (read extra) perspective. Courses and material dealing with feminism are described as peripheral (read unnecessary). Feminist scholarship argues that this exclusion is not accidental; it occurs because the production of knowledge is gendered.

For example, published articles in refereed journals theoretically reflect new, cutting edge knowledge in a discipline. The people who hold the power to decide what gets published in most disciplines, including criminology, are white males (see Eigenberg & Baro, 1992). To publish a journal article, a paper is submitted to the editor, who sends it to two or three people who read it. These reviewers then suggest changes and advise the editor to accept or reject the paper for publication. In essence, an author must generally "please" these reviewers to get the paper published. Theoretically, this process is a blind review, meaning that the reviewers are not supposed to know who the author of the paper is, nor does the author know the identity of the reviewers. However, this system may be undermined (Nebraska Feminist Collective, 1983; Spender, 1981). The more specific and famous the ideas discussed in the article, the more likely that the reviewers know the identity of the author. This may affect decisions about publication positively or negatively since professional networks are often very small within a discipline. Furthermore, editors may select reviewers who are predisposed to recommend against certain perspectives—such as feminist scholarship. Journal editors may use the process to discourage certain perspectives by refusing to publish these papers and by labeling these works as peripheral, unscientific, or biased.

Bowker (Bowker, Arbitell, & McFerron, 1988) has documented an interesting case of bias in the peer review process. A feminist article that he wrote on child abuse was submitted to a journal in early 1985. The editor informed Bowker that the two reviewers had "very divergent opinions" (p. 172). After a third review, Bowker was informed that this review was negative and that the article had been rejected. However, "the editor (or his secretary, most probably) slipped and enclosed, by mistake, a copy of the real third review and an illegitimate, secret fourth review" (p. 172). The correspondence showed that the third review had recommended publication. The editor, apparently predisposed against publication, then sent the paper out for a fourth review and got the intended result: a recommendation against publication. Bowker has published in several fields and reports that 54% of his feminist papers are published compared to 85% of his non-feminist papers. He concludes that there are many academicians "in the world of scholarship whose professionalism is insufficient to keep their anti-feminist attitudes in check" (p. 173).

Feminists have elaborated on the many ways in which women and their concerns have been ignored in the pursuit of "normal" science. Even more controversially they assert that all social interactions, including the process of doing science, is affected by gender and gender relations (Harding, 1986; Keller, 1983; Kitzinger, 1987; Ladner, 1987; Millman & Kanter, 1987; Nebraska Feminist Collective, 1983; Spender, 1981; Stacey & Thorn, 1985). They contend that science is *not* "value free" and note that a researcher's assumptions, beliefs, and values influence her/his work. These assertions challenge both the current status of knowledge in a field and the basic assumptions of positivistic science and the scientific method.

- *Proposition Five: Women should be at the center of intellectual inquiry, not peripheral, invisible, or appendages to men.*

Feminism contends that the marginalization of women in the process of establishing knowledge must be addressed. If women were fully incorporated into the knowledge base of any discipline, much of what we accept as knowledge would be drastically altered. Criminology is no exception. Since most of the discipline was created without information on, by, or for women it is incomplete.

For example, traditional criminological theories are deficient because they have failed to include women in their studies; thus, the research cannot be generalized to explain female criminality (Daly & Chesney-Lind, 1988; Gelsthorpe & Morris, 1990; Heidensohn, 1985). Furthermore, any theory of criminality must explain why women commit so much less crime than do men. If criminological theories cannot account for the vast differences in crime rates by gender, then they cannot claim to explain criminality. Traditional theories generally ignore women or mistakenly rely on stereotypical, biological explanations of gender. They assume that crime is masculine behavior. Feminist scholars have been critical of theoretical development in criminology and argue that new theories should attend to the power of gender stratification in our society. They argue that gender socialization is central to our understanding of crime. As Gelsthorpe and Morris (1990) note: "Despite the fact that its primary subject matter is male offenders, [criminology] focuses hardly at all on men and masculinity. It deals with men without acknowledging this and hence creates theories about criminals without a conceptualization of gender. For feminists this is a key concept" (p. 3).

Gender socialization also affects our understanding of victimization. Prior to the 1970s, very little criminological literature examined how gender influenced victimization (Wright, 1987). Furthermore, the field has ignored those crimes that women most frequently experience: rape, woman battering, child sexual assault, and sexual harassment. There has been a tremendous increase in research on women and victimization; however, most of the field has remained insulated from this proliferation of knowledge. For example, of those crimes most experienced by women, rape is the one most frequently covered in current criminology and criminal justice texts. Even so, only about 1 to 3% of the pages in textbooks are devoted to rape (averaging 6-8 pages per book; Wonders & Caulfield, 1993; Wright, 1992). None of these texts discuss battering, sexual harassment, or child sexual assault in any significant way. The average mainstream criminology course ignores gender in general and violence against women in particular.

In sum, feminism challenges our understanding of crime by asking two questions. First, are gender and the effects of gender socialization examined in this study or theoretical discussion? And second, would the answer to this research question be the same if gender were included in the analysis? It also seeks to transform criminology itself through an examination of the social construction of knowledge. It asks "*whose* social reality is worthy of description and explanation, and *who* can be trusted to get it right" (Daly & Chesney-Lind, 1988, p. 500). Feminism challenges the legitimacy of the scientific method and argues that gender affects all social relationships including the creation of knowledge. It argues that the process of producing knowledge itself is sexist and helps maintain gender oppression. Feminist analysis poses serious epistemological challenges by asking individuals to question how they "know" what they think they know.

Feminist scholarship contends that women are less violent than men and more often victimized by men because gender socialization encourages male violence against women in a social structure that gives men the power to victimize women (Belknap, 1996; Bograd, 1988; Dobash & Dobash, 1979; Yllo, 1993). A feminist analysis of woman battering rejects biological explanations of battering and argues that men do not beat their loved ones because of any physiological difference or hormonal imbalance (Bograd, 1988). Science has been unable to identify any biological characteristics that account for woman battering, and most men who beat their loved ones generally don't beat others in society. If there were a biological explanation for battering, it would have to explain the context-specific nature of the violence. Why is it that batterers tend to express their abuse predominately in the home? For example, if testosterone causes men to beat their partners, one has to be able to account for the fact that testosterone does not cause most batterers to beat up people outside the confines of an intimate relationship—i.e., bosses, strangers, store clerks.

Feminist scholarship on battering looks at the ways in which gender roles are maintained and reinforced in the family and notes that the structure of the family itself is a patriarchal model (Bograd, 1988; Yllo, 1993). Thus, battering is not a private problem. It is a social problem linked to the subordination of women in the larger culture. In fact, violence against women—including woman battering—is not a breakdown of the social order; it is part and parcel of the reproduction of the social order. Violence against women supports patriarchy and is one of the building blocks of this oppressive social system.

Woman battering plays an important role in maintaining a patriarchal social structure. Men beat their wives to control them. The use of force and the threat of violence is an effective way to dominate others; it is called torture when men experience it at the hands of other men in war (NiCarthy, 1986; Pagelow, 1984). When society ignores and/or minimizes the systematic torture of large numbers of women, simply because it occurs at the hands of their loved ones, it sends a clear message to all women (beaten or not). Social tolerance of battering clearly indicates that women are not worth as much as men; they do not count.

Feminist criminologists seek to transform the discipline by addressing the invisibility of women in the field and by making the study of gender central to the study of crime. In doing so, they have challenged the social construction of crime and have pointed to myriad ways in which assumptions about gender influence our understanding of crime as a concept as well as public policies designed to address it.

Social Constructionist Approach

A feminist analysis is, by definition, a social constructionist approach because feminist scholarship contends that gender is a product of social, rather than biological, forces. In other words, most feminists discuss the social construction of gender and agree with the central propositions stated in Lorber's article. However, social constructionism also is a distinct theoretical approach in and of itself. A brief overview of this perspective also is warranted.

Like feminism, a social constructionist perspective suggests that daily events are infused with a variety of social meanings that are organized by people to make sense of their world (Berger & Luckman, 1966; Sarbin & Kitsuse, 1994). "Common knowledge" is the label given to these embedded assumptions. In other words, all social interactions produce and reflect social meanings that rarely are specifically acknowledged. These assumptions are commonly understood to represent "reality"; most people never stop to think about how or why the assumptions became accepted as common knowledge.

Examining the social construction of a social problem allows one to examine everyday events and processes in a different light by highlighting things that often are taken for granted and/or overlooked. The process of examining these assumptions, whether they are called myths (Kappeler, Blumberg, & Potter, 2000), folk constructions (Sarbin & Kitsuse, 1994), or hegemonic assumptions (Arnot, 1994) is called deconstruction. By working backward one is able to gain insight into the social processes and social structures that produce taken-for-granted assumptions about society. Deconstructing a social problem makes the embedded assumptions visible.

Schaef (1985) provides an excellent analogy to explain this idea. Think about pollution. Living in a big city, such as Denver, often means living with pollution. Residents learn to ignore it; soon they stop seeing the pollution. Occasionally, it might cause sinus irritation on a particularly bad day, but people learn to accept it as normal—or at least as normal for city life. However, if these same people travel to the mountains outside Denver, they can view the city below and the brown cloud extending almost 60 miles in either direction. It is a shocking experience to look down on that thick, brown air and to realize that it is an invisible part of normal life in the city. Deconstructing a social problem, then, is like taking that trip up the mountain—a different view allows one to examine what is taken for granted and assumed to be "normal."

According to social constructionists, all "reality" is socially created. Lily Tomlin made this point in her one-woman show on Broadway. One of her characters, Trudy the "bag lady," lives a somewhat eccentric life. For example, she chooses to wear her stockings rolled down around her ankles. While explaining her world to the audience, Trudy asks, "What is reality anyway?", and then answers, "Nothing but a collective hunch." In other words, reality is the product of collective agreement as to the truth of any given situation.

Another short story also conveys this point. Three baseball umpires are reflecting on their professional practice of calling balls and strikes. The first, a self-confident realist, says, "I call 'em the way they are." The second, who leans toward phenomenological analysis, says "I call 'em as I see 'em." The third closes the discussion with, "They ain't nothing until I call 'em" (Sarbin & Kitsuse, 1994, p. 1). The first umpire believes that there is some objective reality out there, and he/she attempts to classify the pitch accurately. The second umpire recognizes that he/she has a role in the process of defining the pitch. The third umpire, the social constructionist, notes that the action has no meaning until he/she assigns the pitch a label—ball or strike.

Like the first umpire, positivists assume there is a given reality to be discovered through scientific examination. Most of the West glorifies science and the use of the scientific method (Harding, 1986). The scientific method relies on the value neutral examination of objective, scientific facts. Scientists observe, theorize, and then attempt to predict phenomena. The process is, supposedly, the epitome of rationality and objectivity. Researchers are detached fact finders who objectively pursue truth based on the latest empirical findings. Theoretically, then, science is insulated from social influences.

Like the third umpire, social constructionists (and feminists for that matter) contend that there is no one way to see the pitch—or the world. In other words, unlike positivists who search for "truth" through empirical and scientific investigation, social constructionists challenge the idea that there is a singular, uniform, and objective reality. For example, scholars from various disciplines are committed to drastically different domain assumptions that, by definition, can never be proven. Psychologists are most apt to view the world based on the assumption that behavior is most influenced by the psychological make-up of an individual. Biologists look for differences in physiology. Sociologists examine the effects of social factors on behavior. One can argue that all of these disciplines are "right" to some degree about different factors. If we put three scholars, one from each discipline, in a room to discuss woman battering we would quickly see how science is used to argue that domain assumptions are correct. A psychologist might argue that men beat their wives because they are unable to control their anger. A biologist might attribute this behavior to testosterone. A sociologist might discuss the ways that socialization teaches men to behave aggressively. Thus, researchers use the science of their disciplines to support their positions. Discussions about the beliefs will be at cross-purposes because each scholar relies on a different truth. Different worldviews lead to different assumptions about the nature of human behavior. Biological research is not likely to convince a sociologist that the majority of behavior is biologically motivated, and biologists are not apt to concede that most disease is a product of psychological factors. There is literature to support each perspective, although science will never resolve these differences in domain assumptions.

From a social constructionist perspective, studying the process of establishing "*the truth*" is, in and of itself, a central focus of study. While positivists, like the first umpire, establish truth by determining how things "are" using science and the scientific method, social constructionists study how things came to be accepted as fact. Thus social constructionists view the use of science as part of the political battle for control over the "truth." These paradigmatic battles reflect the ways in which science is used to create and maintain a reality—a truth—that may or may not reflect the diversity of a particular phenomenon.

Social constructionists note that all reality is socially situated (Berger & Luckman, 1966; Sarbin & Kitsuse, 1994). Each of us, layperson or scholar, processes information through a variety of lenses that are affected by our life experiences. How we process information and attribute "truth" is influenced by a wide variety of characteristics such as age, ethnicity, race, sexual orientation, physical ability, class, and gender because we live in a culture that treats people differently based on these distinctions (and others). As a result of different life experiences—of being differently situated socially in our society—what we assume to be truth and knowledge varies. For example, for some African Americans the verdict in the O. J. Simpson criminal case represented "pay-back time" for a society that has too often incarcerated black men in a city where police violence toward African Americans is legendary. For many women, the case demonstrated that a man still can get away with murdering someone if that someone happens to be his wife. For the poor, the case illustrated all too clearly that "money talks." Many African-American women were torn between the verdict handed down by the largely African-American jury and feminists who noted that the case was a setback for all women. The interpretation of this case depended on one's past experiences with "reality." Instead of expanding the dialogue and allowing for a broader and more complex understanding of social interactions, the media tended to search for the "one" lesson of the case. The tendency to search for an absolute truth interfered with the ability to understand a multiplicity of truths.

For many, giving up the idea that there is some absolute truth out there is disturbing. "The task of suspending belief is not unlike the obverse task of suspending disbelief when reading fairy tales, science fiction, and other contrafactual stories" (Sarbin & Kitsuse, 1994, p. 12). It forces us to think differently. It is like trying to visualize the fourth dimension. Without an ultimate, natural, preordained truth, we must re-evaluate virtually everything we think we know. Confronting the idea that truth is not necessarily a product of scientific investigation shocks many of us to our very foundations. If one cannot rely on science, then what source of knowledge can be trusted?

I cannot assert that the "truth" discussed in this book is more pure, more scientific, more correct, more accurate than another. Everyone's truth is affected by his or her values as well as the historical, social, and political climate. My work is clearly influenced by my experiences as a white, middle-class, professional woman. It is profoundly affected by my past experiences of working with battered women in shelters and by my experiences training police officers about woman battering. It is affected by my definition of myself as a feminist scholar and advocate. It is influenced by my five years of correctional experience, where I learned much about men and masculinity in a hyper-masculine environment. It is influenced by my experience in higher education in a field that is largely dominated by men. All of these experiences and more shape my worldview of gender as well as my understanding of crime, criminality, and victimization. It is my hope that this book will make you think about woman battering and crime from a different perspective. For at its heart, the power of social construction is its ability to make epistemological challenges. By seeing things differently and asking new questions we often are able to come to new and different understandings of a phenomenon.

SOCIAL CONSTRUCTION OF WOMAN BATTERING

In order to examine the social construction of battering, take a moment and think about the image that comes to mind when you hear words like domestic violence, spouse abuse, wife battering, woman battering. Close your eyes and think about an assault between two adults who are in an intimate relationship. Visualize the events leading up to the assault and the event itself. Who is the perpetrator? Who is the victim? What is the context surrounding the assault?

It is likely that there are many similarities in the pictures each of you created. The stereotypical image of the classic battering incident frequently goes something like this. A heterosexual couple is arguing. The intensity of the argument is great, and both parties are verbally aggressive with one another. The woman often is perceived to be demanding, unreasonable, and/or "nagging." The man is provoked; he becomes frustrated and angry. He "loses" it and "slaps" or "shoves" her. Perhaps the image of the couple includes a characterization as economically poor and/or people of color.

The "pictures" we carry with us in our heads represent a set of culturally prescribed values and attitudes about woman battering; they are provided to us by the larger social structure. We share a common image because the ways that we think about battering are defined, refined, and mass produced at the cultural level. As the Martin article illustrates, these pictures are provided to us by the larger social structure.

The tendency to view the couple as engaged in an argument suggests that society is somehow willing to view violence as a natural response to interpersonal conflict, especially when that conflict occurs in the confines of the home. Culturally, violence by family members is allowed under certain circumstances. Historically, battering has been endorsed as a way for men to "discipline" and/or control their wives (as well as children; Pleck, 1987; Stedman, 1996), although violence is rarely accepted as a means to resolve conflict in other situations. We do not assume that it is "normal" for people to get angry and hit their boss in response to interpersonal conflict. We do not accept that the boss might have provoked such an assault by criticizing the employee's work performance. It is only within the family that our society allows, permits, and even encourages the use of physical force to "teach a lesson," "correct wrongdoing," or "stop some particularly irritating behavior" (Gelles & Straus, 1988). In virtually any other situation in society, physical violence is viewed as inappropriate and a criminal offense, but in the family it is accepted as "normal." This notion is exemplified in an old nursery rhyme: "A woman, a spaniel, and walnut tree, the more you beat them the better they be" (Angeli, 1954, p. 9).

The image of victims and perpetrators in this scenario also reflects important cultural assumptions about gender and gender-appropriate behavior. The tendency to identify victims as women in general, and nagging wives in particular, is influenced by the social construction of gender. The image of the "nagging wife" is very powerful and is used to define the woman as blameworthy and unsympathetic. In this scenario it is more reasonable for a man to become angry. He loses control of his temper and lashes out by "slapping" her as a way to get her to "shut up." It may be inexcusable, but it is rationalized because she has "provoked" him. The hegemonic view of battering as something that occurs when men lose control gives permission for the batterer to engage in violence, and the image of the nagging wife turns our attention toward the victim's behavior. As the selection by Martin illustrates, it shifts blame from the perpetrator to the victim and uses a powerful stereotype to hold women accountable for their own victimization.

The hegemonic view of batters as men who lose control ignores the situations in which many batterers evidence a great deal of control. For example, batterers may be calm and charming in public, reserving their violent outbursts for the home front. In addition, some batterers purposely beat women in soft tissue areas—in the stomach, thighs, and buttocks—where it is less apt to show. Doing so decreases the likelihood that friends, family members, neighbors, or others might notice the bruises. It also is less likely to produce "enough" physical damage to qualify as evidence. Some batterers purposely beat their wives in their abdomen during pregnancy, saying things like "I'll knock that baby out of you." This behavior is quite calculated and is evidence of someone in absolute control of the situation, rather than being out of control with anger.

As Martin's article states, the image of battering as minor violence—slapping and/or shoving—trivializes the seriousness of many battering incidents. These words are generally associated with minor physical altercations and minimize both the level of violence and the effects of battering. There is a tremendous difference between someone slapping your arm in jest and someone using his/her entire body weight while backhanding another in the face. The first "slap" may hardly be felt; the other may put one in the hospital or even result in brain damage if it inflicts sufficient trauma to the temple areas. Likewise, it is one thing when a person shoves another so that he or she momentarily loses his or her balance. It is quite another to be shoved into a wall or down a flight of steps. However, because these types of assaults often fail to inflict permanent physical damage, there is a tendency to dismiss them as minor. The use of the words slapping and shoving and other similar nomenclature obscures the vicious nature of the beatings that often occur in battering cases and minimizes the amount of violence committed against women by their loved ones.

Finally, the image of the couple as poor and/or people of color reflects cultural assumptions about race and class. The idea that battering is confined to a particular group of people indicates that definitions of battering are profoundly affected by racist and classist assumptions that make it easier for many of us to believe that battering is an insignificant social problem limited to "other" people. The media lavished attention on the O. J. Simpson case precisely because it captured many hegemonic assumptions about race, class, and gender.

The case provided interesting insight into the social construction of battering in the United States. Nicole Brown, like most women, never imaged that her life would end at age 35 at the hands of her ex-husband. The "fairy-tale" story of the younger homecoming queen and the former captain of the football team had a brutal ending. They had two children and a privileged life with many amenities. He had been an incredible athlete who used that fame to build a media career. He was widely admired, handsome, charismatic, and charming. While many Americans now believe O. J. Simpson is guilty, there was no such support for that attitude when the case initially broke. During the slow-speed police chase, spectators lined the streets cheering him on. During much of the pre-trial coverage, the majority of pundits and commentators pointed to his innocence. The message at that time was clear and powerful. How could he possibly have murdered his ex-wife?

The prosecution presented the following scenario of Simpson's actions on the night of the murder (Bugliosi, 1996; Darden, 1996; Lange & Van Netter, 1997; Schiller & Willwerth, 1996; Toobin, (1996). He left his house dressed in dark clothes, a ski hat, and gloves. He went to the back entrance of his ex-wife's house and got her to come outside. He hit her hard enough to knock her down and then bent over her and stabbed her four times in the neck. As she lay unconscious, he pulled her head back and slit her throat. He was so enraged that he almost severed her head from her body. When Ron Goldman arrived unexpectedly, Simpson turned on him. There were light knife marks on Goldman's neck. The prosecution surmised that Simpson held him from behind and taunted him before administering four fatal wounds: a cut that severed his jugular vein, two that punctured his ribs and lungs, and another that punctured his aorta. Both victims had defensive wounds on their hands indicating that they were conscious and fighting back during at least part of the brutal attacks.

For many, it simply was impossible to believe in the early stages of the case that O. J. Simpson could have committed this brutal and heinous crime. He was one of the most admired football players of all time: a Heisman Trophy winner with numerous records. He was the charming nice man running through airports in commercials and commenting on Monday night football games. He was "The Juice." How could he have butchered his wife and her friend while his children lay sleeping just inside the house? It was not possible. Our collective judgment could not have revered a man who could commit such a chillingly violent and brutal crime? Surely Nicole's life could not have ended at the hands of her husband. Why would he do it? According to the prosecution, the answer is all too familiar: because he is a batterer.

Friends and family members report that Nicole had been physically beaten by O. J. throughout the marriage. Pictures, diaries, and witnesses all corroborate the battering. There were two police reports and 911 calls documenting the abuse; in addition the prosecution submitted evidence of numerous incidents (most of which were never presented to the jury). During one of these police visits in 1989 a bruised and battered Nicole ran from the bushes in a bra and sweat pants repeatedly yelling to the police: "He's going to kill me." (Darden, 1996, p. 363). For this offense, Simpson was arrested, pled no contest, and was sentenced to two years probation and 120 hours of community service. He was fined $470 and ordered to pay $500 to the local women's shelter and assigned to a counseling program—most of which was completed via the telephone (Schmalleger, 1996, p. 4).

In 1990, Nicole rented a safe deposit box; she put her newly executed will and pictures of herself bruised and battered in the box (Darden, 1996, p. 364). In January of 1992 another 911 call was recorded when O. J. Simpson broke in the back door on Nicole's residence, and in February of 1992 Nicole filed for divorce (Schmalleger, 1996, p. 386). In October 1993, 911 tapes capture another violent incident (Schmalleger, 1996, p. 283). In April 1994, after several attempts at reconciliation, Nicole apparently told O. J. that it was over for good and started limiting her contact with him (Resnick, 1994). There is no evidence that she indicated that she would consider going back to him after this time. In early June, O. J. was threatening Nicole with a letter to the IRS exposing tax violations, which would supposedly require her to pay $90,000 or move out of her home (Resnick, 1994, p. 205). Just months before her death, she told her mother that O. J. was stalking her and that she was scared (Darden, 1996, p. 217). She told friends and family that he was going to kill her, and he would get away with it (Resnick, 1994). Four days before her death she allegedly called the local shelter and said she was being stalked (Toobin, 1996, p. 239). On the day of her death, she reasserted her intentions to be free from O. J. when she told him that he could not sit with her family at their daughter's recital or go to dinner afterwards to celebrate (Resnick, 1994). She died that night.

Nicole's death dramatically illustrates what feminists have long noted: that batterers are the most deadly when they feel they have lost control. As reconciliations fail, the battered woman's resolve to leave may strengthen, despite the danger. The batterer may get more and more desperate as he feels his power and control slipping away. Ironically, some pundits asserted that O. J. could not possibly have killed Nicole. He was rich, handsome, and famous and could have any woman in the world. So why kill Nicole? To those familiar with battering, the answer was simple. Perhaps he could have any *other* woman in the world, but not Nicole.

The case and social reactions to it demonstrate that there is much work to be done to educate the public about woman battering. For example, the fact that at least one juror has argued that this case had nothing to do with domestic violence illustrates that some individuals have trouble acknowledging the lethal nature of battering. And while the case has helped renew a much needed national debate on racism in the United States, gender and woman battering did not receive the same attention. Recall for example the barrage of press following the verdict: almost all of it concentrated on how the verdict reflected the country's growing racial tensions. It is important to attend to the racism in this country and the case has opened that debate. However, we also need to incorporate how sexism, racism, *and* classism influenced this case and our understanding of it.

Race issues surround the case. The notion that the defense played the "race card" is code language for discussing the cultural hegemony that surrounds race in this society. Johnny Cochran clearly called for jury nullification when he asked the jury to acquit O. J. to send a message about racism in Los Angeles. Some people find that either offensive or unethical; others might call it justice or "pay-back" time; and still others label it a clever legal strategy. Most analyses ignore the systemic role of race, like class and gender, *in all social interactions in our society*. Class arguably has been the least visible issue, despite the fact that most individuals could never afford the aggressive defense presented in this case. One expert witness alone billed the defense $100,000 for his testimony (Bugliosi, 1996). Nonetheless, there has been no massive outcry to reform the criminal justice system to ensure that all defendants have access to this type of "justice."

If we can see through the pollution, the case offers many critical lessons. It shows that woman battering is everywhere: it exists in wealthy families, not just in lower socioeconomic groups. It also illustrates that batterers often lead a double life. Their public image, that outside the family, is often very different from their private behavior. The case clearly demonstrates that battering is dangerous and often lethal. Ironically (and in contrast to the defense assertions of a frame-up), the case also demonstrates how the criminal justice system often fails to take the problem seriously, especially when the defendant is a powerful, wealthy celebrity. Most profoundly, it demonstrates that the family is a dangerous place for some women.

This book contends that crime is constructed in the United States in ways that deny and minimize women's victimization. As mentioned earlier, the tendency to conceptualize crime largely as violent street crime overemphasizes the experiences of male victims and focuses attention on crime committed by strangers. A feminist analysis of woman battering argues that battering is related to women's status in both society and the family. At its most simplistic level, men beat their wives because they can—because society allows it. Society has endorsed mores and values that have historically endorsed battering as a way to "discipline" and/or control wives/women. Violence by intimates has been tolerated, and even encouraged, in a society that continues to romanticize the image of the "ideal nuclear family." Furthermore, a social system that continues to view the beating and/or murder of a wife, girlfriend, or lover as somehow less criminal, less frightening, less deserving of sanction by the criminal justice system and less worthy of study continues to perpetuate the message that women are less valuable than men.

TREATMENT OF BATTERING
THROUGHOUT HISTORY

Although it is commonly assumed that battering was first detected in the 1960s and 1970s, Americans have discovered and re-discovered the problem at various times in history. For example, the Puritans enacted some of the first laws in the world to restrict wife beating in the 1600s (Pleck, 1987). Likewise, the temperance movement of the 1800s brought renewed interest to the problem, as did the progressive era in the late 1800s and early 1920s. Historically, woman battering has been defined as a social problem when other strong social movements existed in society. Battering reforms have occurred when social groups, especially women's movements, have pursued a variety of issues pertaining to women's equality. Reproductive freedom, divorce reform, and the ability to be financially independent are some of the issues that highlight the inequality of women and their role as defined in traditional marriages. These movements have produced social change because they lift the veil of silence and challenge the sanctity of the family. However, each time society addresses the problem, it tends to be presented as a newly discovered issue. Americans, in general, tend to approach most issues ahistorically, and battering is no exception. Ignoring the resurfacing of the same inequality allows us to hold fast to the hegemonic ideal of the nuclear family that is central to our social and economic structure. If centuries of abuse and the structure that sustains it were acknowledged, the long-standing tradition of social control would be called into question.

Historically women have generally been allotted a very narrow role in society, and this role is based on motherhood and marriage. The only legitimate option available for women, traditionally, has been that of wife and mother. Women were under tremendous pressure to marry as there were few other acceptable alternatives to ensure their social, economic, and legal survival. While men also were expected to marry, it was of secondary importance to them because their social status depended on their work outside the home (their jobs). Furthermore, women were treated as property—first belonging to their fathers and then later to their husbands, but never to themselves. The husband-wife relationship had more in common with a parent-child relationship.

From early Roman law until very recently, men had the legal power —in fact the obligation—to control their wives' behavior (Dobash & Dobash, 1979; Pleck, 1987; Stedman, 1996). Women were like children, considered to be immature and incapable of managing their own affairs. The ideology of "physical chastisement" was a predictable outgrowth of the "obligation" of men to guide those lower in the hierarchy. History is replete with formulas that describe how much physical punishment should be used and under what circumstances (Dobash & Dobash, 1979). For example, the early Romans had laws that allowed wives to be put to death by their husbands for a variety of offenses including adultery, although there were no such penalties for husbands. Furthermore, husbands were allowed to divorce their wives for a variety of reasons, but wives were prohibited from leaving their husbands under any circumstances. Many of these laws emphasized chastity and focused on controlling women's sexuality as a means for husbands to protect their property—and also to protect "property who produced other property (especially male children)" (Dobash & Dobash, 1979, p. 37).

In the 1600s both the Church and the state were used as strong agents of control to ensure that communities lived in peace and harmony. Given the physical isolation in the new colonies, it is hardly surprising that cooperation and mutual dependence were the backbone of social control. Spying on one's neighbors to discover sin and crime was encouraged. Families were not supposed to disturb the domestic tranquility of the settlement, thus both battering and child abuse were, theoretically, discouraged (Pleck, 1986). However, the power of the male dominated church courts and the ability to attribute battering to witchcraft ensured that there was little to no risk to men who battered.

The church exercised tremendous power in dealing with cases of battering and used it in ways that strengthened the patriarchal order of the family (Pleck, 1986). If abuse was detected, it was reported to the minister who would visit with the couple. Clergy would warn the couple and pray with them. They had the power to force the couple before a church court. When cases of battering were disclosed, "the wife who was beaten was considered to be almost as much at fault as her husband" who had the right to "discipline" her (Pleck, 1986, p. 21).

Women also risked being identified as witches, thus all husbands and especially batterers had a tremendous amount of social control at their disposal. A batterer could threaten to denounce his wife as a witch if she failed to obey his every demand (as promised in the wedding vows) or he could use witchcraft to explain the violence. For example, an "abusive husband testified in Connecticut that the bruises on his wife's thighs came not from the beatings he gave her, but from his wife's secret practice of witchcraft" (Pleck, 1986, p. 18). Thus women had little power to protect themselves from abusive men and few options when they were trapped in abusive marriages. Divorce was rare and most petitions did not succeed. For example, no woman was granted divorce in almost a sixty year period in the 1600s based on grounds of cruelty (Pleck, 1986, p. 23). Women's safety was seen as less important than preserving the family. Women were literally trapped.

The late 1700s were times when fundamental principles of liberty and justice were widely debated on a global scale. During this so called Age of Enlightenment, both the French and American revolutions gave voice to the cry for democracy and a focus on liberty and equality—for men. Despite Abigail Adams' urgent plea in 1777 to her husband to "remember the ladies" and to enfranchise them with the vote so that they had a voice in their destiny, the newly created democracy failed to provide legal power for women and people of color.

Most of the legal system in the newly formed United States evolved from English common law. In this system, marriage was viewed as a contract whereby two people were legally united as one, and the one with the legal power was the husband. English common law allowed husbands the power of domestic chastisement as long as it was within reasonable bounds. Common law generally adopted the "rule of thumb" where a man was permitted to assault his wife as long as the rod was no thicker than his thumb (Hart, 1996).

Courts in the United States generally allowed for the physical chastisement of wives throughout the 1700s and 1800s for three reasons (Stedman, 1996). First, they argued that it was a husband's duty to make the wife behave. Second, the private chastisement made less noise and trouble than a public trial. Third, a long line of legal precedent existed that gave husbands legal immunity from chastisement. While the first case recognizing this "right" in the United States was decided by the Supreme Court of Mississippi in 1824, the finding illustrates a line of reasoning that was several centuries old. In this case, the Court held that:

> It is true, according to the old law, the husband might give his wife moderate correction, it was thought reasonable, to intrust him, with a power, necessary to restrain the indiscretions of one, for whose conduct he was to be made responsible. . . . [However], family broils and dissensions cannot be

investigated before the tribunals of the country, without casting a shade over the character of those who are unfortunately engaged in the controversy. To screen from public reproach those who may be thus unhappily situated, let the husband be permitted to exercise the right of moderate chastisement, in cases of great emergency, and use salutary restraints in every case of misbehavior, without being subjected to vexatious prosecutions, resulting in the mutual discredit and shame of all parties concerned. (Bradley v State, 1824, p. 156).

This decision was not overturned until seventy years later (Harris v State, 1871). Almost one hundred years passed before society began to implement legal reforms that undermined a husband's right to "chastise" his wife.

From the early to mid-1800s the temperance movement brought renewed visibility to woman battering as reformers urged family members to call upon the batterers' sense of responsibility to his family (Pleck, 1987). However, when that failed, feminists began to call for divorce reform and demand that women had the right to divorce "drunkards." In doing so, they indirectly argued for women's rights, but they did so based on the evils of alcohol. Temperance advocates believed in a simplistic relationship between alcohol and battering. Alcohol was defined as the problem, thus solutions focused on temperance and prohibition. However, when some temperance advocates began to call for divorce reform, they challenged the prevailing normative structure. In doing so, they placed the safety and happiness of the woman above the preservation of the family.

Other reforms during the mid-1800s also indicated that women were gaining some power in the larger social structure. In 1848 the Seneca Falls Convention was held, and feminists publicly called for equality for women when it published the Declaration of Sentiments. It paraphrased the Declaration of Independence and demanded equality in education, employment, and the law. In 1850 and 1857, Tennessee and Georgia passed laws defining wife beating as a misdemeanor legal violation, and some states began to grant divorce on the basis of cruelty—allowing battered women to legally dissolve their marriages (Pleck, 1987). However, the success of the temperance movement made it much more common and easier to get a divorce on the basis of drunkenness. Ironically, the most common reason for divorce was desertion. Society, which had previously refused to allow battered women to divorce their husbands, now sanctioned divorce when the husband had already left.

In 1868, the first women's suffrage amendment was introduced into Congress. It was defeated. With the passage of the 14th and 15th Amendments in 1869—which gave the right to vote, in theory if not practice, to men of color— the women's movement renewed its commitment to securing the vote, but progress would be slow. The period immediately following the Civil War obscured battering as a social problem (Pleck, 1987).

The Comstock law was passed in 1873 and prohibited use of the mail to distribute sexually explicit information, including information on birth control. Many divorce reforms were repealed. Society became more conservative in response to the massive structural chaos created by the war. Given the severe financial and social upheaval, society had a vested interest in maintaining nuclear families. If society could not provide for families, it certainly had no financial resources to support single women, nor could it afford to have them in the workplace taking jobs from unemployed men.

In the late 1800s and early 1900s, Americans were forced to deal with industrialization, poverty, and immigration. One of the social problems targeted during the Progressive era was child abuse. This topic had originally been linked to heavy drinking, as had woman battering. The explanation soon shifted to immigration (Gordon, 1988; Pleck, 1987). Society was willing to acknowledge child abuse because it served the interests of the powerful by providing a rational for imposing social control. Reformers feared that without intervention children of immigrants would not learn American social values. These families would produce children who would engage in deviancy like crime. Thus the privileged class defined abuse in a way that affected only the immigrant poor, and they then devised mechanisms of social control that allowed for intervention in "those" families. While violence within families was recognized it was done in a way that supported a patriarchal, capitalistic society. Alcohol use and an unruly immigrant population were seen as the root of the problem; there were few demands to alter the nature of the family or women's role in it. Quite the contrary, a middle-class, privileged image of the family was exalted as the national ideal. However, as social workers continued to investigate reported cases of child abuse, they increasingly were confronted with cases of wife abuse (Gordon, 1988).

Women were able to gain some political, economic, and social power during the Progressive era. Reformers like Susan B. Anthony focused on reproductive freedom and attempted to educate women about birth control, even though such efforts were illegal. In 1920, women finally received the right to vote when the 19th Amendment passed. However, the accompanying backlash also helped to shift definitions so that battering soon disappeared from public awareness. The definition of family violence shifted from the physical and sexual abuse of women and children toward neglected children (Gordon, 1988). Society shifted the focus from male perpetrators of family violence to deviant and/or bad mothers. Social mechanisms were used to punish and control mothers for failing to feed their children rather than concentrating on men who abused their children and wives. This shift in the definition also allowed men to avoid financial responsibility by allowing them to abandon their wives and children to a life of abject poverty. The villain was no longer a drunken father but an incompetent, poor, single mother.

The definition of single mothers at the time was quite different from today (Gordon, 1988). They usually were married women who had been abandoned by their husbands or married women who had run away from their abusive husbands. There was great public fear over the rise of single mothers. Even though these women were often technically married, society feared the breakdown of the traditional family when women lived without a male partner. Women in these circumstances were viewed as morally suspect, and reformers made stereotypical assumptions about their lifestyles. Single mothers were vulnerable to social intervention because they were often viewed as loose and promiscuous.

Poor single mothers were trapped. Society provided little to no economic support. If women sought economic relief or love from another man, they were viewed as promiscuous. That, by definition, made them unfit mothers. If they remained on their own they often could not support their children economically. In order to work outside the home, they were often forced to leave children alone, and they often relied on money from child labor to make ends meet—either of which could be used as evidence of neglect. Failing to provide basic needs was another reason for state intervention. Furthermore, mothering was defined as biological and inherent to women's nature, thus women who neglected their kids were seen as double deviants. They violated social rules about sexuality and motherhood, but they also violated the very nature of womanhood. Shifting the focus to child neglect and framing the issues in this way protected men economically from their familial responsibilities. It also obscured the physical and sexual violence committed by men against women and children that had often created the single parent situation.

During the Depression, very little attention was given to battering, and social definitions continued to obscure violence by husbands against their wives (Pleck, 1988). As in the Civil War era, severe economic hardship and massive unemployment demanded the maintenance of a patriarchal family structure. Battering also received very little attention in the 1940s during World War II (Pleck, 1987). Many women experienced more economic independence during this time. The war required a large industrial work force, which was depleted when so many working men were enlisted in the military services. "Rosie the Riveter" stepped in to help build ships and airplanes. Under other circumstances, women would not have had the opportunity to demonstrate their skills. At the end of the war, women were thanked for their help with the "war effort" and were immediately fired. They were forced to return to lesser paying jobs or returned to the home to do their "real work." The end of World War II gave way to the 1950s idealization of motherhood and homemaking.

The idealization of women as homemakers, however, has not been equally possible for all women. While women's participation in the labor force clearly is increasing, the recent focus on this phenomenon is ahistorical and classist. Poor women and women of color have always worked outside the home to put food on the table. African-American women, in particular, often worked in the homes of middle- and upper-class, white women (Coontz, 1992). Somewhere behind Donna Reed's crisp apron and pearls was a poor woman of color on her hands and knees scrubbing the toilets. Thus, despite the tendency to define women as homemakers within the family, this ideal is and always has been reserved for only certain, privileged women.

Women of the 1960s and 1970s carried on the fight for reproductive freedom and equal rights. They advocated a wide range of legal and social reforms that would (and did) have a dramatic impact on the quality of life for women. Some feminist reformers also specifically concentrated on battering. In 1974 Erin Prizzey published *Scream Quietly or the Neighbors Will Hear* in England; Del Martin published *Battered Wives* in 1976 in the United States. Both books broke the silence and exposed woman battering as an extensive, serious, deadly social problem. They also contributed to a new social movement that focused on social services for battered women.

Grassroots feminist organizations led the fight for victim services, developing and providing services where none existed. Women literally reached out to their battered sisters and housed them in sleeping bags on living room floors, providing safe homes for women when there were none (Schechter, 1982). In 1971 the first identified shelter opened in Chiswick, England; two shelters in the United States were opened in 1972. In 1976, the National Organization for Women (NOW) established a task force on woman battering and demanded shelter funding from government sources (Schechter, 1982). That same year, Pennsylvania created the first state coalition against domestic violence, and Nebraska became the first state to make it a crime for a husband to rape his wife (Schechter, 1982). By 1977 there were 89 shelters across the United States and shelter hot lines logged 110,000 calls for service (Roberts, 1996, p. 10).

There has been a continued increase in services for battered women instituted during the past two decades. In 1990 there were approximately 1,250 battered women's shelters in the United States and Canada (Roberts, 1996, p. 10). These organizations offer a broad range of services including emergency shelter, 24-hour hot lines, peer counseling, court advocacy, legal aid, and general referral; they also often are involved in community education and professional training, and generally provide these services free of cost (Roche, 1996). The last two decades have witnessed legislative and systemic reforms that have tried to criminalize battering. Instead of viewing the problem as a private, family matter, advocates have stressed that is it a crime and it needs to be treated as such. As a result, there have been massive reforms in laws and in the ways the criminal justice system operates in response to woman battering.

BATTERING AS A FORM OF SOCIAL CONTROL

"Family" invokes strong symbolic images of love, loyalty, and sentiments of attachment. If one's personal experiences do not match the embedded characterization, the image is so strong that one often mourns the missing symbol rather than questioning its existence. The tendency to "promote" a non-relative to the status of "family" is a common way to proclaim closeness. Widely divergent groups from sororities to prison gangs use the terms like "brother" or "sister" to describe members. This is a powerful indication of the meaning of the symbol. Likewise, children who proclaim that their "nanny" was "like a mother to them" are assigning meaning to relationships using the socially approved metaphor of the family (Holstein & Gubrium, 1994).

Despite the idealized image of the American family as the "source of love, sympathy, understanding, and unlimited support" (Utech, 1994), the family is quite a dangerous place for a number of women. Battering poses a serious challenge to the ideal of the nuclear family. If society acknowledges that women are more likely to be assaulted by loved ones, not strangers, then we as individuals are forced to balance two competing belief systems. How can the family be the sacred bastion of our society if it continues to be dangerous for so many women?

Most people tend to invoke a very narrow definition of the ideal: a nuclear family composed of two adults of the opposite sex married to each other for life with children to complete the picture. Women are responsible for homemaking and childcare, and men are the breadwinners. This ideal ignores a variety of relationships and, in fact, romanticizes a type of family that is and has almost always been quite rare in society. Family is a fluid, dynamic concept that includes a multiplicity of intimate relationships, yet the hegemonic ideal of the family is simplistic and unidimensional (Holstein & Gubrium, 1994). Historically, there is great public concern and a call for a return to family values whenever the hegemony of the family is threatened (Coontz, 1992; Gordon, 1988). There is a tendency to romanticize the past and blame a variety of social problems, including crime, on the decline of the American family. Many 1950s and 1960s sitcoms are experiencing a revival as new generations are introduced to the Brady Bunch and the Cleavers. The popular tendency to romanticize the "traditional nuclear family" is, as one author notes, a longing to return to "the way we never were" (Coontz, 1992). Popular culture and other forces, however, help create and maintain a hegemonic view of the family that is narrowly defined and rarely represents the diversity of familial relationships.

These definitions of family impact our understanding of woman battering. As Lorber's article notes, gender inequality in society is both reproduced and reflected in the family. Some men use battering to achieve power and control at the personal level. It is effective. Physical violence and other abusive tactics (including emotional and sexual abuse) are powerful ways to insure submission. Any analysis of woman battering that fails to concentrate on the effects of the larger social structure leads to the mistaken conclusion that woman battering is committed by a few mentally ill men or a handful of sadistic husbands. This simplistic view ignores a number of factors on the macro level. For example, the lack of adequate, affordable child care, and the poor wages many women earn assures that many women remain financially dependent upon men—even when those men batter them. Likewise, a social structure that conditions women to believe that they have less value if they cannot "get" a man leads some to feel that any man, even a batterer, is better than no man. Religious beliefs that proclaim that marriage is for life and that women should obey their husbands may also cause women to stay in violent and dangerous marriages.

SUMMARY

Society has a long history of legitimizing battering. Laws that charged husbands with the responsibility of disciplining their wives established an attitude that persists today. Even after battering was criminalized, society made no effort to enforce the laws until the 1970s (Buzawa & Buzawa, 1996). While laws have moved toward the criminalization of battering and extensive reforms are attempting to make the criminal justice system respond to battering as a type of crime, progress has been slow.

The existence of woman battering challenges the hegemonic ideal of the nuclear family, which is a fundamental building block of a patriarchal, capitalist social structure. The ways in which battering is named, defined, and measured diminish the magnitude of the problem and deflect the gendered nature of the act. Terms like domestic violence, family violence, and spouse abuse obscure the notion that most victims of heterosexual battering are women who are beaten by their male intimates. If we ever really begin to see through the pollution, we might find that violence is far too "normal" in the "average American home."

REFERENCES

Angeli, M. (1954). *Book of nursery and mother goose rhymes.* New York: Doubleday.

Arnot, M. (1994). Male hegemony, social class, and women's education. In L. Stone (Ed.), *The education feminism reader* (pp. 73–83). New York: Routledge.

Baro, A., & Eigenberg, H. (1993). Images of gender: A content analysis of photographs in introductory criminology and criminal justice textbooks. *Women and Criminal Justice, 5*(1), 3–36.

Belknap, J. (1996). *The invisible woman: Gender, crime and justice.* New York: Wadsworth.

Berger, P., & Luckman, T. (1966). *The social construction of reality.* New York: Doubleday.

Bograd, M. (1988). Feminist perspectives on wife abuse. In K. Yllo & M. Bograd (Eds.), *Feminist perspectives on wife abuse* (pp. 11–26). Thousand Oaks, CA: Sage.

Bowker, L., Arbitell, M., & McFerron, R. (1988). On the relationship between wife beating and child abuse. In K. Yllo & M. Bograd (Eds.), *Feminist perspectives on wife abuse* (pp. 158–174). Beverly Hills: Sage.

Bugliosi, V. (1996). *Outrage: The five reasons why O. J. Simpson got away with murder.* New York: W. W. Norton and Company.

Bureau of Labor Statistics. (1998). Employed persons by occupation, sex, & age. Retrieved February 22, 1999 from the World Wide Web: *http://stats.bls.gov/pdf/cpsaat9.pdf*

Buzawa, E., & Buzawa, C. (1996). *Domestic violence: The criminal justice response* (2nd ed.). Newbury Park, CA: Sage.

Coontz, S. (1992). *The way we never were: American families and the nostalgia trap.* New York: Basic Books.

Daly, K., & Chesney-Lind, M. (1988). Feminism and criminology. *Justice Quarterly, 5*(4), 497–535.

Darden, C. (1996). *In contempt.* New York: Regan Books.

Dobash, R. E., & Dobash, R. (1979). *Violence against wives.* New York: Free Press.

Dolan, K. (1988). Voting for women in the "Year of the Woman." *American Journal of Political Science, 42,* 272–293.

Edwards, A. (1987). Male violence in feminist theory: An analysis of the changing conceptions of sex/gender violence and male dominance. In J. Hanmer & M. Maynard (Eds.), *Women, violence, & social control* (pp. 13–29). Atlantic Highlands, NJ: Humanities Press International.

Eigenberg, H., & Baro, A. (1992). Women and the publication process: A content analysis of criminal justice journals. *Journal of Criminal Justice Education, 3*(2), 293–314.

Eigenberg, H., Scarborough, K., & Kappeler, V. (1996). Contributory factors affecting arrest in domestic and non-domestic assaults. *American Journal of Police, 15*(4), 55–77.

Feminist Majority Foundation. (1999, February 20). More women elected to Congress than ever before. Retrieved February 20, 1999 from the World Wide Web: *http://www.feminist.org/news/newsbyte/april98/0429.html*

Garrison, C., McClelland, A., Dambrot, F., & Casey, K. (1992). Gender balancing the criminal justice curriculum and classroom. *Journal of Criminal Justice Education, 3*(2), 203–222.

Gelles, R., & Straus, M. (1988). *Intimate violence: The causes and consequences of abuse in the American family.* New York: Simon and Schuster.

Gelsthorpe, L., & Morris, A. (1990). *Feminist perspectives in criminology.* Milton Keynes, PA: Open University Press.

Gerwerth, K., & Bachand, D. (1993). Workload and compensation among criminal justice faculty members: A national survey. *Journal of Criminal Justice Education, 4*(1), 43–64.

Glick, P., & Fiske, S. (1999). Gender, power dynamics, & social interaction. In M. Ferree, J. Lorber, & B. Hess (Eds.), *Revisioning gender* (pp. 365–398). Thousand Oaks, CA: Sage.

Goolkasian, G. (1986). Confronting domestic violence: The role of criminal court judges. *National Institute of Justice Research in Brief* (November), 1–8.

Gordon, L. (1988). *Heroes of their own lives: The history and politics of family violence.* New York: Viking.

Harding, S. (1986). *The science question in feminism.* Ithaca, New York: Cornell University Press.

Hart, B. (1996). The legal road to freedom. In N. Lemon (Ed.), *Domestic violence law* (pp. 36–47). San Francisco: Austin and Winfield.

Heidensohn, F. (1985). *Women and crime: The life of the female offender.* New York: University Press.

Holstein, J., & Gubrium, J. (1994). Constructing family: Descriptive practice and domestic order. In T. Sarbin & J. Kitsuse (Eds.), *Constructing the social* (pp. 232–250). Thousand Oaks, CA: Sage.

Kappeler, V., Blumberg, M., & Potter, G. (2000). *The mythology of crime and criminal justice* (3rd ed.). Prospect Heights, IL: Waveland Press.

Keller, E. (1983). Feminism and science. In E. Abel & E. Abel (Eds.), *The signs reader: Women, gender, & scholarship.* Chicago: University of Chicago Press.

Kitzinger, C. (1987). *The social construction of lesbianism.* Beverly Hills: Sage.

Kokepeli, B., & Lakey, G. (1995). More power than we want: Masculine sexuality and violence. In M. Anderson & P. Collins (Eds.), *Race, class and gender* (pp. 450–456). New York: Wadsworth.

Ladner, J. (1987). Introduction to tomorrow's tomorrow: The black woman. In S. Harding (Ed.), *Feminism and methodology* (pp. 29–36). Bloomington: University of Indiana Press.

Lange, T., & Van Natter, P. (1997). *Evidence dismissed.* New York: Pocket Books.

MacKinnon, C. (1987). *Feminism unmodified: Discourses on life and law.* Cambridge: Harvard University Press.

MacKinnon, C. (1989). *Toward a feminist theory of the state.* Cambridge: Harvard University Press.

Martin, D. (1976). *Battered wives.* San Francisco: Glide.

Miller, T. (1997). Sport and violence: Glue, seed, state, or psyche? *Journal of Sport and Social Issues, 21,* 235–238.

Millman, M., & Kanter, R. (1987). Introduction to another voice: Feminist perspectives on social life and social science. In S. Harding (Ed.), *Feminism and methodology* (pp. 29–36). Bloomington: University of Indiana Press.

National Center for Women in Policing. (1997). Equality denied: The status of women in policing. Retrieved May 1, 1999 from the World Wide Web: *http://www.feminist.org/police/status.html*

National Domestic Violence Hotline (No date). Retrieved February 21, 1999 from the World Wide Web: *http://www.ndvh.org/*

Nebraska Feminist Collective. (1983). A feminist ethic for social science research. *Women's Studies International Forum, 6*(5), 535–543.

NiCarthy, G. (1986). *Getting free: A handbook for women in abusive relationships.* New York: Seal.

Pagelow, M. (1984). *Family violence.* New York: Praeger.

Pleck, E. (1987). *Domestic tyranny: The making of American social policy against family violence from colonial times to the present.* New York: Oxford University Press.

Prizzey, E. (1974). *Scream quietly or the neighbors will hear.* Middlesex, England: Penguin Books.

Renzetti, C. (1993). On the margins of the malestream (or they *still* don't get it, do they?): Feminist analyses in criminal justice education. *Journal of Criminal Justice Education, 4*(2), 219–234.

Resnick, F. (1994). *Nicole Brown Simpson: The private diary of a life interrupted.* Beverly Hills: Dove.

Roberts, A. (1996). *Helping battered women.* New York: Oxford.

Roche, S., & Sadoski, P. (1996). Social action for battered women. In A. Roberts (Ed.), *Helping battered women* (pp. 13–30). New York: Oxford.

Rotella, E. (1995). Women and the American economy. In S. Ruth (Ed.), *Issues in feminism,* (3rd ed., pp. 320–333). Mountain View, CA: Mayfield.

Sarbin, T., & Kitsuse, J. (1994). *Constructing the social.* Thousand Oaks, CA: Sage.

Schechter, S. (1982). *Women and male violence: The visions and struggles of the battered women's movement.* Boston: South End Press.

Schaef, A. (1985). *Women's reality: An emerging female system in a white male society.* San Francisco: Harper and Row.

Schiller, L., & Willwerth, J. (1996). *American tragedy: The uncensored story of the Simpson defense.* New York: Random House.

Schmalleger, F. (1996). *Trial of the century: People of the state of California v. Orenthal James Simpson.* Upper Saddle River, NJ: Prentice Hall.

Spender, D. (1981). The gatekeepers. In H. Roberts (Ed.), *Doing feminist research* (pp. 186–202). Boston: Routledge & Keagan Paul.

Stacey, J., & Thorn, B. (1985). The missing feminist revolution in sociology. *Social Problems, 32*(4), 301–316.

Stedman, B. (1996). Right of husband to chastise wife. In N. Lemon (Ed.), *Domestic violence law* (pp. 30–33). San Francisco: Austin and Winfield.

Toobin, J. (1996). *The run of his life: The people v. O. J. Simpson.* New York: Random House.

Utech, M. (1994). *Violence, abuse and neglect: The American home.* New York: General Hall.

West, C., & Zimmerman, D. (1987). Doing gender. *Gender and Society,* (1), 125–151.

Wonders, N., & Caulfield, S. (1993). Women's work? The contradictory implications of courses on women and the criminal justice system. *Journal of Criminal Justice Education, 2*(1), 79–100.

Wright, R. (1987). Are "sisters in crime" finally being booked? The coverage of women and crime in journals and textbooks. *Teaching Sociology, 15,* 418–422.

Wright, R. (1992). From vamps and tramps to teases and flirts: Stereotypes of women in criminology textbooks, 1956 to 1965 and 1981 to 1990. *Journal of Criminal Justice Education, 3*(2), 223–236.

Yllo, K. (1993). Through a feminist lens: Social structure and family violence. In R. Gelles & D. Loseke (Eds.), *Current controversies on family violence* (pp. 47–62). Thousand Oaks, CA: Sage.

COURT CASES

Bradley v. State. 2 Miss. 156 (1824).
Harris v. State. 71 Miss. 464 (1894).

"Night to His Day"
The Social Construction of Gender

Judith Lorber

[Gethenians] do not see each other as men or women. This is almost impossible for our imagination to accept. What is the first question we ask about a newborn baby?

—Ursula Le Guin (1969, p. 94)

Talking about gender for most people is the equivalent of fish talking about water. Gender is so much the routine ground of everyday activities that questioning its taken-for-granted assumptions and presuppositions is like thinking about whether the sun will come up.[1] Gender is so pervasive that in our society we assume it is bred into our genes. Most people find it hard to believe that gender is constantly created and re-created out of human interaction, out of social life, and is the texture and order of that social life. Yet gender, like culture, is a human production that depends on everyone constantly "doing gender" (West & Zimmerman, 1987).

And everyone "does gender" without thinking about it. Today, on the subway, I saw a well-dressed man with a year-old child in a stroller. Yesterday, on a bus, I saw a man with a tiny baby in a carrier on his chest. Seeing men taking care of small children in public is increasingly common—at least in New York City. But both men were quite obviously stared at—and smiled at, approvingly. Everyone was doing gender—the men who were changing the role of fathers and the other passengers, who were applauding them silently. But there was more gendering going on that probably fewer people noticed. The baby was wearing a white crocheted cap and white clothes. You couldn't tell if it was a boy or a girl. The child in the stroller was wearing a dark blue T-shirt and dark print pants. As they started to leave the train, the father put a Yankee baseball cap on the child's

Reprinted with permission from *Paradoxes of Gender* by Judith Lorber, © 1994, pp. 13–16. New Haven: Yale University.

head. Ah, a boy, I thought. Then I noticed the gleam of tiny earrings in the child's ears, and as they got off, I saw the little flowered sneakers and lace-trimmed socks. Not a boy after all. Gender done.

Gender is such a familiar part of daily life that it usually takes a deliberate disruption of our expectations of how women and men are supposed to act to pay attention to how it is produced. Gender signs and signals are so ubiquitous that we usually fail to note them—unless they are missing or ambiguous. Then we are uncomfortable until we have successfully placed the other person in a gender status; otherwise, we feel socially dislocated. In our society, in addition to man and woman, the status can be *transvestite* (a person who dresses in opposite-gender clothes) and *transsexual* (a person who has had sex-change surgery). Transvestites and transsexuals carefully construct their gender status by dressing, speaking, walking, gesturing in the ways prescribed for women or men—whichever they want to be taken for—and so does any "normal" person.

For the individual, gender construction starts with assignment to a sex category on the basis of what the genitalia look like at birth.[2] Then babies are dressed or adorned in a way that displays the category because parents don't want to be constantly asked whether their baby is a girl or a boy. A sex category becomes a gender status through naming, dress, and the use of other gender markers. Once a child's gender is evident, others treat those in one gender differently from those in the other, and the children respond to the different treatment by feeling different and behaving differently. As soon as they can talk, they start to refer to themselves as members of their gender. Sex doesn't come into play again until puberty, but by that time, sexual feelings and desires and practices have been shaped by gendered norms and expectations. Adolescent boys and girls approach and avoid each other in an elaborately scripted and gendered mating dance. Parenting is gendered, with different expectations for mothers and for fathers, and people of different genders work at different kinds of jobs. The work adults do as mothers and fathers and as low-level workers and high-level bosses, shapes women's and men's life experiences, and these experiences produce different feelings, consciousness, relationships, skills—ways of being that we call feminine or masculine.[3] All of these processes constitute the social construction of gender.

Gendered roles change—today fathers are taking care of little children, girls and boys are wearing unisex clothing and getting the same education, women and men are working at the same jobs. Although many traditional social groups are quite strict about maintaining gender differences, in other social groups they seem to be blurring. Then why the one-year-old's earrings? Why is it still so important to mark a child as a girl or a boy, to make sure she is not taken for a boy or he for a girl? What would happen if they were? They would, quite literally, have changed places in their social world.

To explain why gendering is done from birth, constantly and by everyone, we have to look not only at the way individuals experience gender but at gender as a social institution. As a social institution, gender is one of the major ways that human beings organize their lives. Human society depends on a predictable division of labor, a designated allocation of scarce goods, assigned responsibility for children and others who cannot care for themselves, common values and their systematic transmission to new members, legitimate leadership, music, art, stories, games, and other symbolic productions. One way of choosing people for the different tasks of society is on the basis of their talents, motivations, and competence—their demonstrated achievements. The other way is on the basis of gender, race, ethnicity—ascribed membership in a category of people. Although societies vary in the extent to which they use one or the other of these ways of allocating people to work and to carry out other responsibilities, every society uses gender and age grades. Every society classifies people as "girl and boy children," "girls and boys ready to be married," and "fully adult women and men," constructs similarities among them and differences between them, and assigns them to different roles and responsibilities. Personality characteristics, feelings, motivations, and ambitions flow from these different life experiences so that the members of these different groups become different kinds of people. The process of gendering and its outcome are legitimated by religion, law, science, and the society's entire set of values.

In order to understand gender as a social institution, it is important to distinguish human action from animal behavior. Animals feed themselves and their young until their young can feed themselves. Humans have to produce not only food but shelter and clothing. They also, if the group is going to continue as a social group, have to teach the children how their particular group does these tasks. In the process, humans reproduce gender, family, kinship, and a division of labor—social institutions that do not exist among animals. Primate social groups have been referred to as families, and their mating patterns as monogamy, adultery, and harems. Primate behavior has been used to prove the universality of sex differences—as built into our evolutionary inheritance (Haraway, 1978a). But animals' sex differences are not at all the same as humans' gender differences; animals' bonding is not kinship; animals' mating is not ordered by marriage; and animals' dominance hierarchies are not the equivalent of human stratification systems. Animals group on sex and age, relational categories that are physiologically, not socially, different. Humans create gender and age-group categories that are socially, and not necessarily physiologically, different.[4]

For animals, physiological maturity means being able to impregnate or conceive; its markers are coming into heat (estrus) and sexual attraction. For humans, puberty means being available for marriage; it is marked by rites that demonstrate this marital eligibility. Although the onset of physiological puberty is signaled by secondary sex characteristics (menstruation, breast development, sperm ejaculation, pubic and underarm hair), the onset of social adulthood is ritualized by the coming-out party or desert walkabout or bar mitzvah or graduation from college or first successful hunt or dreaming or inheritance of property. Humans have rituals that mark the passage from childhood into puberty and puberty into full adult status, as well as for marriage, childbirth, and death; animals do not (van Gennep, 1960). To the extent that infants and the dead are differentiated by whether they are male or female, there are different birth rituals for girls and boys, and different funeral rituals for men and women (Biersack,

1984, pp. 132–133). Rituals of puberty, marriage, and becoming a parent are gen-dered, creating a "woman," a "man," a "bride," a "groom," a "mother," a "father." Animals have no equivalents for these statuses.

Among animals, siblings mate and so do parents and children; humans have incest taboos and rules that encourage or forbid mating between members of dif-ferent kin groups (Lévi-Strauss, 1956, [1949] 1969). Any animal of the same spe-cies may feed another's young (or may not, depending on the species). Humans designate responsibility for particular children by kinship; humans frequently limit responsibility for children to the members of their kinship group or make them into members of their kinship group with adoption rituals.

Animals have dominance hierarchies based on size or on successful threat gestures and signals. These hierarchies are usually sexed, and in some species, moving to the top of the hierarchy physically changes the sex (Austad, 1986). Humans have stratification patterns based on control of surplus food, ownership of property, legitimate demands on others' work and sexual services, enforced determinations of who marries whom, and approved use of violence. If a woman replaces a man at the top of a stratification hierarchy, her social status may be that of a man, but her sex does not change.

Mating, feeding, and nurturant behavior in animals is determined by instinct and imitative learning and ordered by physiological sex and age (Lancaster, 1974). In humans, these behaviors are taught and symbolically reinforced and ordered by socially constructed gender and age grades. Social gender and age sta-tuses sometimes ignore or override physiological sex and age completely. Male and female animals (unless they physiologically change) are not interchangeable; infant animals cannot take the place of adult animals. Human females can become husbands and fathers, and human males can become wives and mothers, without sex-change surgery (Blackwood, 1984). Human infants can reign as kings or queens.

Western society's values legitimate gendering by claiming that it all comes from physiology—female and male procreative differences. But gender and sex are not equivalent, and gender as a social construction does not flow automati-cally from genitalia and reproductive organs, the main physiological differences of females and males. In the construction of ascribed social statuses, physiologi-cal differences such as sex, stage of development, color of skin, and size are crude markers. They are not the source of the social statuses of gender, age grade, and race. Social statuses are carefully constructed through prescribed processes of teaching, learning, emulation, and enforcement. Whatever genes, hormones, and biological evolution contribute to human social institutions is materially as well as qualitatively transformed by social practices. Every social institution has a material base, but culture and social practices transform that base into some-thing with qualitatively different patterns and constraints. The economy is much more than producing food and goods and distributing them to eaters and users; family and kinship are not the equivalent of having sex and procreating; morals and religions cannot be equated with the fears and ecstasies of the brain; language goes far beyond the sounds produced by tongue and larynx. No one eats "money" or "credit"; the concepts of "god" and "angels" are the subjects of theological disquisitions; not only words but objects, such as their flag, "speak" to the citizens of a country.

Similarly, gender cannot be equated with biological and physiological differences between human females and males. The building blocks of gender are *socially constructed statuses*. Western societies have only two genders, "man" and "woman." Some societies have three genders—men, women, and *berdaches* or *hijras* or *xaniths*. Berdaches, hijras, and xaniths are biological males who behave, dress, work, and are treated in most respects as social women; they are therefore not men, nor are they female women; they are, in our language, "male women."[5] There are African and American Indian societies that have a gender status called *manly hearted women*—biological females who work, marry, and parent as men; their social status is "female men" (Amadiume, 1987; Blackwood, 1984). They do not have to behave or dress as men to have the social responsibilities and prerogatives of husbands and fathers; what makes them men is enough wealth to buy a wife.

Modern Western societies' *transsexuals* and *transvestites* are the nearest equivalent of these crossover genders, but they are not institutionalized as third genders (Bolin, 1987). Transsexuals are biological males and females who have sex-change operations to alter their genitalia. They do so in order to bring their physical anatomy in congruence with the way they want to live and with their own sense of gender identity. They do not become a third gender; they change genders. Transvestites are males who live as women and females who live as men but do not intend to have sex-change surgery. Their dress, appearance, and mannerisms fall within the range of what is expected from members of the opposite gender, so that they "pass." They also change genders, sometimes temporarily, some for most of their lives. Transvestite women have fought in wars as men soldiers as recently as the nineteenth century; some married women, and others went back to being women and married men once the war was over.[6] Some were discovered when their wounds were treated; others not until they died. In order to work as a jazz musician, a man's occupation, Billy Tipton, a woman, lived most of her life as a man. She died recently at seventy-four, leaving a wife and three adopted sons for whom she was husband and father, and musicians with whom she had played and traveled, for whom she was "one of the boys" (*New York Times*, 1989).[7] There have been many other such occurrences of women passing as men to do more prestigious or lucrative men's work (Matthaei, 1982, pp. 192–193).[8]

Genders, therefore, are not attached to a biological substratum. Gender boundaries are breachable, and individual and socially organized shifts from one gender to another call attention to "cultural, social, or aesthetic dissonances" (Garber, 1992, p. 16). These odd or deviant or third genders show us what we ordinarily take for granted—that people have to learn to be women and men. Men who cross-dress for performances or for pleasure often learn from women's magazines how to "do femininity" convincingly (Garber, 1992, pp. 41–51). Because transvestism is direct evidence of how gender is constructed, Marjorie Garber claims it has "extraordinary power . . . to disrupt, expose, and challenge, putting in question the very notion of the 'original' and of stable identity" (1992, p. 16).

GENDER BENDING

It is difficult to see how gender is constructed because we take it for granted that it's all biology, or hormones, or human nature. The differences between women and men seem to be self-evident, and we think they would occur no matter what society did. But in actuality, human females and males are physiologically more similar in appearance than are the two sexes of many species of animals and are more alike than different in traits and behavior (Epstein, 1988). Without the deliberate use of gendered clothing, hairstyles, jewelry, and cosmetics, women and men would look far more alike.[9] Even societies that do not cover women's breasts have gender-identifying clothing, scarification, jewelry, and hairstyles.

The ease with which many transvestite women pass as men and transvestite men as women is corroborated by the common gender misidentification in Westernized societies of people in jeans, T-shirts, and sneakers. Men with long hair may be addressed as "miss," and women with short hair are often taken for men unless they offset the potential ambiguity with deliberate gender markers (Devor, 1987, 1989). Jan Morris, in *Conundrum*, an autobiographical account of events just before and just after a sex-change operation, described how easy it was to shift back and forth from being a man to being a woman when testing how it would feel to change gender status. During this time, Morris still had a penis and wore more or less unisex clothing; the context alone made the man and the woman:

> Sometimes the arena of my ambivalence was uncomfortably small. At the Travellers' Club, for example, I was obviously known as a man of sorts—women were only allowed on the premises at all during a few hours of the day, and even then were hidden away as far as possible in lesser rooms or alcoves. But I had another club, only a few hundred yards away, where I was known only as a woman, and often I went directly from one to the other, imperceptibly changing roles on the way—"Cheerio, sir," the porter would say at one club, and "Hello, madam," the porter would greet me at the other. (1975, p. 132)

Gender shifts are actually a common phenomenon in public roles as well. Queen Elizabeth II of England bore children, but when she went to Saudi Arabia on a state visit, she was considered an honorary man so that she could confer and dine with the men who were heads of a state that forbids unrelated men and women to have face-to-unveiled-face contact. In contemporary Egypt, lower-class women who run restaurants or shops dress in men's clothing and engage in unfeminine aggressive behavior, and middle-class educated women of professional or managerial status can take positions of authority (Rugh, 1986, p. 131). In these situations, there is an important status change: These women are treated by the others in the situation as if they are men. From their own point of view, they are still women. From the social perspective, however, they are men.[10]

In many cultures, gender bending is prevalent in theater or dance—the Japanese kabuki are men actors who play both women and men; in Shakespeare's theater company, there were no actresses—Juliet and Lady Macbeth were played by boys. Shakespeare's comedies are full of witty comments on gender shifts. Women characters frequently masquerade as young men, and other women characters fall in love with them; the boys playing these masquerading women, meanwhile, are acting out pining for the love of men characters.[11] In *As You Like It*, when Rosalind justifies her protective cross-dressing, Shakespeare also comments on manliness:

> Were it not better,
> Because that I am more than common tall,
> That I did suit me all points like a man:
> A gallant curtle-axe upon my thigh,
> A boar-spear in my hand, and in my heart
> Lie there what hidden women's fear there will,
> We'll have a swashing and martial outside,
> As many other mannish cowards have
> That do outface it with their semblances. (I, i, pp. 115–122)

Shakespeare's audience could appreciate the double subtext: Rosalind, a woman character, was a boy dressed in girl's clothing who then dressed as a boy; like bravery, masculinity and femininity can be put on and taken off with changes of costume and role (Howard, 1988, p. 435).[12]

M Butterfly is a modern play of gender ambiguities, which David Hwang (1989) based on a real person. Shi Peipu, a male Chinese opera singer who sang women's roles, was a spy as a man and the lover as a woman of a Frenchman, Gallimard, a diplomat (Bernstein, 1986). The relationship lasted twenty years, and Shi Peipu even pretended to be the mother of a child by Gallimard. "She" also pretended to be too shy to undress completely. As "Butterfly," Shi Peipu portrayed a fantasy Oriental woman who made the lover a "real man" (Kondo, 1990b). In Gallimard's words, the fantasy was "of slender women in chong sams and kimonos who die for the love of unworthy foreign devils. Who are born and raised to be perfect women. Who take whatever punishment we give them, and bounce back, strengthened by love, unconditionally" (Hwang, 1989, p. 91). When the fantasy woman betrayed him by turning out to be the more powerful "real man," Gallimard assumed the role of Butterfly and, dressed in a geisha's robes, killed himself: "because 'man' and 'woman' are oppositionally defined terms, reversals . . . are possible" (Kondo, 1990b, p. 18).[13]

But despite the ease with which gender boundaries can be traversed in work, in social relationships, and in cultural productions, gender statuses remain. Transvestites and transsexuals do not challenge the social construction of gender. Their goal is to be feminine women and masculine men (Kando, 1973). Those who do not want to change their anatomy but do want to change their gender behavior fare less well in establishing their social identity. The women Holly Devor called "gender blenders" wore their hair short, dressed in unisex pants, shirts, and comfortable shoes, and did not wear jewelry or makeup. They described their everyday dress as women's clothing: One said, "I wore jeans all the time, but I didn't wear men's clothes" (Devor, 1989, p. 100). Their gender identity was women, but because they refused to "do femininity," they were constantly taken for men (1987, 1989, pp. 107–142). Devor said of them: "The most common area of complaint was with public washrooms. They repeatedly spoke of the humiliation of being challenged or ejected from women's washrooms. Similarly, they found public change rooms to be dangerous territory and the buying of undergarments to be a difficult feat to accomplish" (1987, p. 29). In an ultimate ironic twist, some of these women said "they would feel like transvestites if they were to wear dresses, and two women said that they had been called transvestites when they had done so" (1987, p. 31). They resolved the ambiguity of their gender status by identifying as women in private and passing as men in public to avoid harassment on the street, to get men's jobs, and, if they were lesbians, to make it easier to display affection publicly with their lovers (Devor, 1989, pp. 107–142). Sometimes they even used men's bathrooms. When they had gender-neutral names, like Leslie, they could avoid the bureaucratic hassles that arose when they had to present their passports or other proof of identity, but because most had names associated with women, their appearance and their cards of identity were not conventionally congruent, and their gender status was in constant jeopardy.[14] When they could, they found it easier to pass as men than to try to change the stereotyped notions of what women should look like.

Paradoxically, then, bending gender rules and passing between genders does not erode but rather preserves gender boundaries. In societies with only two genders, the gender dichotomy is not disturbed by transvestites, because others feel that a transvestite is only transitorily ambiguous—is "really a man or woman underneath." After sex-change surgery, transsexuals end up in a conventional gender status—a "man" or a "woman" with the appropriate genitals (Eichler, 1989). When women dress as men for business reasons, they are indicating that in that situation, they want to be treated the way men are treated; when they dress as women, they want to be treated as women:

> By their male dress, female entrepreneurs signal their desire to suspend the expectations of accepted feminine conduct without losing respect and reputation. By wearing what is "unattractive" they signify that they are not intending to display their physical charms while engaging in public activity. Their loud, aggressive banter contrasts with the modest demeanor that attracts men. . . . Overt signaling of a suspension of the rules preserves normal conduct from eroding expectations. (Rugh, 1986, p. 131)

FOR INDIVIDUALS, GENDER MEANS SAMENESS

Although the possible combinations of genitalia, body shapes, clothing, mannerisms, sexuality, and roles could produce infinite varieties in human beings, the social institution of gender depends on the production and maintenance of a limited number of gender statuses and of making the members of these statuses similar to each other. Individuals are born sexed but not gendered, and they have to be taught to be masculine or feminine.[15] As Simone de Beauvoir said: "One is not born, but rather becomes, a woman . . . ; it is civilization as a whole that produces this creature . . . which is described as feminine." (1952, p. 267).

Children learn to walk, talk, and gesture the way their social group says girls and boys should. Ray Birdwhistell, in his analysis of body motion as human communication, calls these learned gender displays *tertiary* sex characteristics and argues that they are needed to distinguish genders because humans are a weakly dimorphic species—their only sex markers are genitalia (1970, pp. 39–46). Clothing, paradoxically, often hides the sex but displays the gender.

In early childhood, humans develop gendered personality structures and sexual orientations through their interactions with parents of the same and opposite gender. As adolescents, they conduct their sexual behavior according to gendered scripts. Schools, parents, peers, and the mass media guide young people into gendered work and family roles. As adults, they take on a gendered social status in their society's stratification system. Gender is thus both ascribed and achieved (West & Zimmerman, 1987).

The achievement of gender was most dramatically revealed in a case of an accidental transsexual—a baby boy whose penis was destroyed in the course of a botched circumcision when he was seven months old (Money & Ehrhardt, 1972, pp. 118–123). The child's sex category was changed to "female," and a vagina was surgically constructed when the child was seventeen months old. The parents were advised that they could successfully raise the child, one of identical twins, as a girl. Physicians assured them that the child was too young to have formed a gender identity. Children's sense of which gender they belong to usually develops around the age of three, at the time that they start to group objects and recognize that the people around them also fit into categories—big, little; pink-skinned, brown-skinned; boys, girls. Three has also been the age when children's appearance is ritually gendered, usually by cutting a boy's hair or dressing him in distinctively masculine clothing. In Victorian times, English boys wore dresses up to the age of three, when they were put into short pants (Garber, 1992, pp. 1–2).

The parents of the accidental transsexual bent over backward to feminize the child—and succeeded. Frilly dresses, hair ribbons, and jewelry created a pride in looks, neatness, and "daintiness." More significant, the child's dominance was also feminized:

> The girl had many tomboyish traits, such as abundant physical energy, a high level of activity, stubbornness, and being often the dominant one in a girls' group. Her mother tried to modify her tomboyishness: ". . . I teach her to be more polite and quiet. I always wanted those virtues. I never did manage, but I'm going to try to manage them to—my daughter—to be more quiet and ladylike." From the beginning the girl had been the dominant twin. By the age of three, her dominance over her brother was, as her mother described it, that of a mother hen. The boy in turn took up for his sister, if anyone threatened her. (Money & Ehrhardt, 1972, p. 122)

This child was not a tomboy because of male genes or hormones; according to her mother, she herself had also been a tomboy. What the mother had learned poorly while growing up as a "natural" female she insisted that her physically reconstructed son-daughter learn well. For both mother and child, the social construction of gender overrode any possibly inborn traits.

People go along with the imposition of gender norms because the weight of morality as well as immediate social pressure enforces them. Consider how many instructions for properly gendered behavior are packed into this mother's admonition to her daughter: "This is how to hem a dress when you see the hem coming down and so to prevent yourself from looking like the slut I know you are so bent on becoming" (Kincaid, 1978).

Gender norms are inscribed in the way people move, gesture, and even eat. In one African society, men were supposed to eat with their "whole mouth, wholeheartedly, and not, like women, just with the lips, that is halfheartedly, with reservation and restraint" (Bourdieu, [1980] 1990, p. 70). Men and women in this society learned to walk in ways that proclaimed their different positions in the society:

> The manly man . . . stands up straight into the face of the person he approaches, or wishes to welcome. Ever on the alert, because ever threatened, he misses nothing of what happens around him. . . . Conversely, a well brought-up woman . . . is expected to walk with a slight stoop, avoiding every misplaced movement of her body her head or her arms, looking down, keeping her eyes on the spot where she will next put her foot, especially if she happens to have to walk past the men's assembly. (p. 70)

Many cultures go beyond clothing, gestures, and demeanor in gendering children. They inscribe gender directly into bodies. In traditional Chinese society, mothers bound their daughters' feet into three-inch stumps to enhance their sexual attractiveness. Jewish fathers circumcise their infant sons to show their covenant with God. Women in African societies remove the clitoris of prepubescent girls, scrape their labia, and make the lips grow together to preserve their chastity and ensure their marriageability. In Western societies, women augment their breast size with silicone and reconstruct their faces with cosmetic surgery to conform to cultural ideals of feminine beauty. Hanna Papanek (1990) notes that these practices reinforce the sense of superiority or inferiority in the adults who carry them out as well as in the children on whom they are done: The genitals of Jewish fathers and sons are physical and psychological evidence of their common dominant religious and familial status; the genitals of African mothers and daughters are physical and psychological evidence of their joint subordination.[16]

Sandra Bern (1981, 1983) argues that because gender is a powerful "schema" that orders the cognitive world, one must wage a constant, active battle for a child not to fall into typical gendered attitudes and behavior. In 1972, Ms. Magazine published Lois Gould's fantasy of how to raise a child free of gender-typing. The experiment calls for hiding the child's anatomy from all eyes except the parents' and treating the child as neither a girl nor a boy. The child, called X, gets to do all the things boys *and* girls do. The experiment is so successful that all the children in X's class at school want to look and behave like X. At the end of the story, the creators of the experiment are asked what will happen when X grows up. The scientists' answer is that by then it will be quite clear what X is, implying that its hormones will kick in and it will be revealed as a female or male. That ambiguous, and somewhat contradictory, ending lets Gould off the hook; neither she nor we have any idea what someone brought up totally androgynously would be like sexually or socially as an adult. The hormonal input will not create gender or sexuality but will only establish secondary sex characteristics; breasts, beards, and menstruation alone do not produce social manhood or womanhood. Indeed, it is at puberty, when sex characteristics become evident, that most societies put pubescent children through their most important rites of passage, the rituals that officially mark them as fully gendered—that is, ready to marry and become adults.

Most parents create a gendered world for their newborn by naming, birth announcements, and dress. Children's relationships with same-gendered and different-gendered caretakers structure their self-identifications and personalities. Through cognitive development, children extract and apply to their own actions the appropriate behavior for those who belong in their own gender, as well as race, religion, ethnic group, and social class, rejecting what is not appropriate. If their social categories are highly valued, they value themselves highly; if their social categories are low status, they lose self-esteem (Chodorow, 1974). Many feminist parents who want to raise androgynous children soon lose their children to the pull of gendered norms (Gordon, 1990, pp. 87–90). My son attended a carefully nonsexist elementary school, which didn't even have girls' and boys' bathrooms. When he was seven or eight years old, I attended a class play about "squares" and "circles" and their need for each other and noticed that all the girl squares and circles wore makeup, but none of the boy squares and circles did. I asked the teacher about it after the play, and she said, "Bobby said he was not going to wear makeup, and he is a powerful child, so none of the boys would either." In a long discussion about conformity, my son confronted me with the question of who the conformists were, the boys who followed their leader or the girls who listened to the woman teacher. In actuality, they both were, because they both followed same-gender leaders and acted in gender-appropriate ways. (Actors may wear makeup, but real boys don't.)

For human beings there is no essential femaleness or maleness, femininity or masculinity, womanhood or manhood, but once gender is ascribed, the social order constructs and holds individuals to strongly gendered norms and expectations. Individuals may vary on many of the components of gender and may shift genders temporarily or permanently, but they must fit into the limited number of gender statuses their society recognizes. In the process, they re-create their society's version of women and men: "If we do gender appropriately, we simultaneously sustain, reproduce, and render legitimate the institutional arrangements. . . . If we fail to do gender appropriately, we as individuals—not the institutional arrangements—may be called to account (for our character, motives, and predispositions)" (West & Zimmerman, 1987, p. 146).

The gendered practices of everyday life reproduce a society's view of how women and men should act (Bourdieu, [1980] 1990). Gendered social arrangements are justified by religion and cultural productions and backed by law, but the most powerful means of sustaining the moral hegemony of the dominant gender ideology is that the process is made invisible; any possible alternatives are virtually unthinkable (Foucault, 1972; Gramsci, 1971).[17]

FOR SOCIETY, GENDER MEANS DIFFERENCE

The pervasiveness of gender as a way of structuring social life demands that gender statuses be clearly differentiated. Varied talents, sexual preferences, identities, personalities, interests, and ways of interacting fragment the individual's bodily and social experiences. Nonetheless, these are organized in Western cultures into two and only two socially and legally recognized gender statuses, "man" and "woman."[18] In the social construction of gender, it does not matter what men and women actually do; it does not even matter if they do exactly the same thing. The social institution of gender insists only that what they do is *perceived* as different.

If men and women are doing the same tasks, they are usually spatially segregated to maintain gender separation, and often the tasks are given different job titles as well, such as executive secretary and administrative assistant (Reskin, 1988). If the differences between women and men begin to blur, society's "sameness taboo" goes into action (Rubin, 1975, p. 178). At a rock and roll dance at West Point in 1976, the year women were admitted to the prestigious military academy for the first time, the school's administrators "were reportedly perturbed by the sight of mirror-image couples dancing in short hair and dress gray trousers," and a rule was established that women cadets could dance at these events only if they wore skirts (Barkalow & Raab, 1990, p. 53).[19] Women recruits in the U.S. Marine Corps are required to wear makeup—at a minimum, lipstick and eye shadow—and they have to take classes in makeup, hair care, poise, and etiquette. This feminization is part of a deliberate policy of making them clearly distinguishable from men Marines. Christine Williams quotes a twenty-five-year-old woman drill instructor as saying: "A lot of the recruits who come here don't wear makeup; they're tomboyish or athletic. A lot of them have the preconceived idea that going into the military means they can still be a tomboy. They don't realize that you are a *Woman* Marine" (1989, pp. 76–77).[20]

If gender differences were genetic, physiological, or hormonal, gender bending and gender ambiguity would occur only in hermaphrodites, who are born with chromosomes and genitalia that are not clearly female or male. Since gender differences are socially constructed, all men and all women can enact the behavior of the other, because they know the other's social script: "'Man' and 'woman' are at once empty and overflowing categories. Empty because they have no ultimate, transcendental meaning. Overflowing because even when they appear to be fixed, they still contain within them alternative, denied, or suppressed definitions." (Scott, 1988a, p. 49). Nonetheless, though individuals may be able to shift gender statuses, the gender boundaries have to hold, or the whole gendered social order will come crashing down.

Paradoxically, it is the social importance of gender statuses and their external markers—clothing, mannerisms, and spatial segregation—that makes gender bending or gender crossing possible—or even necessary. The social viability of differentiated gender statuses produces the need or desire to shift statuses. Without gender differentiation, transvestism and transsexuality would be meaningless. You couldn't dress in the opposite gender's clothing if all clothing were unisex. There would be no need to reconstruct genitalia to match identity if interests and life-styles were not gendered. There would be no need for women to pass as men to do certain kinds of work if jobs were not typed as "women's work" and "men's work." Women would not have to dress as men in public life in order to give orders or aggressively bargain with customers.

Gender boundaries are preserved when transsexuals create congruous autobiographies of always having felt like what they are now. The transvestite's story also "recuperates social and sexual norms" (Garber, 1992, p. 69). In the transvestite's normalized narrative, he or she "is 'compelled' by social and economic forces to disguise himself or herself in order to get a job, escape repression, or gain artistic or political 'freedom'" (Garber, 1992, p. 70). The "true identity," when revealed, causes amazement over how easily and successfully the person passed as a member of the opposite gender, not a suspicion that gender itself is something of a put-on.

GENDER RANKING

Most societies rank genders according to prestige and power and construct them to be unequal, so that moving from one to another also means moving up or down the social scale. Among some North American Indian cultures, the hierarchy was male men, male women, female men, female women. Women produced significant durable goods (basketry, textiles, pottery, decorated leather goods), which could be traded. Women also controlled what they produced and any profit or wealth they earned. Since women's occupational realm could lead to prosperity and prestige, it was fair game for young men—but only if they became women in gender status. Similarly, women in other societies who amassed a great deal of wealth were allowed to become men—"manly hearts." According to Harriet Whitehead (1981):

> Both reactions reveal an unwillingness or inability to distinguish the sources of prestige—wealth, skill, personal efficacy (among other things)—from masculinity. Rather there is the innuendo that if a person performing female tasks can attain excellence, prosperity, or social power, it must be because that person is, at some level, a man. . . . A woman who could succeed at doing the things men did was honored as a man would be. . . . What seems to have been more disturbing to the culture—which means, for all intents and purposes, to the men—was the possibility that women, within their own department, might be onto a good thing. It was into this unsettling breach that the berdache institution was hurled. In their social aspect, women were complimented by the berdache's imitation. In their anatomic aspects, they were subtly insulted by his vaunted superiority. (p. 108)

In American society, men-to-women transsexuals tend to earn less after surgery if they change occupations; women-to-men transsexuals tend to increase their income (Bolin, 1988, pp. 153–160; Brody, 1979). Men who go into women's fields, like nursing, have less prestige than women who go into men's fields, like physics. Janice Raymond, a radical feminist, feels that transsexual men-to-women have advantages over female women because they were not socialized to be subordinate or oppressed throughout life. She says:

> We know that we are women who are born with female chromosomes and anatomy, and that whether or not we were socialized to be so-called normal women, patriarchy has treated and will treat us like women. Transsexuals have not had this same history. No man can have the history of being born and located in this culture as a woman. He can have the history of *wishing* to be a woman and of *acting* like a woman, but this gender experience is that of a transsexual, not of a woman. Surgery may confer the artifacts of outward and inward female organs but it cannot confer the history of being born a woman in this society. (1979, p. 114)

Because women who become men rise in the world and men who become women fall, Elaine Showalter (1987) was very critical of the movie *Tootsie*, in which Dustin Hoffman plays an actor who passes as a woman in order to be able to get work. "Dorothy" becomes a feminist "woman of the year" for standing up for women's rights not to be demeaned or sexually harassed. Showalter feels that the message of the movie is double-edged: "Dorothy's 'feminist' speeches . . . are less a response to the oppression of women than an instinctive situational male reaction to being treated like a woman. The implication is that women must be taught by men how to win their rights. . . . It says that feminist ideas are much less threatening when they come from a man" (p. 123). Like Raymond, Showalter feels that being or having been a man gives a transsexual man-to-woman or a man cross-dressed as a woman a social advantage over those whose gender status was always "woman."[21] The implication here is that there is an experiential superiority that doesn't disappear with the gender shift.

For one transsexual man-to-woman, however, the experience of living as a woman changed his/her whole personality. As James, Morris had been a soldier, foreign correspondent, and mountain climber; as Jan, Morris is a successful travel writer. But socially, James was far superior to Jan, and so Jan developed the "learned helplessness" that is supposed to characterize women in Western society:

> We are told that the social gap between the sexes is narrowing, but I can only report that having, in the second half of the twentieth century, experienced life in both roles, there seems to me no aspect of existence, no moment of the day, no contact, no arrangement, no response, which is not different for men and for women. The very tone of voice in which I was now addressed, the very posture of the person next in the queue, the very feel in the air when I entered a room or sat at a restaurant table, constantly emphasized my change of status.
>
> And if others' responses shifted, so did my own. The more I was treated as woman, the more woman I became. I adapted willy-nilly. If I was assumed to be incompetent at reversing cars, or opening bottles, oddly incompetent I found myself becoming. If a case was thought too heavy for me, inexplicably I found it so myself. . . . Women treated me with a frankness which, while it was one of the happiest discoveries of my metamorphosis, did imply membership

of a camp, a faction, or at least a school of thought; so I found myself gravitating always towards the female, whether in sharing a railway compartment or supporting a political cause. Men treated me more and more as junior, . . . and so, addressed every day of my life as an inferior, involuntarily, month by month I accepted the condition. I discovered that even now men prefer women to be less informed, less able, less talkative, and certainly less self-centered than they are themselves; so I generally obliged them. (1975, pp. 165–166)[22]

COMPONENTS OF GENDER

By now, it should be clear that gender is not a unitary essence but has many components as a social institution and as an individual status.[23]

As a social institution, gender is composed of:

- *Gender statuses*, the socially recognized genders in a society and the norms and expectations for their enactment behaviorally, gesturally, linguistically, emotionally, and physically. How gender statuses are evaluated depends on historical development in any particular society.

- *Gendered division of labor*, the assignment of productive and domestic work to members of different gender statuses. The work assigned to those of different gender statuses strengthens the society's evaluation of those statuses—the higher the status, the more prestigious and valued the work and the greater its rewards.

- *Gendered kinship*, the family rights and responsibilities for each gender status. Kinship statuses reflect and reinforce the prestige and power differences of the different genders.

- *Gendered sexual scripts*, the normative patterns of sexual desire and sexual behavior, as prescribed for the different gender statuses. Members of the dominant gender have more sexual prerogatives; members of a subordinate gender may be sexually exploited.

- *Gendered personalities*, the combinations of traits patterned by gender norms of how members of different gender statuses are supposed to feel and behave. Social expectations of others in face-to-face interaction constantly bolster these norms.

- *Gendered social control*, the formal and informal approval and reward of conforming behavior and the stigmatization, social isolation, punishment, and medical treatment of nonconforming behavior.

- *Gender ideology*, the justification of gender statuses, particularly, their differential evaluation. The dominant ideology tends to suppress criticism by making these evaluations seem natural.

- *Gender imagery*, the cultural representations of gender and embodiment of gender in symbolic language and artistic productions that reproduce and legitimate gender statuses. Culture is one of the main supports of the dominant gender ideology.

For an individual, gender is composed of:

- *Sex category* to which the infant is assigned at birth based on appearance of genitalia. With prenatal testing and sex-typing, categorization is prenatal. Sex category may be changed later through surgery or reinspection of ambiguous genitalia.
- *Gender identity*, the individual's sense of gendered self as a worker and family member.
- *Gendered marital and procreative status*, fulfillment or nonfulfillment of allowed or disallowed mating, impregnation, childbearing, kinship roles.
- *Gendered sexual orientation*, socially and individually patterned sexual desires, feelings, practices, and identification.
- *Gendered personality*, internalized patterns of socially normative emotions as organized by family structure and parenting.
- *Gendered processes*, the social practices of learning, being taught, picking up cues, enacting behavior already learned to be gender-appropriate (or inappropriate, if rebelling, testing), developing a gender identity, "doing gender" as a member of a gender status in relationships with gendered others, acting deferent or dominant.
- *Gender beliefs*, incorporation of or resistance to gender ideology.
- *Gender display*, presentation of self as a certain kind of gendered person through dress, cosmetics, adornments, and permanent and reversible body markers.

For an individual, all the social components are supposed to be consistent and congruent with perceived physiology. The actual combination of genes and genitalia, prenatal, adolescent, and adult hormonal input, and procreative capacity may or may not be congruous with each other and with sex-category assignment, gender identity, gendered sexual orientation and procreative status, gender display, personality, and work and family roles. At any one time, an individual's identity is a combination of the major ascribed statuses of gender, race, ethnicity, religion, and social class, and the individual's achieved statuses, such as education level, occupation or profession, marital status, parenthood, prestige, authority, and wealth. The ascribed statuses substantially limit or create opportunities for individual achievements and also diminish or enhance the luster of those achievements.

GENDER AS PROCESS, STRATIFICATION, AND STRUCTURE

As a social institution, gender is a process of creating distinguishable social statuses for the assignment of rights and responsibilities. As part of a stratification system that ranks these statuses unequally, gender is a major building block in the social structures built on these unequal statuses.

As a *process*, gender creates the social differences that define "woman" and "man." In social interaction throughout their lives, individuals learn what is expected, see what is expected, act and react in expected ways, and thus simultaneously construct and maintain the gender order: "The very injunction to be a given gender takes place through discursive routes: to be a good mother, to be a hetero-sexually desirable object, to be a fit worker, in sum, to signify a multiplicity of guar-antees in response to a variety of different demands all at once" (Butler, 1990, p. 145). Members of a social group neither make up gender as they go along nor exactly replicate in rote fashion what was done before. In almost every encounter, human beings produce gender, behaving in the ways they learned were appropriate for their gender status, or resisting or rebelling against these norms. Resistance and rebellion have altered gender norms, but so far they have rarely eroded the statuses.

Gendered patterns of interaction acquire additional layers of gendered sexu-ality, parenting, and work behaviors in childhood, adolescence, and adulthood. Gendered norms and expectations are enforced through informal sanctions of gender-inappropriate behavior by peers and by formal punishment or threat of punishment by those in authority should behavior deviate too far from socially imposed standards for women and men.

Everyday gendered interactions build gender into the family, the work pro-cess, and other organizations and institutions, which in turn reinforce gender expectations for individuals.[24] Because gender is a process, there is room not only for modification and variation by individuals and small groups but also for institutionalized change (Scott, 1988a, p. 7).

As part of a *stratification* system, gender ranks men above women of the same race and class. Women and men could be different but equal. In practice, the process of creating difference depends to a great extent on differential evalua-tion. As Nancy Jay (1981) says: "That which is defined, separated out, isolated from all else is A and pure. Not-A is necessarily impure, a random catchall, to which nothing is external except A and the principle of order that separates it from Not-A" (p. 45). From the individual's point of view, whichever gender is A, the other is Not-A; gender boundaries tell the individual who is like him or her, and all the rest are unlike. From society's point of view, however, one gender is usually the touchstone, the normal, the dominant, and the other is different, deviant, and subordinate. In Western society, "man" is A, "wo-man" is Not-A. (Consider what a society would be like where woman was A and man Not-A.)

The further dichotomization by race and class constructs the gradations of a heterogeneous society's stratification scheme. Thus, in the United States, white is A, African American is Not-A; middle class is A, working class is Not-A, and "African-American women occupy a position whereby the inferior half of a series of these dichotomies converge" (Collins, 1990, p. 70). The dominant categories are the hegemonic ideals, taken so for granted as the way things should be that white is not ordinarily thought of as a race, middle class as a class, or men as a gender. The characteristics of these categories define the Other as that which lacks the valuable qualities the dominants exhibit.

In a gender-stratified society, what men do is usually valued more highly than what women do because men do it, even when their activities are very simi-lar or the same. In different regions of southern India, for example, harvesting rice is men's work, shared work, or women's work: "Wherever a task is done by

women it is considered easy, and where it is done by [men] it is considered difficult" (Mencher, 1988, p. 104). A gathering and hunting society's survival usually
depends on the nuts, grubs, and small animals brought in by the women's forag-
ing trips, but when the men's hunt is successful, it is the occasion for a celebration. Conversely, because they are the superior group, white men do not have to
do the "dirty work," such as housework; the most inferior group does it, usually
poor women of color (Palmer, 1989).

Freudian psychoanalytic theory claims that boys must reject their mothers
and deny the feminine in themselves in order to become men: "For boys the
major goal is the achievement of personal masculine identification with their
father and sense of secure masculine self, achieved through superego formation
and disparagement of women" (Chodorow, 1978, p. 165). Masculinity may be the
outcome of boys' intrapsychic struggles to separate their identity from that of
their mothers, but the proofs of masculinity are culturally shaped and usually rit-
ualistic and symbolic (Gilmore, 1990).

The Marxist feminist explanation for gender inequality is that by demeaning
women's abilities and keeping them from learning valuable technological skills,
bosses preserve them as a cheap and exploitable reserve army of labor. Unionized
men who could be easily replaced by women collude in this process because it
allows them to monopolize the better paid, more interesting, and more autono-
mous jobs: "Two factors emerge as helping men maintain their separation from
women and their control of technological occupations. One is the active gendering of jobs and people. The second is the continual creation of sub-divisions in
the work processes, and levels in work hierarchies, into which men can move in
order to keep their distance from women" (Cockburn, 1985, p. 13).

Societies vary in the extent of the inequality in social status of their women
and men members, but where there is inequality, the status "woman" (and its
attendant behavior and role allocations) is usually held in lesser esteem than the
status "man." Since gender is also intertwined with a society's other constructed
statuses of differential evaluation—race, religion, occupation, class, country, of
origin, and so on—men and women members of the favored groups command
more power, more prestige, and more property than the members of the disfa-
vored groups. Within many social groups, however, men are advantaged over
women. The more economic resources, such as education and job opportunities,
are available to a group, the more they tend to be monopolized by men. In poorer
groups that have few resources (such as working-class African Americans in the
United States), women and men are more nearly equal, and the women may even
outstrip the men in education and occupational status (Almquist, 1987).

As a *structure*, gender divides work in the home and in economic production,
legitimates those in authority, and organizes sexuality and emotional life (Connell,
1987, pp. 91–142). As primary parents, women significantly influence children's
psychological development and emotional attachments, in the process reproduc-
ing gender. Emergent sexuality is shaped by heterosexual, homosexual, bisexual,
and sadomasochistic patterns that are gendered—different for girls and boys, and
for women and men—so that sexual statuses reflect gender statuses.

When gender is a major component of structured inequality, the devalued genders have less power, prestige, and economic rewards than the valued genders. In countries that discourage gender discrimination, many major roles are still gendered; women still do most of the domestic labor and child rearing, even while doing full-time paid work; women and men are segregated on the job and each does work considered "appropriate"; women's work is usually paid less than men's work. Men dominate the positions of authority and leadership in government, the military, and the law; cultural productions, religions, and sports reflect men's interests.

In societies that create the greatest gender difference, such as Saudi Arabia, women are kept out of sight behind walls or veils, have no civil rights, and often create a cultural and emotional world of their own (Bernard, 1981). But even in societies with less rigid gender boundaries, women and men spend much of their time with people of their own gender because of the way work and family are organized. This spatial separation of women and men reinforces gendered differentness, identity, and ways of thinking and behaving (Coser, 1986).

Gender inequality—the devaluation of "women" and the social domination of "men"—has social functions and a social history. It is not the result of sex, procreation, physiology, anatomy, hormones, or genetic predispositions. It is produced and maintained by identifiable social processes and built into the general social structure and individual identities deliberately and purposefully. The social order as we know it in Western societies is organized around racial, ethnic, class, and gender inequality. I contend, therefore, that the continuing purpose of gender as a modern social institution is to construct women as a group to be the subordinates of men as a group. The life of everyone placed in the status "woman" is "night to his day—that has forever been the fantasy. Black to his white. Shut out of his system's space, she is the repressed that ensures the system's functioning" (Cixous & Clément, [1975] 1986, p. 67).

THE PARADOX OF HUMAN NATURE

To say that sex, sexuality, and gender are all socially constructed is not to minimize their social power. These categorical imperatives govern our lives in the most profound and pervasive ways, through the social experiences and social practices of what Dorothy Smith calls the "everyday/everynight world" (1990, pp. 31–57). The paradox of human nature is that it is *always* a manifestation of cultural meanings, social relationships, and power politics; "not biology, but culture, becomes destiny" (Butler 1990, p. 8). Gendered people emerge not from physiology or sexual orientation but from the exigencies of the social order, mostly, from the need for a reliable division of the work of food production and the social (not physical) reproduction of new members. The moral imperatives of religion and cultural representations guard the boundary lines among genders and ensure that what is demanded, what is permitted, and what is tabooed for the people in each gender is well known and followed by most (Davies, 1982).

Political power, control of scarce resources, and, if necessary, violence uphold the gendered social order in the face of resistance and rebellion. Most people, however, voluntarily go along with their society's prescriptions for those of their gender status, because the norms and expectations get built into their sense of worth and identity as a certain kind of human being, and because they believe their society's way is the natural way. These beliefs emerge from the imagery that pervades the way we think, the way we see and hear and speak, the way we fantasy, and the way we feel.

There is no core or bedrock human nature below these endlessly looping processes of the social production of sex and gender, self and other, identity and psyche, each of which is a "complex cultural construction" (Butler, 1990, p. 36). *For humans, the social is the natural.* Therefore, "in its feminist senses, gender cannot mean simply the cultural appropriation of biological sexual difference. Sexual difference is itself a fundamental—and scientifically contested—construction. Both 'sex' and 'gender' are woven of multiple, asymmetrical strands of difference, charged with multifaceted dramatic narratives of domination and struggle" (Haraway, 1990, p. 140).

NOTES

1 Gender is, in Erving Goffman's words, an aspect of *Felicity's Condition:* "any arrangement which leads us to judge an individual's . . . acts not to be a manifestation of strangeness. Behind Felicity's Condition is our sense of what it is to be sane" (1983, p. 27). Also see Bem, 1993; Frye, 1983, pp. 17–40; Goffman, 1977.

2 In cases of ambiguity in countries with modern medicine, surgery is usually performed to make the genitalia more clearly male or female.

3 See J. Butler 1990 for an analysis of how doing gender *is* gender identity.

4 Douglas, 1973; MacCormack, 1980; Ortner, 1974; Ortner & Whitehead, 1981a; Yanagisako & Collier, 1987. On the social construction of childhood, see Ariès, 1962; Zelizer, 1985.

5 On the hijras of India, see Nanda, 1990; on the xaniths of Oman, Wikan, 1982, pp. 168–186; on the American Indian berdaches, W. L. Williams, 1986. Other societies that have similar institutionalized third-gender men are the Koniag of Alaska, the Tanala of Madagascar, the Mesakin of Nuba, and the Chukchee of Siberia (Wikan, 1982, p. 170).

6 Durova, 1989; Freeman & Bond, 1992; Wheelwright, 1989.

7 Gender segregation of work in popular music still has not changed very much, according to Groce & Cooper, 1989, despite considerable androgyny in some very popular figures. See Garber, 1992 on the androgyny. She discusses Tipton on pp. 67–70.

8 In the nineteenth century, not only did these women get men's wages, but they also "had male privileges and could do all manner of things other women could not: open a bank account, write checks, own property, go anywhere unaccompanied, vote in elections" (Faderman, 1991, p. 44).

9 When unisex clothing and men wearing long hair came into vogue in the United States in the mid-1960s, beards and mustaches for men also came into style again as gender identifications.

10 For other accounts of women being treated as men in Islamic countries, as well as accounts of women and men cross-dressing in these countries, see Garber, 1992, pp. 304–352.

[11] Dollimore, 1986; Garber, 1992, pp. 32–40; Greenblatt, 1987, pp. 66–93; Howard, 1988. For Renaissance accounts of sexual relations with women and men of ambiguous sex, see Laqueur, 1990a, pp. 134–139. For modern accounts of women passing as men that other women find sexually attractive, see Devor, 1989, pp. 136–37; Wheelwright, 1989, pp. 53–59.

[12] Females who passed as men soldiers had to "do masculinity," not just dress in a uniform (Wheelwright, 1989, pp. 50–78). On the triple entendres and gender resonances of Rosalind-type characters, see Garber, 1992, pp. 71–77.

[13] Also see Garber, 1992, pp. 234–266.

[14] Bolin describes how many documents have to be changed by transsexuals to provide a legitimizing "paper trail" (1988, pp. 145–147). Note that only members of the same social group know which names are women's and which men's in their culture, but many documents list "sex."

[15] For an account of how a potential man-to-woman transsexual learned to be feminine, see Garfinkel, 1967, pp. 116–185, 285–288. For a gloss on this account that points out how, throughout his encounters with Agnes, Garfinkel failed to see how he himself was constructing his own masculinity, see Rogers, 1992.

[16] Paige & Paige (1981, pp. 147–149) argue that circumcision ceremonies indicate a father's loyalty to his lineage elders—"visible public evidence that the head of a family unit of their lineage is willing to trust others with his and his family's most valuable political asset, his son's penis" (p. 147). On female circumcision, see El Dareer, 1982; Lightfoot-Klein, 1987; van der Kwaak, 1992; Walker, 1992. There is a form of female circumcision that removes only the prepuce of the clitoris and is similar to male circumcision, but most forms of female circumcision are far more extensive, mutilating, and spiritually and psychologically shocking than the usual form of male circumcision. However, among the Australian aborigines, boys' penises are slit and kept open, so that they urinate and bleed the way women do (Bettelheim, 1962, pp. 165–206).

[17] The concepts of moral hegemony, the effects of everyday activities (praxis) on thought and personality, and the necessity of consciousness of these processes before political change can occur are all based on Marx's analysis of class relations.

[18] Other societies recognize more than two categories, but usually no more than three or four (Jacobs & Roberts, 1989).

[19] Carol Barkalow's book has a photograph of eleven first-year West Pointers in a math class, who are dressed in regulation pants, shirts, and sweaters, with short haircuts. The caption challenges the reader to locate the only woman in the room.

[20] The taboo on males and females looking alike reflects the U.S. military's homophobia (Bérubé, 1989). If you can't tell those with a penis from those with a vagina, how are you going to determine whether their sexual interest is heterosexual or homosexual unless you watch them having sexual relations?

[21] Garber feels that *Tootsie* is not about feminism but about transvestism and its possibilities for disturbing the gender order (1992, pp. 5–9).

[22] See Bolin, 1988, pp. 149–150, for transsexual men-to-women's discovery of the dangers of rape and sexual harassment. Devor's "gender blenders" went in the opposite direction. Because they found that it was an advantage to be taken for men, they did not deliberately cross-dress, but they did not feminize themselves either (1989, pp. 126–140).

[23] See West & Zimmerman, 1987 for a similar set of gender components.

[24] On the "logic of practice," or how the experience of gender is embedded in the norms of everyday interaction and the structure of formal organizations, see Acker, 1990; Bourdieu, [1980] 1990; Connell, 1987; Smith, 1987a.

A Letter From a Battered Wife

Del Martin

A friend of mine received the following letter after discussing wife-beating at a public meeting.

> I am in my thirties and so is my husband. I have a high school diploma and am presently attending a local college, trying to obtain the additional education I need. My husband is a college graduate and a professional in his field. We are both attractive and, for the most part, respected and well-liked. We have four children and live in a middle-class home with all the comforts we could possibly want.
>
> I have everything, except life without fear.
>
> For most of my married life I have been periodically beaten by my husband. What do I mean by "beaten"? I mean that parts of my body have been hit violently and repeatedly, and that painful bruises, swelling, bleeding wounds, unconsciousness, and combinations of these things have resulted.
>
> Beating should be distinguished from all other kinds of physical abuse—including being hit and shoved around. When I say my husband threatens me with abuse I do not mean he warns me that he may lose control. I mean that he shakes a fist against my face or nose, makes punching-bag jabs at my shoulder, or makes similar gestures which may quickly turn into a full-fledged beating.
>
> I have had glasses thrown at me. I have been kicked in the abdomen when I was visibly pregnant. I have been kicked off the bed and hit while lying on the floor—again, while I was pregnant. I have been whipped, kicked and thrown, picked up again and thrown down again. I have been punched and kicked in the head, chest, face, and abdomen more times than I can count.
>
> I have been slapped for saying something about politics, for having a different view about religion, for swearing, for crying, for wanting to have intercourse.
>
> I have been threatened when I wouldn't do something he told me to do. I have been threatened when he's had a bad day and when he's had a good day.

I have been threatened, slapped, and beaten after stating bitterly that I didn't like what he was doing with another woman.

After each beating my husband has left the house and remained away for days.

Few people have even seen my black and blue face or swollen lips because I have always stayed indoors afterwards, feeling ashamed. I was never able to drive following one of these beatings, so I could not get myself to a hospital for care. I could never have left my young children alone, even if I could have driven a car.

Hysteria inevitably sets in after a beating. This hysteria—the shaking and crying and mumbling—is not accepted by anyone, so there has never been anyone to call.

My husband on a few occasions did phone a day or so later so we could agree on the excuse I would use for returning to work, the grocery store, the dentist appointment, and so on. I used the excuses—a car accident, oral surgery, things like that.

Now, the first response to this story, which I myself think of, will be "Why didn't you seek help?"

I did. Early in our marriage I went to a clergyman who, after a few visits, told me that my husband meant no real harm, that he was just confused and felt insecure. I was encouraged to be more tolerant and understanding. Most important, I was told to forgive him the beatings just as Christ had forgiven me from the cross. I did that, too.

Things continued. Next time I turned to a doctor. I was given little pills to relax me and told to take things a little easier. I was just too nervous.

I turned to a friend, and when her husband found out, he accused me of either making things up or exaggerating the situation. She was told to stay away from me. She didn't, but she could no longer really help me. Just by believing me she was made to feel disloyal.

I turned to a professional family guidance agency. I was told there that my husband needed help and that I should find a way to control the incidents. I couldn't control the beatings—that was the whole point of my seeking help. At the agency I found I had to defend myself against the suspicion that I wanted to be hit, that I invited the beatings. Good God! Did the Jews invite themselves to be slaughtered in Germany?

I did go to two more doctors. One asked me what I had done to provoke my husband. The other asked if we had made up yet.

I called the police one time. They not only did not respond to the call, they called several hours later to ask if things had "settled down." I could have been dead by then!

I have nowhere to go if it happens again. No one wants to take in a woman with four children. Even if there were someone kind enough to care, no one wants to become involved in what is commonly referred to as a "domestic situation."

Everyone I have gone to for help has somehow wanted to blame me and vindicate my husband. I can see it lying there between their words and at the end of their sentences. The clergyman, the doctor, the counselor, my friend's husband, the police—all of them have found a way to vindicate my husband.

No one has to "provoke" a wife-beater. He will strike out when he's ready and for whatever reason he has at the moment.

I may be his excuse, but I have never been the reason.

I know that I do not want to be hit. I know, too, that I will be beaten again unless I can find a way out for myself and my children. I am terrified for them also.

As a married woman I have no recourse but to remain in the situation which is causing me to be painfully abused. I have suffered physical and emotional battering and spiritual rape because the social structure of my world says I cannot do anything about a man who wants to beat me. . . . But staying with my husband means that my children must be subjected to the emotional battering caused when they see their mother's beaten face or hear her screams in the middle of the night.

I know that I have to get out. But when you have nowhere to go, you know that you must go on your own and expect no support. I have to be ready for that. I have to be ready to support myself and the children completely, and still provide a decent environment for them. I pray that I can do that before I am murdered in my own home.

I have learned that no one believes me and that I cannot depend upon any outside help. All I have left is the hope that I can get away before it is too late.

I have learned also that the doctors, the police, the clergy, and my friends will excuse my husband for distorting my face, but won't forgive me for looking bruised and broken. The greatest tragedy is that I am still praying, and there is not a human person to listen.

Being beaten is a terrible thing; it is most terrible of all if you are not equipped to fight back. I recall an occasion when I tried to defend myself and actually tore my husband's shirt. Later, he showed it to a relative as proof that I had done something terribly wrong. The fact that at that moment I had several raised spots on my head hidden by my hair, a swollen lip that was bleeding, and a severely damaged cheek with a blood clot that caused a permanent dimple didn't matter to him. What mattered was that I tore his shirt! That I tore it in self-defense didn't mean anything to him.

My situation is so untenable I would guess that anyone who has not experienced one like it would find it incomprehensible. I find it difficult to believe myself.

It must be pointed out that while a husband can beat, slap, or threaten his wife, there are "good days." These days tend to wear away the effects of the beating. They tend to cause the wife to put aside the traumas and look to the good—first, because there is nothing else to do; second, because there is nowhere and no one to turn to; and third, because the defeat is the beating and the hope is that it will not happen again. A loving woman like myself always hopes that it will not happen again. When it does, she simply hopes again, until it becomes obvious after a third beating that there is no hope. That is when she turns outward for help to find an answer. When that help is denied, she either resigns herself to the situation she is in or pulls herself together and starts making plans for a future life that includes only herself and her children.

For many the third beating may be too late. Several of the times I have been abused I have been amazed that I have remained alive. Imagine that I have been thrown to a very hard slate floor several times, kicked in the abdomen, the head, and the chest, and still remained alive!

What determines who is lucky and who isn't? I could have been dead a long time ago had I been hit the wrong way. My baby could have been killed or deformed had I been kicked the wrong way. What saved me?

I don't know. I only know that it has happened and that each night I dread the final blow that will kill me and leave my children motherless. I hope I can hang on until I complete my education, get a good job, and become self-sufficient enough to care for my children on my own.

In the preceding story one woman tells her secret. It is a secret shared by many women who daily fear for their lives. These women bear the brutality of their husbands in silence because they have no one to turn to and no place to go. They are married women; as such they are untouchables in our society. In the traditional Christian marriage ceremony, the minister warns, "Whom therefore God has joined together let no man put asunder." These words stand between the battered wife and any help she may seek. No one dares to interfere in the intimate relationship between husband and wife, even when the husband's violence and the wife's danger are apparent.

Often the battered woman is completely isolated. She feels she cannot discuss her problem with anyone—she is too embarrassed and humiliated. Besides, who would understand? Alone, in pain and fear, she wrestles with questions of what to do and where to go. Often she wonders whether she should do anything or go anywhere. If she has children she may feel particularly trapped. She might fear for her children's safety and emotional health but be unsure as to how to provide for them alone. When the battered woman becomes desperate enough to reach out for help, she often meets with subtle, and sometimes even hostile, rejection. Her problem may seem insolvable to her. At least with regard to the help and support she can expect from society, she may be right.

The isolation of the battered wife is the result of our society's almost tangible contempt for female victims of violence. Until very recently, the rape victims were believed to be guilty of precipitating the crime against them until proven innocent in a court of law. The rapist had been tantalized, led on, teased, played with until—who could blame him, the argument went—he lost control and forcibly took his temptress. Thanks to efforts growing out of the women's movement, these attitudes are being slowly chipped away. Hopefully, all rapists will soon be looked upon as sex offenders rather than victims of seductive women.

When a woman is a victim of violence in her own home, however, social attitudes as to who is at fault and who deserves help are still very much against her. The woman is often seen as a nagging wife who has driven her husband past all endurance. Having reached the limit of his patience, he "pummels" her into blessed silence. In the stereotyped version of his archetypal scene, words such as "pummel" and "throttle" actually stand for "beat," "assault," "injure," and sometimes even "murder." The violent husband is hardly ever pursued and dealt with as a criminal, and the welfare of the victim has up to now been so far beneath the official concern of society that her needs were simply not acknowledged. Not only did her needs go unmet, they were usually not even considered to be real.

Today, however, women are taking a stand in various parts of the world to liberate themselves. Together they are addressing the problems they face as women. They are seeking solutions by making their issues public and by taking action that will effect social change.

THE NATURE, EXTENT, AND CONTEXT OF WOMAN BATTERING

At first glance, it would seem rather simple to name, define, and measure battering. However, as noted in the previous chapter, no social activity is exempt from the influence of gender. This chapter examines the ways we label, or name, battering. Using a gender-neutral term like domestic violence has a different symbolic meaning than calling the problem wife abuse or woman battering. The choice of words also affects whether or not one sees the gendered nature of the act. This chapter examines how definitions affect conceptualization and measurement of the problem. For example, most research focuses only on physical abuse, which helps maintain the hegemonic assumption that battering is rare. Battering is named, defined, and measured in ways that do not challenge the fundamental sanctity of the family or other patriarchal institutions. It also ensures that women's disproportionate victimization remains disconnected from inequality in the larger social structure.

NAMING THE PROBLEM

Assaultive acts committed on adults by intimates are commonly referred to as "domestic violence," "family violence," or "spouse abuse"—all of which minimize the gendered nature of the act. As Bograd (1988) notes:

> Generic terms ignore the context of the violence, its nature, and consequences, the role obligations of each family member and the different mechanisms or

transactional sequences that lead to various forms of abuse. When gender "neutral" terms mask the dimension of gender, they can lead to biases in how the causes and solutions of wife abuse are conceptualized and treated. (p. 13)

To address this problem some feminist scholars began to use the term wife battering, but it too is inadequate since many women are battered by boyfriends, live-in lovers, dates, and ex-spouses.

Is the use of terms like wife battering inconsistent with a feminist perspective that generally argues for gender-neutral language? Using this terminology is not meant to deny that male victims exist. Clearly some victims are men, and these men also deserve help and protection. Most (perhaps all) social services assist both male and female victims. Women's shelters generally can accommodate men who are in need of shelter (usually by placing them in hotels) and can assist them in numerous other ways (court advocacy, crisis intervention, referrals, etc.). Laws are gender neutral and allow for the arrest and prosecution of both male and female assailants. It is important that male victims of intimate assaults (those assaulted by female or male lovers) receive assistance. However, the proportion of battered men appears to be very small even when one considers their reluctance to report because of the social stigma (as is the case for women victims). Generally, most experts contend that men account for about 5% of all victims of heterosexual battering (Berk et al. 1983; Dobash et al. 1992).

This book uses the term woman battering to emphasize that this social problem disproportionately affects women.[1] This term reflects the domain assumption that intimate assaults generally involve male perpetrators and female victims. Gender-laden pronouns are used throughout the book referring to victims as she or her and to batterers as he or him. Using these gendered terms is a way to fight the minimization of the amount of violence against women and the nature of the victimization. However, the original language used in primary sources is retained because changing the language might change the context in ways that the original source may not have intended. For example, substituting woman battering for the term domestic violence in state legislation might, mistakenly, convey the interpretation that the law is applicable only to female victims. Finally, the term "partner" is used to describe a significant other such as boyfriend, girlfriend, spouse, husband, or wife. This term is used because it is more inclusive; it makes no assumptions about the gender of the partner or the marital status of the couple. Naming anything is a complex social process. In other words, the process of naming is a gendered act that reflects the social construction of any particular issue or problem.

DEFINITIONS OF BATTERING

Defining woman battering also is a complex process; the behavior described varies depending on the name used. For example, definitions of domestic or family violence often include child abuse, elder abuse, sibling abuse, and woman battering. Even when concentrating on the abuse of adult women, the term may refer to a physical beating that would constitute assault under the law. It also might involve actions that are not illegal but that serve as a means to exercise power and control. Unfortunately, there is no universally accepted definition of what constitutes battering and very little research has concentrated on clearly defining the term (Belknap, 1996). In fact, much literature simply fails to provide any definition.

Stark, however, offers a broad, comprehensive, inclusive definition of battering. She contends that:

> Coercive control is the proper frame for understanding male violence against women. . . . When we speak about "battering" we refer to *both* the pattern of violent acts and their political framework, the pattern of social, institutional, and interpersonal controls that usurp a woman's capacity to determine her destiny and make her vulnerable to a range of secondary consequences—attempted suicide, substance abuse, mental illness, and the like. The term "entrapment" describes the cumulative effects of having one's political, social, and psychological identity subordinated to the will of a more powerful other who controls resources that are vital to your survival.

This book relies on Stark's definition. The term battering is used to refer to a pattern of coercive control whereby batterers (who are usually men) use physical, sexual, and emotional abuse to exercise power over their victims (who are usually women). Batterers use a wide variety of techniques to maintain power and control. Some batterers may find physical violence more effective, while others prefer emotional violence; however, it appears that all three types of abuse, used in conjunction with each other, increase the efficacy of the others. Thus, it is important to examine more specifically what is meant by physical, sexual, and emotional abuse.[2]

Physical Abuse

Physical violence is most clearly defined for several reasons. First, it is easier to quantify and count. Second, it receives higher priority than other types of abuse because it has the potential for lethality. Emotional and sexual abuse may be linked to lethal consequences. For example, a woman may commit suicide because of the depression brought on by battering or a marital rape (Stark & Flitcraft, 1995). However, physical violence probably represents a more immediate correlation with the probability of fatality. Third, since it has been studied more frequently, researchers are forced to operationalize their terms and describe their working definition of abuse. Fourth, pragmatically speaking, physical abuse is probably best situated to benefit from intervention by the criminal justice system. For example, the criminal justice system is not equipped to respond to emotional abuse; in fact, there rarely would be instances where emotional abuse would constitute a legal violation. And unfortunately, it is more difficult to address sexual abuse since it often takes women many years to define forced sex inside a marriage as rape (Kelly, 1988), and women are reluctant to reveal this type of victimization in a culture that tends to view sexual access as part of the marriage contract (Russell, 1990).

Despite the attention given to defining physical violence, there is not a universally accepted definition. This book uses the following definition: intentional physical actions that cause pain, injury, or threats of the same directed toward intimate partners (past and present). Physical abuse also exists when a woman is forced by her intimate partner into involuntary action or restrained by force from voluntary action. For example, physical abuse could entail slapping, kicking, hitting, punching, burning, choking, or shoving. Batterers also may throw things at their victims or pull their hair. They may threaten their victims with weapons or may actually use weapons to inflict injury. Batterers might hold victims down on the ground or wrestle with them to prevent them from leaving. Batterers also might force victims into a room or closet against their will. Any of these acts against an intimate partner would constitute physical abuse.

Sexual Abuse

Some studies suggest that a common factor among women who kill their batterers is prolonged sexual abuse (Browne, 1987; Walker, 1989). For some, it appears that women who kill may do so in response to a specific sexual assault—it is the proverbial last straw. Sexual abuse occurs when an intimate partner uses force or the threat of force to engage in any sexual act that occurs against the will of the victim. These acts also often match the legal definition of rape, marital rape, or other types of sexual assault. For example, batterers might require their partners to participate in oral or anal sex against their will. There are other tactics of sexual abuse. Batterers might force their partners to watch pornography. They might force partners to have sex with others and watch. They might force their partners to abstain from (or use) birth control with no regard for the partner's wishes. They might sexually degrade their victims by talking to them in humiliating ways or by making them say things that they find degrading. Batterers may engage in sexual acts with the intent and purpose of making their victims feel shamed and demeaned.

The potential for sexual abuse in intimate relationships is exaggerated by a social structure that socializes men to be sexual aggressors and discourages women from expressing their sexual needs (Stoltenberg, 1989). Here again, it is the lack of power and control that emerge as part of this intricate web that keeps battered women trapped in dangerous situations. While most researchers acknowledge sexual abuse or marital rape, it often is treated as a sub-type of rape and often excluded from the literature on woman battering. More research is needed to ascertain the interactive effects of the various types of violence. At least one study reports that some battered women experience only physical battery and other women are raped by their husbands but experience no other types of physical abuse, while some women experience both types of abuse (Russell, 1990). At a minimum, it seems reasonable to conclude that women are at significant risk of sexual abuse if they are being physically abused. Simply put, if a woman is being physically abused, there is no reason to believe that she will be able to express her wishes and engage in an egalitarian sexual relationship with her partner.

Emotional or Psychological Abuse

Emotional abuse often receives marginal attention outside of the psychological and counseling literature. It can take several forms and occurs when a batterer isolates, degrades, or threatens his intimate partner in order to control her (Sonkin, Martin, & Walker, 1985; Utech, 1994; Walker, 1979). Batterers isolate their victims in a variety of ways. They often become "overly possessive" and "outrageously jealous." They begin to assert that the victim must be having (or wanting to have) affairs and imagine that even the slightest conversation signals a passionate romance. They often monitor the victim's actions and cut off contact with others, leaving victims isolated from any possible support systems. This tactic is especially powerful. The more isolated victims are, the more susceptible they are to the brainwashing that accompanies emotional abuse. It is easier to make a woman believe that it is her fault and that she deserves to be battered if no one else is allowed contact with her. Keeping her isolated ensures that loved ones will be prevented from telling her that no one deserves to be battered and that the problem is his. It also helps ensure that they may not have the support systems necessary if they need to escape an abusive situation.

Batterers use numerous tactics to degrade their partners. Victims might be treated like slaves, forced to wait on the batterers' every whim. Batterers may verbally denigrate and insult their partners—calling them names, saying that they are no good, and claiming that no one else would want them as a partner. The victims' feelings are trivialized; victims often are afraid to express their feelings for fear of physical repercussions. The victim's accomplishments may be minimized or ignored. The victim's worth is constantly destroyed, while the batterer's worth is emphasized and glorified.

Batterers may degrade women by keeping them financially dependent. Batterers may make their partners account for any money spent. They may keep women from working so as to keep them economically dependent. A batterer may control all the couple's assets by placing homes, cars, and bank accounts in his name so that she has little immediate access to any resources. A batterer may "allow" his partner to work and then demand that she turn over all her earnings to him. By keeping their partners financially dependent (childlike), batterers maintain their control and make it difficult for victims to secure the resources needed to escape.

Threats are another powerful type of emotional abuse. Threats terrify and frighten victims into compliance, and they remind victims that their behavior is always under scrutiny and subject to punishment. Threats often focus on retaliatory actions that will occur if victims try to leave or if they tell someone about the abuse. Retaliation might involve violence, or it might include other types of retribution. For example, a batterer may threaten his partner with the loss of their children by telling her that he will fight her in court for custody or that he will kidnap the children and disappear with them. He may threaten to kill her, any children, her family, her friends, and/or himself. Batterers may threaten to harm pets, or they may actually torture or kill them.[3] These threats are especially terrifying if there is a history of violence.

Battering, then, involves a pattern of abuse that occurs when batterers employ physical, sexual, or emotional abuse to exercise power and control over their intimate partners. However, many questions still remain. For example, if a woman has "only" experienced psychological abuse is this battering? Do all battered women experience all types of battering? How often does each type of abuse have to occur for it to constitute battering? Is it battering if a woman is hit "only" once? The answers to these questions are not clear. Additional research is needed so that we can better understand the relationship between physical, sexual, and emotional abuse.

It would be a mistake to assume that all women experience battering similarly. For example, the overwhelming majority of research on battering has concentrated on white women. As the Rasche article indicates, it is possible that the experience of being victimized by a partner is similar for white women and women of color, but the causes, frequency, and solutions may be very different. In a landmark study, Richie (1996) examines the relationship between battering and criminal activity for African-American women. Women in her study were treated especially well in their childhood and were seen as "favorite" children. However, their attempts to find employment often ended badly in a culture where is it difficult for women of color to secure and hold a good job. Because of their upbringing, they felt a strong pressure to succeed. As a result of their failures in the public sphere, these women shifted their focus to the private sphere and became even more committed to marriage and maintaining a traditional nuclear family as a way to gain status. They also had a strong sense of loyalty to African-American men and a keen desire to maintain a nuclear family.

These women were more apt to blame themselves and stay in relationships despite experiencing very serious abuse. In fact, in comparison to other national data, these women experienced more severe abuse including permanent injury and disfigurement. Their criminal activities were, in their eyes, a direct result of their physical abuse. Some women did so to delay or avoid abuse; e.g., they were forced into crime by their batterers. Others engaged in crime to demonstrate their loyalty to their partners in a misguided attempt to try to "fix" their relationships. Still others took the rap for their partners in an attempt to protect them from a racist criminal justice system. Finally, for some women, committing a crime was the only way they knew to escape the abuse—they were safe in jail.

Richie's study illustrates how gender, race, and class combine in unique ways. There is a real need for additional research of this nature. Unfortunately, the tendency to focus on "counting" the amount of abuse and the debate over mutual combat often distracts attention from these types of endeavors.

MEASURING BATTERING

It is very difficult to estimate the frequency of battering even when it is narrowly defined as physical abuse. Very limited data make generalizations difficult. There are too few studies and too many methodological problems. As a result, it is difficult to answer even the most basic questions about battering. How often does it occur? Who are the victims? Who are the perpetrators? To a large extent, the answers to these questions depend on one's theoretical orientation and the type of methodology used.

Statistics on Battering

There are many problems that make it difficult to measure the frequency of battering. Underreporting, narrow definitions of abuse, and a paucity of data make it difficult to provide accurate estimates. Fear is an important barrier to reporting. Battered women are not likely to keep a survey in the house. They may be afraid to talk about it over the phone, and they surely will not reveal it if the batterer is present. Another reason for underreporting is that victims often do not want to disclose their victimization (Walker, 1979). Battered women do not report battering because they are embarrassed, afraid that they will be blamed for causing the problem, or fail to define the behavior as abuse. Some battered women minimize the violence as a survival tactic. Recognizing the magnitude (or even the existence) of the violence may be too frightening to admit. Battered women may not reveal abuse if they define or label it differently. For example, if battered women are asked if they were sexually abused they may say no, but if you ask them about specific behavior they may disclose experiences that they had not labeled as "abuse" (being forced to have sex against their will). Estimates on battering also underrepresent the amount of battering because most figures concentrate exclusively on "counting" instances of physical battering. The estimates of abuse would be much higher if sexual (Russell, 1990) and emotional abuse were included.

This section reviews official sources of data (including the Uniform Crime Report (UCR) and national victimization studies) and the significant shortcomings they pose when trying to assess the frequency of battering. We will also review the debate between researchers who believe that battering is best described as a type of mutual violence among couples and those who believe that it is a result of patriarchal social structures and gender inequality. This section also demonstrates how positivism and science are used to legitimize claims that support patriarchal social arrangements.

Uniform Crime Report (UCR)

The UCR is of limited use because it only measures crimes known to the police. At least one victimization study (NCVS) consistently reports that only about half of battering incidents are reported (see Greenfeld et al., 1998). In addition, the UCR historically lacks information about the relationship between the perpetrator and the offender. The new National Incident-Based Reporting Program (NIBRS), which is a component of the UCR, gathers data on victim-offender demographics, victim-offender relationship, time and place of occurrence, weapon use, and victim injuries. However, only 7% of the U.S. population currently lives in areas where this type of data is being gathered (Greenfeld et al.,

1998, p. vii). Thus, the NIBRS is not representative of the general population and is of limited use at this time.

Another component of the UCR, the Supplementary Homicide Report (SHR), provides data about battering incidents that result in murder. These reports contain detailed information on about 92% of the homicides in the U.S. (Greenfeld et al., 1998, p. viii). The numbers of men and women killed by intimates from 1976 to 1996 were 20,311 and 31,260, respectively. About 9% of all murders nationwide involve intimates (Greenfeld et al., 1998, p. 1). However, 30% of all murdered women (compared to 6% of murdered men) are killed by intimates. In addition, two-thirds of the ex-spouses murdered by intimates were women (Greenfeld et al., 1998, p. 6). These data clearly show that women are more likely to be murdered by intimate partners, especially estranged spouses, but they do not inform us about the risk of experiencing non-lethal battering.

Victimization studies using national, random samples are generally considered the most reliable method to determine the amount of battering in society. Convenience samples from social services, emergency rooms, or shelter records inform us about the number and types of victims who present themselves for these kinds of services; however, they do not allow us to make estimates about the rates of battering in society.

Victimization surveys also provide valuable information about criminal activities not reported to the police—those crimes that have been called the "dark figure of crime" (Biderman & Reiss, 1967, p. 1). Victimization surveys supposedly provide more accurate estimates of the "true" nature of crime (Cohen & Lichbach, 1982; Gottfredson, 1986; O'Brien, 1985, 1986). However, there are problems with such surveys. Response bias is a serious concern. Victims may fail to recall the incident, may erroneously perceive it as a violation of the law, may "telescope" during the interview and report victimizations that occurred outside of the time frame being used for the research, or may simply refuse to reveal their victimization to an interviewer for a variety of reasons (Booth, Johnson, & Choldin, 1977; Gove, Hughes, & Geerken, 1984; Levine, 1976; Hindelang, 1976; Skogan, 1981).

The first national victimization survey was conducted in 1966 by the President's Crime Commission on Law Enforcement and the Administration of Justice (Ennis, 1967). This pioneer survey demonstrated that there was, in fact, a great deal of unreported crime (Lehnen & Skogan, 1981, p. 1). It led to the establishment of the National Crime Survey (NCS) in 1972 that was modified and renamed as the National Crime Victimization Survey (NCVS). A summary of the major components of the various victimization studies are presented in Table 1 and the following sections review each of them.

Table 1. Comparisons of major data sources on physical battering

Methodology	NCVS	VAWS	NFVS
Year Data Collected	1995	1995/96	1985
Sample Population	National Random Sample of 47,600 Households	National Random Sample of 8,000 men and 8,000 women age 18 and over	National Random Sample of 3520 Households
	All individuals age 12 and over interviewed	Only one individual per household interviewed	Only one person in the household interviewed
Incident Rate of Intimate Assault (Victimized in the Past Year)	5.5 p/1000 people rate for women 2.5 p/1000 people rate for men		16% of couples
	953,700 women	1,309,061 women	approximately 1.6 million women
	115,490 men	834,732 men	
Prevalence Rate of Intimate Assault (Victimization in Lifetime)	Not Available	22% of women 8% of men	28% of couples
Major Finding	Women are more likely to experience battering by intimate partners.	Women are more likely to experience battering by intimate partners.	Battering is a result of "mutual combat"; men and women are about equally likely to experience battering by intimate partners.

The National Crime (Victimization) Survey

This survey is administered by the U.S. Census Bureau on behalf of the Bureau of Justice Statistics (BJS). About 50,000 households are randomly selected nationwide, and approximately 100,000 respondents age 12 or older are interviewed annually (see Kindermann et al. selection). Each household remains in the sample for a period of three years. Interviews are conducted every six months. The first interview must be done in person, although the majority of the subsequent interviews (72%) are conducted by telephone. The survey reports a response rate of 95% (BJS, 1997, p. 140).

The survey underwent an extensive re-design in the late 1980s and early 1990s and was renamed the National Crime Victimization Survey. The re-designed survey is the product of a planning process that began in 1979; it took 10 years (until January of 1989) before this new instrument was administered to any respondents. The instrument was gradually phased in by administering it to

5% of the sample in 1989 and another 5% in 1990 (Bachman & Taylor, 1994). From January 1992 until June, 1993 the full sample was divided into two parts— half receiving the old design questions and half the new screening items. All data gathered after June, 1993 are solicited from the new design.

One must be very cautious when interpreting the data (especially between 1991 and 1993) because it is not always readily apparent whether the data source is from the old or new instrument. The Justice department has made this process more confusing by using the same name for both instruments and by failing to clearly identify which of the surveys is being used in any given analysis. Government publications and scholarly materials tend to refer to all data as NCVS data—renaming the NCS after the fact. This book uses NCS when citing information from the old design. NCVS is used only when referring to data from the newly designed instrument. Generally speaking, most data from 1973 to 1992 represent the old design, and data from 1993 through the present represent the new instrument. Because of the massive changes, it is impossible to directly compare rates in order to evaluate crime rates across time. It is, however, informative to compare the instruments to illustrate how the social construction of crime has led to measures that minimize harm to women, including woman battering.

Screening Questions

The NCS used 13 initial screening items to determine whether or not respondents had been victims of crime (see appendix 1 of the Kindermann, Lynch, and Cantor selection). The screening questions did not directly address battering. For example, respondents were asked if anyone beat, attacked, or hit them with something like a rock or bottle. They were asked if anyone knifed, shot at, or attacked them with some other weapon; threatened to beat them up; threatened them with a knife, gun, or some other weapon; had attempted to attack them in any way. Additionally, two broad questions asked if respondents had called the police to report something they thought was a crime or if they believed they had experienced a crime even if they did not report it to the police. If a battered victim answered yes to any of these questions, they then would be asked a series of detailed questions that made it possible to classify the instance as either simple or aggravated assault. Simple assault refers to attacks without a weapon resulting in no or minor injury (misdemeanor) while aggravated (felonious) assaults include all attacks with weapons and those that produce serious injury (BJS, 1997, pp. 147, 149). *Notice, however, that while respondents were asked whether they had been robbed, burglarized, or assaulted they were never directly asked about violence in the home.*

These screening questions over-emphasized street crime and used examples that reinforced this conceptualization of crime. For example, the most direct question on assault asked about being hit with something like a rock or bottle. This question suggests random street violence or bar fights more than assaults that occur in the home. Respondents may have been waiting for a question that would more directly cue them to talk about "family violence." Thus, the survey itself helped confirm the notion that battering is not "real crime" or certainly not one of importance, since the government failed to ask specific questions about these types of incidents.

The re-design made modifications that were intended to address some of the weaknesses of the old screening questions. The NCVS includes two broad questions designed to capture violence committed by relatives and intimates (see appendix 1 in reading 4). Respondents are asked whether anyone "attacked or threatened" them "with any weapon, for instance, a gun or a knife, with anything like a baseball bat, frying pan, scissors, or stick, by something thrown, such as a rock or bottle, any grabbing, punching or choking, any face-to-face threats, or any attack or threat or use of force by anyone at all" (p. 6). Respondents are asked to mention an incident even if they are not certain it was a crime. They are informed that "people often don't think of incidents committed by someone they know." Respondents are also asked whether they had "something stolen" or if they were "attacked or threatened" by "someone at work or school, a neighbor or friend, a relative or family member, or any other person [they've] met or known" (p. 6). These new screening questions are an improvement. They specifically ask victims to think about acts like woman battering that victims might be reluctant to identify as a crime. For the first time, the survey specifically asks "respondents directly about attacks that were perpetrated by relatives or other offenders known to them" (Bachman & Taylor, 1994, p. 504).

As the article by Kindermann and his colleagues demonstrates, the new instrument results in higher rates of violence against women in general and battering in particular. In fact, the most dramatic increases in crimes reported to the NCVS involve crimes that disproportionately affect women. The new instrument resulted in a 157% increase in the amount of rape and a 57% increase in the number of assaults reported. The NCS screening questions resulted in figures that minimized the amount of battering; the NCVS is doing better in capturing intimate violence, although other design flaws remain.

Series Estimates

Another crucial problem of both the NCS and NCVS relates to the definition and measurement of "series" incidents. These incidents involve multiple crimes in which respondents experience similar victimizations but cannot identify dates or details clearly for reporting purposes. For the NCS, when victims reported three or more incidents of battering, the crime was counted as a series incident and detailed information was selected for only the most recent event. In the newly designed NCVS, the threshold for classification as a series incident has been raised to six incidents (Bachman & Taylor, 1994); however, this change is somewhat irrelevant since "series victimizations are excluded from the victimization estimates published in the annual BJS reports on the NCVS" (Greenfeld et al., 1998, p. ix). So those victims who experience the most frequent amounts of intimate violence are excluded from NCVS reports altogether. This omission is especially significant since at least one study reports that series incidents are disproportionately higher in cases of domestic violence (Wiersema, 1993 cited in Bachman & Taylor, 1994, p. 505).

Series victimizations present significant problems for researchers. One does not want respondents to convey unclear information because they cannot remember detailed information. For example, a woman battered on a weekly basis probably cannot identify specifics about the time of day, location, and nature of injuries for each assault. However, excluding them from routine reports ensures that the frequency of battering continues to be underrepresented. Failure to collect more detailed information from victims who are frequently battered also limits our understanding of the phenomenon and denies access to more complex relationships. For example, does the average batterer harm his victim occasionally, monthly, weekly, daily? Does the frequency of abuse correlate with the seriousness of the assault? Are victims more apt to report the crime to the police if they are abused more frequently or more severely? Failing to study victims who experience a series of assaults prohibits a more complex understanding of the issues surrounding battering, in addition to underestimating the amount of battering.

Reporting of the Data

Determining the extent of battering from the NCS or NCVS is difficult because of the way the data are gathered, analyzed, and presented. Reports, especially the comprehensive annual victimization reports, do not specifically create and publish tables that allow one to assess the frequency of battering. These annual reports do offer information on assault, both simple and aggravated, but these figures include all assaults, not just those among partners.

The annual victimization report contains three tables that supposedly address "family violence." Prior to the re-design, these tables were placed in an appendix, separate from the other 120 tables in the body of the annual report. The NCVS publications now place these tables in the main body of the report. Symbolically, battering no longer appears as an afterthought. However, the NCVS has not increased the number of tables or changed the content of the tables. Unfortunately none of the three are useful in determining the amount of battering because of limited information and poor operationalization.

Two of the three tables that supposedly address "family violence" in the annual reports fail to break down the data by sex. The first of the NCVS tables examines the number of victimizations by type of crime and relationship to the offender (see table 2; BJS, 2000, p. 41). One can determine how many spouses, ex-spouses, parents, children, other relatives, well known individuals, casual acquaintances, or strangers have completed a crime of violence including rape, robbery, and assault. Translated, one can determine how many spouses commit assaults on their partners, but not how many husbands beat their wives (or vice versa). The second table of the NCVS tables merely translates the number of victimizations in the first table to percentages and offers no real new information (see table 3; BJS, 2000, p. 42).

The third of the NCVS tables displayed in the annual report does include a breakdown by sex. It presents the victimization rate by victim offender relationship, by type of crime, and selected victim characteristics. It allows one to examine the sex, race, age, marital status, and family income of victims of assault.

Table 2. Number of victimizations, by type of crime and relationship to offender

Type of crime	Total number of victimizations	Related					
		Total	Spouse	Ex-spouse	Parent	Own child	Other relatives
Crimes of violence	**9,604,570**	**876,530**	**333,400**	**125,390**	**86,150**	**68,920**	**262,670**
Completed violence	2,785,570	345,960	178,650	24,520	38,720	16,440 *	87,630
Attempted/threatened violence	6,819,000	530,580	154,750	100,870	47,430	52,480	175,040
Rape/Sexual assault²	340,380	40,840	20,260 *	4,330 *	11,910 *	0.0 *	4,340 *
Robbery	1,141,820	53,430	23,840 *	9,200 *	1,760 *	3,960 *	14,660 *
Completed/property taken	744,810	38,080	21,500 *	2,710 *	1,760 *	0.0 *	12,120 *
Attempted to take property	397,010	15,340 *	2,340 *	6,500 *	0.0 *	3,960 *	2,550 *
Assault	8,122,370	782,270	289,300	111,850	72,480	64,960	243,670
Aggravated	1,882,810	160,280	56,190	12,710 *	3,040 *	11,330 *	77,010
Simple	6,239,560	621,990	233,120	99,140	69,440	53,630	166,660

Type of crime	Number of victimizations				
	Well-known¹	Casual acquaintances	Don't know relationship	Strangers	Don't know number of offenders
Crimes of violence	**2,226,760**	**1,445,140**	**132,700**	**4,754,200**	**169,240**
Completed violence	763,080	354,450	50,630	1,229,100	42,350
Attempted/threatened violence	1,463,680	1,090,690	82,080	3,525,100	126,890
Rape/Sexual assault²	112,550	83,360	2,050 *	96,930	4,650 *
Robbery	127,720	63,320	27,820	848,150	21,400 *
Completed/property taken	88,710	40,300	19,810 *	541,460	16,450 *
Attempted to take property	39,010	23,020 *	8,000 *	306,690	4,950 *
Assault	1,986,490	1,298,460	102,830	3,809,120	143,190
Aggravated	411,330	228,310	32,050	1,012,560	38,290
Simple	1,575,160	1,070,150	70,780	2,796,570	104,910

Note: Detail may not add to total shown because of rounding.
* Estimate is based on about 10 or fewer sample cases.
¹Includes data on offenders well known to the victims whose relationship to the victim could not be ascertained.
²Includes verbal threats of rape and threats of sexual assault.

Table 3. Percent distribution of victimizations, by type of crime and relationship to offender

Type of crime	Total number of victimizations	Total crimes %	Percent of victimizations — Related					
			Total %	Spouse %	Ex-spouse %	Parent %	Own child %	Other relatives %
Crimes of violence	**9,604,570**	**100 %**	**9.1 %**	**3.5 %**	**1.3 %**	**0.9 %**	**0.7 %**	**2.7 %**
Completed violence	2,785,570	100 %	12.4	6.4	0.9	1.4	0.6 *	3.1
Attempted/threatened violence	6,819,000	100 %	7.8	2.3	1.5	0.7	0.8	2.6
Rape/Sexual assault[2]	340,380	100 %	12.0	6.0 *	1.3 *	3.5 *	0.0 *	1.3 *
Robbery	1,141,820	100 %	4.7	2.1 *	0.8 *	0.2 *	0.3 *	1.3 *
Completed/property taken	744,810	100 %	5.1	2.9 *	0.4 *	0.2 *	0.0 *	1.6 *
Attempted to take property	397,010	100 %	3.9 *	0.6 *	1.6 *	0.0 *	1.0 *	0.6 *
Assault	8,122,370	100 %	9.6	3.6	1.4	0.9	0.8	3.0
Aggravated	1,882,810	100 %	8.5	3.0	0.7 *	0.2 *	0.6 *	4.1
Simple	6,239,560	100 %	10.0	3.7	1.6	1.1	0.9	2.7

Type of crime	Percent of victimizations				
	Well-known[1] %	Casual acquaintances %	Don't know relationship %	Strangers %	Don't know number of offenders %
Crimes of violence	**23.2 %**	**15.0 %**	**1.4 %**	**49.5 %**	**1.8 %**
Completed violence	27.4	12.7	1.8	44.1	1.5
Attempted/threatened violence	21.5	16.0	1.2	51.7	1.9
Rape/Sexual assault[2]	33.1	24.5	0.6 *	28.5	1.4 *
Robbery	11.2	5.5	2.4	74.3	1.9 *
Completed/property taken	11.9	5.4	2.7 *	72.7	2.2 *
Attempted to take property	9.8	5.8 *	2.0 *	77.2	1.2 *
Assault	24.5	16.0	1.3	46.9	1.8
Aggravated	21.8	12.1	1.7	53.8	2.0
Simple	25.2	17.2	1.1	44.8	1.7

Note: Detail may not add to total shown because of rounding.
* Estimate is based on about 10 or fewer sample cases.
[1]Includes data on offenders well known to the victim whose relationship to the victim could not be ascertained.
[2]Includes verbal threats of rape and threats of sexual assault.

Furthermore, the assault data are divided into categories so one can examine differences in both simple and aggravated assaults committed by relatives, well known individuals, casual acquaintances, or strangers (see table 4; BJS, 2000, pp. 43–44). However, it is not clear just how these categories are operationalized or what types of relationships are represented. Relatives in this table apparently include spouses, ex-spouses, parents, and children. The membership in this category can be inferred from the previous two tables that break down the subcategories of relatives. Well known individuals are defined by footnots on the previous tables, which states that these individuals are "offenders well known to the victim whose relationship to the victim could not be ascertained" (BJS, 2000, p. 41). The acquaintance category also is problematic. This category includes "friend/ex-friend, roommate/boarder, schoolmate, neighbor, someone at work/customer, or other non-relative" (Rennison & Welchans, 2000, p. 8). It is quite possible that there are significant gender differences in the way this category is applied. For example, it is possible—in fact likely—that a woman who has had a date or two with a man who batterers her would identify that person as an acquaintance rather than a "boyfriend." It also is quite possible that men who are assaulted by acquaintances represent casual associates or drinking buddies. In general, poor operationalization and the way tables are constructed result in annual reports that make it impossible to determine the number of men and women who are physically battered (assaulted) by an intimate partner.

The Bureau of Justice Statistics occasionally publishes special reports that provide some additional data pertaining to interpersonal violence, although even these reports sometimes make it difficult to ascertain the frequency of battering and the sex of victims and perpetrators. For example, a couple of recent reports on violence between intimates fail to break down victimization by *types* of violent victimization (Greenfeld et al., 1998; Rennison & Welchans, 2000). These data need to be disaggregated. While it is quite possible that there are minimal differences between victims who have experienced rape, battering, or robbery at the hands of intimates, it is impossible to evaluate this assumption when all of these types of victimization are lumped into one broad category.

The most recent published data which allow one to specifically examine the sex of the victim based on the relationship of the perpetrator for *assaults* are from the 1994 NCVS (Craven, 1997). Because of the problems associated with interpreting the acquaintance category, however, these data may be summarized in two different ways. First, the victim-offender relationship is divided into two dichotomous categories: strangers versus acquaintances (which includes violence committed by intimates, other relatives, and friends/acquaintances). When this methodology is used, one can conclude that the majority of women are assaulted by someone they know (intimates, other relatives, and friends/acquaintances); 67% of the women experiencing simple assault and 53% aggravated assault. Men are less apt to be victimized by someone they know—42% of men experience simple assault and 35% aggravated assault. The second method of presentation concentrates only on violence committed by intimates (spouses, ex-spouses, and boy/girlfriend). If this approach is used, the same data indicate

Table 4. Victimization rate by victim-offender relationship, by type of crime and selected victim characteristics

Rate per 1,000 persons age 12 and over

Characteristic	Population	Crimes of violence[1]				Assault			
		Relatives	Well-known	Casual acquaintances	Strangers	Relatives	Well-known	Casual acquaintances	Strangers
Sex									
Male	104,268,820	2.5	8.5	8.4	31.8	2.5	7.7	7.8	25.8
Female	111,440,640	5.5	12.0	5.1	12.9	4.7	10.6	4.4	10.0
Race									
White	181,880,850	4.0	9.6	6.5	21.6	3.6	8.6	5.9	18.0
Black	25,998,040	5.1	16.0	8.3	24.8	4.4	13.7	7.1	15.1
Other	7,830,570	2.2 *	9.5	4.9	23.2	2.2 *	8.7	4.6	17.5
Age									
12-15	15,575,940	3.6	37.1	26.2	35.4	3.2	34.5	24.1	29.5
16-19	14,539,170	8.0	28.4	17.8	49.7	6.7	25.8	15.1	42.4
20-24	17,813,630	6.7	16.6	11.1	43.1	5.7	14.1	9.9	34.1
25-34	41,138,060	7.3	10.3	6.3	29.3	6.5	8.8	5.6	23.7
35-49	60,635,010	3.7	6.8	4.3	18.3	3.4	5.9	3.9	13.9
50-64	34,451,280	1.6	1.9	1.2	8.6	1.5	1.9	1.1	6.9
65 and over	31,556,350	0.1 *	1.4	0.7 *	3.2	0.1 *	1.2	0.7 *	2.2
Marital status[2]									
Married	112,722,940	2.3	3.2	2.8	12.6	2.1	3.0	2.7	10.7
Widowed	13,701,130	0.8 *	1.8	1.3 *	4.2	0.8 *	1.7 *	1.2 *	2.3
Divorced or separated	22,574,290	15.9	13.8	8.0	27.9	13.9	11.7	6.8	20.1
Never married	65,997,420	3.7	23.1	14.1	39.9	3.2	20.5	12.4	32.1
Family income[3]									
Less than $7,500	15,917,890	6.4	19.6	11.3	32.4	5.1	15.5	10.0	24.1
$7,500-$14,999	25,169,790	4.8	11.8	5.4	24.9	4.5	10.5	4.8	16.7
$15,000-$24,999	32,095,240	5.5	11.4	6.8	22.5	5.1	9.8	6.1	17.6
$25,000-$34,999	29,608,960	4.1	11.2	8.2	21.3	3.2	10.4	7.6	17.0
$35,000-$49,999	34,914,380	4.5	9.5	7.8	21.1	4.2	8.6	7.0	17.7
$50,000-$74,999	29,657,010	2.2	8.6	5.9	24.4	2.2	8.3	5.3	21.3
$75,000 or more	22,091,400	1.5	7.2	6.1	19.5	1.5	7.1	5.5	17.5

* Estimate is based on about 10 or fewer sample cases.
[1]Crimes of violence includes data on rape, sexual assault, and robbery, not shown separately, as well as assault.

Table 4. (continued)

Rate per 1,000 persons age 12 and over

Characteristic	Aggravated assault				Simple assault			
	Relatives	Well-known	Casual acquaintances	Strangers	Relatives	Well-known	Casual acquaintances	Strangers
Sex								
Male	0.7	2.0	1.5	7.2	1.8	5.7	6.3	18.6
Female	0.8	1.9	0.7	2.3	3.9	8.8	3.7	7.7
Race								
White	0.7	1.7	1.0	4.5	2.9	6.9	4.9	13.6
Black	1.2	3.1	1.7	5.9	3.2	10.6	5.4	9.2
Other	0.4 *	2.4 *	0.6 *	5.8	1.9 *	6.3	3.9	11.7
Age								
12-15	0.2 *	5.3	3.4	5.6	3.0	29.3	20.7	23.9
16-19	1.8	7.3	1.3 *	13.4	4.9	18.5	13.8	29.0
20-24	1.3 *	1.9	1.9	9.6	4.5	12.2	8.0	24.4
25-34	1.1	2.1	1.7	6.3	5.4	6.7	3.9	17.4
35-49	0.8	1.3	0.8	3.6	2.7	4.5	3.1	10.2
50-64	0.4 *	0.3 *	0.1 *	1.6	1.1	1.6	1.0	5.3
65 and over	0.1 *	0.3 *	0.1 *	0.7	0.1 *	0.9	0.6 *	1.5
Marital status[2]								
Married	0.4	0.6	0.6	2.8	1.7	2.4	2.1	7.9
Widowed	0.2 *	0.3 *	0.1 *	0.8	0.6 *	1.3 *	1.0 *	1.5 *
Divorced or separated	3.1	3.0	1.6	5.5	10.8	8.7	5.2	14.7
Never married	0.6	4.1	1.9	8.5	2.6	16.4	10.5	23.6
Family income[3]								
Less than $7,500	1.7	3.7	2.1	8.3	3.4	11.8	8.0	15.8
$7,500-$14,999	1.0	2.7	0.9 *	5.2	3.5	7.8	3.9	11.6
$15,000-$24,999	1.1	2.3	0.9	4.3	4.0	7.5	5.2	13.3
$25,000-$34,999	0.7 *	1.9	1.4	4.4	2.5	8.5	6.2	12.6
$35,000-$49,999	0.5 *	1.6	1.6	5.0	3.8	7.1	5.4	12.8
$50,000-$74,999	0.4 *	1.7	0.7 *	5.1	1.8	6.6	4.6	16.1
$75,000 or more	0.1 *	1.0 *	0.8 *	3.5	1.4	6.1	4.7	13.9

[2]Excludes data on persons whose marital status was not ascertained.
[3]Excludes data on persons whose family income was not ascertained.

that approximately 20% of both aggravated and simple assaults experienced by women are committed by intimates (spouses, ex-spouses, boy/girlfriends) compared to 3% for men. Regardless of the approach the results indicate that women are more often victims of battering, although the magnitude of the finding differs depending on the way the data are presented.

At this time, it is not clear how the acquaintance category affects our estimates of battering. This issue is significant given that almost one-third of the assaults experienced by both men and women fall in this category. As previously noted, it is quite possible that victimizations experienced by women at the hands of friends and acquaintances represent intimate battering that occurs by partners who do not fall into the victim's definition of spouse or boyfriend. It also is possible that these victimizations, for men, represent physical fights with their male friends and casual acquaintances. In other words, for women, the data may be underestimating battering for women, although this may not be true for men. Ultimately, this is an empirical question. Deciphering this friend/acquaintance relationship is a methodological problem that can be resolved by additional refinements to the NCVS. However, given the lengthy process of re-design one can assume that it might well be a decade (or more) before another re-design is implemented.

Major Findings

As the accompanying article by Kindermann and his colleagues demonstrates, the NCVS finds more assaults (and more crime in general) than its predecessor (the NCS), but the general trends are similar for both instruments. The NCVS annual report for 1995 indicates that aggratvated assaults are slightly more likely to be committed by strangers (56% of the cases), but that simple assaults are slightly more likely to occur by someone who is known to the victim (54%; BJS, 2000, p. 37). In general, men are more apt to be assaulted (45.3 per 1000 persons compared to 30.5 per 1000 persons for women; BJS, 2000, p. 9). As Figure 1 shows, men are most apt to be assaulted by strangers (31.8 per 1000 people for men compared to 12.0 for women; BJS, 2000, p. 43). Women are most apt to be assaulted by relatives including intimates (5.5 per 1000 people for women compared to 2.5 for men; BJS, 2000, p. 43). In total, 953, 700 women and 115,490 men were victims of intimate violence in 1995 (Rennison & Welchans, 2000, p. 3).[4] While the quality of the NCVS data and the limited analyses of the results leave estimates of the frequency of battering suspect, one can make a series of deductive assumptions that suggest support for a feminist analysis of battering.

Violence Against Women Survey VAWS

This study was a joint effort of the National Institute of Justice and the Centers for Disease Control (Tjaden & Thoennes, 1998). A random sample of 8000 men and 8000 women over age 18 completed telephone interviews conducted from November 1995 to May 1996. One member of each household contacted was asked to complete the survey.[5] The study used behaviorally specific questions to illicit information about victimization, and details were gathered about the specifics of the assaults.[6] The study examines physical assault experienced as children from adult caretakers, physical assault as adults, and forcible rape or stalking experienced as adults.

Although numerous methodological differences make comparisons precarious, the VAWS generally finds higher estimates of victimization than the NCS and NCVS (see table 1).[7] The VAWS reports that 1,309,061 women and 834,732 men were victims of physical assaults by intimates (spouses, ex-spouses, opposite-sex cohabiting partners, same-sex cohabiting partners, dates, and boyfriends/girlfriends) in the 12 months preceding the survey (Tjaden & Thoennes, 1998, p. 7).[8] These yearly victimization rates, or incident rates, however, underestimate one's lifetime risk of victimization. The VAWS reports that 22% of women (25% if sexual assaults are included) and 8% of men were physically victimized at some point in their lives (Tjaden & Thoennes, 1998, p. 6). This prevalence rate is similar to findings in other studies (see figure 1). For example, Russell (1990) reports that 15% of the women in her random sample drawn from San Francisco had experienced some form of woman battering and 30% of a random sample of Georgia residents reportedly experienced abuse (Buehler, Dixon, & Toomey, 1998). This figure also is similar to findings from other countries. For example, research indicates that 29% of Canadian women (Johnson, 1994), 25% of Turkish women (Feminist Majority Foundation, May 18, 1998), 33% of Japanese women (Feminist Majority Foundation, May 22, 1998) and 38% of Australian women (Domestic Violence & Incest Resource Centre, 1996) report they have experienced some form of woman battering some time in their lifetime. Thus, many victimization studies indicate that a relatively high percentage of women experience abuse by their partners. In addition, the NCS, the NCVS, and the VAWS all provide support for feminist claims that battering is a problem primarily experienced by women at the hands of their intimate male partners. This statement, however, does not apply when one considers the third and remaining national survey.

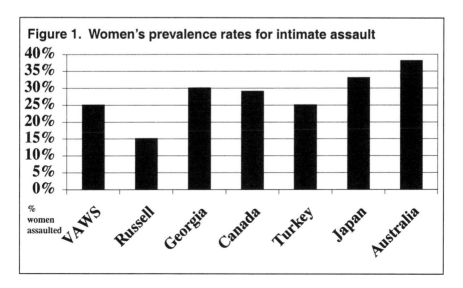

Figure 1. Women's prevalence rates for intimate assault

National Family Violence Survey

Substantial federal funding from several agencies was granted to the Family Research Lab at the University of New Hampshire to conduct a national study on battering. The National Family Violence Survey (NFVS) was created and was administered to a random sample of about 2000 couples in 1975. The study was replicated when about 6000 couples were surveyed in 1985 (Straus & Gelles, 1995).[9]

Reading 5 by Straus and Gelles describes the conflict tactics scales (CTS) designed to measure battering (and child abuse).[10] Cohabitating and married couples were interviewed in person or by phone, but only one member of the couple was questioned. Respondents were asked to "think of situations in the past year when they had a disagreement or were angry with a specified family member and to indicate how often they engaged in each of the acts included in the CTS." Acts were classified as violent if they involved: throwing something at the other person, pushing, grabbing, shoving, slapping, spanking, kicking, biting, hitting with a fist, trying to hit with something, beating up the other, threatening another with a knife or gun, or using a knife or gun. If any of these types of violence occurred, the incident was counted in the overall category of violence; however, this category also was divided into two other subsets of violence: severe and minor. Severe violence included kicking, biting, hitting with a fist or something else, beating someone up, and using or threatening to use weapons. The remaining acts of violence were classified as minor.

As the Straus and Gelles article demonstrates, there was little difference in the overall rate of violence among couples from 1975 to 1985. In other words, there was no statistically significant increase or decrease in the levels of violence reported. In 1986, the survey found that 16% of the *couples* surveyed had experienced some kind of intimate violence in the preceding year and almost one in four (28%) *couples* reported violence sometime in their past (Gelles & Cornell, 1990, p. 69). Their data are reported using couples as the unit of analysis because they find that men and women are about equally violent. This finding, and the notion that there is a "Battered Husband Syndrome" (Steinmetz, 1977), has created much controversy.

In stark contrast to the other studies reviewed, the NFVS finds evidence of mutual combat; "The problem is not wife-beating perpetrated by violent men, but 'violent couples' and 'violent people'" (Dobash et al., 1992, p. 73). In fact, the NFVS actually finds that women commit more violence than do men, although the difference is not statistically significant. As table 2 in reading 5 illustrates, 121 women out of every 1000 couples engaged in *overall violence* against their male partners, while the rate for men was 113 per 1000 couples (overall violence includes all acts of violence measured). Likewise, 44 women in every 1000 couples committed *severe violence* against their male partners while the rate for men was 30 per 1000 couples.

Feminist researchers have been very critical of the NFVS and the use of the CTS instrument (Berk et al., 1983; Breines & Gordon, 1983; Dobash & Dobash, 1992; Dobash et al., 1992; Greenblat, 1983; Kurz, 1993a, 1993b; Saunders, 1988; Schwartz, 1987; Stark & Filcraft, 1985; Yllo, 1988). First, and most seriously, the

NFVS fails to distinguish between acts of aggression and acts of self-defense. If one has engaged in any act of violence in the past year, it is counted as violence regardless of the circumstances leading up to and surrounding the use of force. An example helps to illustrate the problem with this type of measurement. If a male partner severely beats his partner with his fist, punching her in the face, kicking her in the stomach, and choking her until she passes out, he has committed severe violence. If a victim in a similar situation bit her perpetrator, even if it was in self-defense, it would also count as severe violence. The failure to identify the context of the violence is a critical flaw.

When context is provided in the study, it is problematic. Respondents are asked to report their experiences of violence in response to the following statements:

> No matter how well a couple gets along, there are times when they disagree, get annoyed with the other person, or just have spats or fights because they're in a bad mood or tired or for some other reason. They also use many different ways of trying to settle their differences. I'm going to read some things that you and your (spouse/partner) might do when you have an argument. I would like you to tell me how many times . . . in the past 12 months [Read item]. (Straus, 1995, p. 33)

Notice that this statement assumes that battering occurs in the context of a disagreement, despite the fact that battering occurs outside the confines of an argument. Consider the following example. Assume that a male partner comes home and begins complaining about everything in the house. After ranting and raving for a while, he begins to beat her for cooking food he doesn't like and refuses to let her cook him anything else. He overturns the kitchen table and throws her across the room. He is punching her in the face, kicking her with great force, and grinding her face in the food that is all over the kitchen. A woman in this type of circumstance is not a participant in an argument and it is not clear whether women in these situations will report abuse when it is framed as a disagreement.

Second, there are many problems with the acts used in the scale and the definition of serious and minor violence. For example, sexual assaults are not captured in the CTS (Dobash et al., 1992), which leads to underestimates of the amount of violence experienced by women.[11] Furthermore, the distinctions between severe and minor violence are problematic. Remember that severe violence includes kicking, biting, hitting with a fist or something else, beating someone up, and using or threatening to use weapons. In other words, the CTS counts a bite the same as holding a loaded gun to someone's head or stabbing someone. Biting is a type of violence that probably is more consistent with women's socialization than with men's, and it may be used more often as a means of self-defense. For example, it seems reasonable that many women might try to bite a batterer who is choking her. Thus, it is possible that including biting artificially increases women's rates of violence. Regardless, biting hardly seems comparable to the other acts of serious violence in terms of its ability to produce injury.[12]

In a similar vein, slapping is classified as minor violence, yet the definition of slapping is quite broad. "The word encompasses anything from a slap on the hand chastising a dinner companion for reaching for a bite of one's dessert to a tooth-loosening assault intended to punish, humiliate, and terrorize. These are not trivial distinctions; indeed, they constitute the essence of definitional issues concerning violence" (Dobash et al, 1992, p. 79). Likewise, it also may be inappropriate to clas-sify pushing, grabbing, and shoving as minor acts of violence, as discussed in chap-ter 1. While men and women may trade slaps and shoves, they rarely trade injuries. In fact, supplementary questions about injury were added to the 1985 NFVS sur-vey. The results indicate that the injury rate for assaults by men was six times as large as the injury rates for assaults committed by women (Straus, 1993, p. 69).

A third problem with the NFVS is that only one person in the couple is interviewed, making it impossible to assess the reliability of the respondents in the survey. Studies that have examined this issue of interspousal reliability indi-cate that there is little agreement between the evaluation of violence when both parties of the couple are included in studies (see Dobash et al., 1992; Schafer, Caetano, & Clark, 1998; Szinovacz, 1983). Men may underrepresent their use of violence to minimize their behavior and diminish their culpability. It is in their best interest to deny the amount of harm, the extent of injuries, and the level of force. At least one study reports that women are more apt to admit to violence they have committed (Szinovacz, 1983). Thus, it is possible that men underre-port and women overreport, leading to figures that convey mutual combat.

Fourth, the NFVS and its estimates of violence probably fail to capture some cases of severe battering. In the 1975 study, the sample population was limited to those persons who were currently married or cohabiting. While the 1985 study includes persons who have been recently separated or divorced, recently is not defined (Straus & Gelles, 1995, p. 531). By excluding much of the divorced popu-lation, it is possible that many cases of severe violence are excluded since bat-tered women may be more apt to leave—to divorce the batterer—when the violence is extensive.

Data from the NCVS confirm that it is important to include separated and divorced individuals in the sample. Separated women have an extremely high rate of violent victimization—127.8 p/1000 people (Craven, 1997, p. 3). This rate is considerably higher than the rate for separated men (79.1 p/1000) and is, in fact, the third highest crime rate of all groups of men and women. Only men ages 12 to 15 and ages 16 to 19 have higher rates of violent victimization (139.1 and 143.6 p/1000). Thus, while women's victimization rates almost never exceed those of men (with the exception of rape), separated women experience more rapes, rob-beries, and assaults than men regardless of their race or ethnicity, income, resi-dence, educational status or other married status (married, widowed, divorced, etc). While there is no information about the relationship between the offender and the victim in this table, the very high victimization rate for separated women seems to confirm what has long been asserted—that battered women are at most risk when they leave the batterer. If he can't have her, no one will.

In addition, the focus on married or cohabiting adults aged 19–70 (Straus & Gelles, 1995, p. 529) excludes dating violence from the estimates. This omis-sion is problematic given research that indicates between one-fifth and one-third of college students report experiencing non-sexual, physical violence during courtship (Arias et al., 1987; Bogal-Allbritten & Allbritten, 1985; Cate et al., 1982; Knutson & Mehm, 1986; Lane & Gwartney-Gibbs, 1985; Makepeace, 1986; Matthews, 1984; Stets & Pirog-Good, 1987; Sugarman & Hotaling, 1989).[13]

Despite the shortcomings of the CTS, the authors contend that the instrument is both reliable and valid and claim that numerous scholars agree that it is "the best available instrument" (Straus, 1993, p.83). They contend that about 30 other studies support the findings of the NFVS and find that men and women use approximately equal levels of violence in intimate relationships (Straus, 1993, p. 70).

It is certainly possible that the CTS is reliable; that it produces consistent findings. For example, a broken thermometer may consistently register temperatures 10 degrees higher than a properly functioning instrument. That does not mean it is accurate. Validity is quite another issue. There is little evidence that the CTS adequately captures the amount or nature of woman battering. Proponents, however, continue to hold fast to the assumption that battering is most often a case of mutual battering and point to studies using the CTS, which find that men and women are about equally violent in intimate relationships. As reading 5 illustrates, proponents acknowledge that sexism plays an important role in battering, but they view the problem as family violence and focus on violence between partners rather than woman battering.

However, the only studies that find evidence of sexual symmetry or mutual combat are those using the CTS. The NCS and NCVS data, the VAWS and victimization surveys in both Great Britain and Canada (Sacco & Johnson, 1990; Worrall & Pease, 1986) indicate that most victims of assaults in intimate relationships are women. Similarly, studies based on shelter records, emergency room records, police reports, prosecution summaries, judicial records, and homicide data all consistently demonstrate that the vast majority of battering victims are women (Berk et al., 1983; Dobash & Dobash, 1979; Fergusson et al., 1986; Fields & Kirchner, 1978; Goldberg & Tomlanovich, 1984; McLeer & Anwar, 1989; McLeod, 1984; Okun, 1986; Quarm & Schwartz, 1985; Rand, 1997; Vanfossen, 1979; Warshaw, 1989). Likewise, the homicide data discussed earlier also report that women are more likely to be murdered by their intimate partners. The homicide and emergency room data are especially interesting. At a minimum, one would expect to find some substantial evidence of serious battering in these data sets if men are experiencing life threatening injuries and/or deaths at the hands of women. If you are stabbed you need medical treatment. Most homicides are reported and counted because there is a body. If there is some equal proportion of severe, physical battering occurring, these injured and dead men have slipped through the cracks.

SUMMARY

As stated previously, all social activity is affected by gender. How we name, define, and measure a social problem reflects hegemonic assumptions of the larger social structure. Woman battering has often been called by names that obscure the gendered nature of the act. Definitions of the problem are often very narrow and rarely focus on sexual or emotional abuse. Woman battering has been defined and measured in ways that seriously underestimate the amount of abuse. Likewise, seriously flawed science has been used to argue that men and women are equally violent toward their intimate partners.

One might hope that "better science" will produce evidence that dispels the notion of mutual battering. However, the controversy over this issue represents a battle over hegemonic assumptions in our culture. "From a sociological point of view, the debate cannot be easily dismissed as insignificant. It is important because whoever wins this battle earns the right to define the nature of the problem" (Barnett et al, 1997, p. 193). The continued assertion that battering involves mutual combat demands much time and energy. If researchers and/or advocates fail to respond to this assertion there is always the risk that social policies and funding will be eliminated and that battered women will loose support systems that have been hard won (Kurz, 1993). While assuredly some women are violent and some of the time they assault their partners, there is no evidence of the wide-spread use of coercive power exercised by women against men. If the problem is viewed as mutual combat, there is no need to confront the notion that the family is a very violent and dangerous place for women.

The continued battle to count battering more accurately ensures that much needed research on more complex issues will be less likely to occur. When we ask respondents to report whether they have committed or experienced certain acts of violence without measuring their meaning and consequences, there is a risk of distorting these events (Dobash et al, 1992). There is a need for richer data that will result in a more comprehensive description of violence and the explanations for it. There is a need for better theoretical development. For example, Johnson (1995) argues that the debate over *the* nature of "family violence" may have obscured the fact that there are two distinctly different types of partner violence. There may be couples who engage in relatively equal amounts of violence in the family as a way to resolve conflict in a violent prone society; however, there also may be women who experience "patriarchal terrorism" by men who use coercive control to achieve obedience by "any means necessary" (Johnson, 1995, p. 286). It is also possible that there are other types of battering relationships. As Browne (1997) notes, we know little about relationships where violence occurs infrequently. These acts generally are viewed as situational—occurring in response to a particular incident, problem, or set of circumstances—and aberrant in the context of that particular relationship.

We need better theory and research to determine if there are different types of battering relationships. It seems unlikely that battering is a unidimensional problem; however, the stakes are high. "Counting" the amount of abuse does little to address more complex issues, although it does allow advocates to continue to assert a need for services when the problem can be documented in epidemic proportions. As instruments continue to be refined and the estimates of battering (and other violence against women) continue to rise, it also makes it more difficult to maintain the hegemonic assumption that battering is a rare event.

NOTES

[1] Studies have documented the existence of battering in gay and lesbian relationships; however, insufficient data make comparisons difficult. For additional information on this subject see Lobel (1986), Renzetti (1992), and Island and Letellier (1991).

[2] The definitions of abuse here rely heavily upon Tong's (1984) classification scheme. She, however, adds a fourth category—destruction of pets and property. I contend that this behavior is a type of emotional/psychological abuse and do not think it warrants a separate category of its own.

[3] Research indicates that this type of abuse is very common; almost three-fourths of women in shelters report that their partner had threatened or actually harmed a pet (Ascione, 1997, 1998).

[4] These figures include a small number of robberies and rapes. The data are not disaggregated to allow for reporting of battering alone.

[5] In cases where two or more adults were present in the home, the adult with the most recent birth date was used to randomly select a respondent.

[6] The study reports using a modified version of the conflict tactics scale. This scale will be discussed in future sections of this chapter and is much criticized for poor measurement techniques. The study referred to in this section of the paper does not discuss how it modified the scale, but it appears that the study separated acts of self-defense from acts of aggression, given the results that are reported.

[7] Unfortunately, the VAWS data are not presented in ratios (per 1,000 people) making comparisons difficult. The authors of the study, however, report that their estimates are higher.

[8] These figures underestimate physical battering, as cases of rape and assault were counted only as rapes. Furthermore, when rapes are included, the number of women experiencing battering of some form climbs to 1,510,455. The figure for men remains unchanged. The figure for physical battering only is reported in the body of the text to facilitate comparisons.

[9] They report a response rate of 84%, although at least one researcher argues that it might be as low as 60% (Johnson, 1995 p. 292).

[10] The CTS was slightly modified in the 1985 version (see Straus & Gelles, 1995, appendix A and B) and there is a new CTS2, which has just been recently devised (1995).

[11] To be fair, most of the literature on abuse also suffers from this shortcoming as the focus tends to be on physical assaults.

[12] A recent exception might be the case of Mike Tyson biting off part of his opponent's ear in a boxing match. However, this seems to be an atypical type of force used by men—especially when it involves other men.

[13] Like the NFVS, however, they find relatively equal amounts of violence by men and women, which probably is related to their use of the CTS.

REFERENCES

Arias, I., Samios, M., & O'Leary, K. D. (1987). Prevalence and correlates of physical aggression during courtship. *Journal of Interpersonal Violence, 2*(1), 82–90.

Ascione, F. (1997). The abuse of animals and domestic violence: A national survey of shelters for women who are battered. *Society and Animals, 5,* 205–218.

Ascione, F. (1998). Battered women's reports of their partners' and their children's cruelty to animals. *Journal of Emotional Abuse, 1,* 119–133.

Bachman, R., & Saltzman, L. E. (1995). *Violence against women: Estimates from the redesigned survey* (NCJ-15438). Washington, DC: U.S. Department of Justice.

Bachman, R., & Taylor, B. (1994). The measurement of family violence and rape by the redesigned National Crime Victimization Survey. *Justice Quarterly, 11,* 499–512.

Barnett, O. W., Miller-Perrin, C. L., & Perrin, R. D. (1997). *Family violence across the lifespan.* Thousand Oaks, CA: Sage.

Belknap, J. (1996). *The invisible woman: Gender, crime and justice.* New York: Wadsworth.

Berk, R., Berk, S., Loseke, D., & Rauma, D. (1983). Combat and other family violence myths. In D. Finkelhor, R. Gelles, G. Hotaling, & M. Straus (Eds.), *The dark side of families: Current family violence research* (pp. 197–212). Beverly Hills, CA: Sage.

Biderman, A., & Reiss, A. (1967). On exploring the "dark figure" of crime. *The Annals, 374,* 1–15.

Bograd, M. (1988). Feminist perspectives on wife abuse. In K. Yllo & M. Bograd (Eds.), *Feminist perspectives on wife abuse* (pp. 11–26). Thousand Oaks, CA: Sage.

Bogal-Allbritten, R., & Allbritten, W. L. (1985). The hidden victims: Courtship violence among college students. *Journal of College Student Personnel, 26,* 201–204.

Booth, A., Johnson, D., & Choldin, H. (1977). Correlates of city crime rates: Victimization surveys versus official statistics. *Social Problems, 25,* 187–197.

Breines, W., & Gordon, L. (1983). The new scholarship on family violence. *Signs: Journal of Women in Culture and Society, 18,* 490–531.

Browne, A. (1987). *When battered women kill.* New York: Free Press.

Browne, A. (1997). Violence in marriage: Until death do us part? In A. Cardarelli (Ed.), *Violence between intimate partners* (pp. 48–69). Needham Heights, MA: Allyn & Bacon.

Buehler, J., Dixon, B., & Toomey, K. (1998, October 16). Morbidity and mortality weekly report: Lifetime and annual incidence of intimate partner violence and resulting injuries—Georgia, 1995. Retrieved September 5, 1999 from the World Wide Web: *http://www.ama-assn.org/special/womh/newsline/special/mm4740.html*

Bureau of Justice Statistics (2000). *Criminal victimization in the United States, 1995.* Washington, DC: U.S. Department of Justice.

Cate, R. M., Henton, J. M., & Lloyd, S. (1982). Premarital abuse: A social psychological perspective. *Journal of Family Issues, 3,* 79–90.

Cohen, L., & Lichbach, M. (1982). Alternative measures of crime: A statistical evaluation. *The Sociological Quarterly, 23,* 253–266.

Craven, D. (1997). *Sex differences in violent victimization, 1994.* Washington, DC: U.S. Department of Justice.

DeKeseredy, W. S., & Schwartz, M. D. (1998, February). Measuring the extent of woman abuse in intimate heterosexual relationships: A critique of the Conflict Tactics Scales. Retrieved March 17, 1999 from the World Wide Web: *http://www.vaw.umn.edu/Vawnet/ctscrit.html*

Dobash, R. E., & Dobash, R. P. (1979). *Violence against wives: A case against the patriarchy.* New York: Free Press.

Dobash, R. E., & Dobash, R. P. (1992). *Women, violence, and social change.* New York: Routledge.

Dobash, R. P., Dobash, R. E., Wilson, M., & Daly, M. (1992). The myth of sexual symmetry in marital violence. *Social Problems, 39,* 71–91.

Domestic Violence & Incest Resource Centre (1996). Australian statistics on domestic violence. Retrieved September 4, 1999 from the World Wide Web: *http://home.vicnet.net.au/-dvirc/Statistics.html*

Ennis, P. (1967). *Criminal victimization in the United States.* Washington, DC: Report on a National Survey by President's Crime Commission on Law Enforcement and Criminal Justice.

Feminist Majority Foundation (1998, May 9). One third of Japanese women battered by husbands, partners. Retrieved February 20, 1999 from the World Wide Web: http://www.feministorg/news/newsbyte/may98/0522.html

Feminist Majority Foundation (1998, May 18). One in four Turkish women severely beaten by husband, relatives. Retrieved February 20, 1999 from the World Wide Web: http://www.feministorg/news/newsbyte/may98/0518.html

Fergusson, D. M., Horwood, L. J., Kershaw, K. L., & Shannon, K. T. (1986). Factors associated with reports of wife assault in New Zealand. *Journal of Marriage and the Family, 48*, 407–412.

Fields, M. D., & Kirchner, R. M. (1978). Battered women are still in need: A reply to Steinmetz. *Victimology, 3*, 216–226.

Gelles, R. J., & Cornell, C. P. (1990). *Intimate violence in families*. Newbury Park, CA: Sage.

Goldberg, W. G., & Tomlanovich, M. C. (1984). Domestic violence victims in the emergency department: New findings. *Journal of the American Medical Association, 251*, 3259–3264.

Gottfredson, M. (1986). Substantive contributions of victimization surveys. In M. Tonry and N. Morris, *Crime and justice: An annual review of research, Volume 7* (pp. 251–287). Chicago: University of Chicago Press.

Gove, W., Hughes, M., & Geerken, M. (1984). Are uniform crime reports a valid indicator of the index crimes? An affirmative answer with minor qualifications. *Criminology, 23*(3), 451–501.

Greenblat, C. S. (1983). A hit is a hit . . . or is it? In D. Finkelhor, R. Gelles, G. Hotaling, & M. Straus (Eds.), *The dark side of families: Current family violence research* (pp. 235–260). Beverly Hills, CA: Sage.

Greenfeld, L., Rand, M., Craven, D., Klaus, P., Perkins, C., Ringel, C., Warchol, G., Maston, C., & Fox, J. (1998). *Violence by intimates: Analysis of data on crimes by current or former spouses, boyfriends, and girlfriends*. Washington, DC: U.S. Department of Justice.

Hindelang, M. (1981). Variations in sex-race-age-specific incident rates of offending. *American Sociological Review, 46*, 461–474.

Island, D., & Letellier, P. (1991). *Men who beat the men who love them*. New York: Harrington Park Press.

Johnson, H. (1994). Seriousness, type and frequency of violence against wives. Paper presented at the American Society of Criminology Meeting. Miami, FL.

Johnson, M. P. (1995). Patriarchal terrorism and common couple violence: Two forms of violence against women. *Journal of Marriage and Family, 57*, 283–294.

Kelly, L. (1988). *Surviving sexual violence*. Minneapolis: University of Minnesota Press.

Kindermann, C., Lynch, J., & Cantor, D. (1997). *Effects of the redesign on victimization estimates*. Washington, DC: U.S. Department of Justice.

Knutson, J. F., & Mehm, J. G. (1986). Transgenerational patterns of coercion in families and intimate relationships. In G. Russell (Ed.), *Violence in intimate relationships* (pp. 67–90). New York: PMA Publishing Company.

Kurz, D. (1993a). Physical assaults by husbands: A major social problem. In R. Gelles & D. D. Loseke (Eds.), *Current controversies on family violence* (pp. 88–103). Newbury Park, CA: Sage.

Kurz, D. (1993b). Social science perspectives on wife abuse: Current debates and future directions. In P. Bart & E. Moran (Eds.), *Violence against women* (pp. 252–269). Newbury Park, CA: Sage.

Lane, K. E., & Gwartney-Gibbs, P. A. (1985). Violence in the context of dating and sex. *Journal of Family Issues, 6*, 45–59.

Lehnen, R., & Skogan, W. (1981). *The national crime survey: Working papers, Volume I: Current and historical perspectives.* Washington, DC: U.S. Department of Justice.

Levine, J. (1976). The potential for crime overreporting in criminal victimization surveys. *Criminology, 14*(3), 307–330.

Lobel, K. (1986). *Naming the violence: Speaking out about lesbian violence.* Seattle: Seal Press.

Makepeace, J. (1986). Gender differences in courtship violence victimization. *Family Relations, 36,* 87–91.

Matthews, W. J. (1984). Violence in college couples. *College Student Journal, 18,* 150–158.

McLeer, S. R., & Anwar, R. (1989). A study of battered women presenting in an emergency department. *American Journal of Public Health, 79,* 65–66.

McLeod, M. (1984). Women against men: An examination of domestic violence based on an analysis of official data and national victimization data. *Justice Quarterly, 1,* 129–132.

O'Brien, R. (1985). *Crime and victimization data.* Beverly Hills: Sage.

O'Brien, R. (1986). Rare events, sample size, and statistical problems in the analysis of the NCS city surveys. *Journal of Criminal Justice, 14,* 441–448.

Okun, L. (1986). *Woman abuse: facts replacing myths.* Albany: SUNY Press.

Quarm, D., & Schwartz, M. (1985). Domestic violence in criminal court. In C. Schweber & C. Feinman (Eds.), *Criminal justice politics and women* (pp. 29–46). New York: Haworth.

Rand, M. (1997). *Violence-related injuries treated in hospital emergency departments.* Washington, DC: U.S. Department of Justice, Bureau of Justice Statistics.

Rennison, M., & Welchans, S. (2000). *Intimate partner violence.* Washington, DC: U.S. Department of Justice.

Renzetti, C. M. (1992). *Violent betrayal: Partner abuse in lesbian relationships.* Newbury Park, CA: Sage.

Richie, B. (1996). *Compelled to crime: The gender entrapment of battered black women.* New York: Routledge.

Russell, D. (1990). *Rape in marriage.* New York: Collier.

Sacco, V., & Johnson, H. (1990). *Patterns of criminal victimization in Canada.* Ottawa: Statistics Canada.

Saunders, D. B. (1988). Wife abuse, husband abuse, or mutual combat: A feminist perspective on the empirical findings. In K. Yllo, & M. Bograd (Eds.), *Feminist perspectives on wife abuse* (pp. 90–113). Newbury Park, CA: Sage.

Schafer, J., Caetano, R., & Clark, C. (1998). Rates of intimate partner violence in the United States. *American Journal of Public Health, 88,* 1702–1704.

Schwartz, M. (1987). Gender and injury in spousal assault. *Sociological Focus, 20,* 61–75.

Skogan, W. (1981). *Issues in measurement of victimization.* Washington, DC: U.S. Department of Justice.

Sonkin, D., Martin, D., & Walker, L. (1985). *The male batterer: A treatment approach.* New York: Springer.

Stark, E., & Filcraft, A. (1995). Killing the beast within: Women battering and female suicidality. *International Journal of Health Services, 25,* 43–64.

Stark, E., & Filcraft, A. (1983). Social knowledge, social policy, and the abuse of women. In D. Finkelhor, R. Gelles, G. Hotaling, & M. Straus (Eds.), *The dark side of families: Current family violence research* (pp. 330–348). Beverly Hills, CA: Sage.

Steinmetz, S. K. (1977). The battered husband syndrome. *Victimology, 2,* 499–509.

Stets, J. E., & Pirog-Good, M. A. (1987). Violence in dating relationships. *Social Psychology Quarterly, 50,* 237–246.

Stoltenberg, J. (1989). *Refusing to be a man: Essays on sex and justice.* New York: Meridian.

Straus, M. A. (1993). Physical assaults by wives: A major social problem. In R. Gelles & D. Loseke (Eds.), *Current controversies on family violence* (pp. 67–87). Newbury Park: CA: Sage.

Straus, M., & Gelles, R. (1986). Societal change and change in family violence from 1975 to 1985 as revealed by two national surveys. *Journal of Marriage and Family, 48*, 465–479.

Straus, M., & Gelles, R. (1995). *Physical violence in American families: Risk factors and adaptations to violence in 8,145 families.* New Brunswick, NJ: Transaction.

Sugarman, D. B., & Hotaling, G. T. (1989). Dating violence: Prevalence, context, and risk markers. In M. Pirog-Good & J. Stets (Eds.), *Violence in dating relationships* (pp. 3–32). New York: Praeger.

Szinovacz, M. E. (1983). Using couple data as a methodological tool: The case of marital violence. *Journal of Marriage and the Family, 45*, 633–644.

Tong, R. (1984). *Women, sex, and the law.* Totowa, NJ: Rowman & Allanheld.

Tjaden, P., & Thoennes, N. (1998). *Prevalence, incidence, and consequences of violence against women: Findings from the National Violence Against Women Survey.* Washington, DC: U.S. Department of Justice.

Utech, M. (1994). *Violence, abuse and neglect: The American home.* Dix Hills, NY: General Hall.

Vanfossen, B. E. (1979). Intersexual violence in Monroe County, New York. *Victimology, 4*, 229–305.

Walker, L. E. (1979). *The battered woman.* New York: Harper & Row.

Walker, L. (1989). *Terrifying love: Why battered women kill and how society responds.* New York: Harper Perennial.

Warshaw, C. (1989). Limitations of the medical model in the care of battered women. *Gender and Society, 3*, 506–517.

Worrall, A., & Pease, K. (1986). Personal crime against women: Evidence from the 1982 British Crime Survey. *The Howard Journal, 25*, 118–124.

Yllo, K. (1988). Political and methodological debates in wife abuse research. In K. Yllo & M. Bograd (Eds.), *Feminist perspectives on wife abuse* (pp. 28–50). Newbury Park, CA: Sage.

Yllo, K. (1993). Through a feminist lens: Social structure and family violence. In R. Gelles & D. Loseke (Eds.), *Current controversies on family violence* (pp. 47–62). Thousand Oaks, CA: Sage.

Yllo, K., & Straus, M. (1995). Patriarchy and violence against wives: The impact of structural and normative factors. In M. Straus & R. Gelles (Eds.), *Physical violence in American families: Risk factors and adaptations to violence in 8,145 families* (pp. 383–399). New Brunswick, NJ: Transaction.

Minority Women and Domestic Violence
The Unique Dilemmas of Battered Women of Color

Christine E. Rasche

Independent of each other as classes, women, minorities, and victims of domestic assault have been "overlooked" by mainstream criminology in the United States. Though there has been a recent increase in research on each of these classes of persons, modern studies are often still prefaced by acknowledgment that previous criminological interest in the subject was sparse and research prior to the 1970s was scanty. Nothing could be scantier, however, than research on persons simultaneously occupying all three categories—racial or ethnic minority women victimized by domestic violence. This paper examines this gap in the research literature, and draws from the available information to outline some of the special problems faced by this forgotten group of victims.

In some ways, the relative lack of interest in the relationship between minority women and domestic violence may not be surprising at all. Until recently, there has been little published literature on minority women in general. Historians were reproached several years ago for having virtually ignored women of color[1] in historical studies (Winkler, 1986). New writings, particularly on black women, have explained this disinterest in several ways which probably apply to most other minority racial/ethnic groups as well.

First, as Lynora Williams (1981) has noted, minority women in American society may be viewed as bearing a cross "on each shoulder"—racism and sexism. It is what Epstein (1973) has called the "double whammy." Minority women belong to both a devalued race and a devalued gender, by dominant American values, and are therefore of little intrinsic interest to members of the dominant

Reprinted with permission from *Journal of Contemporary Criminal Justice* 4(3) (1989), pp. 150–171.

class. Even when they stand out in some way, such as being disproportionately represented among known female offenders, black women have received little special criminological attention. The criminological literature on women of *other* racial/ethnic backgrounds is virtually nonexistent.

Second, the dual burden of racism and sexism affects not only the interests of the dominant class, but it affects the interests of minority women themselves. Diane Lewis (1977) has observed:

> Black women, due to their membership in two subordinate groups that lack access to authority and resources in society, are in structural opposition with a dominant racial and a dominant sexual group. In each subordinate group they share potential common interests with group members, black men on the one hand and white women on the other. Ironically, each of these is a member of the dominant group: black men as men, white women as whites. Thus, the interests which bind black women together and pull them into opposition against comembers crosscut one another in a manner which often obscures one set of interests over another. (p. 343)

Historically, black women have found that "their interests as blacks have taken precedence over their interests as women" (Lewis, 1977: 343). This primacy of concern for racism over sexism may partially account for the fact that there has been little special interest in minority spouse abuse and domestic violence even among minority researchers (Richie, 1985).

The question which arises of course, is whether there is *in fact* a need to treat minority women in some special way when attempting to understand the causes of and appropriate responses to domestic violence. Might it be perhaps wholly appropriate that no special literature has developed simply because the causes of, the dynamics of, the experience of, and the response to domestic violence are fundamentally the same for all women? Certainly most of the spouse abuse literature makes a point to assert that domestic violence cuts across all racial, ethnic, and class lines, and this may be a third reason for the minimal exploration of minority domestic violence.

However, the women involved on the actual firing line of responding to spousal violence—women who are operating refuges, working in victim's assistance programs, or otherwise fighting the problem—the answer to the question above is clearly "no." When the National Coalition Against Domestic Violence (NCADV) was formed in 1978, a Third World Women's Caucus was immediately formed to share insights about non-white women (Zambrano, 1985). The first National Conference of Third World Women Against Violence was held in Washington, D.C., in August of 1980 (Williams, 1981), and it has been followed by a series of similar conferences in the years since. An example is a two-weekend conference entitled "A Movement of New World Women" held in June 1985, in New York City, sponsored by the Women of Color Caucus of New York Women Against Rape, in cooperation with The Black Women's Development Collective, Inc. The impetus to hold special conferences of this sort is the firm belief on the part of the minority women involved that there *are* special, unique problems faced by minority women victimized by family violence. No empirical evaluation of this belief has ever been undertaken, and most of the concerns remain to date at the grassroots[2] organizing level.

THE EXTENT OF MINORITY VICTIMIZATION

In explaining how the volunteer staff of a newsletter on domestic violence began to explore the special needs of minority victims, Arnold and Perkins (1984–85) describe how the group of minority women found themselves sharing common concerns as well as peculiar ethnic problems. "As the brainstorming continued, a crucial insight was arrived at by the group: for white women and women of color, the *experience* of battering is quite similar but at the point of seeking help or escape from the abuse, women of color face many problems that white battered women generally do not" (Arnold & Perkins, 1984–85:2).

Perhaps it is precisely because the *experience* of being victimized in one's own home is so similar across racial/ethnic lines that possible *differences* in its causes, frequency, and solutions have not yet emerged as issues. But it seems clear that those differences do exist, at least on the level of obtaining solutions to or escape from the abuse.

It is also quite possible that there are real differences in the frequency of spousal violence in different ethnic groups, though the data on this question are quite inconsistent and contradictory. On the one hand, there seems to be no question that minority peoples in America and elsewhere suffer from higher rates of general victimization than do majority members. The higher risk of minority ethnic peoples to both be arrested and be victimized has been well established for some time. Whether it is native Indians in rural Canada (Chimbos & Montgomery, 1978), Maoris and Polynesians in New Zealand (Sullivan, 1977), Hispanics in the Southwest United States, Puerto Ricans in New York City, or blacks in most major U.S. cities, minority persons have been arrested for crimes in greater numbers than their population would warrant, especially for violent crimes. And criminal violence, especially aggravated assault and homicide, is predominantly an *intra*-group event (O'Brien, 1987; Wilbanks, 1985; Wilbanks, 1984; Block, 1977; Curtis, 1974; Savitz, 1973). Though white police have been shown to anticipate more physical danger to themselves in minority areas (Holdaway, 1983; Bayley, 1969) and economically motivated crimes such as robbery are more likely to show *inter*racial features (Wilbanks, 1985; Hindelang, 1976), the fact remains that assault and homicide by minority group members are most likely to be directed toward members of the same group. Where rates of violent crime by minority persons are high, the rate of minority victimization tends also to be high.

Especially for blacks, the largest racial minority group in the United States, crime victimization rates have consistently been shown to be higher than those for whites, especially for personal crimes and crimes of violence (Block, 1985; Hawkins, 1985; Allen, 1980; Hindelang, 1979; Savitz, 1973; Brearley, 1932). Again, most violent crimes among blacks are intraracial; intraracial homicides predominated in both Wolfgang's (1958) and Wilbanks' (1984) samples, and Block (1985) found that homicides committed by blacks were even *more* likely to be intraracial than those committed by whites. An article in the magazine *Ebony* once noted that more blacks were killed by other blacks in the single year of 1977 than were killed altogether during the entire Vietnam War, which spanned a nine-year period! A total of 5,711 blacks died in Vietnam while 5,734 were killed by other blacks in the United States in 1977 (Kirk, 1982).

Certainly more black males than black females are victimized (males of both races generally have higher offender and victimization rates for most offenses than do females of either race). But for the crime of assault and its companion homicide, the victimization rate for black females has frequently been shown to exceed not only the rate for white females but also for white males (Hawkins, 1985; Allen, 1980; Hindelang, 1976; Wolfgang, 1958). Furthermore, black women are victimized by a higher proportion of "assaults judged to be aggravated" than not only whites but women of Spanish origin (Bowker, 1979). By and large, non-homicide assaults upon black women have been shown to be intraracial but cross-sex (Bowker, 1979), and this is certainly true of fatal assaults upon black women (Rasche, 1988; Wilbanks, 1982; Wolfgang, 1958).

Most victimization data report on violations by reference to the crime categories of the *outcome* (assaults, homicides, etc.) rather than by reference to the situational origins. Until recently there has been little attempt to characterize victimizations by their *interactional context* (economically motivated attacks vs. domestic disputes, etc.), though even early empirical studies on homicide observed the important roles of family murder and spousal murder (Wolfgang, 1958; Von Hentig, 1948). The recent work of Straus, Gelles, and Steinmetz (1979) to measure domestic violence not in a clinical or criminal population but in a representative sample of 2,143 American families, has provided some insights into the nature of violence among minority group members. Rates of spousal violence, and in particular wife abuse, were found to be higher for minority groups than for whites. This was recently confirmed by Shoemaker and Williams (1987). Cazenave and Straus (1979) found that blacks had the highest rates, twice that of other racial minorities and four times higher than whites. These findings are consistent with those of Gelles (1980) and Staples (1976). However, other researchers have found no significant differences in rates of domestic violence between racial groups (Lockhart, 1984; Berk et al 1983; Parker & Schumacher, 1979; Walker, 1979; Smith & Snow, 1978), and it must be cautioned that the available data at this point in time is very contradictory.

This may be due, in part, to the fact that even victimization surveys have a very difficult time accurately measuring violence in the home. Probably the vast majority of spousal abuses involve non-fatal assaultive behaviors, acts which would more likely be reported if they were perpetrated between complete strangers. The very fact that such behavior is going on between two persons who have a close, intimate, personal relationship makes for a number of measurement problems. To be sure, police statistics have numerous faults as indicators of crime, not the least of which is their dependence on reporting behavior by victims and observers. In the case of assault, a ". . . simple inspection of existing figures suggests that more victims of spouse abuse do not call the police than do (Bard, 1980). And while victimization survey data are often used to offset the weaknesses of police data, assault is the one offense which has been acknowledged to have the most measurement problems. Assault victims have the poorest "recall rate" in victimization surveys (e.g., failure to report the victimization to the interviewer even though a known offense occurred). Less than half (47 percent) of National Crime Survey Participants who were known assault victims reported the crime to survey interviewers (Hindelang, 1979). Other nonsampling errors in victimization data abound, leading to the conclusion by the Census Bureau that "assault by relatives is the most underreported of all crimes covered by the NCS" (Gaquin, 1977–78).

The fact that assaultive behavior in the home may be severely underreported leads to the question of whether reporting behavior may vary across ethnic/racial lines. While assault and homicide offense and victimization rates may be higher for some groups (such as blacks) than for others (such as Asian Americans), data on clients using refuges or other services for battered women repeatedly report racial/ethnic breakdowns which are similar to the general population characteristics of that area (Walker, 1983; Kuhl, 1982; Brisson, 1981; LaBell, 1979; Rounsaville, 1978–79; Gelles, 1972). Indeed, victimization surveys specifically focusing on spouse abuse (as opposed to the more general category of assault) similarly show that *rates* for blacks and whites are almost the same (Bureau of Justice Statistics, April 1984; Gaquin, 1977–78; Hindelang, 1976), and one survey in Texas showed that whites, blacks, and Mexican Americans each responded affirmatively to the question of spouse abuse in about 6.0% of the cases (Stachura & Teske, 1979).

It seems clear that when attempting to measure spouse abuse or domestic violence, the measurement which is used may have significant consequences. Objective measures of violence, such as the Conflict Tactic Scales developed by Straus and his associates, may "discover" more violence than do inquiries which require the respondent to decide whether or not she has been abused. It has been suggested by more than one observer that different ethnic or cultural groups may have differing definitions of "abuse."

Indeed, there is evidence that some ethnic groups are much more tolerant of, even approving of, familial violence than are others. Several reports point to the relationship between rigid, patriarchal, male-dominated family relationships and high levels of violence in Mexican-American families (Carrol, 1980; Segovia-Ashley, 1978) and other Latin American families (Skurnik, 1983). This has also been reported for Italian-Americans (Spiegel, 1980) and other rural Mediterranean groups (Loizos, 1978), where "family honor" supercedes all other values. Shoemaker and Williams (1987) found that American Indians in their sample were more tolerant of violence than the general population or even blacks and Hispanics. Cazenave and Straus (1979) reported that black respondents in their survey were more approving of slapping between partners than were white respondents, and "Black husbands are also more likely to have actually slapped their wives and engaged in severe violence against them within the last year" (p. 285–286). Williams (1981) describes the frustration of trying to get black community leaders to support spouse abuse prevention campaigns when "beating a wife is something that is tolerated. It's just an okay thing to do" (p. 22). For some minority women, therefore, the first problem in escaping battery may be coming to terms with a cultural tolerance level for violence which is higher than that for other groups. Responses to abuse will be quite different in that context than in situations where violent behavior is viewed as somewhat more abnormal.

It is important to note here in passing, that the cross-cultural data which is available provides some interesting contradictions for a biological theory of ethnic variations in violence. An exception to the Hispanic model of hot-blooded inter-action may be found in the peaceful Tarahumura Indians of Mexico (West, 1980) and in the fact that *lethal* violence against women by Hispanics has been found to be rare (Zahn & Rickle, 1986; Block, 1985a). Wife abuse in Eastern and Central African cultures vary considerably, from high rates among those societies where hitting wives is viewed as no worse than hitting anyone else, to much lower rates among people such as Ankole, who have strong sanctions against violence towards wives (Mushanga, 1977–78). Data such as this strongly supports the etio-logical view that social/ environmental factors are largely responsible for ethnic variations in the United States in violence toleration. Indeed, some evidence sug-gests that social class may have more to do with acceptance of violence than eth-nic/racial traditions or adaption (Cazenave & Straus, 1979; Lockhart, 1984).

It is easy to see that the situation for women in high-violence cultural groups, where abuse is taken for granted, will be quite different than for women in low-violence groups, where even the accusation of battering may be viewed as extraordinary, even inconceivable. Women in both situations may have a hard time either reporting or escaping the violence, though for vastly different reasons.

UNDERREPORTING AMONG MINORITY WOMEN

While levels of abuse and tolerance of violence may vary considerably among different ethnic or cultural groups, there are other reasons why minority women in abusive domestic situations may be underreported. Specific attributes of ethnic or cultural tradition may be the biggest hurdles faced by abused women in getting help.

For example, the native-American woman living on a reservation or in a small rural settlement may find that reservation social service programs are staffed by her own relatives or those of her abuser; similarly, law-enforcement officers (usually county sheriffs department employees but possibly reservation police) may know or be related to her attacker (Feinman, 1985). While this pos-sibility exists in any small town or rural area, the highly interwoven network of Indian society usually makes it much worse. Unfortunately, it is not culturally acceptable to seek help outside of one's own community (American Indian Women Against Domestic Violence, June 1985), and, in any case, there may be no way for the Indian woman to get away from the isolated reservation or rural area when the need for help arises.

In Asian-American communities, presumed to have a fairly low spouse abuse rate, underreporting in fact may be severe. First, there is a tendency for Asian Americans to keep to themselves and shun outside assistance or interfer-ence, partly in response to a perceived hostile white society (Skurnik, 1983).

Asian cultural traditions emphasize respect for and subservience to elders, superiors, and persons in authority; talking back or fighting back even against abusive behavior would be viewed as extremely inappropriate. To seek help outside the community means confronting cultural prohibitions against causing any "loss of face" for oneself or one's family. For the traditionally-trained Asian-American woman, even speaking of such things to an outsider (such as reporting attacks to a victimization surveyor) would be unthinkable.

Even if the abuse were so bad that an Asian-American woman would seek help outside, this may be virtually impossible for immigrant wives who do not speak English. Calling the police in an extreme emergency may prove to be fruitless: "So often Asian batterers, many of whom function daily in the English-speaking work world, are able to out talk their wives in front of the police simply because the women cannot communicate effectively" (Eng, 1985:3). This language barrier exists across a number of ethnic groups, and often the police do not realize that a woman is accusing her spouse of battery simply because they accept the English-speaking husband as translator. Zambrano (1985) warns Latinos:

> Many English-speaking husbands take advantage of the fact that their wives don't speak English. They get to say all they want to the police and the women never get to tell what happened in their own words. If at all possible don't use your husband to translate for you. (p. 170)

Immigrant women face other obstacles in their efforts to escape from abuse as well. Women from foreign countries sometimes come to the U.S. for arranged marriages. Immigrant brides-to-be, even if they did speak English, may still find themselves in a vulnerable legal situation if their visas were sponsored by the men who are now their abusers, who may threaten to withdraw their support and cause instant deportation if the women say anything (Skurnik, 1983). Even if they do not like America, going home may result in an impossible loss of face for the bride's entire family, or may be economically devastating. Silence may seem like the only alternative.

For undocumented workers, of course, the escape from abuse may seem to be impossible. Fear not only of the police, but also of the helping agencies such as hospitals, social service organizations, or lawyers, may keep the illegal alien trapped in silence. For example, one study found that while immigrant Mexican women underutilized available maternal health services in San Diego, *undocumented* Mexican women were even less likely to make use of basic health services (Chavez, Cornelius, & Jones, 1986). Furthermore, the woman without proper documentation is probably thousands of miles from her home and family, and, "if this is your situation, you may find that the closest person to you is the one who is beating you, and he is probably well aware of how isolated you are" (Zambrano, 1985:214). Many such women simply do not know that their men do not have the right to beat them up or that, even if they are not citizens, they are entitled to protection under the law while they are in the United States. Those who do know this still fear that any contact with any official agency will result in their deportation. And their fears are not without warrant.

For those immigrant women with work permits, however, the decisions are still tough. Among Latinos, for example, often the wife was the first family member to come here, alone, to work in an illegal sweatshop and earn enough money to send for the rest of the family. By the time the man comes, he finds a radically restructured gender-role situation, in which he is dependent on a (now stronger) wife. He may resort to physical violence to try to regain his power and control. But for the woman to report him places the man in danger of deportation. "On the other hand a batterer can often threaten to turn the wife's whole family (that she has worked so hard to bring to America) over to immigration if she takes any action against him" (Skurnik, 1983:8). If there is truth to the notion that rates of domestic violence may be higher in Hispanic cultures anyway, the Latina immigrant (especially the illegal alien) may be one of the most abused but underreported battered women in America.

For almost *all* minority women, however, fear of the police may contribute to underreporting. Considerable evidence suggests that a significant proportion of minority group members have a severe distrust of the police and a hesitation to call police in may situations where white majority people would not hesitate to seek help (Carter, 1985; Yates, 1985; Barnett, 1977; Katz, 1973; Bayley & Mendelsohn, 1969). In talking about blacks, Barnett observes that "Based on the historical reputation of the police in the black community, many blacks believe the police function is to support and enforce the political, social and economic interests of the dominant community and only incidentally to enforce the law" (1977:127). This leads to more "negative expectations" of the police on the part of minority people than is true of dominants, and this in turn leads to "a strong disposition to avoid the police" (Bayley & Mendelsohn, 1969:120). As White (1985) notes:

> There is no denying that the relationship between the police and the black community has been a problematic one. Historically, the police have been some of the worst offenders in contributing to or blatantly ignoring the violence in black communities. (p. 40)

Minority women, compared to men, may be especially likely to avoid or become frustrated by police involvement, since police are more likely anyway to discriminate against female than male complainants in domestic disputes (Smith & Klein, 1984; Berk & Loseke, 1981). Though arrest upon demand of the complainant is a more likely outcome when the call for assistance is from a high-status area, indicating that police respond differently to disputes depending on their socioeconomic location, arrests are less likely in general when *women* are the complainants and violence is not obvious. Police also tend to minimize "the legal seriousness of non-violent disputes" involving female complaints (Smith & Klein, 1984: p. 479), and certainly have tended to see domestic disputes as "normal" and unworthy of police action (Edwards, 1986). Only when the situation actually becomes violent do police responses to male and female complainants become the same. The message is clear if you are a woman, any woman, in a low status area (where minorities often cluster), the police may not be much help unless they actually see you being assaulted physically.

Though Smith and Klein (1984) and others have found that race is *not* a factor which independently influences arrest decisions, there may be subtle ways in which racial/ethnic features operate to influence police behavior. In a guidebook for black women dealing with domestic abuse, White (1985) cautions black women to "make sure the officers see your injuries. You may have to explain to them that bruises on blacks are not always as visible or look as dramatic as they do on white people" (p. 39). Or, in a similar handbook for Latinas, Zambrano (1985) warns Hispanic women that the police may not respond to them properly because "they feel that you don't belong in this country or that you are not worth helping," especially if the women do not speak English effectively. In any case, whether police are influenced by race or not, the *belief* that they are and they will behave with prejudice and discrimination may in itself deter minority reporting.

Fear of the police may also derive not so much from concern that they won't do anything, but from concern that they will do too much. If police exhibit sexist devaluations of women's complaints, they are also viewed as being overly zealous and racist toward the minority men they do arrest. Garcia (1985) explains that true fear about what will happen to their men in white-controlled institutions such as the jail or the courtroom keep many minority women silent:

> Not only do we fear that *we* will be mistreated by the institutions, but that our men will be also. *We want the violence in our homes to stop but we do not want to contribute in any way to the unjust treatment of our race or ethnic community.* And so colorful women who are battered may hesitate to call the police or pursue arrest, for example, because we fear that our men will be treated more harshly than white batterers. (p. 2) (Author's emphasis)

White (1979) notes that in responding to black women, police not only typically respond with "traditional macho attitudes" about domestic violence, but "in our communities they have too frequently treated our husbands, sons, and brothers brutally and with racist contempt" (p. 129). One black activist is quoted by Williams (1981) as saying that "All (abusive) men, regardless of race, should be dealt with, but black men are going to be dealt with more severely." As a result, "There's a lot of guilt involved when you're talking about reporting a man. There's a fear that it's not supporting black and other minority men . . ." (p. 22).

Indeed, this concern for how minority men will be treated by police may be wielded by abusive men as a potent psychological weapon. "Your partner may protest about police brutality against blacks or accuse you of 'betraying' the race by calling them," warns White (1985:40). Anecdotal evidence indicates men from all ethnic/racial minority backgrounds utilize the same basic argument and it produces a dreadful conflict for an abused woman with a racial/ethnic conscience. All of the minority feminist literature on domestic abuse, new as it is, addresses this concern, and warns minority women not to be distracted by that ploy. "While it remains critical that black people continue actively struggling against racism and discrimination, it must not be done at the physical and psychological expense of black women," argues Richie-Bush (1983). "We have paid our dues, and black men must be held responsible for every injury they cause" (p.

17–18). Or, as Nkenge Toure of Washington's Rape Crisis Center succinctly put it, "It's a cop-out for brothers to use the issue of racism to make us feel bad" (Williams, 1981: p. 22).

As noted previously, minority women have been more prone to identify with racial/ethnic causes than feminist perspectives, however, and placing their rights as women above their concerns as minorities may not come easily. This is especially true if other components of the minority culture work to keep women in traditional roles. In Latin cultures, for example, women are viewed as being at "the heart" of the family, and the family, in turn, "is the mainstay of Latino culture."

> The Latino culture is a traditional one; in other words, it is a patriarchy with a long-established social system. Although women's roles are critical to the survival of the culture, women are relegated to the less powerful roles of wife and mother, and are often barred from being decision-makers or leaders . . . The authority and dignity of the family is respected. Individuals often defer to family unity and strength. For the battered woman this often means tolerating abuse for the sake of family pride and preservation. (Zambrano, 1985:226–227)

Chai (1987) found that immigrant Korean women in Hawaii were still expected to carry out traditional roles, but had fewer kin supports, less income, much more work, and greater economic dependence on their husbands.

The Catholic religion also plays an extremely important role in Hispanic families, and church teachings will strongly influence individual behavior. Indeed, the parish priest may be the only acceptable non-family authority figure Latinas believe they can consult. The track record for lack of helpfulness by clergy in cases of domestic violence has been documented (Fortune, 1981) and Catholic priests serving Hispanic communities are no exception. Zambrano (1985) notes that the attitudes of clergy at different churches within the same area may be quite different. Zambrano reports that while one church was already mobilizing a support group for battered wives,

> I talked with a group of priests who told me that they had no one in their church who needed "this kind" of help. They told me that women who were beaten could stop it if they really wanted to. They said such women do not honor their husbands and should expect some punishment. (Zambrano, 1985:213)

Little wonder that "Latinas often accept their destiny with resignation, accepting their family life as being the way God wants them to live" (Zambrano, 1985:227). Reaching such women with the message that they need not submit to continuing abuse may be very difficult; getting them to act on that message may be impossible.

The role of the church, and the importance of keeping the family together, has often had a similar impact in black communities. The image of "strong black womanhood," enduring all in the face of incredible racial oppression, is an ideal often held up to long-suffering women victims by the black community itself (Richie, 1985). Asbury (1987) has noted that "When an abused woman believes that strength and independence are expected of her, she may be more reluctant to call attention to her situation, feeling that she should be able to handle it on her own; she may deny the seriousness of her situation. Thus, she may remain immobile, hampered by her belief in inner resources she may not possess" (p. 101). Unfortunately, the traditions of the black church have tended to encourage acceptance of adversity:

> Throughout our history the church has held a predominant place in black people's lives. It was a deep, abiding faith in a "greater good" and a "Higher Power" that gave slave families their spiritual strength and unity. They endured the wrenching pain of losing loved ones on the auction block because they had a firm belief that their families would be reunited in another life . . . [Consequently], instead of seeking active change in the "here and now" some people accept their earthly sufferings and look forward to claiming their reward in heaven. This life, they believe, is a burdensome but necessary cross to bear in order to attain life everlasting. Such is the philosophy of many blacks who because of our oppression and the failing of mankind, have simply chosen to put our trust in the Lord. (White, 1985: 63)

Such emphasis on endurance may be underscored by the sexist attitudes of some black pastors, who may quote scriptures to complaining women which perpetuate male domination and female subservience. In this regard they are no different than their Hispanic counterparts, or for that matter, than white conservative religious leaders. But the role of the black church in most black communities and the power of the black pastor often far exceeds the effects of the church and its pastor in white communities. Since the church (or temple or synagogue) is often an extremely important institution in minority communities, the role of the religious institution and its clergy in either addressing or perpetuating the needs of battered women in those communities deserves far more inquiry.

In some cases, church indifference to the plight of battered women may stem not so much from religious tenets as it does from the unwillingness of community leaders to acknowledge the problem for other reasons. Often minority communities place an extremely high value on setting forth a positive racial/ethnic identity and seek to avoid anything which might reinforce stereotypical images. Egley (1982) has documented how this affects the recognition of spouse abuse among deaf people:

> Since the 1960s deaf organizations have made an effort to recount the successes of deaf individuals. The image of competence fights stigma and supports deaf people seeking achievement . . . Part of the problem for deaf individuals, deaf organizations and deaf communities looking at domestic abuse is whether to seek skills to stop abuse or to avoid stating that such a problem exists. (p. 27)

Similarly, among Indians the issue of violence is particularly difficult. Americans have well-established images of the "howling" and "barbaric" Indians who massacred "helpless" and "peaceable" white pioneers. "Because these images are held by most Americans—mostly in their unconscious—writing about violence against Indian women by Indian men is frightening and dangerous to Indian people; it is dangerous to say anything that can be used to perpetuate negative beliefs" (Allen, 1985: p. 1). Even among activists against domestic violence, this concern for protecting the image of the minority group remains strong. In one case, for example, a group of women from a variety of ethnic/racial backgrounds, who were working on a special newsletter issue on battering and minority women, found consensus when ". . . all agreed that the issue should not reinforce the myth that battering is more prevalent in third world homes than in white homes" (Arnold & Perkins, 1984–85: p. 2).

Among black leaders, the strength and well-being of the family is a very sensitive issue. Richie-Bush (1983) notes that some community agencies focus on strengthening the black family as a way of overcoming many of the needs in black communities. One such agency, at which she was employed, seemed particularly successful at helping black families fight exploitation while maintaining cultural and racial identities. However, "After a period of time, I gradually realized that some of these strong, culturally-identified families, which we had been supporting so vehemently, were dangerous places for some women to live." Richie-Bush notes:

> I found myself caught in a trap . . . It is the trap of silence. Because of the scarcity of agencies such as mine, I hesitated in disclosing my observations. I was immobilized by denial and sadness. Fear of being cast out by the community silenced me in the beginning. Loyalty and devotion are enormous barriers to overcome . . .
>
> Black women be forewarned. It is a painful unsettling task to call attention to violence in our community. You may find yourselves caught by the trap called loyalty. There is already so much negative information about our families that a need to protect ourselves keeps us quiet. (p. 16)

Under these circumstances, recognition and disclosure to the outside world that spouse abuse is a community problem can be, as Richie-Bush describes it, "so easily confused with treason!"

For other minority women, violent stereotypes are not so much the hurdle as is the failure of ethnic leaders to see that a sexist problem within the community may be as important as a racist problem outside of it. Anything which divides the minority community could distract members from the fight for equality which unites them all. As Eng (1985) observes about Asian minorities:

> Battering has not been publicly recognized by the leaders of the Asian communities who are all male. Instead, it has been buried under what are seen as more immediate concerns facing the entire community—low economic status and racial violence. (p. 3)

Since individualism is very suppressed in traditional Asian cultures, women who speak up for themselves against abuse are doubly condemned: for placing their own interests ahead of family interests and for dividing the family and the community (her relatives vs. his relatives, female community members against males).

The fears of minority group leaders are understandable even if they are not laudable. Racial and ethnic subcultures in America, especially those of "people of color," are still surrounded by tremendous walls of prejudice, ignorance, and deprivation. It hardly matters that spouse abuse is prevalent in white house-holds as well, if spouse abuse in the minority community becomes one more ste-reotypical expectation added to the burden.

Conclusion

This preliminary analysis of the available materials on the plight of minority women who are victimized by domestic violence suggests that these women face *three* separate sets of problems.

First, there is the problem of the abuse itself. The available data, admittedly anecdotal, strongly suggest that racial and ethnic minority women experience the battering in much the same way white women do. A punch in the eye or a kick in the stomach is probably the same no matter what color you are or what language is being shouted at the time.

Afterwards, however, minority women find themselves facing problems which may be quite different from those of their white counterparts. A second set of problems for minority women are those which are the product of simple racism. Whether it's fear of police brutality against themselves and their men, or the fear of being viewed as a traitor for disclosing a problem which may tarnish the positive image the minority community has worked so hard to foster, these are problems with which white women simply do not have to contend.

Finally, there are problems typical of or unique to each racial or ethnic group which present special third-level dilemmas to battered women from that group. Some of these problems reflect the traditional cultural heritage or customs of the group, such as the Asian concern about "loss of face." Others reflect the group's par-ticular experience on American soil, such as the destruction of family ties and the cultivation of the image of "strong womanhood" experienced by blacks as slaves. Still others reflect the strong influence of modern institutions which prevail in minority communities, such as the church. Each may work to curtail the recognition among minority women in that cultural group that they do not have to submit to brutaliza-tion or that there are ways of escaping their victimization. These cultural attributes may also serve to retard the actual availability of services for battered women within that community. Asbury (1987) neatly sums up the problems by observing that "For a battered woman to be helped, help must be available; she must know that it is available and how to gain access to it; and she must decide to use it" (p. 99).

Minority women are beginning to speak out on their own behalf against domestic violence, and to form special coalitions to explore their own special problems. It seems clear that those who are concerned about extending assis-tance to battered women must be sensitive to the unique problems of the minor-ity women within their communities, even though these women may not yet have demanded such help. It has been shown here that there are some indica-tions that minority women may be severely underreported in cases of domestic violence, and may be unable or unwilling to make use of traditional helping agencies to escape their victimization.

NOTES

[1] The terms "women of color," "minority women," and "third world women" are here used interchangeably when referring to non-white women in the United States as a large class. The reader should note that some persons to whom these terms apply have specific preferences for one or more of these references.

[2] The term "grassroots" here refers to organizing done by those who are directly affected by the problem and who are not part of the established political system.

REFERENCES

Allen, N. H. (1980). *Homicide: Perspective on prevention.* New York: Human Sciences Press, Inc.

Allen, P. G. (April 1985). Violence and the American Indian woman. *Working Together.* Center for the Prevention of Sexual and Domestic Violence, 1914 N. 34, Suite 205, Seattle, WA 98103.

American Indian Women Against Domestic Violence. (June 1985). Position Paper. In *A Movement of New World Women Conference,* conference packet. (Copies available: Women of Nations, P.O. Box 4637, St. Paul, MN 55704).

Arnold, M. & Perkins, S. (1984–85). Talking about our lives. *Wives Tales: A Newsletter About Ending Violence Against Women in the Home.* Fall/Winter, 2.

Asbury, J. (1987). African-American women in violent relationships: An exploration of cultural differences. In R. L. Hampton (Ed.), *Violence in the Black Family* (pp. 89–105). Lexington, MA: Lexington Books.

Bard, M. (1980). Function of the police and the justice system in family violence. In M. R. Green (Ed.), *Violence and the Family* (pp. 105–120). Boulder, CO: Westview Press.

Barnett, S. (1977). Researching black justice: Descriptions and implications. In C. Owens and J. Bell (Eds.), *Blacks and criminal justice* (p. 24–33). Lexington, MA: Lexington Books.

Bayley, D. H. & Mendelsohn, H, (1969). *Minorities and the police.* New York: The Free Press.

Benedek, E. P. (1982). Women and homicide. In B. L. Danto, J. Bruhns, J. & A. H. Kutscher (Eds.), *The human side of homicide* (pp. 150–164). New York: Columbia University Press.

Berk, S. & Loseke, D. (1981). Handling family violence: Situational determinants of police arrest in domestic disturbances. *Law and Society Review, 15*(2), 317–344.

Berk, R. A., Berk, S. F., Loseke, D. R., & Rauma, D. (1983). Mutual combat and other family violence myths. In D. Finkelhor, R. J. Gelles, G. T. Hotaling & M. A. Straus (Eds.), *The dark side of families: Current family violence research.* Beverly Hills: Sage Publications.

Block, C. R. (1985a). Race/ethnicity and patterns of Chicago homicide 1965 to 1981. *Crime and Delinquency, 31*(1), 104–116.

Block, C. R. (1985b). *Lethal violence in Chicago over seventeen years: Homicides known to the police, 1965–1981.* Chicago: Illinois Criminal Justice Information Authority.

Block, R. (1977). *Violent crime: Environment interaction and death.* Lexington, MA: Lexington Books.

Bonger, W. A. (1943). *Race and crime.* Translated from the Dutch by M. M. Hordyk. New York: Columbia University Press. Reprinted by Patterson Smith, 1969.

Bowker, L. H. (1979). The criminal victimization of women. *Victimology, 4*(4), 371–384.

Brearley, H. D. (1932). *Homicide in the United States.* Chapel Hill: University of North Carolina Press.

Brisson, N. J. (1981). Battering husbands: A survey of abusive men. *Victimology, 6*(1–4), 338–344.

Bruce, D. D. (1979). *Violence and culture in the antebellum South.* Austin: University of Texas.

Bureau of Justice Statistics. (1984). *Special report: Family violence.* Washington, DC: U.S. Department of Justice.

Carrol, J. (1980). A cultural-consistency theory of family violence in Mexican-American and Jewish ethnic groups. In M. A. Straus & G. T. Hotaling (Eds.), *The social causes of husband-wife violence* (pp. 68–81). Minneapolis: University of Minnesota Press.

Carter, David L. (1985). Hispanic perception of police performance: An empirical assessment. *Journal of Criminal Justice, 13*(6), 487–500.

Cazenave, N. A. & Straus, M. A. (1979). Race, class, network embeddedness and family violence: A search for potent support systems. *Journal of Comparative Family Studies, 10*(3), 281–300.

Chai, A. Y. (1987). Freed from the elders, but locked into labor: Korean immigrant women in Hawaii. *Women's Studies, 13*(3), 223–234.

Chavez, L. R., Cornelius, W. A., & Jones, O. W. (1986). Utilization of health services by Mexican immigrant women in San Diego. *Women & Health, 11,* 3–20.

Chimbos, P. D. & Montgomery, R. (1978). Violent crimes in a nonmetropolitan area of Ontario. *Crime and/et Justice, 6*(4), 234–245.

Curtis, L. (1974). *Criminal violence: National patterns & behavior.* Lexington, MA: Lexington Books.

Edwards, S. S. M. (1986). Police attitudes and dispositions in domestic disputes: The London Study. *Police Journal, 59*(3), 230–241.

Egley, L. C. (1982). Domestic abuse and deaf people: One community's approach. *Victimology, 7*(1–4), 24–34.

Eng, P. (1985). Aiding abused Asian women. *Wives Tales: A Newsletter About Ending Violence Against Women in the Home, 11*(1), 3.

Eng, P. & Messing, S. (1987). Shelter Asian women. *New Directions for Women, 16,* 3.

Epstein, C. F. (1973). Black and female: The double whammy. *Psychology Today, 7* (Aug.), 57.

Farley, R. (1980). Homicide trends in the United States. *Demography, 17*(2), 177–188.

Feinman, C. (1985). Domestic violence on the Navajo reservation. Paper presented at the annual meeting of the American Society of Criminology, San Diego, CA. Forthcoming in *Victimology.*

Fortune, M. (1981). *Family violence: A workshop manual for clergy and other service providers.* Rockville, MD: The National Clearinghouse on Domestic Violence.

Gaquin, D. A. (1977–78). Spouse abuse: Data from the National Crime Survey. *Victimology, 12*(34), 632–643.

Garcia, M. (1985). Double jeopardy: Battered women of color. *Wives Tales: A Newsletter About Ending Violence Against Women in the Home, 11*(1), 1–2.

Gelles, R. J. (1972). *The violent home: A study of physical aggression between husbands and wives.* Beverly Hills: Sage.

Gelles, R. J. (1980). Violence in the family: A review of research in the seventies. *Journal of Marriage and the Family, 42,* 873–886.

Hawkins, D. F. (1985). Black homicide: The adequacy of existing research for devising prevention strategies. *Crime and Delinquency, 31*(1), 83–103.

Hindelang, M. (1976). *Criminal victimization in eight American cities: A descriptive analysis of common theft and assault.* Cambridge, MA: Ballinger.

Hindelang, M. (1979). Race and involvement in common law personal crimes. *American Sociological Review, 43*(February): 93–109.

Holdaway, S. (1983). *Inside the British police: A force at work.* Oxford, United Kingdom: Basic Blackwell.

Katz, M. (1973). Family crisis training: Upgrading the police while building a bridge to the minority community. *Journal of Police Science and Administration, 1*(1), 30–35.

Kirk, A. R. (1982). Black homicide. In B. L. Danto, J. Bruhns, & A. H. Kutscher (Eds.), *The human side of homicide.* New York: Columbia University Press.

Kuhl, A. (1982) Community responses to battered women. *Victimology, 7*(1–4), 49–59.

LaBell, L. (1979). Wife abuse: A sociological study of battered women and their mates. *Victimology, 4*(2), 258–267.

Lewis, D. K. (1977). A response to inequality: Black women, racism and sexism. *Signs, 3,* 339–361.

Lockhart, L. L. (1984). A comparative analysis of the nature and extent of spouse abuse (as reflected by several measures) among black and white couples across different social classes. Unpublished dissertation. Florida State University School of Social Work.

Loizos, P. (1978). Violence and the family: Some Mediterranean examples. In J. P. Martin (Ed.), *Violence and the family* (pp. 183–196). New York: Wiley.

Mushanga, T. M. (1977–78). Wife victimization in east and central Africa. *Victimology, 2*(3–4), 479–485.

O'Brien, R. M. (1987). The interracial nature of violent crimes: A reexamination. *American Journal of Sociology. 92*(4), 817–835.

Parker, B. & Schumacher, D. (1979). The battered wife syndrome and violence in the nuclear family of origin: A controlled pilot study. *American Journal of Public Health, 67*(8), 760–763.

Poussaint, A. F. (1972). *Why blacks kill blacks.* New York: Emerson Hall.

Rasche, C. E. (1988). Characteristics of mate-homicides: A comparison to Wolfgang. Paper presented at the annual meeting of the Academy of Criminal Justice Sciences. San Francisco, CA.

Richie-Bush, B. (1983). Facing contradictions: Challenge for black feminists. *Aegis, 37,* 14–20.

Richie, B., (1985). Battered black women a challenge for the black community. *Black Scholar, 16*(March/April), 40–44.

Rounsaville, B. J. (1978–79). Theories in marital violence: Evidence from a study of battered women. *Victimology, 3*(1–2), 11–31.

Savitz, L. (1973). Black crime. In K. Miller & R. M. Dreger (Eds.), *Comparative studies of blacks and whites in the United States* (pp. 467–576). New York: Seminar Press.

Segovia-Ashley. (1978). Shelters—Short-term needs. In *Battered Women: Issues of Public Policy.* Washington, DC: U.S. Commission on Civil Rights.

Shoemaker, D. J. & Williams, J. S. (1987). The subculture of violence and ethnicity. *Journal of Criminal Justice, 15*(6), 461–472.

Skurnik, J. (1983). Battering: An issue for women of color. *Off Our Backs, 13*(5), 8.

Smith, D. & Klein, J. (1984). Police control of interpersonal disputes. *Social Problems, 31*(4), 468–481.

Smith, D. L. & Snow, R. (1978). Violent subcultures or subcultures of violence. *Southern Journal of Criminal Justice, 3,* 1–13.

Spiegel, J. P. (1980). Ethnopsychiatric dimensions in family violence. In M. R. Green (Ed.), *Violence and the family* (pp. 79–89). Boulder, CO: Westview Press.

Stachura, J. S. & Teske, R. H. D. (March 1979). *A special report on spouse abuse in Texas.* Survey Research Program, Criminal Justice Center, Sam Houston State University.

Staples, R. (1973). *The black woman in America: Sex, marriage and the family,* Chicago: Nelson-Hall Publishers.

Staples, R. (1976). Race and family violence: The internal colonialism perspective. In G. E. Lawrence & L. P. Brown (Eds.), *Crime and its impact on the black community.* Institute for Urban Affairs and Development Center. Washington, DC: Howard University.

Straus, M. A., Gelles, R. J., & Steinmetz, S. K. (1979). *Violence in the American family.* New York: Anchor/Doubleday.

Sullivan, D. J. (1977). Violence—an active volcano. In M. G. Kerr (Ed.), *Violence—The community and the administrator* (pp. 70–85). Wellington, New Zealand: New Zealand Institute of Public Administration.

Von Hentig, H. (1948). *The criminal and his victim: Studies in the sociobiology of crime.* New Haven: Yale University Press. Reprinted by Anchor Books, 1967.

Walker, L. E. (1979). *The battered woman.* New York: Harper and Row.

Walker, L. E. (1983). Victimology and the psychological perspectives of battered women. *Victimology, 8*(1–2), 82–104.

West, L. J. (1980). Discussion: Violence and the family in perspective. In M. R. Green (Ed.), *Violence and the family* (pp. 90–104). Boulder, CO: Westview Press.

White, E. C. (1985). *Chain chain change: For black women dealing with physical and emotional abuse.* Seattle, WA: The Seal Press.

White, J. (1979). Women speak. *Essence, 10*(June), 75+.

Wilbanks, W. (1982). Murdered women and women who murder: A critique of the literature. In N. H. Rafter & E. A. Stanko (Eds.), *Judge, lawyer, victim, thief* (pp. 151–180). Boston: Northeastern University Press.

Wilbanks, W. (1984). *Murder in Miami: An analysis of homicide patterns and trends in Dade County (Miami) Florida, 1917–1983.* Lanham, MD: University Press of America.

Wilbanks, W. (1985). Is violent crime intraracial? *Crime and Delinquency, 31*(1), 117–128.

Williams, L. (1981). Violence against women. *Black Scholar, 12*(Jan.–Feb.), 18–24.

Winkler, K. J. (1986). Scholars reproached for ignoring women of color in U. S. history. *Chronicle of Higher Education, 32*(April 23), 6+.

Wolfgang, M. (58). *Patterns in criminal homicide.* Montclair, NJ: Patterson Smith Reprint, 1975.

Wolfgang, M. E., & Ferracuti, F. (1967). Subculture of violence—A socio-psychological theory. In M. Wolfgang (Ed.), *Studies in homicide* (pp. 271–280). New York: Harper and Row.

Yates, D. L. (1985). *Correlates of attitudes towards the police: A comparison of black and white citizens in Austin, Texas.* Unpublished dissertation, University of Texas at Austin. Ann Arbor: University Microfilms International.

Zahn, M. A. & Rickle, W. C. (1986). Murder and minorities: The Hispanic case. Paper presented at the Academy of Criminal Justice Sciences, Orlando, FL.

Zambrano, M. M. (1985). *Mejor sola que mal acompanada.* Seattle, WA: The Seal Press. (Includes English translation.)

Effects of the Redesign on Victimization Estimates

Charles Kindermann, James Lynch, and David Cantor

The National Crime Victimization Survey (NCVS)—a major source of the nation's statistics on criminal victimization—has undergone an extensive rede-sign. A collaborative effort on this redesign among several institutions and agen-cies, including the Bureau of Justice Statistics and the Bureau of the Census, began in the late 1970s and focused principally on improving the accuracy and utility of crime measurement. In 1992 the long-planned redesign of the survey was introduced for half of the sample in such a way that comparisons could be made. This report analyzes the differences in estimates from the two designs. In the discussion that follows, the survey prior to the redesign is referred to as the National Crime Survey (NCS), and that after the redesign is referred to as the National Crime Victimization Survey (NCVS).

IMPROVING THE NCS

The NCS, 1973–92, and the NCVS, 1992 to the present, have each year col-lected crime victimization information from a sample of about 100,000 individu-als living in about 50,000 households. For the NCS the victimizations were categorized as personal crimes of violence (rape, robbery, and assault), personal crimes of theft, and household crimes (burglary, household larceny, and motor vehicle theft).

In the mid-1970s the National Academy of Sciences reviewed the NCS.[1] While the survey was found to be an effective instrument for measuring crime, reviewers identified aspects of the methodology and scope of the NCS that could be improved. The Academy proposed that researchers investigate the following:

Bureau of Justice Statistics: National Crime Victimization Survey. April 1997 NCJ-164381

- an enhanced screening section that would better stimulate respondents' recall of victimizations, thus reducing underreporting due to forgotten incidents

- screening questions that would sharpen the concepts of criminal victimization and diminish the effects of subjective interpretations of the survey questions

- additional questions on the nature and consequences of victimizations that would yield useful data for analysis.

In response, BJS sponsored a research consortium whose purpose was to investigate the issues raised in the review and to make recommendations that would improve the accuracy and utility of the NCVS. The redesign consortium completed its work in 1985.[2]

More recently, the issue of specifically improving the measurement of sex crimes and domestic violence resulted in the formation of a special committee associated with the American Statistical Association's Committee on Law and Justice Statistics. The special committee developed enhanced questions and clarification queries on rape, sexual assault, and domestic violence to get better estimates of these crimes that are difficult to measure. The Bureau of the Census subjected the changes recommended by the special committee, as well as those of the redesign consortium, to additional testing. Modifications proving successful in this testing were introduced into the survey.

From January 1992 through June 1993, the full NCS-NCVS sample was divided into two parts. Half of the sample was administered the NCVS method, and the other half, the NCS method. This overlap procedure was designed to permit the continuous publication of estimates of the year-to-year change in crime rates with comparable data while the new design was introduced. The procedure was also intended to provide measurable differences between the halves (table 1).

Table 1. Comparison of estimated NCS and NCVS victimization rates, 1992

	Number of victimizations per 1,000 persons or households		
	Post-redesign NCVS	Pre-redesign NCS	NCVS/NCS ratio
Personal crimes	49.6	34.4	1.44*
Crimes of violence	47.8	32.1	1.49*
Rape	1.8	0.7	2.57*
Robbery	6.1	5.9	1.03
Assault	40.0	25.5	1.57*
Aggravated	11.1	9.0	1.23*
Simple	28.9	16.5	1.75*
Personal theft	1.8	2.4	0.75
Property crimes	325.3	264.5	1.23*
Household burglary	58.6	48.9	1.20*
Household theft	248.2	195.5	1.27*
Motor vehicle theft	8.5	20.1	0.92

*The ratio of the NCVS to the NCS estimates was statistically significant at the 90-percent level of confidence.

EFFECTS OF THE NEW DESIGN ON ESTIMATES OF CRIME RATES

In general the redesigned procedures achieved their intended effect of pro-ducing higher estimates of crime rates than had the previously used procedures. Estimated rates for the following categories were higher: personal crimes (44% higher), crimes of violence (49%), rapes (157%), assaults (57%), property crimes (23%), burglaries (20%), and thefts (27%). A statistically significant difference could not be found for robbery, personal theft, and motor vehicle theft.

The increase in estimates of crimes of violence largely reflected the increase in assault estimates, especially those for simple assaults, which account for 58% of all violent crimes. Simple assaults, the less serious of the assault categories, are committed by persons without a weapon and result in either no injury or a minor injury.

EFFECTS OF THE NEW DESIGN FOR DIFFERENT TYPES OF EVENTS

The new method results in higher estimates of violent crime rates regardless of the attribute of crime events examined (table 2). However, the new method has a larger impact on the estimates for nonstranger and attempted crimes and crimes not reported to the police than on stranger, completed, and reported crime. The new screening strategy was designed to elicit reports of crime for these categories that were felt to be underreported and appears to have had that effect.

Table 2. Effects of the redesign on victimization rates for total violent crime, 1992

| Attribute | Total violent crime | | NCVS/ NCS ratio | Standard error (SE) of the ratio |
| | Estimated rates per 1,000 persons | | | |
	Post-redesign NCVS	Pre-redesign NCS		
Victim-offender relationship				
Stranger	26.5	19.5	1.4‡	0.09
Nonstranger	22.5	12.8	1.8‡	0.13
Completed	15.8	11.7	1.4‡	0.11
Attempted	33.5	20.4	1.6‡	0.11
Crime reporting to police				
Reported	21.0	16.0	1.3‡	0.10
Not reported	27.5	15.7	1.8‡	0.12

‡The ratio of the NCVW to the NCS estimates was statistically significicatn at the 90-percent level of confidence.

EFFECTS OF THE REDESIGN WITHIN CATEGORIES OF VICTIMS

Ratios of rates from the new method to rates from the old method for selected population groups help to determine if the redesign had a differential effect on population subgroups. To test if there are differential effects, the differences between the ratios were computed and tested for significance. Those that tested significant at the 0.90 confidence level are discussed below.

The number of respondents who provided data for each particular subgroup varied greatly, depending on the size of the subpopulation. Care should taken, therefore, in interpreting the difference in the ratios without considering the standard error of the ratio. Those ratios that appear to be large may be based on a relatively small number of cases. For example, the standard error for the ratio for households with a head age 12 to 17 is relatively large (SE=2.72 for total household crime), especially for crimes with low prevalence, such as household theft (SE=4.78).

In general the redesign had the effect of increasing the number of crimes counted by the survey. In most cases violent crime rates had higher estimates for all groups of respondents when the new methods were used. This was especially true for simple assaults for which nearly every population subgroup that was examined had higher rates when the new method was employed. There was virtually no difference between the new and the old method for robbery for any of the subgroups examined.

For crimes of violence, the new procedures increased victim recounting more for—

- whites than for blacks
- other racial groups than for blacks
- persons age 33 to 44 than for persons 18 to 24 and for persons age 65 or older
- persons with household incomes $15,000 or more than for persons with household incomes below $15,000
- suburban residents than for urban residents.

For robbery and personal theft, the effects of the new procedures did not differ across types of respondents. For aggravated assault, the new procedures increased victim recounting more for whites than for blacks. For simple assault, the increases in victim recall with the new design were greater for—

- persons age 35 to 44 than for persons of other ages
- persons age 12 to 17 than for persons age 65 or older
- persons with household incomes $15,000 or more than for persons with household incomes below $15,000.

In general, except for motor vehicle theft, the new methods had the effect of increasing the number of household crimes recounted to survey interviewers for every group of respondents. Again, all of the following differences in the effect of the new design between respondent groups are statistically significant at the 0.90 level. The new procedures increased recounting more for—

- suburban residents than for urban residents (total household crime)
- blacks than for whites (burglary)

Table 3. Ratios of NCVS rates to NCS rates for violent crimes, by selected victim characteristics, 1992

Victim characteristic	Total violent crime[a]	Robbery	Assault Aggravated	Assault Simple	Personal theft
Age					
12-17	1.6[‡]	1.3	1.1	1.9[‡]	1.2
18-24	1.3[‡]	.9	1.1	1.5[‡]	1.5
25-34	1.6[‡]	1.0	1.4	1.8[‡]	.4[‡]
35-44	1.8[‡]	.8	1.2	2.7[‡]	.6[‡]
45-64	1.6[‡]	1.1	2.0[‡]	1.6[‡]	1.1
65 or older	1.1	1.4	1.1	1.0	.9
Race					
White	1.6[‡]	1.0	1.3[‡]	1.9[‡]	.8
Black	1.2	1.0	.8	1.7[‡]	.6[‡]
Other	2.2[‡]	1.9	2.7	1.9	1.1
Household income					
0-$14,999	1.4[‡]	1.2	1.1	1.5[‡]	.7[‡]
$15,000-$34,999	1.9[‡]	1.1	1.2	1.8[‡]	.9
$35,000-$49,999	1.8[‡]	.9	1.5	2.4[‡]	.4[‡]
$50,000 or over	1.9[‡]	.9	1.8[‡]	2.4[‡]	1.2
Sex					
Male	1.5[‡]	1.0	1.3[‡]	2.0[‡]	.8
Female	1.6[‡]	1.1	1.1	1.7[‡]	.7[‡]
Locality					
Urban	1.4[‡]	1.0	1.2	1.8[‡]	.6[‡]
Suburban	1.7[‡]	1.2	1.4[‡]	2.0[‡]	1.0
Rural	1.5[‡]	1.2	1.0	1.7[‡]	1.1

Note: The standard errors of the estimated ratios are presented on page 7.
[‡]The ratio of the NCVS to the NCS estimates was statistically significant at the 90-percent level of confidence.
[a]Because of an insufficient number of cases, rape is not shown separately but is included in total violent crime.

For household larceny and motor vehicle theft, the new procedures had no differential effect across any of the categories in the variables examined.

The general pattern of the effects of the new design on the recounting to the interviewers by different groups of respondents was to increase recounting more for traditionally low victimization groups than for traditionally high victimization groups. The one exception was the increased recounting of burglary by

black victims. Although the recounting of victimization has increased for virtually all groups, these increases were greater for whites than for blacks, for
higher-income rather than lower-income groups, and for the middle aged, as
opposed to the young or very old.

UNDERSTANDING THE EFFECTS OF DESIGN CHANGES

The changes made in the crime survey were designed to encourage more
complete recall and recounting of crime events.[3] Development work done before
the redesign indicated that a substantial proportion of crimes were not recounted
in the survey for a number of reasons.[4] In some cases, the screening interview did
not provide enough cues to stimulate respondents to recall and recount eligible
events. In others, respondents were uncertain whether they should recount incidents that, although they had all the elements of a crime, did not conform to the
stereotype of crime. Crimes committed by family members, for example, fall into
this gray area. On the basis of this information, changes were made in the screening interview to provide more cues and to clarify that gray-area events should be
recounted. (See the appendix for the altered screener questions.)

Other development work indicated that computer assisted telephone interviewing (CATI) encouraged the recounting of victimization, presumably because
of the enhanced administrative control over the interview process.[5] CATI ensures
that interviewers deliver the cues prescribed in the screening interviews. The
proportion of the sample interviewed with CATI also increased.

In light of these changes in the design, it is understandable that respondents,
in general, recounted more victimizations in the new design than the old. They
were given a larger number of cues to assist in the recall and recounting of eligible
crime events. CATI also provided greater control over the interview process to
ensure that every respondent received all of the additional guidance and cues. It is
less clear why these changes in survey design would increase in varying amounts
the recounting of some crimes by some groups of respondents, and not others.

GRAY-AREA EVENTS: INCIDENTS FAILING TO FIT
POPULAR CONCEPTIONS OF CRIME

One reason for the differential effects of the new survey procedures across
types of events and respondents may be the nature of the cues added to the
screening interview. Particular attention was given to cueing for nonstereotypic
crimes, such as those that involve offenders who are not strangers. There was
good reason to believe that these types of events were not recounted in the old
design. The additional cues for recall of these types of events could have produced greater reporting of these crimes.

This explanation for the differential recounting of events is consistent with
the differences in the patterns of recounting observed in the overlap sample. The

effect of the new design was greater, for example, for crimes involving non-strangers than for those involving strangers. Increases with the new design were greater for attempted as opposed to completed crimes. The new design increased recounting less for stereotypic crimes such as robbery than it did for the more ambiguous crimes such as assault where the inclusion of gray-area events is more of a question.

The increased cueing for gray-area events and the subsequent higher rates of recounting in the new design may also explain the apparent differences in the effect of the design for different types of respondents. The increases in recounting for the new design may be less for young black respondents, for example, than for other age and racial groups because more of the violence that afflicts them involves robbery or some equally unambiguous crime than is the case for young white respondents. The appropriateness of this and other explanations for the differences in the effect of the design for different types of respondents can only be determined with further analysis of these data.

The observed differences between the old and the new design suggest that the changes in the design had the desired effects. The recounting of victimizations to interviewers increased generally. The new design increased the recounting of events reported to the police as well as those not reported to the police. Increases with the new design were greater, however, for gray-area events than for more stereotypic crimes. Recounting also increased, with a few exceptions, more for respondents with traditionally lower rates of victimization than it did for those with traditionally higher rates.

NOTES

[1] Panel for the Evaluation of Crime Surveys, Bettye K. Eidson Penick, ed., *Surveying Crime*, Washington, D.C.: National Academy of Sciences, 1976.

[2] *New Directions for the National Crime Survey*, BJS Technical Report, NCJ-115571, March 1989.

[3] For a discussion of redesign effects not considered in this report, see Michael Rand and Bruce Taylor, "The National Crime Victimization Survey Redesign: New Understandings of Victimization Dynamics and Measurement," Orlando, FL: Annual meetings of the American Statistical Association, August 13–17, 1995.

[4] Albert D. Biderman, et al., *Final Report of Research and Development for the Redesign of the National Crime Survey*, Washington, DC: Bureau of Social Science Research, Inc., 1986.

[5] David Hubble and B. E. Wilder, "Preliminary Results from the National Crime Survey CATI Experiment," New Orleans, LA: Proceedings of the American Statistical Association, Survey Methods Section, August 22–25, 1988.

SOURCES

Biderman, Albert D., David Cantor, James P. Lynch, and Elizabeth Martin. *Final Report of Research and Development for the Redesign of the National Crime Survey*. Washington, DC: Bureau of Social Science Research, Inc., 1986.

BJS. *New Directions for the National Crime Survey.* BJS Technical Report, NCJ–115571, March 1989.

Groves, Robert M. and W. L. Nicholls. "The Status of Computer Assisted Telephone Interviewing: Part II-Data Quality Issues." *Journal of Official Statistics.* Vol. 2, No. 2, 1986, p. 117–134.

Hubble, David. "The National Crime Victimization Survey Redesign: New Questionnaire and Procedures Development and Phase-In Methodology." Orlando, FL: Annual meetings of the American Statistical Association, 1995.

Hubble, David. "National Crime Survey's New Questionnaire Phase-in: Preliminary Results." Tucson AZ: International Conference on Measurement Errors in Surveys, November 11–14, 1990.

Hubble, David and B. E. Wilder. "Preliminary Results from the National Crime Survey CATI Experiment." New Orleans, LA: Proceedings of the American Statistical Association: Survey Methods Section, August 22–25,1988.

Martin, Elizabeth with Robert M. Groves, Jay Matlin, and Carolyn Miller. *Report on the Development of Alternative Screening Procedures for the National Crime Survey.* Washington, DC: Bureau of Social Science Research, Inc., 1986.

Panel for the Evaluation of Crime Surveys, B. K. E. Penick, ed. *Surveying Crime.* Washington, DC: National Academy of Sciences, 1976.

Persley, Carolyn. "The National Crime Victimization Survey Redesign: Measuring the Impact of New Methods." Orlando, FL: Annual meetings of the American Statistical Association, August 13–17, 1995.

Rand, Michael and Bruce Taylor. "The National Crime Victimization Survey Redesign: New Understandings of Victimization Dynamics and Measurement." Orlando, FL: Annual meetings of the American Statistical Association, August 13–17, 1995.

Appendix 1. Comparisons of NCVS and NCS crime screener questions

New (NCVS, beginning January 1992)

1. Has anyone attacked or threatened you in any of these ways—
   a. With any weapon, for instance, a gun or knife—
   b. With anything like a baseball bat, frying pan, scissors, or stick—
   c. By something thrown, such as a rock or bottle—
   d. Include any grabbing, punching, or choking,
   e. Any rape, attempted rape or other type of sexual assault—
   f. Any face to face threats—
   or
   g. Any attack or threat or use of force by anyone at all?
   Please mention it even if you were not certain it was a crime.

2. Incidents involving forced or unwanted sexual acts are often difficult to talk about. Have you been forced or coerced to engage in unwanted sexual activity by—
   a. Someone you didn't know before
   b. A casual acquaintance or
   c. Someone you know well.

Old (NCS, 1972-92)

1. Did anyone take something directly from you by using force, such as by a stickup, mugging, or threat?

2. Did anyone try to rob you by using force or threatening to harm you?

3. Did anyone beat you up, attack you, or hit you with something, such as a rock or bottle?

4. Were you knifed, shot at, or attacked with some other weapon by anyone at all?

5. Did anyone **threaten** to beat you up or **threaten** you with a knife, gun, or some other weapon, **not** including telephone threats?

6. Did anyone **try to attack** you in some other way?

Appendix 1. Comparisons of NCVS and NCS crime screener questions (cont'd)

1. Were you attacked or threatened or did you have something stolen from you—
   a. At home including the porch or yard—
   b. At or near a friend's relative's, or neighbor's home—
   c. At work or school—
   d. In place such as a storage shed or laundry room, a shopping mall, restaurant, bank or airport—
   e. While riding in any vehicle—
   f. On the street or in a parking lot—
   g. At such places as a party, theater, gym, picnic area, bowling lanes, or while fishing or hunting.

   or

   h. Did anyone attempt to attack or attempt to steal anything belonging to you from any of these places?
2. People often don't think of incidents committed by someone they know. Did you have something stolen from you or were you attacked or threatened by—
   a. Someone at work or school—
   b. A neighbor or friend—
   c. A relative or family member—
   d. Any other person you've met or known?
3. Did you call the police to report something that happened to you which you thought was a crime?
4. Did anything happen to you which you thought was a crime, but did not report to the police?

1. Was anything stolen from you while you were away from home, for instance, at work, in a theater or restaurant, or while traveling.
2. Did you call the police to report something that happened to you that you thought was a crime?
3. Did anything happen to you that you thought was a crime, but did not report to the police?

Societal Change and Change in Family Violence from 1975 to 1985 As Revealed by Two National Surveys

Murray A. Straus and Richard J. Gelles

The subordinate status of women in American society, and in most of the world's societies, is well documented (Blumberg, 1978; Chafetz, 1984). Since physical force is the ultimate recourse to keep subordinate groups in their place, women in the history of Euro-American society have often been the victims of physical assault (Straus, 1976).

Blackstone's codification of the common law in 1768 asserted that a husband had the right to "physically chastise" an errant wife, provided the stick was no bigger than his thumb. As recently as 1867 this rule was upheld by an appellate court in North Carolina. It would be bad enough if the violence against women had been limited to this "rule of thumb." However, more severe beatings were common. In the Middle Ages women were burned alive "for threatening their husbands, for talking back to or refusing a priest, for stealing, for prostitution, for adultery, for bearing a child out of wedlock, for permitting sodomy (even though the priest or husband who committed it was forgiven), for masturbating, for Lesbianism, for child neglect, for scolding and nagging, and for miscarrying, even though the miscarriage was caused by a kick or a blow from the husband" (Davis, 1971).

Journal of Marriage and the Family, 48:3 465–479. Copyrighted 1986 by the National Council on Family Relations, 3989 Central Ave. NE, Suite 550, Minneapolis, MN 55421. Reprinted by permission.
Note: The study looked at both child abuse and wife beating. The sections on child abuse have not been reprinted. Omissions have been noted with ellipses, and tables were renumbered.

Burning at the stake is now part of the dim historical past. The *right* to phys-ically chastise has long since disappeared from the common law. However, what actually takes place in American marriages is a different matter. In 1975–76 we carried out a study of a nationally representative sample of 2,143 American cou-ples. That study revealed that at least one violent incident occurred in 16% of American families during the year of the study (1975–76). If the referent period is since the marriage began, the figure is 28% (Straus, Gelles, and Steinmetz, 1980). Although about two-thirds of the violent incidents were minor assaults such as slapping and throwing things, the other third of the incidents were serious assaults such as punching, biting, kicking, hitting with an object, beating up, or assaults with a knife or gun. . . .

Is There an Epidemic of Spouse Abuse?

Until recently, there were no statistics on wife-beating cases known to the police or social service agencies (Lerman, 1981). Consequently, even the data for the three states that now record such cases cannot tell us about trends. How-ever, the number of cases reported in newspapers and the number of magazine articles and television documentaries on wife beating increased dramatically during the 1970s and 1980s. Although most of these articles described an "epi-demic" of wife beating, the apparent increase may reflect a growing awareness and recognition of an already existing high incidence of wife beating, combined with an inability or unwillingness to believe that this much violence could previ-ously have been characteristic of an institution as sacred as the family.

Marital violence may, in fact, be increasing; or it may be declining. An earlier paper argued that both wife beating and child abuse are probably decreasing (Straus, 1981b), but no empirical evidence was presented at that time. The pur-pose of this paper is to report the results of a 1985 replication of the 1975–76 study. This replication enables the first comparison of rates of family violence from surveys at two time points.

Definition and Measurement of Violence and Abuse

The term *abuse* is a source of considerable difficulty and confusion because it covers many types of abuse, not just acts of physical violence, and because there is no consensus on the severity of violence required for an act to be considered "abuse." Since there is no standard definition of abuse, and no consensus on severity, the best that can be done is to make clear the way the terms *violence* and *abuse* are used in this article.

Violence is defined as an act carried out with the intention, or perceived inten-tion, of causing physical pain or injury to another person. See Gelles and Straus (1979) for an explication of this definition and an analysis of alternative definitions.[1]

The term *abuse* is restricted to *physical* abuse because we chose to concen-trate the limited interview time with each family on this phenomenon. This decision was entirely a matter of research strategy. It does not imply that we think physical abuse is more important or more damaging than other types of abuse, such as psychological abuse and sexual abuse. . . .

Operationalizing Violence and Abuse

Violence was measured by the Conflict Tactics Scales (Straus, 1979; 1981a). This instrument has been used and refined in numerous studies of family violence (e.g., Allen and Straus, 1980; Cate, Henton, Koval, Christopher, and Lloyd, 1982; Henton, Cate, Koval, Lloyd, and Christopher, 1983; Giles-Sims, 1983; Hornung, McCullough, and Sugimoto, 1981; Jorgensen, 1977; Straus, 1974; Steinmetz, 1977).[2] Three different studies have established that the Conflict Tactics Scales (CTS) measure three factorially separate variables (Jorgensen, 1977; Schumm, Bollman, Jurich, and Martin, 1982; Straus, 1979): reasoning, verbal aggression, and violence or physical aggression. The violence index and the subindexes used as the measures of child abuse and spouse abuse are described below.

Format of the CTS. The introduction to the Conflict Tactics Scales asks respondents to think of situations in the past year when they had a disagreement or were angry with a specified family member and to indicate how often they engaged in each of the acts included in the CTS. The 1975 version of the CTS consisted of 19 items, 8 of which were acts of violence.

Violent acts. The violent acts in the version of the CTS we used for this study are: threw something at the other; pushed, grabbed, or shoved; slapped or spanked; kicked, bit, or hit with a fist; hit or tried to hit with something; beat up the other; threatened with knife or gun; used a knife or gun.[3]

Violence indexes. The violent acts included in the CTS can be combined to form a number of different violence indexes. The following measures are used in this study:

- *Overall violence.* This measure indicates the percentage of . . . spouses who used *any* of the violent acts included in the CTS during the year covered by the study.

- *Severe violence.* For purposes of this study, *severe violence* was defined as acts that have a relatively high probability of causing an injury. Thus, kicking is classified as severe violence because kicking a child or a spouse has a much greater potential for producing an injury than an act of "minor violence" such as spanking or slapping.[4] The acts making up the severe violence index are: kicked, bit, punched, hit with an object, beat up, threatened with a knife or gun, and used a knife or gun (see footnote 4). . . .

- *Spouse violence and wife beating.* The problem of terminology and norms is even greater for violence between spouses than for violence by parents. Although slapping a child occasionally is not usually considered abuse (or even violence), our perception is that the same act is often considered to be violence if done to a spouse. Thus, in the case of violence between spouses, the "overall violence" rate is more important than is overall violence by parents.

In addition, because of the greater average size and strength of men, the acts in the Severe Violence list are likely to be more damaging when the assailant is the husband. Consequently, to facilitate focusing on the rate of severe violence by husbands, the term *wife beating* will be used to refer to that rate.

THE TWO NATIONAL SURVEYS

Sample and Administration of the 1975 Study

A national probability sample of 2,143 currently married or cohabiting persons was interviewed by Response Analysis Corporation with the use of an interview schedule designed by the authors. . . . A random half of the respondents were women and the other half men. Interviews lasted approximately one hour. The completion rate of the entire sample was 65%. More detailed information on the methodology of the study is given in Straus, Gelles, and Steinmetz (1980).

The 1985 National Family Violence Re-survey[5]

Data on a national probability sample of 6,002 households were obtained by telephone interviews conducted by Louis Harris and Associates. . . . The sample was made up of four parts. The part analyzed for this article is a national probability sample of 4,032 households that were selected in proportion to the distribution of households in the 50 states. The spouse abuse data are based on the 3,520 households containing a currently married or cohabiting couple; households with a single parent or a recently terminated marriage are excluded. The child abuse data are based on the 1,428 of these households with a child aged 3 through 17 and with two caretakers present.[6]

Interviews lasted an average of 35 minutes. The response rate, calculated as "completed as a proportion of eligibles" was 84%. A detailed report on the methodology of the study is available from the authors, and the implications of the differences in methods between the two studies are discussed later in this article. . . .

Violence Between Spouses in 1975 and 1985[7]

Table 1 summarizes the findings on violence between married or cohabiting couples in the form of three indexes (data on each violent act separately is presented in table 2). These indexes differentiate between "minor violence" (pushing, slapping, and throwing things) and "severe violence" (kicking, biting, punching, etc.). All but one of the nine comparisons in table 1 show that the rate of violence was lower in 1985 than in 1975. However, as compared to the changes in parental violence, the decreases from 1975 to 1985 are much smaller.

Husband-to-Wife Violence

The first row of table 1, Part A, shows that the Overall Violence rate of violence by husbands declined from 121 to 113. Thus, the husband-to-wife violence rate declined by 6.6%, which is not statistically significant.

Table 1. Marital violence indexes: Comparison of 1975 and 1985

Violence Index	Rate per 1,000 Couples		t for 1975–1985 Difference
	1975	1985	
A. Husband-to-Wife			
Overall Violence (1–6)	121	113	0.91
Severe Violence (4–8) ("wife beating")	38	30	1.60
B. Wife-to-Husband			
Overall Violence (1–6)	116	121	0.57
Severe Violence (4–8)	46	44	0.35
C. Couple			
Overall Violence (1–6)	160	158	0.20
Severe Violence (4–8)	61	58	0.46
Number of cases[a]	2,143	3,520	

[a]A few respondents were omitted because of missing data on some items, but the *n* is never decreased by more than 10.

The second row of Part A reports the rate of Severe Violence by husbands—our measure of "wife beating." It shows that the rate declined from 38 per thousand couples to 30 per thousand couples in 1985. A decrease of 8 per thousand may not seem large, and it is not statistically significant (p. < 10). However, it is worth interpreting because, relative to the 1975 rate, it represents a 26.6% decrease in the rate of wife beating, and the difference comes close to being significant. In addition, a decrease of 8 per thousand in the rate of wife beating is worth noting because, if correct, it represents a large number of couples. Specifically, if the 1975 rate for husband-to-wife severe violence had remained in effect, the application of this rate to the 54 million couples in the U.S. in 1985 results in an estimate of at least 2,052,000 severely assaulted wives each year. However, if there has been a 27% decrease in the rate, that translates to 1,620,000 beaten wives, which is 432,000 fewer than would have been the case if the 1975 rate prevailed. That would be an extremely important reduction. On the other hand, the 1985 estimate of 1.6 million beaten wives is hardly an indicator of domestic tranquility.[8]

Wife-to-Husband Violence

Although the trend for husband-to-wife violence is encouraging, the situation for wife-to-husband violence is at best mixed. Part B of table 1 shows that the Overall Violence rate actually increased slightly. The rate for Severe Violence against a husband decreased, but only slightly. Neither of these changes is statistically significant.

In addition to the trends, the violence rates in Part B reveal an important and distressing finding about violence in American families—that, in marked contrast to the behavior of women outside the family, women are about as violent within the family as men. This highly controversial finding of the 1975 study is confirmed by the 1985 study and also by findings on other samples and by other investigators (Brutz and Ingoldsby, 1984; Gelles, 1974; Giles-Sims, 1983; Laner and Thompson, 1982; Lane and Gwartney-Gibbs, 1985; Jouriles and O'Leary, 1985; Makepeace,

1983; Sack, Keller and Howard, 1982; Saunders, 1986; Scanzoni, 1978; Steinmetz, 1977, 1977–78; Szinovacz, 1983).

Although the two national surveys and the ten studies just cited leave little doubt about the high frequency of wife-to-husband violence, the meaning and consequences of that violence are easily misunderstood. For one thing, as pointed out elsewhere (Straus, 1977; Straus, Gelles, and Steinmetz, 1980: 43), the greater average size and strength of men, and their greater aggressiveness (Maccoby and Jacklin, 1974; Tavris and Offir, 1977), mean that the same act (for example, a punch) is likely to be very different in the amount of pain or injury inflicted (see also Greenblat, 1983). Even more important, a great deal of violence by women against their husbands is retaliation or self-defense (Straus, 1980; Saunders, 1986). One of the most fundamental reasons why some women are violent within the family, but not outside the family, is that the risk of assault for a typical American woman is greatest in her own home (Straus, Gelles, and Steinmetz, 1980: chapters 1 and 2). Nonetheless, violence by women against their husbands is not something to be dismissed because of the even greater violence by husbands.

On the other hand, the cost of drawing attention to violence by wives is that the information will be used to defend male violence. Our 1975 data, for example, have been used against battered women in court cases, and also to minimize the need for shelters for battered women. However, in the long run, the results of the present study suggest that the cost of denial and suppression is even greater. Rather than attempting to deny the existence of such violence (see Pleck, Pleck, Grossman, and Bart, 1977, for an example and the reply by Steinmetz, 1978), a more productive solution is to confront the issue and attempt to eliminate violence by women. This is beginning to happen. Almost all shelters for battered women now have policies designed to deal with the high rate of child abuse, and some are also facing up to the problem of wife-to-husband violence.

Couple Violence and Specific Violent Acts

Couple violence. Part C of table 1 combines the data on violence by husbands and wives. The first row shows that in 1975, a violent act occurred in 160 out of every thousand families, and that the 1985 rate was almost as high. Similarly, the second row reveals only a small decrease in the rate of *severe* assaults on a spouse—from 61 to 58 per thousand couples. This is a 5% reduction, which is not statistically significant.

Specific violent acts. Table 2 presents the rates for each of the violent acts making up the 1975 and 1985 versions of the CTS. These rates are presented for the record and to show what went into the summary indexes discussed above.

Table 2. Marital violence: Comparison of specific acts, 1975–1985

Type of Violence	Husband-to-Wife		Wife-to-Husband	
	1975	1985	1975	1985
A. Minor Violence Acts				
1. Threw something	28	28	52	43
2. Pushed/grabbed/shoved	107	93	83	89
3. Slapped	51	29**	46	41
B. Severe Violence Acts				
4. Kicked/bit/hit with fist	24	15*	31	24
5. Hit, tried to hit with something	22	17	30	30
6. Beat up	11	8	6	4
7. Threatened with gun or knife	4	4	6	6
8. Used gun or knife	3	2	2	2
Number of cases[a]	2,143	3,520	2,143	3,520

[a]A few respondents were omitted because of missing data on some items, but the n is never decreased by more than 10.
*$p < .05$; **$p < .01$ (two-tailed t tests for 1975–85 differences).

PREVENTION AND TREATMENT PROGRAMS AND CHANGE IN FAMILY VIOLENCE

This section considers the extent to which change in different forms of intrafamily violence parallels the extent of the intensity of prevention and treatment programs. . . .

Wife Beating

The campaign against wife beating, by contrast, began a decade or more later and has been less intensive, and far fewer resources have been invested. Providing shelters has mostly been a private endeavor of the women's movement. Even the feeble effort of the federal government in the form of an information clearinghouse was abolished early in the Reagan administration. Many bills to provide funds for shelters have been introduced and defeated. When a bill appropriating a modest sum was finally passed in 1985, the administration refused to spend the funds. Nevertheless, by 1985 the women's movement succeeded in creating a national consciousness and in establishing hundreds of shelters for battered women (Back, Blum, Nakhnikian, and Stark, 1980; Warrior, 1982); and by 1985 our study found a substantial reduction in the rate of wife beating.

Violence by Wives

Violence by wives has not been an object of public concern. There has been no publicity, and no funds have been invested in ameliorating this problem because it has not been defined as a problem. In fact, our 1975 study was criticized for presenting statistics on violence by wives.[9] Our 1985 finding of little change in the rate of assaults by women on their male partners is consistent with the absence of ameliorative programs. . . .

ALTERNATIVE INTERPRETATIONS OF THE FINDINGS

We have presented some startling and controversial findings. . . . Nevertheless, it is important to regard these results with caution because, with the data available, one can only speculate about the processes that produced the decreases. We will discuss three possible explanations for the findings.

Methodological Differences between the Two Surveys

Data for the 1975 survey were collected by in-person interview, while the 1985 survey was conducted over the telephone. Research on differences between telephone and in-person interviews has shown no major differences in results (Groves and Kahn, 1979; Marcus and Crane, 1986; Smith, in press), and telephone interviewing is now the most widely used method of conducting surveys, including the National Crime Survey. To the extent that there is a difference, we believe, the anonymity offered by the telephone leads to more truthfulness and, therefore, increased reporting of violence. The difference in interview method should have produced *higher*, not lower, rates of reported violence in 1985.

However, a characteristic of telephone surveys that is usually an advantage—the higher rate of completed interviews—might have affected the difference between the 1975 and 1985 rates. The 1985 survey had an 85% completion rate, versus 65% for the 1975–76 survey. Assuming that a higher completion rate means a more representative sample, the question is whether this makes for a lower or a higher rate of reported violence. That depends on whether those who refused to participate are more or less likely to be violent. If those who refused are less likely to be violent, then the fact that there were fewer refusals in 1985 would tend to reduce the violence rate. However, we think it more likely that the violence rate is higher among those who refuse to participate. If so, a reduction in refusals would tend to produce a higher rate of violence, whereas we found a lower rate of violence in 1985 despite the much lower number of refusals.

Another methodological difference is that, in the 1975–76 survey, respondents were handed a card listing the response categories for the Conflict Tactics Scales. All possible answers, including "never," were on the card. For the 1985 telephone survey, interviewers read the response categories, beginning with "once" and continuing to "more than 20 times." Respondents had to volunteer "never" or "don't know" responses. Experience has shown that rates of reported sensitive or deviant behavior are higher if the subject has to volunteer the "no" or "never" response (see, for example, Kinsey, Pomeroy, and Martin, 1948).

These differences in methodology between the two studies should have led to higher, not lower, rates of reported violence. Since the rates of child abuse and wife beating decreased, it seems unlikely that the change is due to the different methods of data collection.

Reluctance to Report

A second plausible explanation for the decline in the rate of . . . wife beating is that respondents may have been more reluctant to report severe violence in 1985 than in 1975. As indicated above, the last 10 years have seen a tremendous increase in public attention to the problem of . . . wife beating. National media campaigns, . . . hot-lines, and almost daily media attention have transformed behaviors that were ignored for centuries into major social problems. The decrease in . . . wife beating may reflect a "moral passage" (Gusfield, 1963), as family violence becomes less acceptable and consequently fewer . . . husbands are willing to admit to participating in violence. The implications of such a change in American culture are discussed at the conclusion of this article.

Change in Behavior

The third explanation is that there has indeed been a decline in . . . wife beating. This explanation is consistent with changes in the family and other developments during the last 10 years that might have served to reduce the rate of family violence. These fall into five broad categories: changes in the family and the economy that are associated with less violence, more alternatives for abused women, treatment programs, and deterrence.

Change in family structure. There have been changes in a number of aspects of the family that are associated with violence, including: a rise in the average age at first marriage, an increase in the average age for having a first child, a decline in the number of children per family, and therefore, a corresponding decrease in the number of unwanted children (Statistical Abstract, 1985: Tables 120, 92, 63, 97). Parents in 1985 are among the first generation to be able to choose a full range of planned parenthood options (including abortion) to plan family size. All these factors are related to lower rates of child abuse and may have an indirect effect on spouse abuse by lowering the level of stress.[10] In addition, later marriage and the greater acceptability of divorce tend to equalize the balance of power between husband and wife.

The fact that, bit by bit, American marriages are becoming more equalitarian (Thornton, Alwin, and Camburn, 1983) has important implications for family violence because previous research shows that male-dominant marriages have the highest, and equalitarian marriages the lowest, rate of violence (Coleman and Straus, 1986; Straus, 1973; Straus, Gelles, and Steinmetz, 1980). There are many reasons for the increasing equality between husbands and wives in addition to the two mentioned above. For the decade in question, two of the most important factors are the diffusion of feminist ideology to a broader population base, and the increase in the percentage of women with paid jobs. Moreover, we found that full-time housewives experience a higher rate of wife beating (Straus, Gelles, and Steinmetz, 1980); thus the rapid increase in paid employment (Statistical Abstract, 1985: Tables 669–672) might also be associated with a lower rate of wife beating.

Economic change. Both child abuse and wife beating are associated with unemployment and economic stress. The economic climate of the country is better in

1985 than in 1975 (at least for the population we are examining intact families). The rate of employment and inflation is down compared to 10 years ago (Statistical Abstract, 1985: Table 777). The one-year referent period used for the 1985 survey coincided with one of the more prosperous years in the past decade. Thus, the lower level of economic stress in 1985 may have contributed to the decline in severe violence.

Alternatives for battered women. As noted earlier, there were only a handful of "safe houses" or "shelters" for battered women in 1975, as contrasted with about 700 in 1985 (Back et al., 1980; Warrior, 1982). The existence of shelters provides an alternative that did not exist in 1975. In addition, the fact that shelters provide an alternative may have emboldened more women to tell their partner that his violence is unacceptable, and to make this more than an idle threat. Similarly, the tremendous growth in paid employment of married women in the 1975–85 period not only helped rectify the imbalance of power between spouses, but also provided the economic resources that enable more women to terminate a violent marriage (Kalmuss and Straus, 1982). Finally, the increased acceptance of divorce probably also helped more women to terminate violent marriages.

Treatment programs. New and innovative prevention and treatment programs for . . . wife beating proliferated during or immediately before the 1975–85 decade. . . . Whereas no treatment programs for men who assault their wives existed in the early 1970s, many such programs were available by 1985 (Pirog-Good and Stets-Kelly, 1985), including a number of court-mandated programs; and there is some evidence of their effectiveness (Lerman, 1981). Finally, family therapy of all types has grown tremendously. It was probably the fastest-growing human service profession in the 1975–85 decade.[11] The increased use of family counseling and the increasing proportion of therapists who directly raise the issue of violence may have had a part in reducing intrafamily violence.

Deterrence. Deterrence of a crime depends on the perception of potential offenders that the act is wrong and that there is a high probability of being apprehended and punished (Williams and Hawkins, in press). The decade in question has been characterized by activities that were intended to change both internalized norms and objective sanctions about family violence. Extensive efforts have been made to alert the public to the problem of child abuse and wife beating. In addition, shelters for battered women may have an indirect effect. The process of publicizing the availability of a shelter can contribute to a husband's redefining "I just slapped her a few times" to "I was violent." Each of these activities probably contributed to a changed perception of the legitimacy of violence against children and wives and therefore plays a preventative or deterrent role. Public opinion poll data suggest that those programs seem to have been effective. A 1976 study found that only about 10% of Americans considered child abuse a serious problem (Magnuson, 1983), whereas a 1982 poll conducted by Louis Harris and Associates found that 90% felt that child abuse was a serious national problem. This is a huge increase in public awareness. The problem of wife beating, although emphasized less than child abuse, has also received a major amount of publicity. It is not implausible to suggest that the advertising campaigns and media attention have had some effect in making parents more cautious about assaulting children and husbands more cautious about severely assaulting wives.

Another important change affects the certainty and severity of legal sanctions for wife beating. The police are gradually changing methods of dealing with wife beating. At the time of the 1975 study, the training manual for police officers prepared by the International Association of Chiefs of Police recommended separating the warring parties and leaving the scene of the marital violence. That manual now recommends dealing with all assaults on the same bases, irrespective of whether they are in the home or elsewhere (International Association of Chiefs of Police, 1976). A growing number of police departments are doing that. To the extent that this change in police policy was known to potential offenders, it is not implausible to think that it has had an effect. Indeed, a study comparing three different methods used by the police to deal with domestic violence suggests that there is a lower recidivism rate when wife beating is treated as a criminal act rather than a private problem (Sherman and Berk, 1984).

SUMMARY AND CONCLUSIONS

This article compares the rates of physical violence against . . . spouses from a 1975–76 survey with the rates from a 1985 study that used the same instrument to measure violence. . . . Wife beating . . . decreased by 27%, but similarly severe assaults by wives on husbands decreased only 4.3%. . . . Even with these reductions, the rates of . . . wife beating remain extremely high.

Factors Underlying the Findings

The lower rates of severe violence in the 1985 study could have been produced by a number of factors, including: (a) differences in the methodology used in the two surveys, (b) a greater reluctance on the part of the respondents to report violence, or (c) a decrease in the amount of . . . wife beating. Our interpretation is that the decrease is probably not due to differences in the methods used in the two surveys because those differences would tend to increase rather than decrease the 1985 rate. This leaves two plausible explanations—the decrease could reflect a change in reporting behavior or a change in violent behavior.

From the perspective of the welfare of children and families, the most desirable interpretation is that the differences between 1975 and 1985 represents fewer . . . beaten wives. However, even if the reduction is entirely due to a greater reluctance to report violence, that is also important. It suggests that the effort to change public attitudes and standards concerning family violence have achieved a certain measure of success. In view of the fact that this decrease refers to changes in a relatively short period of 10 years, perhaps it could even be considered a remarkable degree of success. Moreover, a change in attitudes and cultural norms is an important part of the process leading to change in overt behavior. If all that has been accomplished in the last 10 years is to instill new standards for . . . husbands about the inappropriateness of violence, that is a key element in the process of reducing the actual rate of . . . wife beating.

Most likely the findings represent a combination of changed attitudes and norms along with changes in overt behavior. This interpretation is based on a number of changes in American society that took place during or immediately before the decade of this study, including: changes in the family, in the economy, in the social acceptability of family violence, in alternatives available to women, in social control processes, and in the availability of treatment and prevention services. . . .

NOTES

[1] As pointed out in a previous theoretical article (Gelles and Straus, 1979), the fact of a physical assault having taken place is not sufficient for understanding violence. Several other dimensions also needed to be considered. However, it is also important that each of these other dimensions be measured separately so that their causes and consequences and joint effects can be investigated. Among the other dimensions are the seriousness of the assault (which can range from a slap to stabbing and shooting); whether a physical injury was produced (which can range from none to death); the motivation (which might range from a concern for a person's safety, as when a child is spanked for going into the street, to hostility so intense that the death of the person is desired); and whether the act of violence is normatively legitimate (as in the case of slapping a child) or illegitimate (as in the case of slapping a spouse), and which set of norms are applicable (legal, ethnic, or class norms, couple norms, etc.).

[2] The reliability and validity of the Conflict Tactics Scales have been assessed in several studies over the 15-year period of their development. See Straus (1979) for evidence of internal consistency, reliability, concurrent validity, and construct validity. Other investigators have confirmed some of these findings. See, for example, Jouriles and O'Leary (1985), Jorgensen (1977), and Schumm et al., (1982).

[3] The 1985 version contains an additional item for parent-child violence (scalding or burning) and an additional item for husband-wife violence (choking). These items are excluded from comparisons of 1975 rates with 1985 rates but will be presented in a later paper (Straus and Gelles, 1986). In addition, the 1985 CTS was supplemented by questions intended to assess the consequences or outcomes of acts of violence. We added a series of questions that asked whether an act of violence produced an injury that required medical attention—either seeing a doctor or overnight hospitalization—and also questions on depression and other possible mental health effects. These data will also be reported in a later paper.

[4] It should be recognized that in most instances, being kicked, although painful, does *not* result in an injury. However, the absence of injury does not make it less abusive an act. Our distinction between minor and severe violence parallels the legal distinction between a "simple assault" and an "aggravated assault." An aggravated assault is an attack that is likely to cause grave bodily harm, such as an attack with a knife or gun, irrespective of whether the object of the attack was actually injured.

[5] The 1985 survey differs from the 1975–76 study in a number of important ways. It includes several groups that were omitted from the first survey, such as single parents; and it includes additions to the CTS Violence Index. However, the instrumentation was designed to permit the comparable questions to be selected, and the sample was

chosen in a way that permits selection of a comparable part of the 1985 sample to be used for the 1975-to-1985 change analysis. Unless otherwise indicated, the material reported in this article is restricted to the comparable parts of the 1985 sample and the comparable parts of the instrumentation. See also footnote 3.

6   The other three parts consisted of oversamples for specific purposes. First, certain states were oversampled because one objective of the second national survey was to collect data that could be aggregated by state for analysis of state-level trends and relationships. The oversample consisted of 958 households in 25 states. This was done to assure that there would be 36 states with at least 100 completed interviews per state. Finally, two additional oversamples were drawn—508 black and 516 Hispanic households. Future analyses that include these oversamples will be weighted to take into account the state, black, and Hispanic oversamples.

7   For convenience and economy of wording, terms such as *marital, spouse, wife,* and *husband* are used to refer to couples, irrespective of whether they are married or nonmarried cohabiting persons. For an analysis of differences and similarities between married and cohabiting couples in the 1975–76 study, see Yllö (1978); Yllö and Straus (1981).

8   In addition, the 1985 rate presented in this article is restricted to the comparable part of the sample and the comparable list of violent acts. The figures to be presented in a later paper using all couples and the enlarged CTS list of violent acts yields a somewhat higher rate.

9   For a few years, the advocacy of karate on the part of some in the women's movement put women on record as favoring violence as a means of ending violence. The futility of such an approach is indicated by the fact that the willingness of men to use force does not protect them from assault. Three times is many men are murdered as women (Riedel and Zahn, 1985: Table 3-2), and three times as many men are victims of assault (Bureau of Justice Statistics, 1985: Table 3). Readiness to use force, in our opinion, is no more likely to provide security for women than it does for men.

10   Although this section focuses on changes in the family that are associated with a reduction in violence, there have also been changes in aspects of the family that are plausibly associated with an increase in violence (see Straus, 1981b, for a listing and discussion).

11   For example, membership in the American Association of Marriage and Family Therapists tripled from 3,373 in 1975 to 12,302 in 1985 (information provided by telephone to Straus, 11 March 1986).

REFERENCES

Allen, Craig, and Murray A. Straus. 1980. "Resources, power, and husband-wife violence." Chapter 12 in Murray A. Straus and Gerald T. Hotaling (eds.), *The Social Causes of Husband-Wife Violence.* Minneapolis: University of Minnesota Press.

American Humane Association. 1983. *Highlights of Official Child Neglect and Abuse Reporting.* Denver, CO: American Humane Association.

Back, Susan M., Judith Blum, Ellen Nakhnikian, and Susan Stark. 1980. *Spouse Abuse Yellow Pages.* Denver, CO: Denver Research Institute, University of Denver.

Blumberg, Rae Lesser. 1978. *Stratification: Socioeconomic and Sexual Inequality.* Dubuque, IA: Wm. C. Brown.

Brutz, Judith, and Bron B. Ingoldsby. 1984. "Conflict resolution in Quaker families." *Journal of Marriage and the Family* 46: 21–26.

Bureau of Justice Statistics. 1985. Criminal Victimization in the United States, 1985. Washington, DC: U.S. Department of Justice.

Cate, Rodney M., June M. Henton, James Koval, F. Scott Christopher, and Sally Lloyd. 1982. "Premarital abuse: A social psychological perspective." *Journal of Family Issues 3*: 79–90.

Chafetz, Janet Salzman. 1984. *Sex and Advantage: A Comparative Macro-Structural Theory of Sex Stratification.* Totowa, NJ: Rowman and Allanheld.

Coleman, Diane H., and Murray A. Straus. 1986. "Marital power, conflict, and violence." *Violence and Victims 1*: 139–153.

Davis, Elizabeth Gould. 1971. *The First Sex.* New York: Putnam.

Gelles, Richard J. 1974. *The Violent Home: A Study of Physical Aggression between Husbands and Wives.* Beverly Hills, CA: Sage.

Gelles, Richard J., and Murray A. Straus. 1979. "Determinants of violence in the family: Towards a theoretical integration." Chapter 21 in Wesley R. Burr, Reuben Hill, F. Ivan Nye, and Ira L. Reiss (eds.), *Contemporary Theories about the Family* (Vol. 1). New York: Free Press.

Gelles, Richard J., and Murray A. Straus. 1985. "Is violence toward children increasing? A comparison of 1975 and 1985 national survey rates." Paper presented at the Seventh National Conference on Child Abuse and Neglect, Chicago.

Gelles study strikes discordant note. 1985. Child Protection Report, 22 November, p. 3.

Giles-Sims, Jean. 1983. *Wife Battering: A Systems Theory Approach.* New York: Guilford Press.

Greenblat, Cathy. 1983. "Physical force by any other name . . .: Quantitative data, qualitative data, and the politics of family violence research." In David Finkelhor, Richard J. Gelles, Gerald T. Hotaling, and Murray A. Straus (eds.), *The Dark Side of Families: Current Family Violence Research.* Beverly Hills, CA: Sage.

Groves, R. M., and R. L. Kahn. 1979. *Surveys by Telephone: A National Comparison with Personal Interviews.* New York: Academic Press.

Gusfield, J. 1963. *Symbolic Crusade: Status Politics and the American Temperance Movement.* Urbana, IL: University of Illinois Press.

Haeuser, Adrienne A. 1985. "Social control over parents' use of physical punishment: Issues for crossnational child abuse research." Paper presented at the United States-Sweden Joint Seminary on Physical and Sexual Abuse of Children, Satra Bruck, Sweden (June).

Henton, June, Rodney Cate, James Koval, Sally Lloyd, and Scott Christopher. 1983. "Romance and violence in dating relationships." *Journal of Family Issues 4*: 467–482.

Hornung, Carlton A., B. Claire McCullough, and Taichi Sugimoto. 1981. "Status relationships in marriage: Risk factors in spouse abuse." *Journal of Marriage and the Family 43*: 675–692.

International Association of Chiefs of Police. 1976. *Wife Beating.* Training Key 245. Gaithersburg, MD.

Jorgensen, Stephen R. 1977. "Societal class heterogamy, status striving, and perception of marital conflict: A partial replication and revision of Pearlin's contingency hypothesis." *Journal of Marriage and the Family 39*: 653–689.

Jouriles, E. N., and K. D. O'Leary. 1985. "Interspousal reliability of reports of marital violence." *Journal of Consulting and Clinical Psychology 53*: 419–421.

Kalmuss, Debra S., and Murray A. Straus. 1982. "Wives' marital dependency and wife abuse." *Journal of Marriage and the Family 44*: 277–286. Also reprinted in Bert N. Adams and John L. Campbell (eds.), *Framing the Family: Contemporary Portraits.* Prospect Heights, IL: Waveland Press, 1985.

Kempe, C. Henry, Frederic Silverman, Brandt Steele, William Droegernueller, and Henry Silver. 1962. "The battered child syndrome." *Journal of the American Medical Association* 181: 17–24.

Kinsey, Alfred C., Wardell B. Pomeroy, and Clyde E. Martin. 1948. *Sexual Behavior in the Human Male.* Philadelphia: W. B. Saunders.

Lane, Katherine E., and Patricia A. Gwartney-Gibbs. 1985. "Violence in the context of dating and sex." *Journal of Family Issues* 6: 45–59.

Laner, Mary Riege, and Jeanine Thompson. 1982. "Abuse and aggression in courting couples." *Deviant Behavior: An Interdisciplinary Journal* 3: 229–244.

Lerman, Lisa G. 1981. *Prosecution of Spouse Abuse: Innovations in Criminal Justice Response.* Washington, DC: Center for Women Policy Studies.

Lung cancer in white men declines in U.S. 1985. *New York Times*, 3 December, p. Al.

Maccoby, Eleanor Emmons, and Carol Nagy Jacklin. 1974. *The Psychology of Sex Differences.* Stanford, CA: Stanford University Press.

Magnuson, E. 1983. "Child abuse: The ultimate betrayal." *Time*, 5 September, 122: 20–22.

Makepeace, James M. 1983. "Life events stress and courtship violence." *Family Relations* 32: 101–109.

Marcus, Alfred C., and Lori A. Crane. 1986. "Telephone surveys in public health research." *Medical Care* 24: 97–112.

Nagi, Saad Z. 1976. *Child Maltreatment in the United States: A Challenge to Social Institutions.* New York: Columbia University Press.

Pirog-Good, Mureen, and Jan Stets-Kealey. 1985. "Domestic violence victimization: A multiyear perspective." Paper presented at the 1985 annual meeting of the American Society of Criminology, San Diego.

Pleck, Elizabeth, Joseph H. Pleck, Marlyn Grossman, and Pauline B. Bart. 1977. "The battered data syndrome: A comment on Steinmetz' article." *Victimology: An International Journal* 2: 680–683.

Radbill, Samuel X. 1980. "Children in a world of violence: A history of child abuse." Chapter 1 in C. Henry Kempe and Ray E. Helfer (eds.), *The Battered Child* (3rd ed.). Chicago: University of Chicago Press.

Reidel, Mark, and Margaret A. Zahn. 1985. *The Nature and Pattern of American Homicide.* Washington, DC: National Institute of Justice.

Sack, Alan R., James F. Keller, and Richard D. Howard. 1982. "Conflict tactics and violence in dating situations." *International Journal of Sociology of the Family* 12: 89–100.

Saunders, Daniel G. 1986. "When battered women use violence: Husband-abuse or self-defense?" *Violence and Victims* 1: 47–60.

Scanzoni, John. 1978. *Sex Roles, Women's Work, and Marital Conflict.* Lexington, MA: Lexington Books.

Schumm, Walter R., Stephan R. Bollman, Anthony P. Jurich, and Michael J. Martin. 1982. "Adolescent perspectives on family violence." *Journal of Social Psychology* 117: 153–154.

Sherman, Laurence, and Richard A. Berk. 1984. "The specific deterrent effects of arrest for domestic assault." *American Sociological Review* 49: 261–272.

Smith, Michael D. 1985. "Woman abuse: The case for surveys by telephone." Paper presented at the 1985 meeting of the American Society of Criminology, San Diego.

Statistical Abstract of the United States (105th ed.). 1985. Washington, DC: U.S. Government Printing Office.

Steinmetz, Suzanne K. 1977. *The Cycle of Violence: Assertive, Aggressive, and Abusive Family Interaction.* New York: Praeger.

Steinmetz, Suzanne K. 1977–78. "The battered husband syndrome." *Victimology: An International Journal* 2: 499–509.

Steinmetz, Suzanne K. 1978. "Services to battered women: Our greatest need. A reply to Field and Kirchner." *Victimology: An International Journal* 3: 222–226.

Straus, Murray A. 1973. "A general systems theory approach to a theory of violence between family members." *Social Science Information* 13: 105–125.

Straus, Murray A. 1974. "Leveling, civility, and violence in the family." *Journal of Marriage and the Family* 36: 13–29.

Straus, Murray A. 1976. "Sexual inequality, cultural norms, and wife-beating." *Victimology* 1: 54–76.

Straus, Murray A. 1977. "Wife-beating: How common, and why?" *Victimology* 2: 443–458.

Straus, Murray A. 1979. "Measuring intrafamily conflict and violence: The Conflict Tactics (CT) Scales." *Journal of Marriage and the Family* 41: 75–88.

Straus, Murray A. 1980. "Victims and aggressors in marital violence." *American Behavioral Scientist* 23: 681–704.

Straus, Murray A. 1981a. "Re-evaluation of the Conflict Tactics Scale." Paper presented at the National Conference for Family Violence Researchers, University of New Hampshire (July).

Straus, Murray A. 1981b. "Societal change and change in family violence." Paper presented at the National Conference for Family Violence Researchers, University of New Hampshire (July).

Straus, Murray A. 1983. "Ordinary violence, child abuse, and wife beating: What do they have in common?" In David Finkelhor, Richard J. Gelles, Gerald T. Hotaling, and Murray A. Straus (eds.), *The Dark Side of Families: Current Family Violence Research.* Beverly Hills, CA: Sage.

Straus, Murray A. In press. "Domestic violence and homicide antecedents." Bulletin of the New York Academy of Medicine.

Straus, Murray A., and Richard J. Gelles. 1986. "How violent are American families: Estimates based on two national surveys and other studies." Paper in progress.

Straus, Murray A., Richard J. Gelles, and Suzanne K. Steinmetz. 1980. *Behind Closed Doors: Violence in the American Family.* Garden City, NY: Doubleday, Anchor Press.

Szinovacz, Maximiliane E. 1983. "Using couple data as a methodological tool: The case of marital violence." *Journal of Marriage and the Family*: 633–644.

Tavris, Carol, and Carole Offir. 1977. *The Longest War: Sex Differences in Perspective.* New York: Harcourt Brace Jovanovich.

Thornton, Arland, Duane F. Alwin, and Donald Camburn. 1983. "Causes and consequences of sex-role attitudes and attitude change." *American Sociology Review* 48: 211–227.

"2 researchers say violence has plunged in the last 10 years, but . . ." 1985. *Christian Science Monitor*, 18 November, pp. 3–4.

U.S. Department of Justice. 1985. "Criminal victimization in the U.S., 1983." National Crime Survey Report NCJ–96459. Washington, DC: Government Printing Office.

Warrior, Betsy. 1982. *Battered Women's Directory* (8th ed.). Cambridge, MA: Author, 46 Pleasant Street, Cambridge, MA 02139.

Williams, Kirk R., and Richard Hawkins. In press. "Perceptual research on general deterrence: A critical review." *Law and Society Review.*

Yllö, Kersti. 1978. "Nonmarital cohabitation: Beyond the college campus." *Alternative Lifestyles* 1: 37–54.

Yllö, Kersti, and Murray A. Straus. 1981. "Interpersonal violence among married and cohabiting couples." *Family Relations* 30: 339–345.

CHAPTER THREE

EXPLAINING BATTERING

As discussed in the last section, how we name, define, and measure something is affected by hegemonic assumptions about gender. Similarly, our explanations of battering are affected by these same stereotypes. An examination of the various explanations for battering is informative, regardless of the empirical evidence supporting any particular causal factor. By looking at the way we frame the questions and the answers, we can dissect the social construction of the problem.

This chapter contends that the most common explanation for battering is that the primary fault is with the victim; she asked for it, provoked it, or must somehow deserve it if she chooses to stay in the relationship. If the blame is not placed on the victim, the explanation is usually that the batterer is a deviant, "sick," or out of control individual. Rarely are social-structural-level analyses employed, especially in everyday discourse. Common-sense responses to this problem create a climate that blames the victim and rarely assigns responsibility to the perpetrator.

When batterers are held accountable, there is a tendency to resort to micro-level analyses that explain battering in the context of a rare and aberrant event. While this conceptualization does place responsibility for the behavior on the perpetrator, it also allows society to avoid the more difficult process of examining the ways in which the social structure contributes to woman battering. Micro-level assessments of blame allow us to avoid the onerous process of changing society itself. We have bad individuals, not a deficient society. Individuals need therapy, but social structures need no attention. In other words, we don't need to bother to rearrange social organizations to pay women equally so that they can afford to leave their batterer. Instead, we can invest in counseling so that the marriage can be saved and the family (as conceived by the patriarchy) remains intact.

129

IT'S HER FAULT

Scientific studies have been unable to isolate common traits shared by victims with any real success. If, in fact, victims cause their victimization, one should theoretically be able to detect many shared common characteristics. A comprehensive review of over 400 studies on battering suggests that of 97 possible characteristics (often called risk markers), only one factor apparently distinguished battered women from non-battered women: witnessing violence between one's parents (Hotaling & Sugarman, 1986).

Not surprisingly, battered women are a heterogeneous group. Battered women fail to share common characteristics that can be used to explain the cause of the behavior because the underlying assumption is flawed. The tautological thinking that women somehow cause their own victimization (that there is something wrong with women that causes them to get involved with batterers) crumbles when actual circumstances are examined. As the United Nations article points out, theories based on victim precipitation are dangerous because they excuse the perpetrator's behavior and place the blame for the abuse on the woman.

The nagging wife is a powerful image that society invokes to blame women for their victimization (Adams, 1988; Dobash & Dobash, 1979; Ptacek, 1988). Clearly the image of a nagging wife is associated with gender assumptions about femininity and the roles of women in relationships. "Understanding the woman's 'nagging' from a less male-defined perspective, for instance, may reveal that the woman is repeating herself because he does not listen to her" (Adam, 1988, p. 187). Nagging may be nothing more than "continued discussion once he has made up his mind" (Dobash & Dobash, 1979, p. 133). There is, however, a strong historical tradition of accepting the idea that nagging causes men to lose control and lash out by "slapping" or "shoving." Lost in this image is the reality of an enraged man slamming his wife against a concrete wall, screaming that she has no right to ask where he's been or what he's been doing until 4:00 a.m. in the morning. Instead of being shocked by the violence, too often society has been willing to buy into the justification that she kept at him until he couldn't take it anymore. This idea of loss of control is a central explanation for men's violence and will be discussed in more detail shortly. However, it dovetails with the explanation of the nagging woman. These two hegemonic views minimize men's violence against their intimates. At best, she deserved it; at worst, he lost control—it was something he could not help.

Another powerful way in which the hegemony is maintained is by focusing on why women stay. Asking this question conveys that there is something wrong with her and implies that she is responsible for the behavior because she would leave if she really didn't like being battered. This view is so widespread that readers often have difficulty considering alternative explanations for battering until they can find a plausible answer.

Why Does She Stay?

It is often hard to understand why someone would stay in a relationship where there is battering. However, many feminists note that the very question is problematic. It tends to focus on the wrong population. Instead of asking why he batters, there is a tendency to ask why she stays (Bograd, 1988; Hoff, 1990). The nature of the question frames the debate to focus on her role in the relationship and obscures the actions of the batterer. Furthermore, it implies that battered women can and should simply walk away from these violent relationships. We forget that many, perhaps most, battered women do leave these situations at considerable risk to their safety. Since batterers use a variety of controlling and violent tactics to drag women back into the relationship when they do try to leave (Ptacek, 1997), a more appropriate research question might be: why won't he let her go? Unfortunately, social debate rarely focuses on this issue.

Once battered women leave, batterers tend to use a rather consistent approach to getting their partners back (Ptacek, 1997). Batterers may coax friends and family members to pressure victims to return home. Batterers also may coerce relatives and/or friends into revealing where the victims are living. Batterers devise ways to follow and harass their victims. They may use child visitations as a means to manipulate the legal system to maintain contact with their partners and to learn their whereabouts. Batterers may take off with the children, kidnap them from school, and surrender them only when victims return home. Batterers may stalk their victims, threatening to kill them if they don't come home. Thus many battered women do leave, but they return because they are afraid of the batterers' violence. Research suggests this fear is not unfounded (Craven, 1997; Browne, 1993). In fact, the most severe violence and the greatest threat of fatality may exist when a battered woman leaves, (Mahoney, 1981; Ptacek, 1997) and this threat may exist for months and even years after she has gone (Wilson & Daly, 1993).

Emotional Factors

At the micro level, there are several psychological or emotional factors that contribute to staying in the relationship. Some battered women may stay because they are trapped in the "cycle of violence." Walker (1979) coined this term and contends that battering occurs in three phases: the tension-building phase, the acute-battering incident, and the honeymoon phase (Walker, 1979). In the first stage, tension builds as the batterer becomes tense and short-tempered. The battered woman tries to calm him down to avoid battering. In the second phase, generally the briefest, he batters her. In the final stage the batterer tries to beg, plead, and otherwise ingratiate himself so as not to lose her. He begs for forgiveness and often is quite conciliatory—bearing gifts and compliments. The cycle then begins again.

This explanation is widely accepted and often cited; however, there is insufficient empirical research on the cycle of violence. Some studies suggest that the violence tends to increase in frequency and severity as time passes (see Dobash & Dobash, 1979). The tension-building phase becomes longer, and the reconciliation attempts are less apologetic in nature as batterers turn to providing justification for their actions (Browne, 1987; Walker, 1983, 1984). However, we know little about the length and nature of these phases. While some battered women acknowledge this explanation of their behavior and profess it is difficult to leave when batterers are charming and contrite following a beating, other battered women have expressed feelings of oppression by manipulative attempts to balance the abuse. The description of the honeymoon phase may well be more related to the batterer's behavior than to the victim's experiences. While he may feel that he is winning her back with flowers, fine dining, and dancing, she may well be highly resentful of having to pretend that all is well for fear of further retribution. It may be difficult to enjoy this reconciliation if her head throbs every time she bends over to smell the flowers, if she can't swallow the food because of a swollen throat, or if her ribs ache as he spins her around the dance floor.

Walker has also argued that women in battering relationships lose their ability to develop a plan for leaving. Battered women learn a variety of coping techniques to minimize their risk of harm. This "learned helplessness" ensures that women become preoccupied with surviving, which causes them to lose sight of the future and makes it difficult to plan for escape (1979). While some researchers report that battered women experience clinical depression (Riggs et al., 1992), there is controversy over the idea that battered women have poor problem-solving abilities (Orava, McLeod, & Sharpe, 1996). In contrast, empirical studies find that battered women are quite persistent in seeking help (Bowker, 1983; Gondolf, 1988a). As the article by Campbell and her colleagues suggest, the image of battered women as passive victims is far from accurate.

Walker (1984, 1993) also argues that battered women experience battered women's syndrome (BWS), a form of post-traumatic stress disorder similar to that experienced by Vietnam veterans. The stress associated with battering manifests itself in several ways and may result in cognitive distortions including difficulty concentrating and confused thinking. Victims may experience memory distortions in the form of flashbacks or repressing the victimizations through disassociation. They may experience a variety of emotional reactions including depression, irritability, anger, and anxiety. They may experience sleep and eating disorders and often demonstrate hypervigilance to danger—that is, carefully monitoring their environment for the slightest hint of danger.

Unfortunately, Walker is not clear whether she means some women or all battered women suffer from BWS (Bowker, 1993). She asserts that some unidentified percentage of women experience BWS and that the symptoms may abate when the woman leaves the battering situation, or it may require additional counseling. Walker argues that "there are psychological effects to being battered [and] that such effects are predictable and have a name": BWS. It appears, however, that Walker's work lacks conceptual integrity if she intends to argue that all battered women experience a clinical diagnosis of mental illness (Bowker, 1993). Some battered women may be mentally ill as a result of living in a battering relationship, or they may experience stress related symptoms. However, it is dangerous to assert that all battered women are mentally ill. This inference translates that battered women stay because they are "sick" and ignores other social factors that may explain their continued presence in the relationship.

A variety of other emotional factors also may contribute to a woman's reluctance to leave (Dutton-Douglas, 1991; Ferraro & Johnson, 1983; Frisch & MacKenzie, 1991; Kaner et al., 1993; Pagelow, 1981; Strube & Barbour, 1984; Vaughn, 1987). Battered women sometimes minimize the abusive behavior to avoid confronting the painful truth: that the man she loves beats her. Some battered women may be insecure and lack self-confidence in their ability to take care of themselves and their children. Battered women may fear the unknown. Battered women who hope that batterers will change often hear such promises—especially after severe beatings or after leaving. Sometimes battered women need time to work on the relationship to be sure that they have done what they can to try to make the relationship work. Some battered women are still in love with their batterers.

Social Factors

At the macro level, there are structural arrangements that encourage battered women to stay with their batterers. First and foremost, battered women may be economically dependent on their batterers (Aguirre, 1985; Bowker, 1993; Frisch & MacKenzie, 1991; Pagelow, 1981; Strube & Barbour, 1983, 1984; Wilson et al., 1989). We live in a culture that has discouraged and prevented women from working outside the home. Instead, women have been taught to marry in order to ascertain their financial security. Hence the idea that women should try to "marry up." Women, especially poor women and women of color, have been denied access to education and are relegated to jobs that pay poorly. Poor women, under-educated women, and women of color have less economic opportunities in our culture, making it more difficult for these women to escape batterers if they are financially dependent on them. Women may well choose to be battered rather than risk homelessness, especially when children are involved.

Another attitude that contributes to women staying is the considerable pressure in our society for women to attract a partner. Some women may believe what society often conveys: that any man is better than no man. Is it really surprising that some battered women stay in violent situations in a culture where women are taught to "stand by their man" no matter what. In addition, battered women worry about losing custody of their children (Geffner & Pagelow, 1990).

Women's responses to violence are shaped by various racial, ethnic, and class factors (Miller, 1989), including religion. As noted in previous chapters religious institutions often emphasize the permanency of marriage and support patriarchal values that assert men are the family decision makers (Dobash & Dobash, 1979; Martin, 1978). In some cases, women may believe that divorce is prohibited once a couple is united in the eyes of God, that it is a mortal sin.

Most of us can relate to the explanations battered women offer if we take a minute to think about it. Many of us ignore negative traits in our partners and hope that these behaviors will change. Many of us have made poor choices in the name of love. Many of us have returned to a relationship in the hopes of reconciling with a loved one, even when we knew that it was not good for us to do so.

Many of us have tried to re-build relationships even when all available evidence suggested that it was not going to work. Leaving is often a process that takes some time. For battered women, their safety and/or their lives may be in jeopardy if the reconciliation fails.

Many battered women recognize this threat and flee when they are able to do so. For the most part, researchers have not concentrated on studying the women who escape. The article by Campbell and her coauthors examines the process of leaving. They found that battered women use a variety of strategies that involve active problem solving. Campbell notes that leaving was rarely immediate or linear and cautions against using dichotomous measures that focus on whether a woman is "in" or "out" of the violent relationship. This is consistent with other studies that found battered women left and returned to a relationship an average of six times (Gondolf, 1988b; Okun, 1986).

We need additional research like the study by Campbell and her colleagues so we can better understand the process of leaving. Studies of this nature might identify coping strategies that lead women to freedom. However, we must not forget that simply leaving does not solve the problem; in fact, it may make it worse (Browne, 1997). While it may be in the best interests of the battered victim to leave at any sign of abuse, to expect all victims to act this way is unrealistic and unsophisticated. Most profoundly, this attitude ignores the fact that many battered women do not leave because they are terrified of their batterers. The risk of being battered or even killed after leaving is not insignificant (Jurik & Winn, 1990). For some women, the fear of reprisals for leaving is more frightening than confronting the known danger present in the relationship (Browne, 1997). Furthermore, even if a particular woman escapes a battering relationship, in all probability the battering does not end; he finds a new partner and a new victim. The root problem remains. Asking why she stays ignores a more pressing question: why does he batter?

HE'S DEVIANT, SICK, OR OUT OF CONTROL

Very little research has concentrated on studying batterers. Since we have rarely studied batterers, it has been difficult to formulate theories that explain their behavior. Just as powerful hegemonic assumptions are used to create the nagging wife, the image of the out of control batterer defines the situation very narrowly in ways that minimize the social structural arrangements that support, encourage, and endorse battering.

Individual Psychopathology

As the articles by the United Nations and Healey, Smith, and O'Sullivan demonstrate, research has been unable to isolate any particular mental illness associated with battering despite the popular hegemonic assumption that portrays batterers as a few deviant, psychologically ill men. In other words, batterers do not share any identifiable mental illness such as schizophrenia, neurosis, or depression. Furthermore, since only a small proportion of the mentally ill are violent in any situation, why would mental illness provide the primary explanation of violence within the home (Burgess & Draper, 1989)?

Stress has been a popular explanation for woman battering. As the United Nations article points out, economic conditions, poor wages, and limited job opportunities have all been used to "explain" battering, although this approach has minimal empirical support (Schwartz, 1990). The 1990s version of the deviant batterer revolves around two popular explanations for battering: that batterers are substance abusers and that they lack the ability to control their anger.

Substance Abuse.   As the United Nations article notes, there appears to be a link between substance abuse and woman battering, but the nature of this relationship has yet to be determined. Alcohol use has long been a favorite explanation for battering. "Demon rum" has been blamed for woman battering since the 1700s (Gelles, 1993; Pleck, 1987). The current war on drugs, now 15 years old, has linked drugs and crime in the minds of most Americans and battering is no exception. The hegemonic assumption is that batterers use drugs (legal and illegal) that cause them to lose control of their inhibitions, which leads to battering. The solution is equally simplistic: eliminate drug use and the battering will stop. In other words, these men are sick and/or deviant, and if they were able to conquer the substance abuse they would not engage in battering.

Batterers who are under the influence of substances may loose their ability to perceive their actions accurately. For example, a drunken batterer may hit his partner harder than he realized because he is too drunk to judge the amount of force that he is using. Like any substance abuser, batterers would probably be better equipped to deal with their problems if they were sober; however, there are many problems with this simplistic view of drug use and battering.

First, little evidence suggests that there is a direct causal relationship between substance use and battering (Edleson et al., 1985; Gelles & Cornell, 1985; Gelles, 1993; Kantor & Straus, 1995; Tolman & Bennett, 1990; Zubretsky & Digirolamo, 1994). In order to establish causal order, one must demonstrate that the cause occurs before the effect. It is possible that the temporal order of this hypothesis may be incorrect (it may be backwards). Perhaps offenders batter because they use drugs, but it also is possible that batterers use drugs because they batter. Drug use may be used an excuse to mediate responsibility for their behavior or to block out pain that they experience when they come face to face with their actions. Perhaps a third intervening variable is the cause of both behaviors and drug use only appears to be responsible for battering. For example, perhaps men with low self-esteem are more apt to use drugs *and* they are more apt to batter. The drug use may have nothing to do with battering but if the study does not measure and control for the effects of this variable it may appear as if these two factors have a causal relationship. Thus the old adage that correlation does not mean causation.

Second, our understanding of the relationship between drugs and abuse is hampered by an overly broad definition of substance use (Gelles, 1993). Generally speaking, this relationship is examined by measuring the correlation between the frequency of drug use and the frequency of battering. These types of studies fail to determine whether the drug use is actually occurring during the assault or if it is occurring differently during the assault. For example, is the batterer only abusive when using the substance or does he become abusive if he uses more of the substance than at other times? Does he only beat her when he drinks or when he drinks "too much"? Simply asking about whether or not one uses drugs and whether or not one engages in battering does not allow us to determine the relationship between substance abuse and battering.

In addition, researchers tend to dichotomize drug use into two categories: alcohol use and "other drug use" (Gelles, 1993). In other words, they tend to group all drugs together with little regard for pharmacological differences. However, it would be remarkable if all substance use affected battering similarly. For example, perhaps drugs that have depressant effects such as heroin and marijuana would be unrelated to battering while drugs such as amphetamines might facilitate battering. If drug use contributes to battering, it seems likely that this relationship would vary depending upon the biochemical response produced by particular drugs. More complex research needs to be conducted to allow us to understand this phenomenon.

Finally, and perhaps most importantly, even if drug use "caused" battering, one would still need to explain the context-specific nature of the abuse. As the United Nations article asks, why is it that substance abuse seemingly produces violence specifically in the home? Why does it cause men to batter their wives but not others in society?

Drug use is a popular explanation for battering partially because it is consistent with larger social expectations about the effects of drugs. As anthropologists MacAndrew and Edgerton (1969) have pointed out, how drugs affect us is related to the social construction of drug use. For example, in the United States, we associate drug use, especially alcohol use, with the loss of control. We give permission for people to act in fundamentally different ways—hence the stereotype of dancing with a lamp shade on one's head at a party. In other cultures, alcohol has different effects because the participants are socialized to believe that they will act differently (MacAndrew & Edgerton, 1969).

Substance abuse is a very popular explanation for battering. One of the most attractive aspects of this explanation is that it does not require macro-level solutions. We live in a culture that reveres individual accountability. It is much easier to define the problem as a matter of individual deviance. If the problem lies at the micro or individual level, society can continue to focus on "abnormal" people and seek solutions that leave the social structure unchanged. The focus on drug and alcohol use/abuse restricts the problem to the individual level.

Anger Management.   Another popular explanation for battering falls in the micro-level, psychopathological approach to battering. Batterers abuse their partners because of poor anger control management. Here again, battering can be explained as the pathology of a few deviant individuals. "Rather than being depicted as rational and unemotional, violent husbands are characterized as extremely emotional and highly sensitive to situational stress, and their violence is primarily expressive rather than instrumental" (Hotaling, Straus, & Lincoln, 1995, p. 439). In other words, their deficient personalities lead them to victimize those they have power over in the family.

While the empirical support for this explanation is mixed (Barnett et al., 1991; Dutton & Strachan, 1987; Hasting & Hamberger, 1988; Maiuro et al., 1988; Telch & Lindquist, 1984; Tolman & Bennett, 1990), many treatment programs for batterers focus on anger management. Batterers are taught how to maintain control over their anger, frequently by keeping anger control logs to learn to recognize cues that cause them to lose their temper and become violent. The success of these programs is controversial. Batterer treatment programs, in general, tend to experience high drop out rates; these rates have been reported to range from 40% (Pirog-Good & Stets, 1986) to over 90% (Gondolf & Foster, 1991). Thus, while programs often report successful outcomes ranging from 50 to 85% of the participants (Tolman & Bennet, 1990) one must evaluate these figures with great caution given the high percentage of men who drop out of the program. The majority of treatment evaluations only follow batterers for 6 to 12 months after completion of the treatment (see Tolman & Bennett, 1990). Recidivism rates often appear artificially low. Evaluators sometimes rely on the batterer's self reports to measure success. Others use arrest rates, which also may overestimate the success of the program. Men may well be able to escape police detection for beatings administered while in treatment. Even victim surveys may fail to capture relapses if women are embarrassed or afraid to report the violence.

In addition, anecdotal data from victims indicates that many men in treatment learn to postpone the physical violence and "use" the program to abuse her emotionally. For example, a batterer may walk out the door every time the couple disagrees about a subject. Couples frequently have to make complicated decisions about finances, children, and employment. In the ideal, they can negotiate differences, but in battering situations batterers may use treatment to avoid any difficult or unpleasant discussion. For example, a woman may confront her batterer about his failure to do his share of household tasks or for not assisting with child care duties. He, in turn, may become angry and justify leaving without having to discuss the problem because he has been taught to leave rather than risk hitting her. He then is free to escape any discussion about responsibility for his actions in the relationship by pointing out that the alternative is for him to stay, get angry, lose control, and hit her. The batterer then may take refuge in the pool hall and leave the battered woman alone with her anger, unable to confront him about any behavioral patterns in the relationship.

While there may be value in teaching men to better manage their anger, this psychopathological approach is quite limited from a theoretical standpoint. It ignores the larger social structural support for battering and fails to explain why this personality defect apparently only affects men primarily in the context of marriage. Why is it that most batterers do not suffer from poor anger control management in other social situations causing them to batter their bosses or strangers with equal regularity as their partners?

Both drug use and the failure to manage anger are popular explanations for battering because they share a domain assumption—that men who batter do so because they lose control. Batterers and clinicians alike are prone to use and accept metaphors that imply a loss of control (Ptacek, 1988); therefore, it should come as no surprise that the general public also adopts a similar view. Batterers then become "walking time bombs" until they "go berserk," "blow up," or just generally "lose it." In contrast, Ptacek reports that batterers in his study exhibited a pattern of "intentional, goal-oriented violence," including punishing their partners for failing to be "good wives" (1988, p. 150–151). Research on batterers suggests that they minimize the violence, deny their responsibility, offer excuses and justifications for their behavior, and blame their victims for precipitating the abuse (Adams, 1988; Barrera et al., 1994; Dutton, 1986, 1988; Edleson & Tolman, 1992; Gondolf, 1985; Ptacek, 1988; Pence & Paymar, 1986).

Culture provides the framework for these scripts. Much masculine behavior is excused by the idea that men sometimes lose control. For example, it is often assumed that men cannot control their sexuality, and if women "tempt" them by dressing or acting in certain ways then they have caused their own victimization. The idea that men batter because they lose control is consistent with larger social values that allow men to act out. It makes it easier to assert that women are to blame. After all, if she knows that her "nagging" will "set him off," she should simply avoid bugging him about things he does not want to discuss.

As Healey and her colleagues note, a feminist analysis of battering challenges these micro-level explanations of battering and contends that battering is not abnormal behavior. Quite the contrary, the extensive nature of the problem and the widespread social and legal acceptance of it indicate that wife battering "may be more a function of the normal psychological and behavioral patterns of most men than of the aberrant actions of a very few husbands" (Bograd, 1988, p. 17). Clearly, psychological factors play a role in battering because not all men batter, but psychological perspectives fail to include an adequate understanding of the ways in which patriarchal social structures encourage violence that is specifically directed toward women in the family. In contrast, all sociological approaches, to some extent, shift the focus from deviant individuals and concentrate on the ways that battering is maintained by society and social forces. A sociological analysis recognizes that change may occur at the individual level but suggests that social arrangements must change to eradicate battering. However, sociologists do not agree about which types of social arrangements contribute most to woman battering.

Sociological Explanations

Numerous sociological theories have been devised to explain battering. As the United Nations article demonstrates, cultural factors and underdevelopment have been offered as potential explanations. Exchange theory has been used to argue that family members will use violence as long as the rewards outweigh the consequences (Gelles, 1983; 1993). Other researchers have asserted that certain subcultures in society are more accepting of violent behavior (Wolfgang & Fer-racuti, 1967). Proponents of resource theory assert that all social systems rely on some degree of force and that the more resources one has the more apt they are to use violence. Thus men who lack prestige and income are more apt to batter to gain power at home to compensate for their lack of power in the public arena (Blood & Wolfe, 1960; Goode, 1971; Warner, Lee, & Lee, 1986). As noted in read-ing 8, a general systems theory approach asserts that the family operates as a sys-tem and the violence is functional in that it often produces the desired outcome (Straus, 1973). Three sociological approaches have received the most attention.

Intergenerational Abuse or Social Learning Theory.   A very popu-lar explanation for battering involves childhood socialization and the idea that battering is part of a cycle of abuse passed from generation to generation.[1] As the United Nations article points out, this explanation is very popular and is perpet-uated by folk wisdom. Theoretically, violence can be "learned" in several ways. Both male and female children who witness their father battering their mother may learn that violence is an acceptable way to deal with conflict in the family; therefore, the boys may grow up to be batterers and the girls may grow up to marry batterers. Or, if one contends that battering is mutual combat, both girls and boys may grow up and use violence to solve disputes with their partners. Or, children who experience abuse at the hands of their parents may grow up to be abusive to their partners. The empirical data on this perspective is mixed. While some studies report that children who witness parental violence are more prone to experience violence in their own relationships (Straus et al., 1980), others find that male children are more apt to become batterers if they both experienced and witnessed violence (Caesar, 1988; Hotaling & Sugarman, 1986; Pagelow, 1981; Rosenbaum & O'Leary, 1981). Other studies report that any effect is more pro-nounced when children view paternal rather than maternal violence (Barnett et al., 1991; Caesar & Hamberger, 1989; Choice et al., 1995; Widom, 1989). Other lit-erature reports that there is no evidence of intergenerational transmission (Cap-pell & Heiner, 1990; Frieze & Browne, 1989; Herzberger, 1983; Weis, 1989).

As the United Nations article notes, more sophisticated research is needed in this area. We need to understand how gender affects possible intergenera-tional transmission; that is, does it matter who is committing the violence—fathers or mothers—and does it vary by the sex of the child witnessing the acts. It is interesting to note, however, that this explanation for battering is one of the most popular sociological theories. To some extent, it challenges the sanctity of the nuclear family by identifying it as the root cause of the problem; however, it does not contest the very structure of the family. Instead of sick individuals, we now have sick or deviant families. Here again, there is no challenge to the patri-archal nature of society or the family itself.

Family Violence Perspective.   Another sociological approach, some-times called the family violence perspective (Kurz, 1993a, 1993b), has been devel-oped by the authors of the conflict tactics scale and the national family violence surveys: Straus and Gelles (Gelles, 1974, 1979, 1983, 1985; Gelles & Cornell, 1990;

Gelles & Straus, 1988; Straus, 1980a, 1980b, 1980c). These authors focus on three factors which produce family violence: (1) the unique structure of the family, (2) social acceptance of violence as a means of solving conflict, and (3) the important role corporal punishment of children plays in the social acceptance of violence (Kurz, 1983b).

Straus and Gelles contend that the unique structure of the family contributes to its nature as a "violence prone" institution (Gelles, 1993, p. 35). Families spend a great deal of time together, and their interactions involve a wide range of activities and situations. In addition, there are often limited opportunities for win-win situations in family activities when disputes arise. For example, if family members fight over which television program to watch, one party generally wins and another loses. Family involvement is uniquely intense so that actions by family members carry more power; for example, insults by a family member often carry more weight. Likewise, we assume that family members have more of a right to influence other family members even though membership is involuntary. The family is composed of people of different ages and sexes, which set the stage for conflicts that occur in part because roles are ascribed based on these differences.[2] Families are very private institutions and are thereby insulated from the public view, although the amount of intimacy assures that family members have a great deal of knowledge about other family members. Finally, families are subjected to much stress because of the constant change they experience related to the birth and maturation of children, aging, retirement, and death. The stress experienced by one family member (e.g., unemployment, bad grades at school, illness, etc.) affects the remaining members. Stressors present in the larger society—job related difficulties, financial woes, and other stressful events—increase the likelihood of violence in the family in a society where physical violence is condoned.

While Straus and Gelles contend that these unique factors make the family prone to conflict, they argue that social acceptance of familial violence also must exist in order for violence to occur. In other words, the family is subject to a variety of serious stressors that lead to battering *provided* there is a cultural belief that violence in the family is accepted, tolerated, and even required. They note the widespread acceptance of violence in fairy tales, cartoons, television programs, and movies. However, they contend that the extensive use of corporal punishment in the United States ensures that most of us, through experience of one kind or another, learn that violence in families is acceptable under certain conditions. Specifically it teaches children (and all of us) that it is acceptable: "(a) to hit people you love, (b) for powerful people to hit less powerful people, (c) to use hitting to achieve some end or goal, and (d) to hit as an end in itself" (Gelles & Cornell, 1990, p. 110). Parents who hit their children, at some level, teach children that violence and love can (and do) co-exist. There is widespread social acceptance for the use of violence in the family especially when someone is "wrong" or "will not listen."

While Straus and Gelles often note that sexism plays a role in "family violence," they do so in a limited way. They believe that it is only one factor among many and that the most powerful family member is most apt to use violence. They note that wives are victimized more often in homes where they have less power, but that husbands are victimized in homes that are "wife dominant" (Straus et al., 1980, p. 193). It is important to remember that these researchers also view battering as mutual combat (as noted in the previous section). In a very real sense, proponents of the family violence perspective could not argue that patriarchy is central to woman battering as long as they are willing to view findings from the conflict tactics scale (CTS) as valid. Sexism could not be viewed as the primary contributory factor since their data find that men and women use equal levels of violence.

The family violence perspective, unlike the psychopathological approaches, shifts the focus from the micro-level of analysis to the macro-level. Instead of asking why some people batter or what is wrong with abnormal men who batter, this perspective asks about the structure of the family in a particular society that encourages or contributes to family violence. The authors advocate altering structural factors rather than changing individuals in order to reduce battering. They predict that attacking sexism is one way to help reduce this violence, but that social reform must also concentrate on undermining all types of social violence. Feminists agree with a great deal of this theoretical orientation, although there are subtle but critically important differences in the emphasis given to sexism and patriarchy.

The Feminist Perspective

Feminists make assumptions that challenge the family violence perspective and have been critical of this approach (Bowker, 1986; Breines & Gordon, 1983; Dobash & Dobash, 1979; Kurz, 1993a, 1993b; Pagelow, 1981; Russell, 1982; Stanko, 1985). As Healey and colleagues note, feminist scholarship places patriarchy at the center of any explanation for woman battering. It is based on the domain assumption that sexism is not *a* factor contributing to woman battering but *the* factor (Dobash & Dobash, 1979; Martin, 1976; Pagelow, 1981; Russell, 1982; Schechter, 1982). Feminists contend that men who beat their partners are not committing a random, deviant act but one that must be interpreted in light of the particular social structural arrangement that gives all men power over women in society. While race and class differences exist, all men have the power and opportunity to use violence against women to oppress them. Even when individual men do not use this type of power, all men benefit from the ways in which women's lives are restricted in a society where violence is an important part of oppression. Feminist approaches point to the ways that social institutions have supported and condoned woman battering. They point to the historical traditions that have treated women as children in need of supervision and discipline. Laws and social customs clearly have endorsed the use of "corporal punishment" for wives, and social structures keep women dependent on men for economic survival. These values are still prevalent in our society today. Male violence is not only tolerated but encouraged by a variety of forces ranging from popular culture to organized religion. While we may no longer have laws that permit woman battering, in practice the criminal justice system and many other institutions have failed to respond to the needs of battered women. At its heart, a feminist approach contends that it is no accident that our society has empha- sized street crime and minimized intimate violence. Acknowledging the over- whelming magnitude of woman battering would openly contradict the hegemonic assertion that violence of this nature is rare and aberrant.

SUMMARY

Instead of concentrating on sick/psychopathological men or deviant families and problems with familial structure, a feminist perspective concentrates on the ways in which society is organized to allow for and encourage woman battering. Instead of seeing battering as mutual violence or individual pathologies, feminist scholarship concentrates on the ways in which the institution of marriage itself has been organized, defined, and socially reproduced to facilitate the battering of women. The family reflects the larger social, political, and economic arrange- ments in society.

In doing so, it draws back the curtain on hegemony. Think of the pollution analogy introduced in the first chapter. Acknowledging the extent of battering and accepting the idea that women are more at risk from intimates than strang- ers is as revealing as the view from the mountains. The pollution is visible; the patriarchal social structure is exposed. How can one continue to support a return to "family values" if this institution is dangerous for women and not for men? What does it say about society that we have constructed marriage in ways that have empowered men and disempowered women? What does it say about economic arrangements of our society when financially dependent women live with batterers in order to feed their children? What does it mean if women of color are reluctant to report their batterers to the police because they fear racial discriminatory law enforcement for men of color? Why have women historically had to fight for the "right" to divorce an abusive man, but divorce was readily available if men "deserted" their wives? It is clear that society, in general, con- structs battering in ways that obscure these issues, and the pollution allows us to avoid troubling questions.

NOTES

[1] This theory is often referred to as the cycle of violence—the same term that Walker uses to describe the cyclical nature of abuse as experienced by battered women. This can lead to confusion if one is not sure of the context of the term.

[2] Note that the assumption of intergenerational conflict assumes that the family includes children.

REFERENCES

Adams, D. (1988). Treatment models of men who batter. In K. Yllo & M. Bograd (Eds.), *Feminist perspectives on wife abuse* (pp. 176–199). Newbury Park, CA: Sage.

Aguirre, B. (1985). Why do they return? *Social Work, 30,* 350–354.

Barnett, O., Fagan, R., & Booker, J. (1991). Hostility and stress as mediators of aggression in violent men. *Journal of Family Violence, 6,* 219–241.

Barrera, M., Palmer, S., Brown, R., & Kalaher, S. (1994). Characteristics of court-involved men and non-court involved men who abuse their wives. *Journal of Family Violence, 9,* 333–345.

Blood, R., & Wolfe, D. (1960). *Husbands and wives: The dynamics of married living.* Glencoe, IL: Free Press.

Bograd, M. (1988). Feminist perspectives on wife abuse. In K. Yllo & M. Bograd (Eds.), *Feminist perspectives on wife abuse* (pp. 11–26). Thousand Oaks, CA: Sage.

Bowker, L. (1983). *Beating wife beating.* Lexington, MA: Lexington.

Bowker, L. (1986). *Ending the violence.* Holmes Beach, FL: Learning Publications.

Bowker, L. (1993). A battered woman's problems are social, not psychological. In R. Gelles & D. Loseke (Eds.), *Current controversies on family violence* (pp. 154–166). Newbury Park, CA: Sage.

Bowker, L., & Mauer, L. (1986). The effectiveness of counseling services utilized by battered women. *Women and Therapy, 5,* 65–82.

Breines, W., & Gordon, L. (1983). The new scholarship on family violence. *Signs: Journal of Women in Culture and Society, 8,* 490–531.

Browne, A. (1987). *When battered women kill.* New York: Free Press.

Browne, A. (1993). Violence against women by male partners: Prevalence, outcomes, and policy implications. *American Psychologist, 48,* 1077–1087.

Browne, A. (1997). Violence in marriage: Until death do us part? In A. Cardarelli (Ed.), *Violence between intimate partners: Patterns, causes, and effects* (pp. 48–69). Boston: Allyn & Bacon.

Burgess, R., & Draper, P. (1989). The explanation of family violence: The role of biological, behavioral, and cultural selection. In L. Ohlin & M. Tonry (Eds.), *Family violence* (pp. 56–116). Chicago: University of Chicago Press.

Cappell, C., & Heiner, R. (1990). The intergenerational transmission of family aggression. *Journal of Family Violence, 5,* 135–152.

Caesar, P. (1988). Exposure to violence in the families of origin among wife abusers and maritally non-violent men. *Violence and Victims, 3,* 36–49.

Caesar, P., & Hamberger, L. (1989). *Treating men who batter.* New York: Springer.

Choice, P., Lamke, L., & Pittman, J. (1995). Conflict resolution strategies and marital distress as mediating factors in the link between witnessing interparental violence and wife battering. *Violence and Victims, 10,* 107–119.

Craven, D. (1997). *Sex differences in violent victimization, 1994* (NCJ-164508). Washington, DC: U.S. Department of Justice.

Dobash, R., & Dobash, R. (1979). *Violence against wives: A case against the patriarchy.* New York: Free Press.

Dutton-Douglas, M. (1991). Counseling and shelter services for battered women. In M. Steinman (Ed.), *Woman battering: Policy responses* (pp. 113–130). Cincinnati, OH: Anderson.

Dutton, D. (1986). Wife assaulters' explanations for assault: The neutralization of self-punishment. *Canadian Journal of Behavioral Sciences, 18,* 381–390.

Dutton, D. (1988). *The domestic assault of women.* Boston: Allyn & Bacon.

Dutton, D., & Strachan, C. (1987). Motivational needs for power and spouse-specific assertiveness in assaultive and nonassaultive men. *Violence and Victims, 2,* 145–156.

Edleson, J., & Tolman, R. (1992). *Intervention for men who batter.* Newbury Park, CA: Sage.

Ferraro, K., & Johnson, J. (1983). How women experience battering. *Social Problems, 30,* 325–339.

Frieze, I., & Browne, A. (1989). Violence in marriage. In L. Ohlin & M. Tonry (Eds.), *Family violence* (pp. 163–218). Chicago: University of Chicago Press.

Frisch, M., & MacKenzie, C. (1991). A comparison of formerly and chronically battered women on cognitive and situational dimensions. *Psychotherapy, 28,* 339–344.

Geffner, R., & Pagelow, M. (1990). Victims of spouse abuse. In R. Ammerman & M. Hersen (Eds.), *Treatment of family violence: A sourcebook* (pp. 81–97). New York: John Wiley.

Gelles, R. (1974). *The violent home: A study of physical aggression between husbands and wives.* Beverly Hills, CA: Sage.

Gelles, R. (1979). *Family violence.* Beverly Hills, CA: Sage.

Gelles, R. (1983). An exchange/social control theory. In D. Finkelhor & M. Straus (Eds.), *The dark side of families: Current family violence research* (pp. 151–165). Beverly Hills, CA: Sage.

Gelles, R. (1985). *Intimate violence in families.* Beverly Hills, CA: Sage.

Gelles, R. (1993). Alcohol and other drugs are associated with violence—They are not the cause. In R. Gelles & D. Loseke (Eds.), *Current controversies on family violence* (pp. 182–196). Newbury Park, CA: Sage.

Gelles, R., & Cornell, C. (1980). *Intimate violence in families.* Newbury Park, CA: Sage.

Gelles, R., & Straus, M. (1988). *Intimate violence.* New York: Simon & Schuster.

Gondolf, E. (1985). *Men who batter: An integrated approach for stopping wife abuse.* Holmes Beach, FL: Learning Publications.

Gondolf, E. (1988a). *Battered women as survivors: An alternative to treating learned helplessness.* Lexington, MA: Lexington.

Gondolf, E. (1988b). The effect of batterer counseling on shelter outcome. *Journal of Interpersonal Violence, 33,* 275–289.

Gondolf, E., & Foster, R. (1991). Pre-program attrition in batterer programs. *Journal of Family Violence, 6,* 337–349.

Goode, W. (1971). Force and violence in the family. *Journal of Marriage and Family,* (November), 624–636.

Hastings, J., & Hamberger, L. (1988). Personality characteristics of spouse abusers: A controlled comparison. *Violence and Victims, 3,* 31–48.

Herzberger, S. (1983). Social cognition and the transmission of abuse. In D. Finkelhor, R. Gelles, G. Hotaling, & M. Straus (Eds.), *The dark side of families: Current family violence research* (pp. 317–329). Beverly Hills, CA: Sage.

Hoff, L. (1990). *Battered women as survivors.* London: Routledge & Kegan Paul.

Hotaling, G., Straus, M., & Lincoln, A. (1995). Intrafamily violence and crime and violence outside the family. In M. Straus & R. Gelles (Eds.), *Physical violence in American families: Risk factors and adaptations to violence in 8,145 families* (pp. 431–470). New Brunswick, NJ: Transaction Books.

Hotaling, G., & Sugarman, D. (1986). An analysis of risk markers in husband to wife violence: The current state of knowledge. *Violence and Victims, 1,* 101–124.

Jurik, N., & Winn, R. (1990). Gender and homicide: A comparison of men and women who kill. *Violence and Victims, 5,* 227–242.

Kaner, A., Bulik, C., & Sullivan, P. (1993). Abuse in adult relationships of bulimic women. *Journal of Interpersonal Violence, 8,* 52–63.

Kantor, G., & Straus, M. (1990). The "drunken bum" theory of wife beating. In M. Straus & R. Gelles (Eds.), *Physical violence in American families: Risk factors and adaptations to violence in 8,145 families* (pp. 203–224). New Brunswick, NJ: Transaction.

Kurz, D. (1993a). Physical assaults by husbands: A major social problem. In R. Gelles & D. D. Loseke (Eds.), *Current controversies on family violence* (pp. 88–103). Newbury Park, CA: Sage.

Kurz, D. (1993b). Social science perspectives on wife abuse: Current debates and future directions. In P. Bart & E. Moran (Eds.), *Violence against women* (pp. 252–269). Newbury Park, CA: Sage.

MacAndrew, C., & Edgerton, R. (1969). *Drunken comportment: A social explanation.* Chicago: Aldine.

Mahoney, M. (1991). Legal images of battered women: Redefining the issue of separation. *Michigan Law Review, 30,* 97–102.

Maiuro, R., Cahn, R., & Vitaliano, P. (1988). Anger, hostility, and depression in domestically violent versus generally assaultive men and nonviolent control subjects. *Journal of Consulting and Clinical Psychology, 56,* 17–23.

Martin, D. (1978). Battered women: Society's problem. In J. R. Chapman & M. Gates (Eds.), *The victimization of women* (pp. 111–141). Beverly Hills, CA: Sage.

Miller, S. (1989). Unintended side effects of pro-arrest policies and their race and class implications for battered women: A cautionary note. *Criminal Justice Policy Review, 3,* 299–316.

Okun, L. (1986). *Woman abuse: facts replacing myths.* Albany: SUNY Press.

Orava, T., McLeod, P., & Sharpe, D. (1996). Perceptions of control, depressive symptomatology, and self-esteem of women in transition from abusive relationships. *Journal of Family Violence, 11,* 167–186.

Pagelow, M. (1981). *Woman-battering: Victims and their experiences.* Beverly Hills, CA: Sage.

Pence, E., & Paymar, M. (1986). *Power and control: Techniques of men who batter.* Duluth: Minnesota Program Development, Inc.

Pleck, E. (1987). *Domestic tyranny: The making of American social policy against family violence from colonial times to the present.* New York: Oxford University Press.

Pirog-Good, M., & Stets, J. (1986). Programs for abusers: Who drops out and what can be done. *Response, 9*(2), 17–19.

Ptacek, J. (1988). Why do men batter their wives? In K. Yllo & M. Bograd (Eds.), *Feminist perspectives on wife abuse* (pp. 133–157). Newbury Park, CA: Sage.

Ptacek, J. (1997). The tactics of men who batter: Testimony from women seeking restraining orders. In A. Cardarelli (Ed.), *Violence between intimate partners: Patterns, causes, and effects* (pp. 104–123). Boston: Allyn and Bacon.

Riggs, D., Kilpatrick, D., & Resnick, H. (1992). Long-term psychological distress associated with marital rape and aggravated assault: A comparison to other crime victims. *Journal of Family Violence, 7,* 283–296.

Rosenbaum, A., & O'Leary, K. (1981). Marital violence: Characteristics of abusive couples. *Journal of Consulting and Clinical Psychology, 49,* 63–71.

Russell, D. (1982). *Rape in marriage.* New York: Macmillan.

Schechter, S. (1982). *Women and male violence: The visions and struggles of the battered women's movement.* Boston: South End Press.

Schwartz, M. (1990). Work status, resource equality, injury and wife battery: The National Crime Survey data. *Free Inquiry in Creative Sociology, 18,* 57–61.

Stanko, E. (1985). *Intimate intrusions.* London: Routledge & Kegan Paul.

Straus, M. (1973). A general systems theory approach to a theory of violence between family members. *Social Science Information, 12,* 105–125.

Straus, M. (1980a). The marriage license as a hitting license: Evidence from popular culture, law, and social science. In M. Straus & G. Hotaling (Eds.), *The social causes of husband-wife violence* (pp. 39–50). Minneapolis: University of Minnesota Press.

Straus, M. (1980b). A sociological perspective on the prevention of wife beating. In M. Straus & G. Hotaling (Eds.), *The social causes of husband-wife violence* (pp. 39–50). Minneapolis: University of Minnesota Press.

Straus, M. (1980c). Victims and aggressors in marital violence. *American Behavioral Scientist, 23,* 681–704.

Straus, M., Gelles, R., & Steinmetz, S. (1980). *Behind closed doors: Violence in the American family.* New York: Anchor Press/Doubleday.

Strube, M., & Barbour, L. (1983). The decision to leave an abusive relationship: Economic dependence and psychological commitment. *Journal of Marriage and the Family, 45,* 785–793.

Strube, M., & Barbour, L. (1984). Factors related to the decision to leave an abusive relationship. *Journal of Marriage and the Family, 46,* 837–844.

Telch, C., & Lindquist, C. (1984). Violent versus non-violent couples: A comparison of patterns. *Psychotherapy, 2,* 242–248.

Tolman, R., & Bennett, L. (1990). A review of quantitative research on men who batter. *Journal of Interpersonal Violence, 5,* 87–118.

Vaughn, D. (1987, July). The long goodbye. *Psychology Today,* 37–38, 42.

Walker, L. (1979). *The battered woman.* New York: Harper & Row.

Walker, L. (1983). The battered woman syndrome study. In D. Finkelhor, R. Gelles, G. Hotaling, & M. Straus (Eds.), *The dark side of families: Current family violence research* (pp. 31–49). Beverly Hills, CA: Sage.

Walker, L. (1984). *The battered woman syndrome.* New York: Springer.

Walker, L. (1993). The battered woman syndrome is a psychological consequence of abuse. In R. Gelles & D. Loseke (Eds.), *Current controversies on family violence* (pp. 133–153). Newbury Park, CA: Sage.

Warner, R., Lee, G., & Lee, J. (1986). Social organization, spousal resources, and marital power: A cross-cultural study. *Journal of Marriage and the Family, 48,* 121–128.

Weis, J. (1989). Family violence research methodology and design. In L. Ohlin & M. Tonry (Eds.), *Family violence* (pp. 117–162). Chicago: University of Chicago Press.

Wilson, M., Baglioni, A., & Downing, D. (1989). Analyzing factors influencing readmission to a battered women's shelter. *Journal of Family Violence, 4,* 275–284.

Wilson, M., & Daly, M. (1993). Spousal homicide risk and estrangement. *Violence and Victims, 9,* 3–16.

Widom, C. (1989). Does violence beget violence? A critical examination of the literature. *Psychological Bulletin, 106,* 3–28.

Wolfgang. M., & Ferracuti, F. (1972). *Delinquence in a birth cohort.* London: Tavistock.

Zubretsky, T., & Digirolamo, K. (1994). Adult domestic violence: The alcohol connection. *Violence Update, 4*(7), 1–2, 4, 8.

Violence Against Women in the Family
What Causes Violence Against Women in the Home

The United Nations

Violence against women in the home is a widespread problem that has serious consequences for the individual woman, her family, and society at large. Responses to the problem are essential, but in order for these responses to be both effective and appropriate, it is critical that the cause of the violence should be isolated. Indeed, many attempts have been made to establish the cause of the phenomenon, the search producing a spectrum at the ends of which stand two main theoretical frameworks.

The first, and the earliest, seeks the origins of domestic violence in some form of eradicable cause. It focuses attention on the characteristics of the wife, husband and family, and finds the cause of the violence in the personal inadequacy of the husband or wife or in external stresses that affect the family. Thus, theorists argue that men are violent towards the women with whom they live "because of some internal aberration, abnormality or defective characteristic."[1] These vary, but include alcoholism, a violent upbringing, mental illness, and poor self-control. Others suggest that wives provoke their husbands to beat them or are predisposed to violence, being attracted to violent men and addicted to abuse. Further variations on this analysis based on external causes find the etiology of wife abuse in stress, frustration and blocked goals, often resulting from unemployment or poverty, which in turn can depend on ethnicity and social class, or on the psychological effects of violent practices or deprived culture.

The second theoretical framework goes beyond an analysis based on psychological or social causes, noting the pervasiveness and acceptability of violence

United Nations Office at Vienna, Centre for Social Development and Humanitarian Affairs, # E.89.IV.5. Copyright 1989, 1993, 1994, United Nations.

against women in the home and roots its cause in the structure of society itself. It suggests that wife battery is neither a private nor a family problem, but rather a reflection of the broad structures of sexual and economic inequality in society. Indeed, it suggests that violence by husbands against wives is not a breakdown of the social order at all, not an aberration, but rather, "an affirmation of a particular social order,"[2] arising out of the socio-cultural belief that women are less important and less valuable than men and so are not entitled to equal respect. Domestic violence, therefore, is seen as a part of a total social context that tolerates the subordination of women and the use of violence against them as a solution to frustration and conflict. In this analysis, wife abuse is seen as the product of an interrelated and complex set of values wherein women are regarded as inferior to men, suffering discrimination in employment and education and being grossly underrepresented in all areas of social and political life. This inferiority is confirmed particularly within intimate relationships wherein men are assumed to be dominant and women are legally and financially dependant. The analysis further suggests that the subordination of women within relationships and therefore, domestic violence, is condoned by cultural values that emphasize the privacy and autonomy of the family, rendering outside agencies loath to interfere, or if they do so, to stress reconciliation.[3] This theoretical framework can be best summarized as follows:

> We propose that the correct interpretation of violence between husbands and wives conceptualizes such violence as the extension of the domination and control of husbands over their wives. This control is historically and socially constructed. The beginning of an adequate analysis of violence between husbands and wives is the consideration of the history of the family, of the status of women therein and of violence directed against them. This analysis will substantiate our claim that violence in the family should be understood primarily as coercive control.[4]

While other theories have been advanced to explain domestic violence, most locate themselves along this broad spectrum. The following thus attempts to survey the literature that has analyzed the causes of violence against wives, starting first with those explanations that find the causes in external factors.

ALCOHOL AND DRUGS

Research has shown that there is a close relationship between the consumption of alcohol and drugs and violence in the home, such substances playing as significant a role in the instigation of domestic violence as they do in violence in other contexts. Thus, Hilberman's study of 60 battered women in a general medical clinic revealed that drinking accompanied 93 percent of the incidents,[5] while Renvoize indicated that alcohol was a factor in 40 percent of the cases she investigated.[6] Similarly, Gelles discovered, in his 1974 study of violence in families in New Hampshire, that drinking accompanied violence in 48 percent of the families where assaults had occurred.[7] Indeed, many of the women in his sample revealed that their husbands only hit them when they were drunk. Further evidence supporting the link between alcohol and assaults against wives can be found in Gayford's study,[8] where 52 percent of his sample of women who had been abused stated that their husbands were drunk at least once a week, while another 22 percent indicated that the violence only occurred when the man was under the influence of alcohol; Scott's study of the wives of 100 alcoholics; Pahl's study[10] of 42 women who had used a women's refuge in the United Kingdom; and evidence gleaned from surveys in Australia.[11] Studies from Poland indicate that the one cause of violence against wives is alcoholism and that this is endemic in the country.[12]

Although research into the subject is very new in developing countries, similar findings have been made in Papua New Guinea,[13] Samoa,[14] Uganda,[15] Chile,[16] Kuwait,[17] and Colombia.[18]

It is clear that there is an association between alcohol use and violence against wives, but the precise role of alcohol in the domestic context has yet to be determined. It has been suggested that re-analysis of studies that stress the link between wife abuse and alcohol may reveal that the relationship is meaningless as very little distinction is made in such studies between alcoholism or pathological drinking and episodic drinking associated with violence.[19] Moreover, while the studies that do exist reveal that many abusive husbands are heavy drinkers, many of the men who beat their wives when they are drunk, also beat them when they are sober.[20] Further, drunkenness exists in many families that are non-violent and violence is present in others where there is no alcohol abuse.[21]

The studies suggest that in cases where violence is associated with alcohol, the link is peculiarly male as wives rarely become violent towards their husbands and children when inebriated.[22] Some evidence also exists that links male drunkenness, ultimately resulting in an assault on the wife, with male drinking parties, during which men give each other support and encouragement and reaffirm their role as breadwinner and boss.[23]

Drunkenness, therefore, is perhaps best seen not as a "cause" of violence, but as a condition that coexists with it. Indeed, men who wish to carry out a violent act may become drunk in order to perform the act. After the violence has occurred, both the man and his wife may excuse his behavior on the ground that he was drunk and therefore not responsible for his actions. In the end analysis, all that the studies which put forward the view that there is a connection between alcohol or drug abuse and wife beating indicate is that men who are drunk or drugged do beat their wives. They do not show us that they beat them because they are under the influence of alcohol or drugs. It may well be that they drink or take drugs in order to justify beating their wives.

CYCLE OF VIOLENCE: VIOLENCE AS LEARNED BEHAVIOR

A number of researchers locate the origins of wife assault in the childhood of the abusive man, suggesting that the violence occurs because he has witnessed or experienced violence in his family of origin. Thus, Straus, Steinmetz and

Gelles[24] concluded from their survey of intact couples in the United States that "the majority of today's violent couples are those who were brought up by parents who were violent to each other"[25] and that there is a "clear trend for violence in childhood to produce violence in adult life . . . violence by parents begets violence in the next generation."[26] They reported that compared to men from non-violent families of origin, men who saw their parents attack each other were 3 times as likely to hit their wives and 10 times more likely to attack them with a weapon. Even if they had only witnessed "wife beating"—hitting without punching or weapons—they were more likely to be violent adults, only 2 percent of men from non-violent homes hitting their wives, while 20 percent of men from the "most violent" families did so. Moreover, among 13 percent of their sample who reported being hit as teenagers, fully 35 percent indicated that they hit their wives, as opposed to only 11 percent of those who were not so hit.

Similar conclusions were reached by Stacey and Shupe[27] who determined from their research sample that 6 out of 10 abusive men had witnessed physical violence between their parents, 4 out of 10 had been neglected by their parents and 4 out of 10 had been abused by their parents. They found, further, that 1 out of 3 of the batterers' brothers and sisters had been abused by their parents and in two-thirds of the childhood homes where the batterers had been abused their siblings had been also.[28]

The theory that violence is learned behavior and is cyclical is a popular one and has tended to be perpetuated by folk wisdom and personal impressions. A number of writers have, however, questioned its validity, particularly attacking the studies that are presented to support it.

It is suggested that many of the publications widely cited to support the theory present no empirical data,[29] often relying on self-reports from small criminal subgroups, anecdotal information from battered women on their husbands, individual case histories and reports from service providers.[30] Of those that produce data, a number draw on samples that are small and unrepresentative, frequently being based on groups of people known either to be violent in some way, or to be the victims of violence, whose backgrounds are then examined for evidence of violence in their families of origin.[31] Further, even those studies that draw on a wide data base are problematic. No consistent definition of violence is used, rendering such studies inappropriate for comparative research, and most definitions used are ambiguous.[32] If, as Dobash and Dobash point out, the definition is sufficiently vague, almost everyone will come from a violent family. Thus, information that a mass murderer was sometimes slapped as a child will lend support to the cycle of violence theory, but will hardly be concrete confirmation.[33] Moreover, it is rare to find studies that are designed to include comparisons or controls. Little attention has been paid, for example, to the siblings of the individuals studied, so it is often unknown whether they too have violent families. Results, therefore, which indicate that one in three husbands who are abusive were themselves abused will suggest that the cycle of violence thesis is accurate, but at the same time will case doubt on the analysis as two out of three, or the majority, of such husbands come from non-violent homes.[34]

It seems, thus, that while there is support for the theory that violence is cyclical, much more sophisticated research, which compares violent and non-violent individuals from violent and non-violent homes, is required to test it. Certainly, it is wrong to assume that all children of men who abuse their wives or all men that have themselves been abused will abuse their wives. The most that can be said is that a violent family of origin is yet another variable that may be involved in the etiology of violence against wives.

VICTIM PRECIPITATION

Suggestions have been made that wife battery is caused by the behavior or personality of the victim. Hence, some researchers believe that violence arises when the victim reduces her husband's self-control by verbally tormenting him until he is no longer in control of his responses.[35] Others conclude that women have a psychological need for domination, excitement and attention,[36] one theory going so far as to hypothesize that women become addicted to the excitement and stimulation brought about by the violence because of some form of chemical reaction.[37]

Research indicates that while patterns of this nature may exist, they are not the norm. Often a man will abuse a woman without any warning, let alone provocation, sometimes waking her from sleep to do so. Further, there is evidence which indicates that women do not seek out successive abusive relationships, which casts doubt on these psychological theories. Pahl's study, for example, of 42 women who had used a refuge in the United Kingdom, revealed that not one of the women who went on to another relationship was abused in that partnership; however, their abusers went on to replicate the pattern of abuse in their new relationships.[38]

As Dobash and Dobash observe, moreover, the types of behavior defined by researchers and husbands as provocative are diverse, ranging from aggression, nagging and emasculation, to submission. Thus, they point out:

> Being too talkative or too quiet, too sexual or not sexual enough, too frugal or too extravagant, too often pregnant or not frequently enough, all seem to be provocative. The only pattern discernible in these lists is that the behavior, whatever it might be, represents some form of failure or refusal on the part of the woman to comply with or support her husband's wishes and authority.[39]

They point out, also, and this must be stressed, that explanations of wife abuse that rely on victim precipitation are dangerous. Such explanations accept the use of violence and also perpetuate the stereotype of female submission in intimate relationships.[40] As such, they absolve the man of his responsibility and place blame for the abuse on the woman.

MENTAL ILLNESS

Some theorists have characterized men who are violent in the home as passive, indecisive and sexually inadequate. Their wives, by contrast, are seen as aggressive, masculine and masochistic. Others see men who abuse their wives as psychopaths.[41] While some violent men are indeed sick, the widespread incidence of domestic violence against women and the variety of personality types, both women and men, who are involved in it, suggests that this is not a common cause of the conduct.

STRESS, FRUSTRATION, ROLE FRUSTRATION

Early scholarship on violence against wives emphasized the role of stress in its etiology. Thus, the British Association of Social Workers stated:

> Economic conditions, low wages, bad housing, overcrowding and isolation: unfavorable and frustrating work conditions for the man: lack of job opportunities for adolescents/school-leavers and lack of facilities such as day care (e.g., nurseries), adequate transport, pleasant environment and play space and recreational facilities, for mother and children were considered to cause personal desperation that might precipitate violence in the home.[42]

Explanations indicating stress as the cause of domestic violence, at the outset, directed attention to stresses derived from economic and social disadvantage. As such, violence against wives was seen as a primarily lower class phenomenon, as this class was most susceptible to such pressures. Again, however, while it is possible for economic and social stresses to incite violence, theorists who rely on stress as the explanation for such violence are unable to explain why all men subject to such pressure do not abuse their wives.

UNDERDEVELOPMENT

Research into family violence is very new in developing countries. A number of scholars have, however, addressed the issue and see family violence as a particular by-product of underdevelopment. Thus, research from Chile[43] points to the subsistence existence and economic dependence of many families involved in domestic abuse; Nigeria,[44] to the economic crisis of many such families; Kenya,[45] to the gaps between the rich and the poor, the urban and the rural, and the powerful and powerless; and Egypt[46] and Bangladesh[47] to tensions in society. It is suggested that in situations of underdevelopment violence becomes inherent as the result of a system wherein there is political and economic deprivation and oppression of individuals leading to social injustice.[48] In many developing countries, traditional social norms and practices, which may have once served to restrain wife abuse, are in the process of disintegration,[49] populations in the cities have swollen as migration from the rural areas has taken place as people have sought individual economic opportunities, and basic resources and services have proved to be inadequate. In such societies, poor housing and a precarious economic existence appear inevitable and violence becomes almost a way of life.[50] Such violence is vented against the most powerless who are inevitably women.[51]

This theory, which is a variation on the theme that stress and frustration produce wife abuse, may well have some validity. Again, however, it fails to explain why all men in deprived circumstances are not violent to their wives and why many men in economically privileged positions in both industrialized societies and developing countries are violent to their wives.

CULTURAL FACTORS

In a number of societies customs or beliefs are offered to explain the existence of wife abuse. Thus, it is common for African surveys to indicate that wife abuse occurs because beating shows that the man loves the woman, that this is expected by her and that she will feel rejected if she is not beaten.[52] Similarly, it is suggested that wives need beating.[53]

South Asian studies point to the custom of dowry as a precipitating factor in wife abuse. Dowry is an important part of the negotiations for an arranged marriage, parents accepting that if they wish their daughters to be married, they must provide a suitable dowry. Recently, the custom has combined with the growth in consumerism and has become, in some cases, a life and death matter for the bride. This is because her husband or his family may consider the dowry that has been provided to be inadequate and harass the woman, sometimes to the point of death by murder or suicide, in order to extract more from her natal family.[54]

Again, while certainly such customs may be factors in wife abuse, they do not explain why only some husbands in such systems abuse their wives.

STRUCTURAL INEQUALITY: THE POSITION OF WOMEN IN THE FAMILY AND SOCIETY

The overwhelming pervasiveness of violence against wives in the family led scholars to question the validity of explanations for the phenomenon that were based on an external cause. Further, studies that sought such causal explanations had discovered some "causes" for such violence that when taken together led inevitably to a new analysis.

For example, some researchers concluded that violence occurred when men failed to live up to the traditional stereotype of male superiority. Such could occur if the man believed he was an under achiever in employment or education,[55] if he were denied access to power and prestige outside the home,[56] or if his wife were perceived to be a superior achiever.[57] Others pointed to jealousy,[58] disputes over money,[59] and the wife's right to personal autonomy.[60] Surveys of women who were abused revealed that their husbands liked to dominate financial management within the family,[61] often keeping them chronically short of money and even forcing them to give them their wages or, if available, their government benefits.[62] Other surveys indicated that very often the abuser was unemployed.[63]

Treated separately, such indications would result in a "cause"-based analysis, but looked at in aggregate they revealed a common thread, such being that there was an assumption by the man that he should be the dominant party in a relationship that was traditionally unequal and that where such dominance was threatened by some factor, even the woman's separateness as a human being, dominance would be reasserted, if necessary, by violence.[64]

This common thread opened the way to an analysis that found the origins of violence against women in the family in the structure of the family itself, a structure that is mirrored and confirmed in the structure of society, which condones the oppression of women and tolerates male violence as one of the instruments in the perpetuation of this power balance. Hence, Straus concluded[65] "... wife beating is not just a personal abnormality, but rather it has its roots in the very structuring of society and the family; that is, the cultural norms and in the sexist organization of society."

This analysis has been taken even further by scholars, primarily feminists, who suggest that wife abuse is typical, not rare behavior and, indeed, behavior consistent with and condoned by general attitudes. They stress that economic, social and political factors are all interconnected, creating a structure wherein the low economic position of women is linked with their vulnerability to violence within the household. This, in turn, is connected to their powerlessness in relation to the State and men in general,[66] thereby resulting in a tacit acceptance by the community of abusive conduct within the home. This acceptance becomes manifest in societal attitudes that allow husbands to view their wives as chattels and that stress the privacy and autonomy of the family.[67]

The analysis of wife abuse as a structural rather than a causal phenomenon began in the industrialized West. However, studies from developing countries have served to confirm rather than cast doubt on its validity. Thus, studies from India[68] suggest that family violence may be a by-product of the societal structure where authority lies in the male with the female conditioned to accept her secondary role. A Chinese study similarly finds the root of such behavior in the male-centered ideology in China where a husband will abuse his wife when something is not done to his satisfaction, even, for example, if the wife gives birth to a girl.[69] Confirmation is found in other studies from developing countries which reveal that violence often occurs when the man wishes to take another wife,[70] where he suspects his wife of infidelity[71] and where he sees his wife as "rebellious," because of her ascending liberation[72] or because of her "nagging."[73]

This analysis, which goes beyond the search for an external cause and locates the origin of violence against women in the family in the structure of marriage and the family and in the wider society, in sum, argues that it is impossible to understand the nature of wife assault without taking account of the social and ideological context within which it occurs.[74] The analysis leads us to question the family as an institution and also leads us to question the role of society, particularly the helping professions, such as the police, the courts, the medical profession, in the tacit condonation of a structure that "supports the male's use of violence to maintain his dominance over his mate."[75]

Conclusion

Explanations of violence against women move, therefore, from explanations that seek the origin of the abuse in an individualized cause to an approach that sees the issue as located in a broader social-structural context, focusing upon the entire social situation within which the violence takes place. This approach stresses the subordination of women within society that allows them to become the "appropriate"[76] victims of marital violence.

While this analysis is helpful, the fact remains that although violence against women in the family is common it is not universal, thus explanations of such violence must go beyond a mere assertion that violence against women arises out of structural inequality and will exist as long as men are regarded as more important than women. Certainly, such inequality is the context in which such violence is condoned and even encouraged and the context in which violence against women in the home becomes crystallized as a cultural and societal norm. Notwithstanding this, the analysis fails to explain how sociological and cultural factors that are universal, interact with individual personal behavior.[77]

One commentator has attempted to grapple with this difficulty and while basing her analysis in the theory that domestic violence arises out of a social structure that perpetuates the subjugation of women as a community to the overall dominance of men as a community, she suggests that there are three particular situations wherein the social and cultural norm will result in violence against the wife.[78] Thus, she hypothesizes that wife assault is most likely to occur in three "milieus," a term she uses to encompass the norms, values, and attitudes of a particular cultural context, the traditional, transitional, and modern industrial.

In the traditional milieu, where social norms and customary law tolerate some use of physical force as a means of disciplining female members of the family in certain circumstances, the man is usually afforded a right to sanction what is regarded as unsuitable behavior, the sanctionable behavior being primarily sexual and being regarded as involving the man's honor. Here, clearly, violence against the wife will arise out of her subordination, but if the man who perpetrates the violence is traditionally assigned authority over her, such violence will be considered legitimate and, indeed, not even defined as violence. If, however, a man who has not been granted authority over her performs the same act, as the purpose of the violence is not in accordance with tradition, sanctions may be available.

Migrant populations, refugees and others in situations where the modes of living and authority structures are in transition and flux come within the definition of the transitional milieu. Here, attitudes, mores and roles are changing rapidly, and frequently the male's position is threatened, as often he is no longer in a position to support the family, and the woman may be obliged to undertake tasks and responsibilities that challenge previously held beliefs and attitudes. In this context, the man may seek to establish his dominance within the relationship by means of force.[79]

The third situation wherein domestic violence is common is the modern, industrial milieu. Here the official ideology proclaims the equality of the sexes,

permitting neither the expression of male authority over women, nor any coercive measures to maintain such authority. In this milieu, however, there is a gap
between prevalent attitudes and the law, the legal system being characterized by
unevenness and contradictions. Hence, while the expressed philosophy is that
violence against women in the family is unacceptable, the law may still tacitly
condone such violence by, for example, not criminalizing marital rape.

The approach outlined above confirms and extends the analysis of violence
against women in the domestic context as arising out of a power structure where men
are traditionally dominant within the family and society. Other analyses that similarly
accept this structural background suggest that violence erupts because of the general
acceptance of violence as a reasonable response to frustration, conflict or despair,
such acceptance being manifested in the existence of war, sport, the encouragement
of violence in various sub-cultures, and its popularity and celebration in the media.[80]

The combination of structural inequality within the family and society and
the general acceptability of violence as a method of conflict resolution within
society as the fundamental cause of violence against wives is attractive, appearing to be a rational and logical explanation. However, there is no empirical data
to support it as there have been no studies that have compared the level of violence against wives in societies at war with societies at peace; the level of violence against wives in societies with violent punishments with those without
them; and societies with standing armies with those without. Finally, there is
little empirical data linking violence in the media with violence in the home.[81]

In sum, it would appear that there is no simple explanation for violence
against women in the home. Certainly, any explanation must go beyond the individual characteristics of the man, the woman and the family and look to the
structure of relationships and the role of society in underpinning that structure.
In the end analysis, it is perhaps best to conclude that violence against wives is a
function of the belief, fostered in all cultures, that men are superior and that the
women they live with are their possessions or chattels that they can treat as they
wish and as they consider appropriate.

In some societies, this philosophy is reinforced by devices such as bride
price[82] that lead a man to believe that he has bought his wife and thus his conduct
towards her should not be open to question. Even in those societies where there
are no such overt indications of subordination, the social framework relegates the
woman, nonetheless, to the level of a chattel. Here structures place her in a position of dependence on the man and predict that she will fulfill certain roles. This
combines with the isolation of the family as an institution and the respect that is
offered to it in terms of privacy and autonomy by all agents within the society, to
allow violence to occur if the wife is seen to overstep her traditional role.

The collected scholarship that seeks to explain violence against women in
the home indicates that the explanation is complex and certainly multi-factorial.
Any explanation must, however, be seen against a background of gender inequality, wherein the victim of such violence is most often the woman and the perpetrator most often the man and wherein the structures of society—be they
economic, political or legal—act to confirm this inequality.

NOTES

[1] M.D.A. Freeman, "Legal ideologies, patriarchal precedents and domestic violence," in *State, Law and Family* (London, Tavistock, 1984), p. 69.

[2] *Ibid.*, p. 52.

[3] J. Pahl, ed., *Private Violence and Public Policy: The Needs of Battered Women and the Response of the Social Services* (London, Routledge and Kegan Paul, 1985), pp. 187–188.

[4] Dobash and Dobash, *Violence Against Wives: A Case Against the Patriarchy* (London, Open books, 1980), p. 15. See also M.D.A. Freeman, "Violence against women: does the legal system provide solutions or itself constitute the problem?", *British Journal of Law and Society*, No. 7, 1980, p. 216.

[5] E. Hilberman and F. Munson, "Sixty battered women," *Victimology*, No. 2, 1978, p. 460.

[6] J. Renvoize, *Web of Violence: A Study of Family Violence* (London, Routledge and Kegan Paul, 1978).

[7] R. J. Gelles, *Family Violence* (Beverly Hills, Sage, 1979).

[8] J. J. Gayford, "Wife battering: a preliminary survey of 100 cases," *British Medical Journal*, No. 1, 1975, p. 194.

[9] P. D. Scott, "Battered wives," *British Journal of Psychiatry*, No. 125, 1974, p. 433.

[10] Pahl, *op. cit.*, p. 9.

[11] See, for example, Domestic Violence Phone-In Report (Adelaide, Australia, Women's Information Switchboard, 1980); Report on Phone-In on Domestic Violence (Victoria, Australia, 1985).

[12] W. Stojanowska, case study from Poland (Warsaw, Instytut Badania Prawa Sadowego, 1987).

[13] S. Ranck and S. Toft, "Domestic violence in an urban context with rural comparisons," in *Domestic Violence in Urban Papua New Guinea*, Occasional Paper No. 19 (Boroko, Law Reform Commission of Papua New Guinea, 1986), p. 3.

[14] N. P. Simi, case study from Samoa (Prime Minister's Department, Apia); See also Report in Conference on Alcohol Related Problems on Pacific Island Countries, sponsored by the South Pacific Commission and the World Health Organization, Noumea, New Caledonia, 9–13 September 1985. This Conference stressed the link between alcohol abuse and domestic violence in the Pacific.

[15] L. E. M. Mukasa-Kikonyogo, Ugandan case study (Kampala, High Court of Uganda, 1987).

[16] ISIS Internacional, case study from Chile.

[17] B. A. Al-Awadi, Kuwaiti case study (Safat, University of Kuwait).

[18] M. I. Plata, case study from Colombia (Bogota, Population Concern, 1987).

[19] J. Downey and J. Howell, *Wife Battering—A Review and Preliminary Enquiry into Local Incidents, Needs and Resources* (Vancouver, B.C., Social Policy and Research Department, United Way of Greater Vancouver and the Non-Medical Use of Drugs Directoreate, National Department of Health and Welfare), p. 56.

[20] L. H. Bowker, *Beating Wife-Beating* (Lexington, MA, 1983), p. 467.

[21] Downey and Howell, *op. cit.*

[22] R. Gelles, *The Violent Home* (Beverly Hills, Sage, 1972).

[23] R. Epstein, R. Ng and J. Trebble, *The Social Organisation of Family Violence: An Ethnography of Immigrant Experience in Vancouver* (Vancouver, B. C., Women's Research Centre, 1978), p. 27.

[24] M. Straus, R. J. Gelles and Steinmetz, *Behind Closed Doors: Violence in the American Family* (New York, Anchor Books, 1980).

[25] *Ibid.*, p. 100.

[26] *Ibid.*, p. 113.

[27] W. Stacey and A. Shupe, *The Family Secret: Domestic Violence in America* (Boston, Beacon Press, 1983), p. 93.

[28] See also Gelles, *The Violent Home*...; J. J. Gayford, "Battered wives," *Medical Science and Law*, No. 15, 1975, p. 237; B. F. Steele, "Violence within the family," in *Child Abuse and Neglect: The Family and the Community*, R. E. Helfer and C. H. Kempe, eds. (Cambridge, MA, Ballinger, 1976).

[29] D. Potts and S. Herzerberger, "Child abuse: a cross generational pattern of child rearing?", a paper presented at the Annual Meeting of the Midwest Psychological Association, Chicago, May 1979.

[30] Dobash and Dobash, *Violence Against Wives*..., p. 22; E. Stark and A. Flitcraft, "Women battering, child abuse and social heredity: what is the relationship?", in *Marital Violence*, N. Johnson, Ed., Sociological Review Monography No. 31 (London, Routledge and Kegan Paul, 1985), p. 155.

[31] *Ibid.* See also W. Brienes and L. Gordon, "The new scholarship on family violence," *Signs*, No. 8, 1983, p. 561, who further argue that the database is likely to be skewed to poor and multi-problem families.

[32] Stark and Flitcraft, "Women battering, child abuse . . ."

[33] Dobash and Dobash, *Violence Against Wives*..., p. 155.

[34] *Ibid.* Stark and Flitcraft, "Women battering, child abuse . . ."

[35] W. J. Goode, "Force and violence in the family," *Journal of Marriage and the Family*, No. 33, 1971, p. 624.

[36] A. Storr, *Human Aggression* (London, Penguin, 1974), p. 95; J. Jobling, "Battered wives: a survey," *Social Service Quarterly*, No. 47, 1974, p. 146; J. Gayford, "Ten types of battered women," *Welfare Officer*, 1976.

[37] E. Pizzey and J. Shapiro, *Prone to Violence* (London, Hamlyn, 1982).

[38] Pahl, *op. cit.*, p. 5. See also B. Andrews and G. W. Brown, "Marital violence in the community: a biographical approach," *British Journal of Psychiatry*, vol. 153, 1988, which reports that of 72 women found to have been involved in a violent relationship, 32 had cohabited with more than one man, but of these only three had been involved in more than one relationship.

[39] Dobash and Dobash, *Violence Against Wives* . . . , p. 135.

[40] *Ibid.*, pp. 135–137; note also Andrews and Brown, *op. cit.*, which investigated 72 abused women who had been culled from a random survey. Of these women, only two ever physically provoked an attack and, far from being "addicted" to or "prone" to violence, most came from families which were neglectful rather than abusive. The researchers concluded that a woman's neglectful family of origin may make her susceptible to involvement in unsatisfactory relationships.

[41] E. Pizzey, *Scream Quietly or the Neighbours Will Hear* (London, Penguin, 1974).

[42] British Association of Social Workers, Discussion document of B.A.S.W. Working Party on Home Violence, *Social Work Today*, No. 6, 1975, p. 409. See also Gelles, *The Violent Home*... , p. 185; L. MacLeod, *Wife Battering in Canada: the Vicious Circle*, (Ottawa, Canadian Advisory Council on the Status of Women, 1980), p. 26.

[43] ISIS Internacional, case study from Chile.

[44] J. O. Akande, case study from Nigeria (reviewed Social Service files and conducted informal interviews).

[45] B. N. Wamalwa, case study from Kenya (Nairobi, Public Law Institute, 1987).

[46] M. El Husseiny Zaalouk, case study from Egypt (Cairo, National Center for Social and Criminal Research, 1987).

[47] I. Shamim, case study from Bangladesh (Dhaka, University of Dhaka, Department of Sociology, 1987).

[48] *Ibid.*

[49] Wamalwa, *op. cit.*

[50] *Ibid.*

[51] El Husseiny Zaalouk, *op. cit.*

[52] Wamalwa; Mukasa-Kikonyogo, *op. cit.*

[53] Wamalwa.

[54] H. Singh, case study from India (New Delhi, National Institute of Social Defence, Ministry of Welfare); and *Bangladesh Economist*, 22 August 1987.

[55] J. E. O'Brien, "Violence in divorce-prone families," *Journal of Marriage and the Family*, No. 33, 1971, p. 692.

[56] W. J. Goode, "Force and violence in the family," *Journal of Marriage and the Family*, No. 33, 1971, p. 624.

[57] M. Pagelow, *Battered Women: A New Perspective* (Dublin, International Sociological Association, 1977).

[58] S. Toft, ed., *Domestic Violence in Papua New Guinea*, Monograph No. 3 (Boroko, Papua New Guinea Law Reform Commission, 1986). This monograph contains eight studies of the incidence, causes and approaches to domestic violence in Papua New Guinea. Sexual jealousy is revealed to be one of the major contexts in which such violence is manifested.

[59] Pahl, *op. cit.*, p. 33.

[60] Dobash and Dobash, *Violence Against Wives...*, p. 98; M. Roy, ed., *Battered Women: A Psychosociological Study of Domestic Violence* (London, Van Nostrand Reinhold, 1977).

[61] E. Evason, *Hidden Violence* (Belfast, Farset Press, 1982).

[62] M. Homer, A. Leonard and R. Taylor, "The burden of dependency," in *Marital Violence*, N. Johnson, ed., Sociological Review Monograph 31 (London, Routledge and Kegan Paul, 1985), p. 77.

[63] Pahl, *op. cit.*, p. 42.

[64] *Ibid.*, p. 43.

[65] M. Straus, "Sexual inequality, cultural norms and wife beating," in *Women into Wives*, J. R. Chapman and M. Gates, eds. (Beverly Hills, Sage, 1976), p. 59. See also MacLeod, *Wife Battering in Canada...*, p. 31: "To understand violence in the family, we must look at the way the family is kept isolated, the woman dependent and family violence legitimated through family roles, mandates and restrictions and through other institutions in their normal operation."

[66] D. Martin, *Battered Wives* (San Francisco, Glide, 1976); J. Hammer, "Violence and the social control of women," in *Power and the State*, G. Littlejohn, ed. (London, Croom Helm, 1977); M.D.A. Freeman, "Violence against women: does the legal system provide solutions or itself constitute the problem?", *British Journal of Law and Society*, No. 7, 1980, p. 215; J. Scutt, *Even in the Best of Homes: Violence in the Family* (Sidney, Penguin, 1982); S. Jackson and P. Rushton, "Victims and villains: images of women in accounts of family violence," *Women's Studies International Forum*, No. 5, 1982, p. 7.

[67] Dobash and Dobash, *Violence Against Wives...*; Freeman, "Violence against women...," p. 215.

[68] Singh, *op. cit.*

[69] Wu Han, case study from China (Shanghai, Criminology and Crime Investigation Department, East China Institute of Law and Politics).

[70] El Husseiny Zaalouk, *op. cit.*; Akande, *op. cit.*

[71] Mukasa-Kikonyogo, *op. cit.*; Al-Awadi, *op. cit.*; El Husseiny Zaalouk, *op. cit.*; Plata, *op. cit.*

[72] Akande, *op. cit.*

[73] Al-Awadi, *op. cit.*; Mukasa-Kikonyogo, *op. cit.*; Wamalwa, *op. cit.*; Akande, *op. cit.*; El Husseiny Zaalouk, *op. cit.*

[74] Pahl, *op. cit.*, pp. 18–19.

[75] M.D.A. Freeman, *Violence in the Home* (Farnborough, Saxon House, 1979), pp. 141–142.

[76] R. E. Dobash and R. Dobash, "Wives: the 'appropriate' victims of marital violence?", *Victimology*, No. 2, 1978, p. 426.

[77] R. Leonard and E. MacLeod, *Marital Violence: Social Construction and Social Service Response* (University of Warwick, 1980).

[78] C. Benard, "Patterns of violence against women in the family," Working Paper on the Nature and Effects of Physical Violence and Coercion Against Women in the Family, Expert Group Meeting on Violence in the Family with Special Emphasis on its Effects on Women, Vienna, 8–12 December 1986.

[79] Developing societies are typically in a state of transition. This may go some way to explain the prevalence of domestic violence in such societies. See Indian, Chinese, Colombian and Kenyan case studies.

[80] M. Straus, "A sociological perspective in the prevention of wife beating," in *Social Causes of Husband-Wife Violence*, M. Straus and G. Hotaling, eds. (Minneapolis, University of Minnesota Press, 1980), pp. 211–232.

[81] Brienes and Gordon, *loc. cit.*, p. 503.

[82] Mukasa-Kikonyogo, *op. cit.*; Wamalwa, *op. cit.*

The Causes of Domestic Violence
From Theory to Intervention

Kerry Healey, Christine Smith, and Chris O'Sullivan

The origins of domestic violence are the subject of active debate among victim advocates, social workers, researchers, and psychologists concerned with batterer intervention. More than in most fields, the theoretical debate affects practice. Over the last two decades, a number of practitioners representing divergent theoretical camps have begun to move toward a more integrated "multidimensional" model of batterer intervention in order to better address the complexity of a problem that has psychological, interpersonal, social, cultural, and legal aspects. Two practitioners who advocate an eclectic approach to batterer intervention describe the dilemma of practitioners looking for a single explanation for battering as follows:

> During a recent conversation, a respected colleague of ours suggested that marital aggression was rooted in a need for control. "Men," he said, "use aggression to control their female partners." We agreed. Control is certainly an important factor in the dynamics of marital violence. His treatment approach, well known and effective, focused on helping abusers relinquish control and share power with their spouses. Several weeks later, we discussed the same topic with the director of a treatment program for wife abusers, who stated that "poor impulse control" and "defective self-concept" were the critical factors. We agreed. Abusers are certainly impulsive and often have poor self-esteem. Her treatment program, which focused on these factors was, she claimed, very successful. Sometime later, one of our graduate students, well aware of these previous conversations, reported on a workshop she had attended. The model presented at the workshop conceptualized marital violence as a couples' problem and suggested that communication between spouses was the critical factor. Conjoint couples'

National Institute of Justice, Issues and Practices in Criminal Justice. Batterer Intervention: Program Approaches and Criminal Justice Strategies, chapter 2.

counseling was suggested as an effective intervention for violent couples. Again, we could agree. The safest conclusion would appear to be that there are numerous routes by which husbands come to be wife abusers and a multitude of variables that increase the likelihood of violence.[1]

In practice, few batterer programs represent a "pure" expression of one theory of domestic violence; the majority of programs contacted for this report combine elements of different theoretical models. As a result, when discussing program theory with batterer intervention providers, criminal justice professionals need to understand not only the primary theory the program espouses but also the program's content, because programs may identify with one theory but draw on or two more theories in their work. Experts caution criminal justice agencies against accepting an eclectic curriculum uncritically: program components borrowed from different theoretical perspectives should be thoughtfully chosen to create a coherent approach, not a scattershot attempt hoping to hit some technique that works.

Criminal justice professionals are likely to encounter programs based on one or more of the following theories of domestic violence. Each theory locates the cause of the violence differently:

- Society and culture—Social theories of domestic violence attribute the problem to social structures and cultural norms and values that endorse or tolerate the use of violence by men against women partners. For example, the *feminist model* of intervention educates men concerning the impact of these social and cultural norms and attempts to resocialize them emphasizing nonviolence and equality in relationships.

- The family—Some sociologists locate the cause of domestic violence in the structure of the family, the interpersonal interactions of families, and the social isolation of families. For example, *family systems theory* attributes the cause to communication problems and conflict within intimate relationships and teaches communication skills to help partners avoid violence. As noted below, couples counseling, an intervention based on family systems theory, is controversial because of its failure to assign blame for the abuse to one person and to identify a victim. Couples counseling is also considered dangerous to the victim because it encourages the victim to discuss openly issues that may spark later retaliation by the batterer.

- The individual—*Psychological theories* attribute domestic violence to the individual batterer's predispositions and experiences. Battering may be attributed to personality disorders and biological dispositions to violence or, as *social learning theory* suggests, to the role of the batterer's social environment during childhood. *Attachment theory*, a form of social learning theory, focuses on the interaction of caregivers with their children and the impact of that first attachment on an individual's ability to establish safe and healthy relationships later in life. Batterer interventions based on this theory attempt to facilitate secure attachments between batterers and loved ones (intimate partners, children, and parents). Psychodynamic approaches target the underlying psychological cause of the violence, while cognitive behavioral approaches teach batterers new patterns of nonviolent thinking and behavior.

It is important for criminal justice professionals to understand the assumptions and goals of service providers whose interventions have divergent theoretical bases, because not all intervention approaches employ techniques that are equally compatible with the goals of the criminal justice system—protecting the victim as well as rehabilitating the offender.

The Language of Batterer Intervention

The shift in providers of help to batterers and their partners from psychotherapists to feminist social activists to professional mental health providers has created tensions in the field that are exhibited in the language of batterer interventions. Criminal justice professionals need to be aware of the connotations of various terms so that they can communicate effectively with service providers.

For example, the term "domestic violence" itself has a gender-neutral connotation. A number of feminists, seeing a link with other violence against women and noting the severity of injuries inflicted on women by male partners, prefer such terms as "wife abuse" and "woman abuse."[2] Programs based on feminist theories of battering are often described as "profeminist," indicating male support for feminist goals. Mental health professionals may talk about "counselors" or "therapists" providing "treatment" to "clients," while profeminist "facilitators" or "teachers" provide an "intervention" to "batterers" using a didactic format described as "classes." Feminist-based programs object especially to the word "treatment" and may not consider rehabilitation the program's primary goal, as Red Crowley of Atlanta's Men Stopping Violence program explains:

> Let's start with the word *treatment*. We do not see our work as therapy. Battering is the natural outgrowth of patriarchal values. We want to change those values. Batterers' intervention classes serve a number of purposes: they, like shelters, make visible what has been systematically concealed, that is, the horrendous problem of violence against women; create an opportunity to engage the community and the criminal justice system in the effort to stop the violence; and contribute to research. Giving men who want to change the opportunity to do so is just one purpose of the intervention.

The three most widely used intervention approaches—"educational" or "psychoeducational classes," "couples therapy," and "group process"—are each associated with a theory of the cause of domestic violence. Thus, "educational programs" are most often based on feminist theory; "couples therapy" may suggest a link with family systems theory; and "group process" programs base their work on either psychodynamic or cognitive behavioral theories. Some practitioners—especially those with eclectic programming—may use terms interchangeably; others harbor strong objections to mislabeling their approach and consider some terms to have great symbolic meaning. Criminal justice professionals need to be sensitive to the language used by intervention providers and to ask practitioners to explain the importance of unfamiliar terminology.

OVERVIEW OF THEORIES AND RELATED INTERVENTIONS

Feminist (or profeminist; see box, "The Language of Batterer Intervention"), family systems, and psychotherapeutic theories of domestic violence offer divergent explanations of the root causes of battering and lead to distinct intervention models. The following section outlines the basic tenets of each theory, illustrates how these assumptions influence the choice of intervention strategies, and notes the advantages and disadvantages of each theoretical and treatment approach. As noted previously, however, examples of programming based exclusively on one theory are becoming increasingly rare.

Feminist Approaches: The Social Problem Approach

Batterer intervention programs originated in the early 1970s, as feminists and others brought to public attention the victimization of women and spawned grass roots services such as rape hot lines and battered women's shelters.[3] According to Anne Ganley of Seattle's Veteran Administration Medical Center and David Adams of EMERGE in Boston, providers of services to battered women felt that victims who had received services either returned home to face the same destructive environment or left the relationship—and the batterer found a new victim. To help victims, advocates realized, it was also necessary to address the root cause of their problems—the perpetrators of violence. Profeminist men concerned with sexism in themselves and society felt a particular responsibility for working with male abusers. As a result, some of the first systematic interventions for batterers developed from a profeminist perspective.

What Is a Feminist Model of Battering?

Central to the feminist perspective on battering is a gender analysis of power.[4] According to this view, domestic violence in intimate relationships mirrors the patriarchal organization of society in which men play a dominant role in most social institutions. Along with verbal, emotional, and economic abuse, violence is a means of maintaining male power in the family when men feel their dominance is being threatened. Economic roles have left women dependent on men and unable to escape abusive situations.[5] Men's superior physical strength may enable them to dominate women through violence.

Feminists argue that a consequence of the social arrangement in which men hold the positions of respect and power is that men and women alike devalue the feminine and overvalue the masculine. To the batterer, women are childlike and incompetent. It is not uncommon for batterers to convince their wives that they are not capable of adult activities, such as driving a car or holding a job.[6] For example, a former victim reported that her husband had convinced her that she could not turn on the washing machine without breaking it, so she had to wait until he returned from work before she could do the laundry for their seven children. Similarly, in disputed custody cases when a batterer and partner separate, the husband often contends that his wife is incapable of taking care of the children.[7]

In the feminist view, batterers feel that they should be in charge of the family: making decisions, laying down rules, disciplining disobedient wives and children, and correcting unsatisfactory performance of duties.[8] Batterers may typically exercise control over the family in nonviolent, coercive ways and only sometimes resort to violence. As men, batterers feel entitled to gender-based respect and obedience; therefore, what they perceive to be disrespect and disobedience infuriates them. Batterers often rationalize their violence on the grounds that it was necessitated by their partner's actions: she provoked or caused it, and they simply reacted as any man would.

Feminist programs attempt to raise consciousness about sex role conditioning and how it constrains men's emotions and behavior (through education around sexism, male privilege, male socialization). Programs with a feminist philosophy present a model of egalitarian relationships along with the benefits of nonviolence and of building relationships based on trust instead of fear (see exhibit 2-1, "Equality Wheel"). Most feminist approaches support confronting men over their power and control tactics in all domains of the relationship, including verbal and psychological abuse, social isolation, the undermining of the victim's self-confidence, and sexual coercion. A particular concern of profeminist male group facilitators is the constant risk and temptation of colluding with batterers. For example, a male facilitator at Family Services of Seattle reported that when his female cofacilitator was absent at one session, the men in

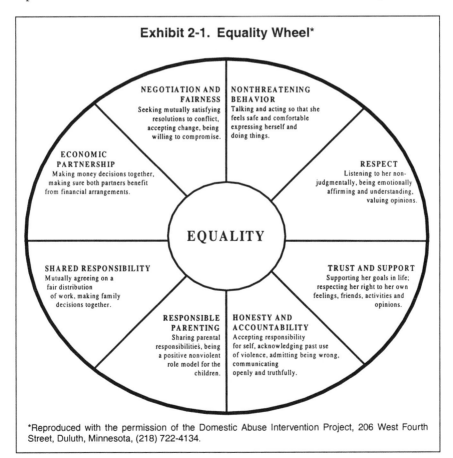

Exhibit 2-1. Equality Wheel*

NEGOTIATION AND FAIRNESS
Seeking mutually satisfying resolutions to conflict, accepting change, being willing to compromise.

NONTHREATENING BEHAVIOR
Talking and acting so that she feels safe and comfortable expressing herself and doing things.

ECONOMIC PARTNERSHIP
Making money decisions together, making sure both partners benefit from financial arrangements.

RESPECT
Listening to her non-judgmentally, being emotionally affirming and understanding, valuing opinions.

EQUALITY

SHARED RESPONSIBILITY
Mutually agreeing on a fair distribution of work, making family decisions together.

TRUST AND SUPPORT
Supporting her goals in life; respecting her right to her own feelings, friends, activities and opinions.

RESPONSIBLE PARENTING
Sharing parental responsibilities, being a positive nonviolent role model for the children.

HONESTY AND ACCOUNTABILITY
Accepting responsibility for self, acknowledging past use of violence, admitting being wrong, communicating openly and truthfully.

*Reproduced with the permission of the Domestic Abuse Intervention Project, 206 West Fourth Street, Duluth, Minnesota, (218) 722-4134.

the group expected him to drop his profeminist "guise" and participate in or agree with their negative characterizations of women.

Advantages and Criticisms of the Feminist Model.   Perhaps because work with batterers was originated by battered women's advocates and feminists, the feminist perspective has influenced most programs. A national survey conducted in 1986 found that 80 percent of programs attempt to change sex role attitudes, stop violence, and increase self-esteem.[9] Even programs adopting a family systems model (see below) may advocate an egalitarian and democratic relationship to couples in treatment. Support for the feminist analysis of the role of power in domestic violence comes from the observation that most batterers are able to control their anger and avoid resorting to violence when "provoked" by someone more powerful than they, such as their work supervisors, police officers, or judges. Further support for the feminist analysis comes from research showing that batterers are less secure in their masculinity than nonbatterers[10]— the theory being that men who do not feel masculine will need to assert their masculinity more forcefully to compensate for their sense of inadequacy. Other studies have documented the sense of *entitlement* batterers feel in controlling their partners' behavior and in justifying violence if these women deviate from the female sex role.[11]

Critics have claimed that the feminist perspective overemphasizes sociocultural factors, such as patriarchal values, to the exclusion of individual factors like growing up abused.[12] Men's behavior in intimate relationships varies across individuals, and broad cultural factors cannot explain this variability. Feminist theory predicts that *all* men in our society will be abusive, claim its critics, adding that besides being untrue, this theory makes it impossible to predict *which* men will be violent. To make individual predictions, a model must assign a role to other factors including, but not limited to, psychological deviance.

Other criticisms center not on the validity of feminist explanations of battering but on the translation of that theory into programming. For example, some observers argue that feminist educational interventions are too confrontational in tone and, as a result, are ultimately self-defeating, alienating batterers, increasing their hostility, and making them less likely to become engaged in treatment. It is possible that the goal of the feminist model—to rebuild the batterer's belief system in order to achieve nonviolence—may be unnecessarily ambitious and adversarial. Batterers' existing value systems may be more easily fine-tuned to emphasize nonviolence (e.g., building on religious convictions or humanism) without a feminist overlay.

Another concern is that educational programs may effectively transmit information without deterring violent behavior. A 1991 evaluation of three short-term psychoeducational batterer programs in Baltimore found that while batterers considered the curriculum helpful, they recidivated at a higher rate than batterers who did not receive treatment.[13] A study of graduates of Duluth's Domestic Abuse Intervention Project found that completion of the feminist educational intervention had no impact on recidivism after five years.[14] Outcomes such as these point to the need for broader evaluations that examine the impact of systemic factors—

arrest and prosecution policies, court procedures, and probation supervision—on intervention effectiveness, as well as a clarification of the goals of feminist-based interventions. If deterrence is not a likely outcome of an intervention, other goals, such as punishment, education, behavioral monitoring, or social change, must be explicitly advanced. (A few practitioners are in fact shifting their primary focus away from individual change in batterers in favor of social change through a coordinated community response. See chapter 5, "Criminal Justice Response").

The Family Systems Model

The family systems model regards individual problem behaviors as a manifestation of a dysfunctional family unit, with each family member contributing to the problem. Rather than identifying one individual as the cause of the violence and removing that person from the home or singling that person out for treatment, the model advocates working with the family or couple together, providing support with the goal of keeping the family intact.

According to the family systems (or "interactional") model,[15] both partners may contribute to the escalation of conflict, with each striving to dominate the other. Family systems theorists believe that most abuse is verbal and emotional, but as the conflict escalates, either partner may resort to violence. Because, from this perspective, *interactions* produce violence, no one is considered to be the perpetrator or victim, even if only one person is physically violent. Family systems theory also suggests that interactions may permit or facilitate abusive behaviors in one person, such as a nonabusive parent's failure to intervene in child abuse or a family member's failure to establish appropriate personal boundaries, thus setting the stage for their own victimization. Family systems therapists criticize psychological approaches that focus on individual deficits (low self-esteem, dependence, anger) while neglecting to teach interpersonal skills that could promote safety. Family systems theory leads to treatment that involves improving communication and conflict resolution skills. Both members of the couple can develop these skills through "solution-focused brief therapy" that:

- locates the problem in the interaction rather than in the pathology of one individual;
- focuses on solving the problem, rather than looking for causes; and
- accentuates the positive—for example, examining occasions when the couple avoided violence.

Advantages and Criticisms of the Family Systems Model.   Advocates of the family systems approach note that many violent couples would like to remain together and that there may be positive aspects to the relationship that counseling can build on. However, while some observers report that over half of domestic violence couples remain together,[16] a study of abused wives whose husbands did become nonviolent found that most of the women subsequently terminated the marriage because of other marital problems that became apparent after the violence ended.[17]

Both feminist and cognitive-behavioral approaches agree that partner abuse does not involve shared responsibility. Both approaches firmly hold that batterers bear full responsibility for the violence, victims play no causal role, and no one incites violence. Of particular concern to both feminist and cognitive-behavioral proponents is the format of couples counseling: encouraging each partner to discuss problems openly with the other partner can put the victim at risk after the session if the woman expresses complaints. Furthermore, no frank exchange between counselor and victim concerning the abuse is likely to be possible in the presence of the batterer. Moreover, the format is conducive to victim-blaming. Finally, if the court prohibits the batterer from contacting the victim, the family systems approach will violate the court order. For these reasons, couples counseling is expressly prohibited in 20 State standards and guidelines (see box, "Controversial Approaches to Batterer Intervention"). Judges involved with partner abuse cases that also involve child abuse need to pay particular attention to safety issues raised by family systems interventions, which may be the treatment approach recommended by child welfare workers who are working toward a goal of family reunification. In such cases, issues of victim and child safety must be weighed carefully, and if a family systems approach is chosen, close monitoring is needed.

Psychological Approaches: A Focus on Individual Problems

Psychological perspectives hold that personality disorders or early experiences of trauma predispose some individuals to violence.[18] Being physically abusive is seen as a symptom of an underlying emotional problem.[19] Parental abuse, rejection, and failure to meet a child's dependence needs can be the psychological source of battering. People with these underlying problems may choose partners with whom they can reenact the dysfunctional relationship they had with their parents. Two forms of batterer intervention have evolved from this perspective: individual and group psychodynamic therapy and cognitive-behavioral group therapy.

Individual and Group Psychodynamic Counseling.   Psychoanalysis can be undertaken not only in individual counseling but also in unstructured batterer groups that allow members to explore their life experiences. Psychodynamic therapies involve uncovering the batterer's unconscious problem and resolving it consciously. Proponents of psychodynamic therapy for batterers believe that other interventions are superficial: since other therapies are unable to eliminate the abuser's deep-rooted and unconscious *motive* for aggression, they cannot end violence but only suppress it temporarily. Long-term change requires exposing and resolving the root cause of the violent behavior.

Advantages and Criticisms of Psychodynamic Approaches.   Browne and Saunders recently conducted a study comparing a "process psychodynamic treatment model" with a feminist/cognitive-behavioral intervention and found no difference in recidivism rates based on partners' reports. Nevertheless, they argue:

> [T]here were two advantages to the process-psychodynamic model. It retained a significantly higher percentage of men in treatment and it was

more successful with men who had dependent personality disorders. *Regard-less of the treatment approach used, more self-disclosure and less lecturing were related to greater group cohesion, which in turn was related to lower recidivism rates.*[20] (Emphasis added)

Critics argue that psychodynamic therapy merely assigns a psychiatric label to people who batter (e.g., insecure, narcissistic, dependent, compulsive, or suffering from intermittent explosive disorder) without explaining how they got that way or what can be done about it.[21] The psychodynamic approach has also been criticized for allowing batterers to continue the behavior until the underlying psychological problem is resolved.[22] David Adams, director of EMERGE, gives the example of a batterer mandated to treatment who had already learned in individual psychotherapy that he battered because he was insecure. At the intake interview for the batterer program, the counselor asked the man whether he was going to continue to choose to be violent until he resolved his insecurity. The man said that he had never thought of battering as a choice, but now he would reconsider the notion.[23] Feminists argue that labeling batterers as having psychological problems not only exonerates them in their own eyes but also ignores the cultural acceptability of male dominance in the family and how it serves to keep the batterer in control of his partner. The approach pays attention to *internal* psychological functions of abuse for the batterer but ignores the *interpersonal* function of controlling the other person's behavior.

In practice, many psychologically oriented programs have moved away from the original stance that battering is caused primarily by psychological disorder and always indicates an emotional problem. Instead, they have integrated social explanations with psychological explanations. For example, some psychologically oriented theorists propose that it is the combination of a man's low self-esteem and a cultural expectation that men should be dominant and successful that produces a batterer.

Cognitive-Behavioral Model of Change.   Cognitive-behavioral therapy is used in the treatment of violent offenders. Whereas the psychoanalytic tradition focuses on psychological disorders based in the unconscious and early childhood experiences, the cognitive-behavioral model focuses on conscious material in the present: therapy is intended to help individuals function better by modifying how they think and behave in current situations. The theory behind cognitive-behavioral batterer interventions maintains that behaviors are learned as a result of positive and negative reinforcements (rewards and punishments) for engaging in particular behaviors under particular circumstances (e.g., parental pride or praise for aggressive behavior). Behavior is also influenced by how people mentally construct and interpret their environment and experiences— that is, the way they think about themselves, other people, and their relationships. The cognitive-behavioral theory postulates that men batter because:

- they are imitating examples of abuse they have witnessed during childhood or in the media;

- abuse is rewarded;
- it enables the batterer to get what he wants; and
- abuse is reinforced through victim compliance and submission.

Attachment Abuse

A small number of practitioners base batterer interventions on psychological theories of attachment, affect, and individuation. These interventions consider battering to be "attachment abuse"—that is, abusive behaviors toward intimates arising from the individual's insecure attachment to his or her caregivers as a child. Attachment theory describes two broad categories of attachment relationships: *secure attachments* that result from the caregiver's responsiveness to the child's emotional and physical needs, and a range of *insecure attachment* patterns that may develop if a child's emotional and physical needs are not met by caregivers. Insecure attachments in childhood may lead, in adult relationships, to emotional distress, anxiety, anger, depression, and emotional detachment when the specter of loss or separation arises in an intimate relationship. These feelings may lead to attachment abuse.

Batterer interventions based on theories of attachment, such as the Compassion Workshop, seek to enhance the batterers' ability to regulate their own emotions and to stimulate a sense of "compassion" for both themselves and their intimates (partners, children, and elders) using cognitive behavior techniques that are designed to interrupt the batterers' violent emotional response to guilt, shame, and fear of abandonment.

Cognitive-behavioral interventions focus on "cognitive restructuring" and skill building. Counselors focus on identifying the chain of events that lead each batterer to violence, starting with beliefs and "self-talk"—the way we talk to ourselves in our minds (see exhibit 2-2, "A Cognitive Model of Woman Abuse"). For example, a batterer whose partner is ten minutes late may tell himself, "She's out with her boyfriend" or "She can't be trusted." The programs attempt to restructure the beliefs and "self-talk" that lead to violence; for example, "I don't know why she's late, but I'm sure she's trying to get here." The programs help batterers to analyze the thought patterns underlying violent reactions (e.g., "Dinner isn't ready because my wife doesn't respect me") and learn new ways of understanding situations that trigger violence (e.g., "Dinner isn't ready because my wife had a busy day"). The program teaches nonviolent alternative behaviors, such as conflict-resolution tactics, relaxation techniques, and communication skills.[24]

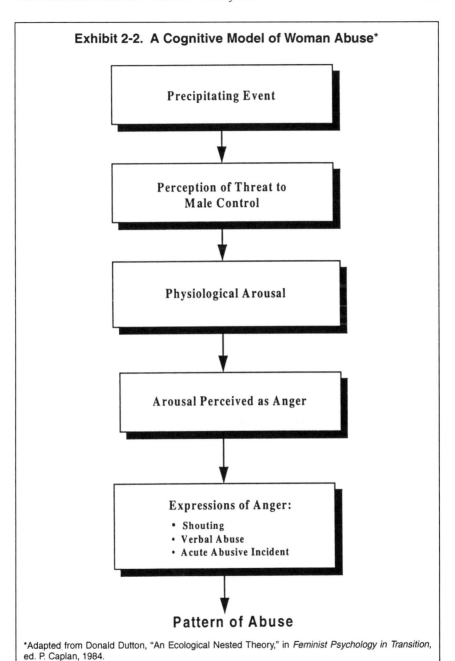

Exhibit 2-2. A Cognitive Model of Woman Abuse*

Precipitating Event

Perception of Threat to Male Control

Physiological Arousal

Arousal Perceived as Anger

Expressions of Anger:
- Shouting
- Verbal Abuse
- Acute Abusive Incident

Pattern of Abuse

*Adapted from Donald Dutton, "An Ecological Nested Theory," in *Feminist Psychology in Transition*, ed. P. Caplan, 1984.

Controversial Approaches to Batterer Intervention

The following approaches, although commonly used, are controversial. Criminal justice professionals referring batterers to programs that feature these techniques must be careful to learn how these approaches are being integrated into the programs and be wary of programs using these methods as their primary intervention.

Anger Management

While some researchers have suggested that a small percentage of battering may be attributable to a psychological disorder involving uncontrollable rage,[25] the "anger management" model attributes battering to out-of-control (rather than uncontrollable) anger. Anger management programs offer a short-term intervention that teaches batterers to recognize the physiological signs of anger and to then implement relaxation techniques to defuse the anger.[26] The intervention may also teach stress management and communication skills.[27] Many batterer treatment providers disavow the single-focus "anger management" treatment, instead incorporating anger management as one component of their intervention, sometimes under another name.

Critics have raised several concerns about the anger management approach—even as a component of more comprehensive treatment:

- Anger management programs address a single cause of battering, ignoring other, perhaps more profound, causes.[28]

- According to the feminist model, although they may claim to feel out of control, batterers are *not* out of control: battering is a decision, a choice. The social learning model adds that batterers choose to use or threaten violence because of its effectiveness in controlling their partners. The violence persists because it is rewarded.

- Anger management programs teach batterers nonviolent ways to control their partners. If the underlying issue of batterer control of the victim is not addressed, critics maintain, men will misuse the techniques used to "control" anger—stress management and communication skills—to continue to control the victim. For example, a batterer could refuse his childcare responsibilities on the grounds that it is stressful.

- According to "misattribution of arousal" theory, men learn to label all strong emotional states as anger when they are, in fact, experiencing feelings of betrayal or hurt.

- Interventions therefore need to focus on identifying the underlying emotion men are feeling in situations in which they batter rather than on means of controlling the mislabeled anger.[29]

- Two studies of anger management interventions that were parts of comprehensive batterer treatment programs found that men who completed the programs but whose violence continued reported that they had used anger management techniques to attempt to control their violence, whereas men who were successful in avoiding violence after the program said they ended their abuse through empathy, a redefinition of manhood, and cooperative decision making.[30]

Finally, some practitioners are concerned that any short-term, single-focus approach can be dangerous because it gives victims, judges, and batterers the illusion that the problem has been solved. Some practitioners feel that the availability of brief, inexpensive anger management programs even undermines the credibility of the more difficult, lengthy, and expensive treatments other programs provide. One-time "Saturday Afternoon Special"-style anger management programs arouse particular concern among practitioners who feel that such short-term programs trivialize the severity of the problem in the eyes of the batterer and are unlikely to have any deterrent effect.

Individual and Couples Counseling

Many practitioners disapprove of—and at least 20 State standards and guidelines expressly prohibit—couples counseling for batterers. In addition, a number of program directors disapprove of individual counseling as the sole intervention for battering. Group work is considered important in helping abusers to overcome their denial by hearing other men acknowledge and deal with their behavior, and to break the isolation that is considered part of the syndrome of abuse.

Although systematic research comparing couples and group interventions has not been conducted,[31] anecdotal evidence and the beliefs of providers (many of whom serve on committees to draft or approve State standards or guidelines) have limited the utilization of couples therapy for domestic violence. The practitioners' disapproval is based on a belief that victims of abuse are intimidated and cannot fully participate in therapy in the presence of their abusers. If victims do reveal the batterer's violence or disclose other problems, they face the threat of reprisal. Restrictions on couples therapy and individual psychotherapy for battering are a point of contention between feminist-oriented batterer intervention providers and mental health providers in many communities.

Self-Help Groups: Batterers Anonymous

Self-help batterer groups are modeled on Alcoholics Anonymous and Parents Anonymous. Member-run support groups are facilitated by former batterers who have been nonviolent for at least a year.[32] Although there are some ground rules and facilitators may introduce specific topics, the approach is unstructured, with members setting the agenda, usually addressing their personal concerns.

Self-help or support groups are an accepted model of *follow-up* for batterers who have completed a program and want continued support to prevent relapse, to continue the change process, or to have a place to address ongoing problems. Self-help groups are controversial as an *initial* intervention, however, because it is questionable whether former batterers—especially those who have been nonviolent for only a year—are qualified to conduct groups, unless they have been extensively involved with a program, have been trained, and are supervised. In addition, facilitators tend to use an aggressive, even belligerent, style of confrontation that more traditional programs view as inappropriate modeling of antagonistic behavior that borders on abuse. By contrast, other professionals are concerned that support groups run by former batterers may be insufficiently confrontational about members' excuses for violence and too supportive of batterers' hostility toward women.

Advantages and Criticism of the Cognitive-Behavioral Models. One advantage of the cognitive-behavioral model is that its analysis of battering and its intervention strategy are compatible with a criminal justice response to domestic violence. The approach holds the batterer fully responsible for his violence and fully responsible for learning and adopting nonviolent alternatives. Without trying to solve larger issues of social inequality on the one hand, or delving into deep-seated psychological issues on the other, the cognitive-behavioral approach simply focuses on the violent acts themselves and attempts to change them. The model also offers a straightforward intervention that can be implemented in a limited period of time.

The feminist perspective criticizes the cognitive-behavioral approach for failing to explain why many men with thought patterns or skills deficits that allegedly explain their domestic violence are not violent in other relationships, how culture or subcultures influence patterns of violence, and why some men continue to abuse women even when the behavior is not rewarded.[33] These criticisms are usually moot because most cognitive-behavioral programs integrate the feminist analysis of domestic violence, both in the cognitive component (for example, by examining thoughts that encourage wife-beating, such as "She should obey me. I'm the man of the household.") and the social learning aspects (for example, by discussing how sexism in the media and in society provides models of social support for abusing and degrading women). (See exhibit 2-3, "Example of an Integrated Feminist/Cognitive-Behavioral Strategy.")

Exhibit 2-3. Example of an Integrated Feminist/Cognitive-Behavioral Strategy

Teach him to be mindful of perception but suspicious of the conclusions he comes to

CONTROL LOG

He notices something

Confront with evidence that his behavior is criminal and hurtful, and that he is responsible for his behavior

He minimizes his abusive behavior and blames her for his action

Challenge belief system

He makes an assumption

He denies the hurt he has caused

Compulsion to Control

He has an emotional reaction ◄— Control plan

Arrest him. Negative social/legal sanctions. Safety planning with victim ——► He abuses her

He begins negative self-talk

He decides he is justified in abusing her

His body reacts to emotional tension and his negative self-talk

Teach positive self-talk

Confront his entitlement and belief system

Teach time-out

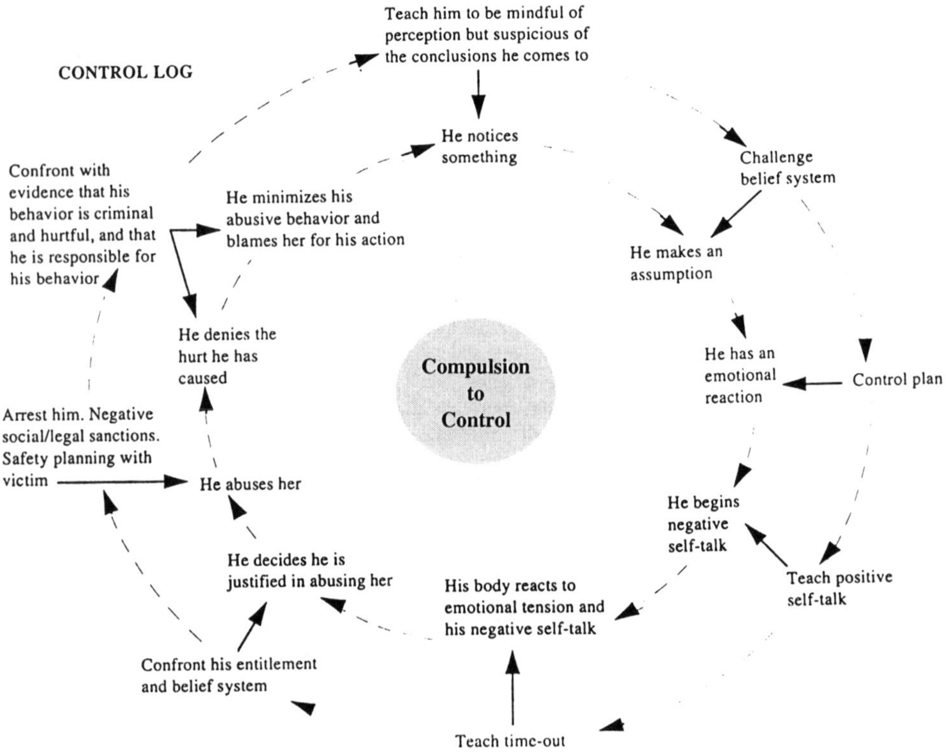

Source: Wil Avery, House of Ruth, Baltimore, Maryland

COMPATIBILITY OF THE MODELS WITH CRIMINAL JUSTICE GOALS

The feminist educational approach to batterer intervention is theoretically more compatible with a criminal justice perspective than either the family systems or psychotherapeutic approaches in several respects.[34]

- The feminist educational view of domestic violence is that the behavior is criminal, not just the result of faulty couple interactions or mental illness.

- The feminist educational view is that consequences are appropriate. By contrast, the psychotherapeutic explanation results in a treatment approach that is designed to modify the inner emotional life of the batterer through insight and possibly medication. Changing the inner person and prescribing medication to alter behavior may be considered by some to be beyond the scope of a criminal justice intervention.

- The primary goal of feminist educational programs is to hold batterers responsible for their violence. While most psychological programs also make this claim, feminists believe that the psychotherapeutic view of batterers as victims of childhood trauma or other mistreatment undercuts a program's ability to hold batterers responsible. The family systems approach—unlike the criminal justice system—holds the victim as well as the batterer accountable.

- The explicit goal of feminist educational approaches is to end the abusive behavior rather than to heal the batterer (the psychotherapeutic goal) or to improve relationships (the family systems goal).

A case can be made, however, that psychological interventions can also meet the needs of the criminal justice system. The aim of the criminal justice system in sending men to batterer programs is to reduce recidivism; for this to happen, the intervention has to be effective. While advocates of the feminist educational model criticize the psychotherapeutic model for failing to hold batterers responsible for their behavior, advocates of the psychotherapeutic approach respond that educational interventions are not successful in deterring or rehabilitating batterers because they are too short and superficial and do not address the needs of batterers with severe mental illness, who may comprise up to 25 percent of all batterers.[35] Indeed, the "confrontational" and didactic process of the feminist model—as well as the feminist rhetoric in which it is framed—may alienate the batterer and increase his hostility and resistance. For example, an assistant group facilitator for the Compassion Workshop in Silver Spring, Maryland, reported that, when he was in treatment, feminist interventions had only increased his anger and denial, while subsequent, nonconfrontational, compassion-based treatment had helped him become nonviolent. His wife, a cofacilitator of the group whose role was to give the perspective of the victim, agreed that the feminist education model had exacerbated her husband's abuse but that after psychologically oriented counseling, he was now violence free.

While the narrow treatment goals of the strictly educational feminist programs are compatible with the criminal justice view—simply stopping the abusive behavior as expeditiously as possible and holding the batterer responsible—the feminist theory of domestic violence also has broad social goals that may be seen as going beyond the purview of the criminal justice system. Because feminist theory locates the cause of domestic violence in social structures and the organization of society, social change may be seen as the ultimate goal of the curricula. In a sense, though, even this broad goal is consistent with a criminal justice agenda in that it suggests that broad-based community education and a coordinated community response are necessary for preventing domestic violence. In contrast, it is difficult to identify a broad prevention strategy that follows from either the individualistic psychotherapeutic theory of domestic violence or the family systems model.

Finally, some practitioners and criminal justice professionals are beginning to regard any form of batterer intervention as a proxy for intensive probation. While the curriculum may not deter reoffenses over time, at least during program participation batterers are being monitored closely, and their victims are receiving at least minimal attention and referrals. This heightened vigilance with regard to the batterer's behavior and the victim's welfare is compatible with criminal justice goals. However, theoretical compatibility with the criminal justice system is not the only important factor in selecting a batterer intervention. On a practical level, interventions must be able to retain batterers in treatment and address any obstacles to program participation.

CONCLUSION: MULTIDIMENSIONAL MODELS DOMINATE THE FIELD

Many practitioners accept that there are compelling features in more than one theoretical model. In practice, regardless of their primary perspective, most programs have adopted some tenets of the feminist model. For example, they view sexual inequality and masculine role expectations of dominance as core issues to address—along with cognitive-behavioral techniques for modifying behavior—and they teach batterers to use "time-outs" (a behavioral technique for controlling emotional outbursts). Longer-term programs may progress through the feminist and cognitive models in stages, and some even progress to a psychotherapeutic group process model for aftercare. These programs have a brief initial phase using a feminist educational model to tackle denial of responsibility, a longer second phase teaching cognitive-behavioral techniques for skill-building, and a third phase delving into individual psychological issues in an unstructured format for those men identified as having psychological problems contributing to battering. Other programs blend treatment modalities and approaches by combining individual, group, and couples treatment sequentially over an extended period of two to three years.

Programs may also use different models or materials to accommodate the special needs of specific types of batterers, most commonly substance abusers, African Americans, Asians, Latinos, recent immigrants, female offenders, gay and lesbian batterers, or batterers with poor literacy skills.

Some practitioners may resist incorporating consideration of individual psychology and cultural differences in interventions because they are concerned that the individual approach will eclipse consideration of the sociological factors emphasized by the prevailing feminist model. However, the critical issue from a criminal justice perspective is simply "what works"; if mixed-model interventions that incorporate psychotherapeutic elements or cultural competence are shown to be more effective in retaining and engaging batterers in treatment, questions of theory are likely to become secondary.

NOTES

[1] Rosenbaum, A. and R. D. Maiuro, "Eclectic Approaches in Working With Men Who Batter," in *Treating Men Who Batter: Theory, Practice, and Programs*, ed. P. L. Caesar and K. L. Hamberger. New York: Springer, 1989: 65–195.

[2] Mary Russell, for example, justifies her use of the expression "wife assault" on the grounds that "domestic violence" and "family violence" ignore the "male to female direction" of most violence between partners. See Russell, M., "Wife Assault Theory, Research, and Treatment: A Literature Review." *Journal of Family Violence*, 3 (3) (1988): 193–208.

[3] Schechter, S., *Women and Male Violence: The Visions and Struggles of the Battered Women's Movement*. Boston: South End Press, 1982.

[4] Pence, E. and M. Paymar, *Education Groups for Men Who Batter: The Duluth Model*. New York: Springer, 1993.

[5] In support of the point that women may remain with men who abuse them because of economic dependence, Ida Johnson found in a study of 426 battered women leaving a Central Florida battered women's shelter that a woman was more likely to return home if the batterer had a high income and the woman was unemployed; if she had an independent income and his income was insufficient to support a family, the woman was unlikely to return home. Johnson, I. M., "Economic, Situational, and Psychological Correlates of the Decision-making Process of Battered Women." *Families in Society: The Journal of Contemporary Human Services*, (March 1992): 68–176.

[6] There is disagreement over whether batterers actually believe that women are incompetent or whether promoting that notion merely serves their needs to control their wives in order to restrict their activities. Rusbult and Martz, in a study of women leaving a domestic violence shelter in Lexington, Kentucky, found that the strongest predictor of whether women would return to the batterer was whether they had a driver's license and access to a car. Rusbult, C. E. and J. M. Martz, "Remaining in an Abusive Relationship: An Investment Model Analysis of Nonvoluntary Dependence." *Personality and Social Psychology Bulletin*, 21 (1995): 558–571.

[7] O'Sullivan, C. and B. Birns, *Contested Custody Cases When Violent Marriages End*. Paper presented at the First National Conference on Children Exposed to Family Violence, Austin, Texas, June 1996.

[8] Browne, K., D. G. Saunders, and K. M. Staecker, "Process-Psychodynamic Groups for Men Who Batter: Description of a Brief Treatment Model," University of Michigan, January 26, 1996.

[9] Gondolf, E. W. and J. Hanneken, "The Gender Warrior: Reformed Batterers on Abuse, Treatment, and Change," *Journal of Family Violence*, 2 (2) (1987): 177–191.

[10] Gondolf and Hanneken, "The Gender Warrior." The measure is Bem's Sex Role Inventory.

[11] Browne, Saunders, and Staecker, "Process-Psychodynamic Groups for Men Who Batter."

[12] Dutton, D., "Patriarchy and Wife Assault: The Ecological Fallacy," *Violence and Victims*, 9 (2) (1994): 167–182.

[13] Harrell, A., "Evaluation of Court Ordered Treatment for Domestic Violence Offenders," Final Report, Washington, DC: The Urban Institute, 1991.

[14] A 1990 evaluation of the Duluth Domestic Abuse Intervention Project (DAIP) found that program participation had no impact on recidivism. Shepard, M., "Predicting Batterer Recidivism Five Years After Community Intervention," Report, Duluth, Minnesota, 1990.

[15] Giles-Sims, J., *Wife-battering: A Systems Theory Approach*, New York: Guilford, 1983.

[16] While it is true that many victims who seek services want to maintain the relationship while eliminating the abuse, and that most programs report that 30 to 40 percent of the men in treatment are separated, no long-term data show what percent of relationships in which there has been battery last. See Sirles, E. A., S. Lipchik, and K. Kowalski, "A Consumer's Perspective on Domestic Violence Interventions," *Journal of Family Violence*, 8 (3) (1993): 267.

[17] Bowker, L., *Ending the Violence: A Guidebook Based on the Experience of 1,000 Battered Wives*. Holmes Beach, FL: Learning Publications, 1986.

[18] Russell, "Wife Assault Theory."

[19] Specific disorders that have been found in batterers are post-traumatic stress disorder (probably due to childhood trauma), depression, low self-esteem, and personality disorders. Personality disorders usually mentioned by therapists who work with batterers are antisocial personality disorder, narcissism, and borderline personality disorder. In addition, passive-aggression, paranoia, obsessive-compulsive disorder, and intermittent explosive disorder have been said to foster aggression. A psychotherapeutic reference describes the personality disorders as follows: People with antisocial personality disorder are irresponsible, irritable, and aggressive; they are not sadistic but are reckless and have no remorse; they are unable to maintain friendships or romantic relationships. Narcissists are hypersensitive but lack empathy; they have difficulty with relationships because they expect others to meet their special needs. Borderline personalities are characterized by instability of identity, self-image, and relationships; they want to be alone but fear abandonment; they are often moody and depressed and, in severe cases, self-destructive and suicidal. Reid, W. H. and M. G. Weise, *The DSM-III-R Training Guide*, New York: Brunner/Mazel, 1989. See also Dutton, D., "Trauma Symptoms and PTSD-like Profiles in Perpetrators of Intimate Abuse." *Journal of Traumatic Stress*, 8 (2)(1995): 299–316; and Maiuro, R., T. S. Cahn, P. P. Vitaliano, B. C. Wagner, and J. B. Zegree, "Anger, Hostility, and Depression in Domestically Violent Versus Generally Assaultive and Nonviolent Control Subjects," *Journal of Consulting and Clinical Psychology*, 56 (1) (1988): 17–23.

[20] Browne, Saunders, and Straecker, "Process-Psychodynamic Groups for Men Who Batter."

[21] See Dutton, "Patriarchy and Wife Assault."

[22] Adams, D., "Treatment Models for Men Who Batter: A Profeminist Analysis," in *Feminist Perspectives on Wife Abuse*, ed. K. Yllo and M. Bograd. Newbury Park, CA: Sage Publications, 1988: 176–199.

[23] Adams, "Treatment Models for Men Who Batter," 176–177.

[24] Hamberger, K. L. and J. E. Hastings, "Recidivism Following Spouse Abuse Abatement Counseling: Treatment Program Implications," *Violence and Victims*, 5 (3) (1990): 160.

[25] Information provided by Roland Maiuro.

[26] Hamberger, K. L. and J. E. Hastings, "Court-Mandated Treatment of Men Who Assault Their Partner: Issues, Controversies, and Outcomes," in *Legal Responses to Wife Assault*, ed. Z. Hilton, Newbury Park, CA: Sage Publications, 1993: 188–229.

[27] Tolman, R. M. and D. G. Saunders, "The Case for the Cautious Use of Anger Control With Men Who Batter," *Response*, 11 (2) (1988): 15–20.

[28] Tolman and Saunders articulate this concern, while accepting anger management as part of a cognitive-behavioral intervention: "The use of anger control techniques with batterers is problematic when battering is framed exclusively as an anger problem, when the issues of dominance and control of women by men are ignored in treatment, and when practitioners fail to address societal reinforcements for battering." Tolman and Saunders, "The Case for the Cautious Use of Anger Control With Men Who Bat-

ter," 19. See also Ptacek, J., "The Clinical Literature on Men Who Batter, A Review and Critiques," in *Family Abuse and Its Consequences: New Directions in Research*, ed. B. T. Hotaling, D. Finkelhor, J. T. Kirkpatrick, and M. A. Straus. Newbury Park, CA: Sage Publications, 1986: 149–162.

29 Dutton, D., *The Domestic Assault of Women: Psychological and Criminal Justice Perspectives* (revised). Vancouver: University of British Columbia, 1995.

30 Two studies showing a recurrence of violence among program participants who said they used anger management to reduce their violence are: Gondolf, E., "Men Who Batter: How They Stop Their Abuse," Paper presented at the Second National Conference for Family Violence Researchers, Durham, NC, 1984; and Kelso, D. and L. Personette, *Domestic Violence and Treatment Services for Victims and Abusers*. Anchorage: Altam, 1985.

31 Daniel O'Leary's studies comparing single-sex group and couples-group interventions were unable to retain couples when the batterer had a history of severe violence. Rosenbaum, A. and K. D. O'Leary, "The Treatment of Marital Violence," in *Clinical Handbook of Marital Therapy*, ed. N. S. Jacobsen and A. S. Gurman, New York: Guilford, 1986. Gondolf studied 12 men who had been through a men's group program and were deemed to be fully reformed (versus 38 who were not). Several of these highly motivated men had sought professional help before coming to the batterer program but they had found no improvement after individual or couples therapy. According to their self-reports, the batterer group they subsequently attended gave them what they needed to stop battering. Gondolf and Hanneken, "The Gender Warrior."

32 Edelson, J. L. and M. Syers, "Relative Effectiveness of Group Treatments for Men Who Batter." *Social Work Research and Abstracts*, (June 1990): 10–17.

33 According to social learning theory, a retaliatory attack should *decrease* future abuse. However, two national surveys found that when women resist violently, the batterer's violence usually increases in severity. This result is consistent with the feminist view that the intent of physical abuse is to punish resistance and disobedience. Bowker, L., *Ending the Violence: A Guidebook Based on the Experience of 1,000 Battered Wives*. Holmes Beach, FL: Learning Publications, 1986; Feld, S. L. and M. A. Straus, "Escalation and Desistance From Wife Assault in Marriage," in *Physical Violence in American Families*, ed. M. A. Straus, and R. J. Gelles. New Brunswick, NJ: Transaction, 1990: 489–505.

34 Edelson and Syers, "Relative Effectiveness of Group Treatments for Men Who Batter." This article reports an experiment in which all comers to a program were assigned to a brief or intense intervention and to one of three models: the Duluth "educational" model, a self-help group, and a combined group process-educational model. The results showed no difference between the brief and intense programs, except for the few men of color who were less likely to recidivate if they completed the long program; the structured feminist educational model was found to be most effective.

35 Gondolf, E., "Multi-Site Evaluation of Batterer Intervention Systems: A Summary of Preliminary Findings." Working Paper, Mid-Atlantic Addiction Training Institute, October 24, 1996.

Voices of Strength and Resistance

A Contextual and Longitudinal Analysis of Women's Responses to Battering

Jacquelyn Campbell, Linda Rose, Joan Kub, and Daphne Nedd

A recent national probability study of women estimates that at least 4.4 million women are physically assaulted in the United States each year (Plichta, 1996). There is substantial evidence demonstrating that battered women are seriously at risk for homicide as well as a wide range of physical and mental health problems (Campbell, 1995; Eby, Campbell, Sullivan, & Davidson, 1995; McCauley et al., 1996; Plichta, 1996; Ratner, 1993). In spite of this knowledge, there is a paucity of information about women's responses to battering over time that integrates physical, emotional, social, and behavioral reactions within complex familial and environmental contexts. A study was undertaken to examine women's responses at three points in time over a 3 ½ to 4-year period, using both in-depth interviews and standardized instruments. This article reports the component of the study combining qualitative and quantitative data analysis to illustrate the complexity of women's decision making in terms of the relationship status and continuing or cessation of abuse.

LITERATURE REVIEW

The traditional picture of battered women as passive victims has been counteracted at least partially in recent years by a variety of studies using both quali-

Journal of Interpersonal Violence, Vol. 13, No. 6, December 1998, 743–762. ©1998 Sage Publications, Inc.

tative and quantitative data. Gondolf, Fisher, and McFerron (1988) and Okun (1986) both used large-record reviews from wife-abuse shelters to demonstrate survival strategies of battered women in the face of serious terrorism. Hoff (1990), in an ethnographic analysis, documented the importance of women's social support systems—especially family, friends, and shelters—in helping them to survive and escape the abuse. Okun (1986) and Campbell, Miller, Cardwell, and Belknap (1994) found that the majority of battered women do leave an abusive relationship but generally leave several times before they leave permanently. In the recent Jacobson, Gottman, Gorner, Berns, and Wu Shortt (1996) study, 42% left or achieved nonviolence. It also has been demonstrated that women's risk for abuse continues after they leave (Kurz, 1996; Wilson, Johnson, & Daly, 1995).

Several investigators have used qualitative approaches to examine these processes. Merritt-Gray and Wuest (1995) found women actively counteracted abuse from the first appearance of violence. Women first relinquished parts of themselves, minimized the abuse, and fortified their defenses as the first part of their process of breaking free. Landenburger (1989) and Mills (1985) described abused women as losing a sense of self or identity, either early in the relationship or during what Landenburger calls an "entrapment" phase. Her study showed subsequent stages of disengaging and recovery. Lempert (1996) developed a central concept of agency to describe the strategies and processes women used to "halt, change or cope with their partner's violence." Her study redefined seemingly passive actions as active survival strategies and seemingly self-erasures as face-saving strategies to maintain invisibility. These studies have been instrumental in demonstrating the interactive and complex processes that characterize abusive relationships and women's responses to them. All of these qualitative studies, however, were cross sectional accounts and included primarily well-educated White women, most of whom had left the abusive relationships and retrospectively were recounting the events and their responses. The current study addresses these gaps by interviewing primarily African American women over three points in time.

METHOD

The study was conducted over 3 years, with interviews conducted every 8 to 12 months. A total of 164 women were recruited at Time 1, and 96 women returned for the third interview. Although 38% of the overall sample was lost by Time 3 due to safety issues and transience, there were no significant differences in demographic or major predictor and outcome variables (abuse, stress, self-care agency, self-esteem, depression, health symptoms) between those who returned and those who did not. The data for this analysis are from a subset of 32 of the women randomly selected from the 96 battered women that were followed at all three points in time.

Women who "had serious problems in an intimate relationship with a man" were recruited with newspaper advertisements and bulletin board postings in places frequented by women, such as child care centers, community centers, laundromats, and university women's restrooms in the metropolitan area of a large midwestern city. Because prior research has shown that committed relationships are more likely to be characterized by violence (Fagan & Browne, 1994), only women who had been in a relationship for at least 1 year were included.

Women were screened for battering using the conflict tactics scale, developed by Straus and Gelles (1990). The scale assessed conflict tactics directed toward the woman only and was modified by adding the question, "Has your partner ever forced you into sex that you did not wish to participate in?" This question originally was used by Russell (1982) in her study of marital rape and subsequently used by Campbell (1989) to successfully determine forced sex in battering relationships. Battering was defined in this study as repeated physical and/or sexual assault within a context of coercive control (Campbell & Humphreys, 1993). A woman was categorized as battered if there were more than one instance of minor violence or at least one major violence tactic or forced sex perpetrated by her partner against her during the past year. The coercive control aspects of the relationship were determined by responses on the Index of Spouse Abuse (ISA) (Hudson & McIntosh, 1981). Coercive control includes emotional abuse, threats, and intimidation, as well as financial control and social isolation (Pence & Paymer, 1993). Identifying self as battered was not used as an inclusion criteria, as many women subjected to violence in intimate relationships do not put those labels on themselves (Schechter & Jones, 1992).

The methodology was enacted as feminist action research as described across disciplines by such scholars as Reinharz (1992), Small (1995), Lather (1991), and Henderson (1995). The term can be said to encompass a group of evolving methodologies that are striving to create change as the result of the research (action research) and/or have participants both be changed and create change as part of the research process (participatory research). The feminist specificity of this particular strand of action research adds that it is research for women, is reflexive, represents human diversity, strives to equalize power relationships both within research teams and between researchers and participants, critiques prior scholarship (especially for andocentric and ethnocentric bias), uses both qualitative and quantitative data, and portrays women's strengths (Bunting & Campbell, 1994).

Data were collected with in-depth structured, semistructured, and open-ended interviews that used a dialogic approach (give-and-take discussion rather than traditional question and answer). Each interview lasted approximately 2 hours. Interview topics included relationship history, relationship problems and problem-solving strategies, attributions, and cultural norms about abuse. They also included safety planning and referrals as requested by the participants. Because of safety concerns, many women were only contacted through work or a family member or friends and were never called at home.

INSTRUMENTS

Severity of physical and emotional abuse was assessed using the modified version of the ISA (Hudson & McIntosh, 1981) and interview questions about abuse experience by the women. The ISA (Hudson & McIntosh, 1981) is a 30-item scale designed to measure the severity or magnitude of physical and nonphysical abuse inflicted on a woman by her spouse or partner using a frequency and weighting of tactics. Two scores are computed for each respondent: severity of physical abuse (ISA-P) and severity of nonphysical abuse (ISA-NP). Scores on both scales range from 0 to 100. The ISA has been validated partially in four studies (Hudson & McIntosh, 1981). Campbell et al. (1994) found independent reliability and factor analysis support in a sample of African American women. Internal consistency of the ISA for this sample was alpha =.937.

SAMPLE DESCRIPTION

Thirty-two women, ranging in age from 18 to 53 years (mean = 32.5 years), comprised the sample. They were relatively well educated, with a mean educational level of 13.5 years and a range between the fourth grade to an earned doctorate. The women had an average of 2 children, with 48% having children under 5 years of age. The majority of the women were single (58%) but had been in the relationship from 1 to 17 years (mean = 4.4 years). The majority (61%) were employed or were in school full-time, and the average family income was $18,800 per year, with 54% being below the official poverty level. The majority (74%) of the women were African American, with 23% European American (Eastern European ancestry was the most frequent ethnic group), and 1 woman was of Puerto Rican descent.

DATA ANALYSIS

All interviews were audiotaped and/or transcribed verbatim. Manifest and latent content analysis were used to analyze the interview data. Thematic analysis consisted of a process of coding, clustering, "subsuming particulars into the general," and confirming (Miles & Huberman, 1994). Each interview was read by three of the investigators who met regularly to discuss coding of relevant passages. Two types of codes were used: descriptive codes that identified contextual aspects of the woman's personal situation, such as relationship parameters (marital status, length of time in relationship, presence of children), and process codes that were reflective of the women's responses to the abusive relationship over time. Process codes were not generated a priori, although some codes were suggested by the question that had been asked during the interview, for example, "Who have you talked to in the last 6 months about the relationship problems?" was initially coded as "social support." As additional interviews were analyzed, the codes became increasingly interpretive as the investigators reflected on the context of the woman's responses. A more conceptual level of codes thus emerged, such as a relationship status that we called "in-out," to reflect the complexity of the attachment between the woman and her partner that changed over time.

Each participant's interviews (Time 1, Time 2, Time 3) were read as a whole, and patterns over time were identified. In addition, the Time 1 interviews were considered together, Time 2 together, and Time 3 together. In this way, we considered the contextual aspects of each woman's situation and their impact on her responses to the abusive relationship.

Trustworthiness of the findings was addressed in several ways. A computer program was used to assign codes to specific passages of interviews. As codes were identified, definitions were discussed until agreement was reached. In addition, researchers' responses to the data were recorded in memos that were attached to the individual interviews. This documented the analysis process and the emerging conceptualizations of the women's experiences. Finally, the interview segments that were coded in the same way were compiled together by the NUDIST program and reviewed in a separate phase of the analysis.

RESULTS

In examining the women's stories of their relationships with their partners, as well as their stories about and reflections on other aspects of their lives, the complexity of battering relationships was evident. The analysis of the verbatim responses identified two primary themes: the "fluidity of the relationship status" and "women engaged in a process of achieving nonviolence."

FLUIDITY OF RELATIONSHIP STATUS

Although only 13% of the sample were married at Time 1, all were in a committed, sexually intimate, and for most a monogamous relationship that had lasted at least 1 year. Approximately two thirds of the unmarried women were living with their partner all the time, whereas the remainder were in relationships that involved him staying in her domicile or vice versa at least part of the time. Women and their male partners were intertwined in sexually intimate relationships in many nontraditional ways, eluding the usual marital status categories.

The status of the relationship between the woman and her partner also did not fit into a dichotomous variable of "in" and "out." The women described their relationships and their attachment to the partners in much more fluid terms. The notion of being in a state of flux, or what we have called an "in/out" relationship status, was an important component of women's responses to the abuse.

Relationships status over time. The in/out relationship status described women who still had some expectation of the relationship continuing or who were ambivalent about the relationship ending but had made attempts to leave or were in the process of leaving. Some women had physically left a shared residence or had thrown him out, but their ambivalence about the relationship was evident in their descriptions of goals for the relationship, continued feelings of love for him, or expressed doubts about what would happen in the future. They were seen as in/out because they were actively engaged in the process of leaving but had not yet made a final break. For example, some women took legal action to dissolve the relationship, others focused on getting custody or child support payments, and still others concentrated on making plans to leave as soon as a specific event occurred. For all of these women, there was a fundamental change in the status of the relationship that they were cognizant of, but on some level, there was still attachment or connection. Tables 1 and 2 illustrate these aspects of the process over time.

At the first interview, 2 women were out of the relationships while 5 were in the in/out status. At Time 3, more than half (53.1%) of the battered women were totally out of the relationship while almost a third (28.1%) were in/out (see Table 1). Although individual relationships took varying trajectories, including 1 woman who went from in/out to "out" (and a new nonviolent relationship) to "in" with the abusive partner who continued coercive control, the overall pattern of the sample clearly went from being committed to the violent relationship to an in/out status to an out status and/or a nonabused status.

Table 1. Relationship status/interview

	1		2		3	
	N	%	N	%	N	%
In	25	78	7	21.9	6	18.8
In/Out	5	15.6	13	40.6	9	28.1
Out	2	6.3	12	37.5	17	53.1

Table 2. Abuse status over time (*N* = 32)

	Time		
	1	2	3
No abuse	0	10 (31.2%)	14 (43.8%)
ISA-NP emotional > 25	7 (21.8%)	7 (21.8%)	11 (34.4%)
> 20 (ISA-P)	25 (78.1%)	14 (43.8%)	9[a] (28.1%)
M of ISA-P	35	17.9	14.4
	(2-86)	(0-65)	(0-63)

NOTE: ISA = Index of Spouse Abuse; ISA-P = ISA–severity of physical abuse; ISA-NP = ISA–severity of nonphysical abuse.
a. Four have totally ended relationship.

Characteristics of in and in/out relationship. The majority of women who were in the in or in/out categories at Time 2 and Time 3 seemed to adopt a stance that could be described as "making do in the relationship" (deciding to physically remain in the relationship while being emotionally removed), "watching and waiting" (being vigilant about his behavior while staying in), or "keeping it under control" (continuing the emotional connection but being aware that if the abuse continued or got worse, the relationship would have to end). Others communicated a moral sense of staying in the relationship because it was the right thing to do" or they had to "learn to tolerate" the abuse. For many of these women, financial constraints were a major issue in keeping them in the relationship. In contrast, a small group were in/out because they had left physically but had a lingering emotional and/or sexual attachment to the partner.

Relationship status/abuse status. An important contextual reality of the process of achieving nonviolence was that leaving the relationship and ending the violence were often independent. In fact, for many of the women, the violence escalated after the woman left, as is being increasingly documented in other studies (Bachman & Saltzman, 1995; Kurz, 1996; Wilson et al., 1995). As Table 2 shows, slightly less than half (43.8%) of the women achieved a state of no violence (and no coercive control) for at least 1 year, as assessed by the ISA (physical and nonphysical) and by in-depth interview. Another third (34.4%) were emotionally abused but no longer physically abused according to the ISA. Several relationships had moved from severely abusive relationships (more than 20 on the ISA-P—above the 20th percentile from the overall sample and twice the cutoff score of 10) at Time 1, through emotional abuse (below the cutoff score of 10 on the ISA-P but above the cutoff score of 25 on the ISA-NP) at Time 2, to no abuse at the third interview. In addition, the mean on the ISA-P and ISA-NP were both significantly lower at Time 3 than at Time 1 in both this analysis and in the larger sample, and significantly fewer (chi-square) were in the severely abused category (Campbell & Soeken, in press).

Of the 6 women who were still in the relationship at Time 3, 3 had not been abused (either emotionally or physically) for at least 1 year. On the opposite end of the spectrum, of the 9 women who were still severely abused (according to ISA scores) at Time 3, 4 had totally ended the original relationship, but the same abuser was still hitting her. But for the majority of the women who were totally out of the relationship, there was no consistent pattern of abuse or harassment from their former partner at Time 3.

THE PROCESS OF ACHIEVING NONVIOLENCE

In response to the violent relationship, most women initiated a process of achieving nonviolence rather than necessarily leaving the intimate relationship. This process of achieving nonviolence was not linear with easily identifiable stages. The women described going back and forth, both in external acts such as leaving and returning but also in their internal thinking and feeling processes. The process included a number of elements: responding to turning points by thinking about, labeling, and conceptualizing what was happening to them; negotiating internally with self and externally with the abuser; and trying various strategies and combinations of strategies to improve the relationship and decrease the abuse.

Turning points. A turning point was a specific incident or process that was seen as pivotal to how the relationship was viewed, how the woman viewed herself, or a major influence in her decision to leave the relationship. There were many types of turning points, most often more than one for each woman, and because of this variety we have presented types and examples in table 3. The most significant and obvious identifiable event was an instance of escalation of his abuse, such as being threatened with death. "I really saw the light when he drew a gun on me," said one woman. For others, it was property damage, serious injury, or a more serious type of physical abuse. For instance, one woman who at first was being emotionally abused, said, "When the physical abuse started, that was it." For another woman, it was the second incident of hitting that caused her to think about the relationship and start seeing herself as abused. Being hit during and after pregnancy for some led to the decision to "get out of there."

For a few women, the turning point was becoming violent themselves. One women explained that although the emotional abuse made her see herself as abused, it was her own thoughts of hate toward him that was pivotal in her decision to leave: "It [seeing self as abused] made me hate him and plot to kill him. I knew it was time to leave when I started plotting to kill him—I burned him bad with grease." At Time 2, this woman remained physically out of the relationship but described an emotional attachment: "I get lonesome for him sometimes. I make myself remember that the bad was worse than the good." At Time 3, she was still out of the relationship.

Another frequent type of turning point was a psychological one that involved the woman's own labeling of herself as abused or the relationship as abusive at Time 2 or Time 3. Initially, when asked if they saw themselves as bat-

Table 3. Turning points in deciding to leave or change

	N	Example Quote
Her violence	3	"I was starting to think about killing him."
Financial independence	2	"I am more independent now—I was financially dependent when I got pregnant. I was an L.P.N. and then got my R.N." "Financial independence is very important. I decided to put my social security check in direct deposit because he would check when he knew the day would come."
His infidelity	2	"I tolerated a few affairs in the relationship—I have since found out there were more than a few."
His abuse or violence	7	"I really saw the light when he drew a gun on me." (Three women were threatened with death; with others, it was property damage, serious injury, or a more serious type of abuse.) "When the physical abuse started, that was it." (After being sexually abused.) "I changed the lock."
Defining self as abused	4	"It helped me; I moved out. I decided I had to get out of there."
Child related	4	"He hit me right after the baby was born." "He hit me while I was pregnant. I ended up in the hospital after overdosing on aspirin." "The effects on the kids could be seen."

tered or abused, the majority of the women responded "yes" but qualified their answer by saying it was limited to psychological or mental abuse, even though scores on the Conflict Tactics Scales (CTS) and ISA indicated that physical abuse was present. A few women resisted the abuse label altogether, either because they felt they had already done something to change the abusive situation or because they felt it would mean they were not a strong person. A change in thinking for some women by Time 2 or Time 3 was seen as pivotal because once it occurred, it either provided the impetus to leave or influence her decision to stay. Women were able to identify a specific event or time when the relationship had a turning point, and reactions about these events was evident: As one woman noted, "After the first really bad fight, I realized how upset he can be. I changed my thinking. It made me reevaluate my husband and my situation." This woman did leave the relationship at Time 2 but came back, indicating that the change in thinking did not immediately translate to permanent change in behavior. At Time 3, she was able to identify another turning point that helped her to leave for good: "He started drinking, what I thought was excessive. It aggravated his mood swings and his bad temper." Turning points could also be small incremental changes that, taken together, resulted in a shift in thinking and a move toward leaving. For example, one woman described her reactions this way:

> I decided to go because of the benefits to me and my kids. If I stayed with him, it would have just gone down further. I was so run down. The effects on the kids could be seen—my daughter talked about it in school—the teachers asked her. The kids said we should leave. I started to think about ways to kill him.

Financial independence was also very important—"I decided to put my social security check in direct deposit because he would check when he knew the day it would come. I also set goals in support group, and I reached them all."

Negotiating with self or partner. Negotiating as a strategy for achieving nonviolence was also complex in that it involved the woman negotiating with herself first and then negotiating with the partner. Part of the negotiating with the self (sometimes with the help of family, friends, shelter advocates, support groups, or therapists at various stages) included convincing herself that either "it's not that bad" or there was a serious relationship problem because of certain behaviors and/or their severity. For some, the negotiating process was an essential step that preceded coming to terms with the notion that the problem was abuse and/or control and deciding that some sort of action was necessary.

Negotiating with self continued as women negotiated with their partner. Negotiating involved setting up a scenario, "when this happens, I will leave" or "if that happens, I will confront him." There was an element of bargaining—waiting until a daughter goes off to college or until the woman was able to go back to school. Women decided that if they saw or continued to see certain behaviors in him that affected themselves or their children, they would need to do something else. Some plans were concrete, others more vague in terms of whether the outcome could be realized. Examples of the concrete negotiating were offering to do something he wanted or correcting something he identified as a major problem in exchange for him ending the abusive behavior and/or seeking help from a professional—most often for substance abuse or a mental health problem.

Selecting strategies to decrease abuse. Most often, women used a combination of strategies designed to decrease the abuse in the relationship. The strategies were chosen through an active, conscious, evaluative process of decision making, revising, and choosing new strategies when old ones failed. The women monitored the effects on their partners, their children, and themselves. Although most of the women admitted they did things they had not intended to do, such as not carrying through with resolutions or decisions, they kept trying to make it better. Even those who were "making do in the relationship" monitored the situation and recognized their deliberate passivity.

A group of strategies that emerged in terms of women working to achieve nonviolence were categorized as active problem solving, in direct response to the abuse. Examples included (a) calling the police, (b) seeking advice or help from others, (c) fighting back or hitting first, (d) leaving, (e) financial actions, (f) self-talk, (g) acts of finality, and (h) avoiding or hiding. They were used with varying degrees of success. Finally, a strategy labeled "subordinating self" was identified as a critical component of the active problem-solving process.

More than half of the women had "called the police" at least once, and another small group had used the tactic of threatening to call the police. For close to half of those who called, the police were helpful, taking or precipitating actions such as taking the partner's gun, taking the woman to a shelter, or getting an order of protection. For another group, calling the police made no difference or was detrimental because "they told me nothing could be done," or the police did not even show up. Some women resorted to subversive methods to deal with the nonresponsive system: "I told them there was a gun to get them to come, and they got mad at me."

Close to half of the women in this sample had "sought advice and/or help from others." Female friends were identified most often as a source of support. Other women spoke about isolation or decisions to not seek out others for support due to embarrassment, critical responses of others, or responses from others that seemed to minimize the problem or impeded the woman's own help seeking.

Approximately half the women had tried "fighting back" (hitting back at least occasionally), some reported hitting him first most of the time, and two women usually hit first since the beginning of the relationship. However, whether they continued being the one to hit first depended on how well it worked for them in keeping them from getting hurt. One woman said, "I used to be the first one to hit, although it was usually minor, and I always ended up getting hurt." The consequences of fighting back were often substantial, such as increasing the partner's anger toward the woman. Another woman decided that her partner deliberately provoked her to initiate aggression so he could strike back at her. For a small minority, the fighting back was a very effective strategy because it decreased the violence. One woman said her fighting back "surprised him" and another realized that it gave her a greater sense of control.

Close to half of the women had tried "leaving" at some point, some leaving for a few days to get his attention and then returning, whereas another had a clear intent of leaving forever and going as far away as possible. Leaving was used as a problem-solving strategy but was not an easy strategy to embrace. Women talked about "getting on with my life" and "having a job to do—raising my kids." The process of leaving was not linear, and it was not always immediate. For some, a turning point, discussed earlier, changed the thinking, but it took additional time for the act of leaving to actually occur.

The women took "financial actions" before and/or after leaving. For example, one woman gave up child support because "it gave him control and occasions for contact and argument." Because financial independence was seen as critical to leaving the relationship, the women focused on achieving it as much as possible and through whatever means available such as getting a job, going after his income tax, or simply not buying things jointly. Women who were in the process of leaving engaged in "self-talk" as a way to try to make objective decisions about the relationship. For example, one woman made lists of advantages and disadvantages of the relationship, while others who left reminded themselves how bad the relationship was. Other women said they took "acts of finality," as if to symbolize to themselves and/or to their partners that the relationship was over. Such acts included filing divorce papers or destroying gifts that she had received from or given to him. "Avoiding and hiding actions" were necessary for some of the women who left a violent man. For example, one woman hid her car whenever she went out. Another woman stopped answering the phone and kept her lights on a timer.

"Subordinating the self" was an internal problem-solving strategy. Subordinating was a term used by one woman who described her decision to use it as a strategy "to avoid making a scene" in public. It was classified as active because it resulted from a conscious choice, a proactive decision, to try a strategy to address a problem that had been recognized as abuse or controlling behavior. Subordinating thus was defined as a defensive strategy, designed to avoid physical harm or intense verbal altercations that might lead to harm. Approximately half of the women who were subordinating themselves at Time 1 were still subordinating themselves at Time 3.

Subordinating thus was characterized as a conscious decision to be as nonresponsive as possible to stop the escalation of his anger. It is important to note that the women made choices regarding when to resist and when to adopt a subordinating posture. One woman decided, "Keeping feelings in is keeping things under control." This was not a consistent pattern of responding; rather, it was tied to particular events, times, and spheres of contention. This same woman explained about her job: "He might pressure, but I wouldn't quit—it's my livelihood." Another woman was able to "stand her ground" in disagreeing with her partner about child issues but subordinated herself to avoid being hit in other arguments.

There were different types of subordinating. The first was doing what the partner wanted, illustrated by statements such as "I did things to please him that I would not have ordinarily done," "I did try to change things that irritated him," and "had to do everything alone for . . . an ill child not readily accepted by hus-band." Another type was actively silencing themselves, such as "keeping feelings in" quoted above, and also "I clam up," and "I avoid discussing it . . . don't know what else to do." A third mode was taking a stance of passivity, illustrated by phrases such as "act docile," "tried not to provoke him," and "back off." Finally, ignoring his behavior was exemplified by phrases such as "ignore it," "pretend it doesn't exist," and by the woman who said, "I loved him, so I let him do whatever made him happy so he would not leave me."

In summary, the overall theme was women initiating and sustaining a pro-cess of achieving nonviolence through active problem solving. This is not to say that the women were uniformly strong; that they did not "make mistakes"; that they did not use violence themselves, sometimes to a frightening extent; or that they always made healthy choices for themselves or their children. Even so, the overall picture over time was one of strength, resistance, and resourcefulness in the face of frightening circumstances.

DISCUSSION

A strength of this study was that it used a prospective rather than retro-spective design, with the women describing the process as it occurred rather than after they had processed the events and their feelings. This resulted in sto-ries that were sometimes contradictory rather than coherent. They were more difficult to categorize but were more likely closer to the actual presentation of battered women. Another strength of this study was that it included women who had not achieved nonviolence at the end of the time period, whereas most of the other qualitative studies were limited to women who were totally out of the violent relationship.

As has been noted in other studies, dealing with abuse is a complex process, and achieving nonviolence is neither strictly linear nor necessarily progressive in all instances. The majority of the women in this study had indeed either left the abusive relationship, almost a third were in the process of leaving the abusive relationship, and 3 women were still in the relationship after almost 4 years and were not being abused. To be considered nonabused, women had to have been free of all forms of coercive control (physical, sexual, psychological, and emo-tional) for at least 1 year. The trajectory of achieving nonviolence for the women was also true of the entire sample according to quantitative analysis (Campbell & Soekin, in press) as well as in an earlier investigation of a different sample by the same investigator (Campbell et al., 1994) and others (Feld & Straus, 1989; Okun, 1986). However, this study has demonstrated that categories of relation-ship status should not be combined or confused with violence status categories. One of the most important implications for research is that dichotomous mea-sures of being in or out of the relationship or being violence free or still abused do not adequately capture the complexity of relationship status and violence presence, absence, and severity demonstrated in this study.

It was striking that severity of abuse did not always influence women's decisions about leaving until it reached an extreme level. At these times, a critical event was an important turning point and impetus to leave. There were also very different thresholds for abuse, different definitions of severity, different perceptions of what made the abuse intolerable, and what made the relationship intolerable. Abuse was clearly part of the picture but clearly not the only factor and often not the most important.

We need to continue our safety planning with women during and after the actual leaving and to be clear that leaving is not a static event. Relationships involve emotional commitment, sexual intimacy, legal processes, and financial arrangements that may be more important than, and independent from, actual living arrangements and legal marital status. Our safety planning may occur at one point in time, but women need to know that it is an ongoing process for them. It is also important to realize that it indeed is possible for relationships to become violence free (and noncontrolling) as well as for the violence to decrease to a point that women consider tolerable. This is not to say that women should remain in abusive relationships, but that we need to offer women creative interventions that help them to monitor their ongoing physical safety and emotional safety, as they negotiate their own individual process toward freedom from violence (e.g., Sullivan, Campbell, Angelique, Eby, & Davidson, 1994). We need to help them understand that there are no easy answers or pathways and that individual stories are unique. Relationships can become nonabusive, and the majority of women do find freedom from violence and control from intimate partners by leaving the relationship. However, it often takes time after the relationship is over for the violence to end and for the emotional connection to disseminate.

Theoretical implications. This study explicates further the stage of the process of entrapment and recovery that Landenburger (1989) identified as "disengagement," because all the women in this study recognized that there were "serious problems" in the relationship. It is also similar to Merritt-Gray and Wuest's (1995) well-described first phase of the process of "breaking free." Their description of women minimizing abuse and fortifying their defenses was echoed by the women in this study as they talked about being "only" psychologically abused (in spite of reporting physical violence against them) and "making do" in the relationship. However, this sample was not recruited on the basis of a self-ascribed label of abused or battered woman, and the majority of the women did not identify violence as the major problem of the relationship. Therefore, they may have been less severely abused than women in the other samples.

We found clear support for "agency" in Lempert's (1996) terminology, whereby women used conscious decision making to take action, not only active behaviors (e.g., calling the police) but other actions that would be defined as passive (e.g., subordinating the self) in most theoretical schemas. In the face of potential danger to both herself and her children, such decisions were clearly intelligent, courageous, and healthy, rather than passive. Our analysis was that the passive approaches were driven by an intricate interplay of external circumstances as well as an interior style of coping, attributional style, or mental status (explored during the interview). The most salient issues were related to how she labeled and conceptualized the violent behavior, an awareness of the possibility of death, her level of violence, her degree of commitment to and hope for the relationship, concerns about the children, financial issues, and mostly what seemed to be helping the most in improving the relationship and minimizing the abuse. This is important clinically and theoretically, especially for professionals who have not worked with battered women extensively or are accustomed to thinking of them as having unhealthy coping styles. At the same time, we theorize that the subordinating strategy, although entered into purposively, may over time result in the disappearance of the self, noted by Mills (1985), Landenburger (1989), and Jack (1991), and contribute to depression (Campbell, Kub, Belknap, and Templin, 1997).

Abuse or battering labeling. The majority of these women labeled themselves as primarily psychologically or emotionally abused at the beginning of the study but not battered, in spite of the violence and controlling behavior. It may be that the majority of the women were in the disengagement phase according to Landenburger's (1989, 1993) conceptualization because it is in the earlier "entrapment" stage that women generally do not think of themselves as abused. A few women actively resisted such labels, apparently finding them shameful or not conveying the resistance that they saw in themselves. This may reflect increased public awareness of domestic violence (Klein, Soler, & Campbell, 1997). The clinical implication seems to be that labels of "battered" or "abused" should not be applied unless the women come to this label themselves. However, helping women label the partner's behavior as abusive can be important, as it may help women explore how to make decisions about what and who needs to change.

Ethnicity. The majority of the women in the sample were African American. The data of the 7 White women were examined to determine if their stories were different from the African American women. No clear differences emerged. We heard occasional references from the African American women to race and racism, in terms of police response and a concern about society's destruction of Black men, but these were not themes that predominated. In this study, we conclude, as others have, that there were more similarities than differences between abused women of different ethnic backgrounds (Moss, Pitula, Halstead, & Campbell, 1997; O'Keefe, 1994; Sorenson, 1996). At the same time, we recognize the multiple oppression faced by women of color who are also in abusive relationships (Richie, 1996).

SUMMARY

The generalizability of the findings is limited by the small sample size, the high rate of attrition, and the self-selected nature of the study. Nevertheless, when considered in conjunction with other studies, they show that women's responses to abusive relationships are never static or unidimensional. Ending the relationship does not necessarily end the violence, nor does the relationship have to end for the abuse to stop. They were engaged in an ongoing process of considering options, making choices, and dealing with daily-life issues. They described active—and effective—strategies of dealing with problems in ways that might be viewed as passivity or denial of the severity of their situation. They were aware that the relationship had to change, but they also made decisions about when and to what extent those changes would occur. Self-talk, decisions to subordinate and negotiate, were essential to many women in staying safe as they moved through the process of achieving nonviolence. Recognizing the importance of these responses in the process will provide women with support, advocacy, and partnership in realizing the goal.

REFERENCES

Bachman, R., & Saltzman, L. E. (1995). *Violence against women: Estimates from the redesigned survey*. Washington, DC: U.S. Department of Justice.

Bunting, S., & Campbell, J. C. (1994). Through a feminist lens: A model to guide nursing research. In P. Chinn (Ed.), *Advances in methods of inquiry for nursing* (pp. 75–87). Gaithersburg, MD: Aspen.

Campbell, J. C. (1989). Women's responses to sexual abuse in intimate relationships. *Women's Health Care International, 8*, 335–347.

Campbell, J. C. (1995). *Assessing dangerousness: Violence by sexual offenders, batterers, and child abusers*. Newbury Park, CA: Sage.

Campbell, J. C., & Humphreys, J. H. (1993). *Nursing care of survivors of family violence*. St. Louis: Mosby.

Campbell, J. C., Kub, J., Belknap, R. A., & Templin, T. (1997). Predictors of depression in battered women. *Violence Against Women, 3*(3), 271–293.

Campbell, J., Miller, P., Cardwell, M., & Belknap, R. A. (1994). Relationship status of battered women over time. *Journal of Family Violence, 9*, 99–111.

Campbell, J., & Soekin, K. (in press). Women's responses to battering: A test of a model. *Research in Nursing and Health*.

Eby, K., Campbell, J. C., Sullivan, C., & Davidson, W. (1995). Health effects of experiences of sexual violence for women with abusive partners. *Women's Health Care International, 16*, 563–576.

Fagan, J., & Browne, A. (1994). Violence between spouses and intimates: Physical aggression between women and men in intimate relationships. In Albert J. Reiss & Jeffrey A. Roth (Eds.), *Understanding and preventing violence Vol. 3: Social influences* (pp. 115–292). Washington, DC: National Academy Press.

Feld, S. L., & Straus, M. A. (1989). Escalation and desistance of wife assault in marriage. *Criminology, 27*(1), 141–161.

Gondolf, W., Fisher, E., & McFerron, R. (1988). Racial difference among shelter residents. *Journal of Family Violence, 3*, 39–51.

Henderson, D. J. (1995). Consciousness raising in participatory research: Method and methodology for emancipatory nursing inquiry. *Advances in Nursing Science, 17*, 58–69.

Hoff, L. A. (1990). *Battered women as survivors*. London: Routledge.

Hudson, W. W., & McIntosh, S. R. (1981). The assessment of spouse abuse: Two quantifiable dimensions. *Journal of Marriage and the Family, 43*, 873–885.

Jack, D. C. (1991). *Silencing the self*. Cambridge, MA: Harvard University Press.

Jacobson, N. S., Gottman, J. M., Gorner, E., Berns, S., & Wu Shortt, J. (1996). Psychological factors in the longitudinal course of battering: When do the couples split up? When does the abuse decrease? *Violence and Victims, 11*, 371–392.

Klein, E., Soler, E., & Campbell, J. (1997). *Ending domestic violence: Changing public perception about domestic violence.* Newbury Park, CA: Sage.

Kurz, D. (1996). Separation, divorce and woman abuse. *Violence Against Women,* 2(1),63–81.

Landenburger, K. (1989). A process of entrapment in and recovery from an abusive relationship. *Issues in Mental Health Nursing,* 3, 209–227.

Landenburger, K. (1993). Exploration of women's identity: Clinical approaches with abused women. In J. Campbell (Ed.), *Empowering survivors of abuse: Health care, battered women and their children.* Philadelphia, PA: Lippincott.

Lather, P. (1991). *Getting smart: Feminist research and pedagogy with/in the postmodern.* New York: Routledge.

Lempert, L. B. (1996). Women's strategies for survival: Developing agency in abusive relationships. *Journal of Family Violence,* 11, 269–290.

McCauley, J., Kern, D., Kolodner, K., Dill, L., Schroeder, A., DeChant, H., Ryden, J., Bass, E., & Derogotis, L. R. (1996). The "Battering Syndrome": Prevalence and clinical symptoms of domestic violence in primary care internal medicine practices. *Annals of internal Medicine,* 123, 737–746.

Merritt-Gray, M., & Wuest, J. (1995). Counteracting abuse and breaking free: The process of leaving revealed through women's voices. *Health Care for Women International,* 16, 399–412.

Miles, M. B., & Huberman, A. M. (1994). *Qualitative data analysis.* Thousand Oaks, CA: Sage.

Mills, T. (1985). The assault on the self: Stages in coping with battering husbands. *Qualitative Sociology,* 8, 103–123.

Moss, V. A., Pitula, C., Halstead, L. K., & Campbell, J. (1997). The experience of terminating an abusive relationship from an Anglo and African-American perspective. *Issues in Mental Health Nursing,* 18(5), 433–454.

O'Keefe, M. (1994). Racial/ethnic differences among battered women and their children. *Journal of Child and Family Studies,* 3(3), 282–305.

Okun, L. E. (1986). *Woman abuse: Facts replacing myths.* Albany, NY: SUNY Press.

Pence, E., & Paymer, M. (1993). *Education groups for men who batter.* New York: Springer.

Plichta, S. B. (1996). Violence and abuse: Implications for women's health. In M. M. Falik & K. S. Collins (Eds.), *Women's health: The commonwealth fund survey.* Baltimore: Johns Hopkins University Press.

Ratner, P. A. (1993). The incidence of wife abuse and mental health status in abused wives in Edmonton, Alberta. *Canadian Journal of Public Health,* 84(4), 246–249.

Reinharz, S. (1992). *Feminist methods in social research.* New York: Oxford University Press.

Richie, B. (1996). *Compelled to crime.* New York: Routledge.

Russell, D. (1982). *Rape in marriage.* New York: MacMillan.

Schechter, S., & Jones, A. (1992). *When love goes wrong.* New York: HarperCollins.

Small, S. (1995). Action-oriented research: Models and methods. *Journal of Marriage and the Family,* 57, 941–955.

Sorenson, S. (1996). Violence against women, examining ethnic differences and commonalities. *Evaluation Review,* 2(2), 123–145.

Straus, M. A., & Gelles, R. J. (Eds.). (1990). *Physical violence in American families: Risk factors and adaptations to family violence in 8,145 families.* New Brunswick, NJ: Transaction.

Sullivan, C., Campbell, R., Angelique, H., Eby, K., & Davidson, W. (1994). An advocacy intervention program with abusive partners: Six-month follow-up. *American Journal of Community Psychology,* 22, 101–122.

Wilson, M., Johnson, H., & Daly, M. (1995). Lethal and non-lethal violence against wives. *Canadian Journal of Criminology,* 37, 331–362.

CHAPTER FOUR

LEGAL ASPECTS OF BATTERING

Like theoretical explanations, the law provides insight into the social construction of battering. There often is disagreement about whether the law can be used to mandate social change and whether legislation can fundamentally alter a patriarchal institution like the criminal justice system. If the law is a tool of the oppressors (one which is used to maintain patriarchy) how useful can it be in attempts to reform the system? Furthermore, there is always the risk of unintended consequences. The path is not always clear, and simplistic responses can actually increase the risk for individual battered women. Too little research and too little data make it difficult to determine the efficacy of many reforms, and hegemonic assumptions often frame the debate in ways that fail to concentrate on the safety of battered women.

This chapter explores several legal aspects of battering. It reviews major changes in state legislation and highlights the importance of reforming laws on misdemeanor assault to facilitate arrest. It examines the ways in which state laws have moved from prohibiting arrest in misdemeanor assaults toward encouraging and even mandating arrest in domestic violence cases and the controversy surrounding arrest practices. It also reviews recent federal reforms and examines their impact. It discusses the advantages and disadvantages of these legislative reforms and examines the debates endemic to them.

STATE LEGISLATIVE REFORM

As noted previously, legislation historically failed to make assaulting one's wife a crime. In the past two or three decades, state legislators have taken several actions to address this legacy. First, they have written specific domestic violence statutes. While batterers may be prosecuted for a wide variety of offenses including homicide, assault and battery, and criminal trespass, many states have adopted laws that make domestic violence a separate and unique crime (as distinguished from a "regular" assault charge). As of 1997, twenty-five states have implemented this type of legislation, and several of these laws allow for enhanced penalties for repeat offenders (a second and third misdemeanor charge may result in a felony charge). Second, most states (49) have abolished the marital rape defense that prohibited women from filing rape charges against their husbands, although many conditions still apply (Miller, 1997). For example, in some states the rape must be reported within 30 days, and others require that the couple be living apart. Third, there have been major changes in legislation that allows officers to make arrests in misdemeanor assaults. This last change, arguably, has had the most dramatic effect on the day-to-day operations of the criminal justice system and will be discussed in some detail.

Changes in Misdemeanor Legislation

Criminal violations generally are divided into two classifications: misdemeanor and felony. Felonies are considered to be more serious crimes and usually carry the potential of a prison sentence of one year or longer. Misdemeanors are theoretically less serious violations. Generally, at most, one may be sentenced for up to a year in jail for these types of violations. Normally, police officers may arrest perpetrators who have apparently committed a felony if they have probable cause to believe that a crime occurred, regardless of whether or not they actually witnessed the crime. In contrast, statutes historically have required that police officers actually witness a misdemeanor offense in order to make an arrest. Officers were required to witness these crimes because, by definition, they were supposed to be minor crimes—crimes that placed an unnecessary burden on police resources. These laws, however, also effectively prohibited the prosecution of the vast majority of battering cases.

In theory, many battering cases rise to the level of a felony because they involve serious bodily injury or the threat of the same. In reality, most police and prosecutors rarely take such action and the overwhelming majority of battering cases are processed as misdemeanors (see Buzawa & Buzawa, 1996; Dobash & Dobash, 1979; Ferraro, 1989; Stanko, 1985). For example, data from the National Crime Victimization Survey indicate that one-third of the domestic violence cases would have been classified as felonies if they had been committed by strangers (i.e., they would have been identified as rape, robbery, or aggravated assault; Langan & Innes, 1986). Since batterers were rarely charged with felonies, most batterers were not held accountable for their actions under the old laws. Even the most "out of control" batterer generally had the good sense not to beat the victim in the presence of the police. Since police rarely witnessed the violation, most batterers were never arrested, prosecuted, or convicted. The only action available to police officers was to advise victims to go to the courthouse, perhaps days later if the beating took place on a Friday night, and apply for a warrant.[1]

Some of the early reform efforts focused on changing these laws. By 1983, 28 states had legislation that allowed the police to make warrantless arrests in cases of domestic violence where officers had probable cause to believe that batterers had committed misdemeanor assaults, regardless of whether or not they witnessed the assault (Lerman and Livingston, 1983). By 1997, all states had made this change (Miller, 1997). In fact, some state legislators have gone beyond simply *allowing* police officers to arrest in these cases; some states are *requiring* arrest.

Mandatory Arrest Laws

Some states have simply revised laws to allow for arrest; others have declared arrest as a preferred response (sometimes referred to as pro-arrest laws); and still others require arrest (sometimes referred to as mandatory arrest laws). In the face of continuing evidence of inadequate policing practices and because of pressure by some domestic violence advocates, several states have moved toward requiring arrest in misdemeanor battering cases as a way to eliminate—or more precisely—control police discretion. As of 1992, fifteen states mandated arrest in cases of misdemeanor battering (Zorza, 1996). By 1997, nineteen states mandated arrest and seven more states had preferred arrest legislation (Miller, 1997). It is important to remember that no law allows for or mandates arrest without probable cause. Translated, mandatory arrest laws do not mean that officers must arrest every time they respond to a domestic violence call. They are, however, required to do so when there is reason to believe that an assault took place.

There are a variety of controversies that have influenced legislation and police policy regarding arrest. At the heart of the debate, many experts question whether arrest does any good, especially in misdemeanor cases. Does it prevent battering and does it protect battered women? As the accompanying article by Lerman suggests, the answer lies in the different underlying assumptions one has about the nature of policing and the context of battering. In general, it seems that there is little controversy when the assault is a felony. However, failing to provide sufficient attention to the issue of felonious assaults allows us to ignore the fact that many a misdemeanor case should be tried at the felony level. Society, though, has not engaged in this debate. Instead, the overwhelming majority of the discussions examine the utility and effectiveness of arrest as it applies to misdemeanor assault.

One of the reasons that the debate has remained narrowly focused on the efficacy of arrest is the Minneapolis Police Foundation Study. Well publicized, this study argued that arrest *alone* deterred battering. This finding has had an inordinate effect in framing the dialogue about reforms to facilitate arrest at the misdemeanor level, although interestingly enough the original study "arose not out of express concern for victims of domestic violence" but rather from a more general publication and study on deterrence theory (Buzawa & Buzawa, 1996, p.107).

In 1981 a study was conducted in Minneapolis by Sherman and Berk (1984) to determine what effect arrest had upon batterers. Police officers randomly performed one of three different responses when they responded to misdemeanor domestic assaults. They were to (a) arrest the batterer, (b) require the batterer to leave the premises for 24 hours, or (c) restore order by talking to the parties involved (mediation) depending on the color code of the incident report. The conclusion was that batterers who were arrested were less likely to commit additional acts of violence. Official police reports demonstrated that 19% of those advised, 24% of those ordered to leave for eight hours, and 10% of those arrested committed a subsequent criminal act against the victim in the six months following intervention. Interviews with victims demonstrated similar findings; 37% of those advised, 33% of those ordered to leave for eight hours, and 19% of those arrested committed another battering within six months.

There were many problems with the Minneapolis study (Binder & Meeker, 1988; Elliot, 1989; Fagan, 1989; Lempert, 1989; Miller, 1993). One of the most serious was that three officers accounted for 28% of the cases in the study (Sherman & Berk, 1984). Gartin (1995) contends that a large percentage of the officers in the study ignored research protocols to apply the dictated outcome based on random assignment. He re-analyzed the original data, using only those cases where officers appear to have conformed to the experimental protocol and found no significant differences in the three treatments. In other words, he reports that arrest did not deter future battering.

Despite the many shortcomings of the study and contrary to "normal scientific practice," findings from one study were heralded in the criminological literature and in the popular press as "gospel." Pursuant to this study, many states revised their laws pertaining to arrest in misdemeanor assaults, and police departments nationwide altered their policies to facilitate arrest (Sherman & Cohn, 1989). One of the authors (Sherman) of the study has been publicly criticized for appearing on many popular television shows and overgeneralizing the findings (Lempert, 1989). While it is easy to attribute blame here, the authors of the study were not the only people who were "prematurely and unduly" (Lempert, 1989, p. 145) publicizing the findings. Many feminists and domestic violence advocates proclaimed the study as a breakthrough. They had been arguing, begging, and pleading for police departments to make arrests for over a decade and finally could point to "scientific proof" to argue that arrest was the most effective response to battering. It is, however, dangerous to glorify science. As illustrated in the Lerman article, this same body of research would ultimately be used to argue against arrest in misdemeanor battering cases in the subsequent studies that sought to replicate this finding.

Five replication studies were funded by the National Institute of Justice to test the generalizability of the Minneapolis experiment. Research conducted in Omaha, Nebraska (Dunford, Huizinga, & Elliott, 1990); Colorado Springs, Colorado (Berk et al., 1992); Dade County (Miami), Florida (Pate & Hamilton, 1992); Milwaukee, Wisconsin (Sherman, Smith et al., 1992; Sherman, Schmidt et al., 1992); and Charlotte, North Carolina (Hirschel et al., 1991) have not provided support for the Minneapolis findings. While the Lerman article discusses these findings in more detail, it appears safe to conclude that none of the replication studies finds that arrest deters battering.

Despite many significant weaknesses in the replication studies (Zorza, 1994), there has been a tendency to cite the replication studies as evidence that society should move away from arrest as a response to battering in misdemeanor cases (Buzawa & Buzawa, 1993; Hirschel et al., 1992). As Lerman notes, this approach fails to take several things into account, including the context of the arrest and the behavior of police officers at the scene. The tendency for scholars to move away from arrest is problematic for several reasons (Berk, 1993; Stark, 1996; Zorza, 1994).

First, this literature fails to note that about half of all batterers are no longer at the scene by the time the police arrive (Dunford, 1990; Feder, 1996; Ferraro & Pope, 1993; Sherman, Schmidt et al., 1992), thus half of the study population is missing from the sample. One notable exception exists. In the Omaha replication study (Dunford, 1990), officers were instructed to issue a warrant in cases where the suspect was no longer at the scene when the police arrived. Batterers arrested in this manner were significantly less likely to re-offend in the following 12 months; thus, arrest in these cases apparently had a deterrent effect. In a similar vein, Feder (1996) compared offenders who were on the scene to those who had left by the time the police arrived to look for distinguishing characteristics. Offenders who had left the scene were similar to those who had absconded with one exception— those who had left the scene were less apt to be married to their intimate victims. Thus, offenders who leave the scene of the crime greatly reduce the risk of arrest since few jurisdictions bother to issue a warrant when the perpetrator is absent, even though the vast majority of them can be located easily through the assistance of victims. If we are to move away from arrest as a preferred response based on social science, it seems that we ought to at least determine what affect this "missing" population has upon our understanding of arrest as a deterrent.

Second, the replication studies found non-significant differences between arrest and other police responses. Translated, the other options such as mediation and ordering the batterer to leave the home worked no better *or no worse* than arrest in deterring future violence. If the studies had found that mediation, for example, worked better than arrest then it would be more difficult to assert that one should continue to pursue arrest policies that made matters worse than taking some other action. However, this was not the case in the replication studies. Since arrest worked as well as other alternatives, it is unfounded to contend that we should abandon pro-arrest legislation and policies.

Third, just because arrest fails to deter is, in and of itself, insufficient grounds to move away from arrest. There is little evidence that drug use, for example, is deterred by arrest (Lyman & Potter, 1996) and yet we have not hesitated to employ a law enforcement response. No other crime requires a demonstration that arrest, in and of itself, deters future criminality in order to justify a response by the criminal justice system.

Fourth, research suggests that police officers typically fail to arrest batterers (Bachman & Coker, 1995; Belknap, 1995; Brown, 1984; Erez, 1986; Gondolf & Fisher, 1988; Worden & Politz, 1984; Zorza, 1994) and fail to comply with pro-arrest policies (Balos & Trotzky, 1988; Bourg & Stock, 1994; Ferraro, 1989;

Lawrenz, Lembo, & Schade, 1988; Websdale, 1995; Websdale & Johnson, 1997). If arrest were used more consistently by officers, the results might be more positive. In other words, pro-active arrest practice is a good idea that hasn't been tried in most jurisdictions, making it premature to call for a return to mediation and crisis intervention (see Eigenberg, Scarborough, & Kappeler, 1996).

Fifth, research on the deterrent power of arrest places too heavy a burden on this phase of the process. As Lerman notes, if the rest of the system does not respond—does not prosecute and convict—batterers may come to see arrest more as an inconvenience than as punishment.

Sixth, there may be more than one way to measure the effectiveness of an arrest. For example, some studies find that pro-arrest policies reduced domestic homicides (Jolin, 1983). Arresting batterers may prevent homicides because some victims escape death when the police interrupt the battering. In addition, it is possible that the subsequent assaults were less violent or that there were longer periods of time between incidents (Martin, 1997). The exclusive concentration on arrest as a deterrent ignores the context of the victim's level of satisfaction or her definition of "success" (Martin, 1997).

Seventh, batterers should be arrested to safeguard police officers and their departments from legal liability. Just as some state legislatures have passed bills requiring arrest in cases of battering where probable cause can be established, police departments also have moved toward pro and mandatory arrest policies, in part, to protect themselves from legal liability. A police chief can go beyond state law and implement a mandatory arrest policy even if state law only requires a pro arrest response. In other words, a chief can go further than the law when establishing policy as long as s/he does not contradict state law. In fact, chiefs may have good reason for doing so; it may help limit the agency's exposure to legal liability. This will be discussed in more detail in the next section.

Finally, batterers should be arrested because doing so reflects the moral values and principles of our society and conveys the message that battering is criminal behavior that is socially unacceptable. Even if arrest (and conviction for that matter) fails to deter future battering, arguments against arrest reinforce the attitude that battering is not a crime—that it is somehow acceptable or at least tolerable. The very fact that one of the central debates in this battle for hegemonic control focuses on whether arrest serves a deterrent effect, again, leads us away from other issues more directly relevant—such as whether arrest helps protect battered women and increases their safety. The pollution clouds the air and most of us do not examine the ways that this type of social construction allows us to lose sight of the danger that non-arrest policies have posed to women in the past.

Arrest, however, is not a panacea. As with any legislation, there are often unintended consequences. For one thing, there have been problems associated with mutual arrest (see Buzawa & Buzawa, 1996). Police officers who are poorly trained or hostile to implementing pro-arrest policies may decide to simply arrest both parties. Instead of bothering to figure out who is the aggressor and who is the victim, some officers simply arrest both parties leaving it to the courts to "sort it all out." Ignoring the context of the violence, officers may arrest victims whose only crime was to inflict minor injuries in self-defense. In addition, there is some evidence that African-American women are especially vulnerable when it comes to dual arrest. Not only are they arrested more frequently than white women, but they tend to be charged with felony battery (Bourg & Stock, 1994).

In addition, there is evidence that these policies are implemented unfairly. Men of color and poor men are more likely to have the policy used against them, while wealthier white men are more likely to avoid arrest (Miller, 1989, 1993). Such disparate treatment may actually inhibit poor women and women of color from calling the police for assistance. Poor women who will not see a paycheck from jailed batterers may refuse to call for help. Likewise, women of color may refuse to call the police, fearing that these laws will provide the police with yet another means to oppress men of color rather than offering any real protection to battered women (Rasche, 1988).

Third, victims may be disempowered by polices that require arrest and refuse to call the police (Buzawa, 1982). For example, a battered woman may be right when she tells the police officer that arrest will make things worse. She may know that batterers are not detained, prosecuted, or convicted in her jurisdiction; therefore, her risk increases, not decreases, if he is arrested. In some cases, mandatory arrest laws or policies contribute to an increased exposure to violence.

We need to work to ensure that laws are enforced equitably so that victims are not arrested and so that poor men and men of color are not arrested more frequently than wealthy, white men. We also need to make certain that other aspects of the criminal justice system are responding to battering. As Lerman notes, mandatory arrests will be useless if prosecutors fail to prosecute and if judges fail to sentence. Arrest alone cannot compensate for an ineffective system.

Protective Orders

Similar to legislation on arrest, legislation on protective orders has experienced considerable reform in the past few decades (Finn & Colson, 1990; Grau, Fagan, & Wexler, 1984). Protective orders have different names in different states and sometimes are referred to as restraining orders, emergency orders, domestic violence orders, or peace bonds. Victims seeking a protective order usually go through a two-step process. In the first stage victims can secure a temporary order (sometimes called an *ex parte* order) that usually is good for only a short time and often relies only on the petitioner (or victim's) testimony (Fischer & Rose, 1995). The victim makes out a statement and is guaranteed some limited protection until the batterer is served with the order. In the second phase, the batterer is notified of a court hearing and has due process rights to present evidence. If the order is granted, judges have more discretion in remedies, and stronger sanctions are available for violators.

Historically, protective orders were issued in civil court and carried only civil sanctions (Finn & Colson, 1990); therefore, the police were not allowed to enforce them. Victims had to go to court and report any violations to the judge, who could then impose sanctions, usually limited to relatively small fines. Protective orders were not very helpful in improving the safety of battered women. To the contrary, some battered women suffered when the court imposed fines and an already thin family budget was reduced or the fine did little to deter the batterer from committing additional acts of violence.

In the 1980s, however, legislators began to alter laws to authorize arrest by the police and to impose criminal penalties for the violation of protective orders (Finn & Colson, 1990). By 1997, 49 states allowed for the warrantless arrest of perpetrators who violated protective orders (Miller, 1997). States also began to grant judges more discretion to tailor remedies to assist victims (Finn & Colson, 1990). While orders historically only prohibited contact and/or further violence, new legislation began to offer a broader scope of assistance.

A comprehensive national study of protective orders (Finn & Colson, 1990) conducted on 1988 legislation found that 48 states and the District of Columbia authorized civil protection orders. In all of these jurisdictions, spouses were allowed to file for protection, and most states allowed victims to file if they were former spouses (45), cohabiting couples (38), former cohabitators (35), or other family members (41). States were less likely to ensure that couples with a child in common received protection (29 states doing so). All states with statutes allowed for orders if there was physical abuse, and most did so even if there were "only" threats or attempted abuse. Most states did not technically require the victim to have experienced abuse. The majority of the states also had moved toward increased use of criminal sanctions. Violation of protective orders amounted to civil contempt in 31 states and could result in criminal contempt or a misdemeanor charge in 39 states (some states allow either criminal or civil penalties). This trend has continued; in 1997, 41 states made violation of a protective order a separate criminal offense (Miller, 1997). In three states, a violation constitutes a felony, and six more states allow for felony charges for repeat violations (Miller, 1997). Furthermore, in 1992, legislators in 19 states had passed mandatory arrest laws pertaining to the violation of protective orders (Zorza, 1996, p. 524). By 1997, 28 states required arrest, and two made arrest a preferred response in response to violation of orders (Miller, 1997). Thus, just as there has been an increased movement toward requiring police officers to arrest in cases of misdemeanor assault, reforms also have concentrated on requiring police officers to make arrests when protective orders are violated.

Protective orders are an important tool to protect battered women, although one study (Fernandez, Iwamoto, & Muscat, 1997) suggests that women who may need them most may be the least apt to obtain them. This study found that the more dependent the woman was on the abuser and the more severe the abuse, the least likely she was to follow through to secure an order. Nonetheless, at the most basic level, orders are useful because they prohibit the batterer from having contact with the victim. Batterers who are harassing their victims may be arrested for behavior that traditionally the police were powerless to prevent. As a result, in most states, batterers may be arrested, convicted, and sentenced to jail (or even prison) for simply showing up at the victim's house even if they have not committed a new assault. In other words, police officers no longer have to inform battered women that they can do nothing until he commits a new crime—until he beats her up again. In addition, many states offer a wide variety of relief that would greatly assist battered women if judges were willing to grant it. For example, many statutes allow judges to order eviction of the residence (47), prohibit batterers from going to the victim's residence (38), provide for temporary custody of any children (39), provide for temporary child support (27 states) or spousal support payments (29 states), and order disposition of property (16 states; Finn & Colson, 1990).[2] Unfortunately, judges appear to be reluctant to use sanctions that include ordering financial support, allocating property, or providing temporary child custody arrangements (Gondolf et al., 1994). Thus, while judges appear to be willing to provide orders that address physical battering, they seem less willing to take measures that would involve altering the family structure or diminishing the power of the abuser as "head of the family."

Protective orders apparently deter some batterers (Chaudhuri & Daly, 1992; Horton, Horton & Simonidis, 1987) and may increase successful prosecutions of batterers (Weisz, Tolman, & Bennett, 1998); however, they are not a panacea (Adhikari, Reinhard, & Johnson, 1993; Klein, 1996). For example, one study reports that 60% of the battered women in the sample reported that their batterers violated protective orders (Harrell, Smith, & Newmark, 1993). Other evidence suggests that judges in many states issue mutual orders even though only one party petitioned (see Hemmens, Strom, & Schlegel, 1998), thereby subjecting victims to the purview of the criminal justice system. Orders appear to be less useful when there is an extensive history of serious violence (Chaudhuri & Daly, 1992; Harrell & Smith, 1996; Keilitz et. al., 1998), and many victims experience difficulties in getting protective orders enforced (Fagan, 1996; Ferraro & Pope, 1993; Finn & Colson, 1990; Harrell & Smith, 1996; Hart, 1999; Hemmens, Strom, & Schlegel, 1998; Lerman, 1980), especially poor women and women of color (Kinports & Fischer, 1993). However, some research suggests that battered women pursue protective orders, in part, because it returns some sense of power and control to their lives (Caringella-MacDonald, 1988; Fischer & Rose, 1995; Keilitz et. al., 1998). As such, it may play an important step in the process of leaving and may offer women one of many tools they will need to accomplish that goal.

Stalking

Another new type of legislative reform that also may facilitate arrests of batterers pertains to stalking. California became the first state to pass stalking legislation in 1990 and by 1997 all states had stalking statutes; 21 of these treat stalking as a felony and a second or third offense can result in felony charges in the remaining 29 states (Miller, 1997). Also, by 1997, 21 states authorized protective orders for stalking victims, regardless of whether there was any domestic violence (Miller, 1997). In addition, in 1996 it became a federal crime for perpetrators to cross state lines to stalk someone (Interstate Stalking Punishment and Prevention Act). While the impetus for creating these new laws apparently came about as a result of public attention to famous cases involving celebrity victims (Kappeler, Blumberg, & Potter, 2000), the legislation has the potential to offer another vehicle to address domestic violence.

The National Violence Against Women Survey (discussed in chapter 2) offers the first national data on stalking that indicate it is highly related to domestic violence. The definition used in the survey closely resembles that of the federal antistalking model code. Stalking is "a course of conduct directed at a specific person that involves repeated visual or physical proximity, nonconsensual communication, or verbal, written or implied threats, or a combination thereof, that would cause a reasonable person fear," with repeated meaning on two or more occasions (Tjaden & Thoennes, 1998, p. 2). Stalkers do not have to make a credible threat against victims, who must report feeling a high level of fear. The study finds that eight percent of American women and two percent of men have experienced stalking sometime in their lives (p. 2). Seventy-eight percent of stalking victims are women and 94% of their stalkers were men (p. 5). About three-fourths (77%) of the women knew their stalkers (p. 5) and the majority of the perpetrators (59%) were intimate partners (current or former husbands, cohabitating partners, or dates/boyfriends, p. 6). Victims are most apt to report they were stalked because their perpetrator wanted to control them or to keep them in the relationship (p. 8). On average, the stalking lasts 18 months (p. 12). A little over one-fourth (28%) of the women sought a protective order, although 69% of these women reported that the order was violated (p. 11).

Some critics argue that these new stalking laws are overly broad and vague (Kappeler, Blumberg, & Potter, 2000) and contend that there already were laws on the books to deal with this type of criminal activity (e.g., trespass, vandalism, terroristic threatening, and harassment). They also contend that these laws give police extraordinary powers of arrest. It remains to be seen whether or not these statutes will withstand the inevitable constitutional challenges that will be made (Buzawa & Buzawa, 1996). In the meantime, it is important to establish the link between stalking and domestic violence, as the current data indicate that the vast majority of stalking victims are battered women. In fact, these victims appear to be at the most serious end of the continuum of abuse. At least one study (Coleman, 1997) reports that women who experienced more verbal and physical abuse during the relationship were more likely to experience stalking after the relationship ended. Thus, stalking laws may provide yet another way for battered women to seek protection under the law. In some instances these statutes may be preferable to traditional domestic violence legislation. For example, violation of a protective order prohibiting stalking is a criminal offense that generally carries greater penalties than violations of protective orders based on domestic violence alone (Miller, 1997).

Federal Legislative Reform

Until the Violence Against Women Act passed in 1994, no federal legislation directly addressed woman battering. This is particularly ironic since the federal government declared "war on crime" in the 1960s. President Johnson established the Law Enforcement Assistance Administration (LEAA) as part of the Omnibus Crime Control and Safe Streets Act of 1968. It was responsible for providing federal funding to the states to "fight crime," although it is clear that the definition of crime rarely has included woman battering.

LEAA

The creation and funding of LEAA marked the first time in the history of the United States that federal funds were allocated for state and local law enforcement (Feeley & Sarat, 1980). While LEAA was amended and modified several times, it provided billions of dollars in federal funding to state and local law enforcement efforts from 1968 to 1984. The level of LEAA funding varied over the years and was at its highest in the mid 1970s. By any standard, however, it was generous. For example, $100 million was allocated for 1969, $300 million for 1970, and $1.75 billion in 1973 (Feeley & Sarat, 1980, p. 47).

In general, much of this money was spent outfitting the police in hardware. Almost none of it—certainly nothing significant—was allocated to battered women's organizations. While it is difficult to track, it appears that programs for woman battering received their largest allocation in 1980. Even then, these programs received only about $3 million out of a discretionary budget of almost $30 million and a total agency appropriation of almost $500 million (Schechter, 1982, p. 186). Ironically, funding for battered women's programs under LEAA was peaking at the very time that LEAA as a whole was grinding to a halt. LEAA began to dissolve in the late 1970s during the Carter administration, and it was formally abolished during the first Reagan administration as part of the Crime Control Bill of 1984. That bill included other federal legislation that assisted victims of crime, including battered women.

The Victims of Crime Act (VOCA)

Even though VOCA legislation benefited battered women, the legislation did not develop out of a specific concern for women or violence against women per se. VOCA was developed by President Reagan's administration to address the concerns of a growing and more general victim's rights movement. VOCA established the Crime Victim's Fund, which collects fines, penalties, and forfeitures from federal offenders to finance grants for victim services (Parent, Auerbach, & Carlson, 1992). The federal government then allocated money to the states to provide services to victims of state and federal crimes. The fund is distributed almost equally between victim compensation funds and victim assistance programs (Office for Victims of Crime, [a]).

Victim compensation programs are required to reimburse victims for medical expenses, mental health counseling fees, wage losses due to injuries, and funeral expenses. Unfortunately, though, most programs do not provide victim compensation for victims of misdemeanor crimes (McGillis & Smith, 1983). Since most batterers are not charged at the felony level, many battered women are ineligible for any victim compensation benefits. In addition, victims usually are ineligible for compensation if they are related to or reside with the offender, or if they are engaging in a sexual relationship with the offender (McGillis & Smith, 1983). Thus, most battered women who remain with their batterers also are ineligible.

VOCA also allocates funds for victim assistance programs. Victim assistance programs are defined broadly as programs that provide services to victims of crime, but states initially were required to give funding priority to programs that provided services to victims of child abuse, spouse abuse, and sexual assault. States could accomplish this by (a) allocating 10% of their funds to each of the three categories, (b) conducting a needs assessment to determine the appropriate allocation of funds in these categories, or (c) require every agency receiving VOCA funds to include at least one category of priority victims (Finn & Lee, 1987). Public agencies and private organizations including non-profit organizations like shelters were eligible for funding if: they had a record of providing services to victims; a history of utilizing volunteer labor; promoted community responses; and assisted victims in securing victim compensation benefits (Finn & Lee, 1987). These funds also made it possible for many criminal justice agencies to hire victim coordinators. These agents often are located in law enforcement or prosecutor's offices, and they help victims understand and negotiate the criminal justice system. They keep victims notified of scheduling and progress on the case and can provide referral to other social services agencies. While most of these programs were not designed specifically to provide services to battered women, they are frequent clients; thus, VOCA was the first federal legislation to allocate funds for services to battered women.

VOCA has been modified several times over the past 15 years, but it continues to fund battered women's services and other organizations that serve battered women. While it is difficult to locate precise data to ascertain just how much money VOCA has spent to address battering specifically, it clearly has been important to victim services agencies nationwide. During the first ten years, VOCA generated more than $1 billion to support crime victimization programs. Today, it "provides substantial funding for approximately 2,300 victim assistance programs serving more than 2 million crime victims each year; state victim compensation programs that serve an additional 200,000 victims; and training and technical assistance on crime victims issues for thousands of diverse professionals across the country, including 70 federal law enforcement agency personnel" (Office for Victims of Crime, [b]).

The Violence Against Women Act (VAWA)

VAWA was passed as part of the 1994 Crime Bill and is the first federal legislation created specifically to address violence against women. It has three missions: to change public attitudes, to reform the criminal and civil justice systems, and to provide leadership working with states and communities to develop appropriate innovative solutions.

The Act is a direct product of Senate hearings held for several years and directed by Senator Joseph Biden to "respond both to the underlying attitude that this violence is somehow less serious than other crime and to the resulting failure of our criminal justice system to address such violence" (Staff of Senate Committee on the Judiciary, cited in Klein, 1995, p. 254). VAWA is organized into five broad areas.

Title I, Safe Streets for Women, increases sentences for repeat offenders who commit various kinds of sexual abuse. It requires restitution for victims of sex offenders and requires states to pay for rape exams. Title II, Safe Homes for Women, creates federal penalties for spouse abusers who cross state lines to continue their abuse. It requires states to enforce protective orders issued in other jurisdictions including other states. It authorizes funding for programs that promote arrest and prosecution for battering, increases shelter funding, and establishes a national hotline. Title III, Civil Rights for Women, creates the first civil rights remedy for violent, gender-based discrimination. It makes gender-based crimes a violation of federal civil rights laws and allows victims to bring civil suits against their assailants. Title IV, Safe Campuses, grants funds to create rape prevention programs on college campuses. Title V provides training for state and federal judges on gender bias in the courts—programs to sensitize judges about crimes against women.

VAWA, as signed in 1994 theoretically committed 1.6 billion dollars to combat all types of violence against women; however, actual allocations have been much smaller. The Act had limited funding in 1995, which was to be used as a start up period. For example, the Violence Against Women Office was not created and staffed until Bonnie Campbell, former Iowa Attorney General, was appointed as its director in March of 1995 (Violence Against Women Office, 1996). Furthermore, fiscal year 1996 funds were delayed and tied up along with all other federal monies in the fight over the federal budget. Nonetheless, VAWA has provided unprecedented levels of funding for violence against women. Congress appropriated $26 million in fiscal year 1995, $166 million in 1996, and $193 in 1999 (Robinson, July 27, 1995); these funds are distributed over a wide number of programs that address the entire spectrum of violence against women. There are no specific figures for the amount devoted only to battering-related programs. VAWA clearly has brought additional assistance to battering victims by funding direct services, and it has increased public visibility of the issue.

FEDERAL LAWS THAT ADDRESS BATTERING

In addition to providing funding for services, VAWA and several other pieces of federal legislation have made some significant changes that affect enforcement efforts against battering.

Full Faith and Credit in Protective Orders

Historically, states have resisted enforcing protective orders across local jurisdictional lines. If a woman was assaulted in another county, law enforcement officials often lacked access to official records to verify the status of any protective order. Women who routinely crossed jurisdictional boundaries or who lived on state lines were particularly vulnerable. For example, women often work in another county or even another state; therefore, women risk having orders be relatively useless if they travel often outside of their home county or state.

Matters also are complicated if a woman moved to another state to put distance between herself and the batterer. She usually had to petition for a new order in the new location. Prior to VAWA, the court in the new state had no jurisdiction. The court would then notify the batterer of the petition, and the batterer had due process rights that required a new hearing. Notifying him of the petition for the new order then alerted him to her new location. Therefore, most battered women who relocated failed to file for a new order. When battered women were forced to choose between a valid enforceable order and the secrecy of their location, they most often chose secrecy and safety.

Numerous other difficulties were created when battered women were required to re-file for protective orders following a move. These factors, including "additional filing fees; language barriers; the difference in each state's domestic violence laws regarding availability, duration, and scope of protection; inadequate transportation; access to legal assistance; and child care facilities" (Klein, 1995, p. 255) placed a burden on battered women.

The full faith and credit provision of the 1994 VAWA was designed specifically to address these problems (18 U.S.C. Section 2265). VAWA requires states to honor orders issued by other states, tribes, or nations: both *ex parte* or temporary orders as well as permanent orders and to administer them *as if they were issued by the enforcing state*. Thus the current state of residence is required to enforce any existing protective order just as if it had originally issued the order and in accordance with state law in the new state of residence. The order is valid until the expiration date of the original order.

There are two exceptions to the rule. First, states are not required to enforce a protective order issued in another jurisdiction if the batterer's due process rights were violated in the original order. It is not clear how states will ensure that due process requirements have been met in another state or jurisdiction. Second, states are prohibited from providing full faith and credit to mutual protective orders unless both parties submitted a written request for the orders and unless the order was issued based upon a judicial finding of mutual violence that did not involve self-defense. In the past, some courts routinely entered mutual orders assuming that it was easier to order both parties to stay away from one another rather than sort out who was hitting whom and under what circumstances. VAWA prohibits the interstate enforcement of these types of orders and allows that full faith and credit be provided only if both parties were aggressors. Here again, the bill fails to determine how police officers on the street will identify that an order was a mutual order and to ascertain whether or not it meets the exception to the rule.

VAWA does not specify how jurisdictions must comply with this new provision and there is a great deal of diversity in responses. Thirty-four states have passed some type of full faith and credit enabling legislation (Zeya, 1998). Five states direct officers to enforce orders if they appear to be valid on their face, and three states allow police officers to rely solely on the statement of the protected party (Zeya, No Date, 1998). However, it also appears that some states are implementing the law in ways that overtly or covertly contradict either the spirit or the letter of the law. Eleven states (Arkansas, Colorado, Delaware, Iowa, Maryland, Missouri, Montana, Nevada, Oregon, Pennsylvania, and Rhode Island) require that victims file and/or register orders from outside the jurisdiction before they will be enforced (Zeya, No Date, 1998). Three states (Colorado, Louisiana, Missouri) send notice to the perpetrator when orders are filed or registered in their state (Zeya, 1998).

The federal government has created a computerized registry for protective orders; however, the database is only as good as the local or state registries used to create it (Hart, 1999). Many problems have already surfaced (Hart, 1999). The system does not include orders that do not include certain "vital" information such as social security number and date of birth. If this information is not on the local order, it does not mean the order is invalid—only that the system is an unreliable means of verifying orders. There also may be significant delays between issuing the order and getting it onto a state and/or local registry, which then can submit it to the federal registry. Furthermore, this reliance on computerized checks will surely lead to officers discounting paper copies of certified orders, which appears to be allowed under the law. States who are concerned about legal liability for police officers should enact legislation to provide immunity for officers who act in good faith; eight states, in fact, have done so (Websdale, 1998; Zeya, 1998). Clearly, it will take some time to get this verification system up and going and to work out any inevitable bugs to ensure that officers in all states have easy access to the information. Even then, it will not be foolproof. This type of legislation is unprecedented in the history of law enforcement, and it undoubtedly will take time for officers to adapt to these new procedures. To assist in this effort, the Violence Against Women Office in the U.S. Department of Justice has joined forces with the Pennsylvania Coalition Against Domestic Violence (PCADV, No Date) to form the Full Faith and Credit Project. The Project offers technical assistance including training and has developed materials such as an overview of law enforcement responsibilities, case scenarios that illustrate how the law should be enforced, model standardized forms, and a model state code. The International Association of Chiefs of Police (IACP) also has posted some excellent guidelines to its web page where officers may request a pocket guide designed to help officers enforce this provision (IACP, No Date)

Firearms Provision

In addition to making it easier to enforce protective orders, the 1994 Crime Bill prescribes some new consequences associated with having a valid protective order lodged against an individual.[3] The law prohibits the purchase and possession of firearms and/or ammunition by individuals who have a protective order issued against them, although the order must state that defendants pose a threat to the physical safety of the victim or that they are not allowed to use any force that would cause injury to the victim (18 U.S.C. Section 922). Law enforcement officers and military personnel are exempt from the law (18 U.S.C. Section 925). In addition, the person must have received notice of the order and must have had the opportunity to present his/her side prior to having the order issued. Thus, in most jurisdictions this provision excludes temporary or ex-parte orders.

The first case processed under this VAWA provision occurred when Robert Goben of South Dakota pled guilty to illegal possession of a firearm (Violence Against Women Office, 1996). A protective order was issued against him in October, 1994. Approximately 5 months later police found he possessed a loaded .22 caliber magnum revolver. He was sentenced to one year in prison to be followed by two years of supervised release during which he was prohibited from contacting his former wife.

Another more controversial law also limits firearms possession by batterers. An amendment to the Omnibus Consolidated Appropriations Act of 1997, sometimes referred to as the Lautenberg Act, modifies the Gun Control Act of 1968. This Act is discussed in detail in the Eigenberg and Kappeler reading. Briefly, it prohibits possession of firearms and/or ammunition by anyone who has been convicted of misdemeanor domestic violence. Furthermore, unlike the other firearms provision, this law does *not* exempt law enforcement or military personnel; therefore, these employees are no longer able to carry a weapon or possess ammunition, even while on duty or at work. Possession of firearms or ammunition when one has had a prior misdemeanor conviction is punishable by a fine of $250,000 and/or imprisonment of up to 10 years. While no existing data offer reliable estimates about the amount of battering committed by police officers, opponents of the law were quick to argue that large numbers of police officers would be affected and forced to resign—possibly even leading to shortages of police personnel. As Eigenberg and Kappeler make clear, there is no danger of this threat materializing. Only a handful of police officers nationwide appear to be affected by the law. Even then, most of them have been successful in having their convictions expunged so that they can keep their jobs. This task is apparently easier for officers residing in California, as the state has passed legislation that allows batterers to have their conviction expunged if they have had a clean record since their conviction and if they can afford the $100 fee (Mecka, 1998).

As the Eigenberg and Kappeler article notes, within one year of its passage, there were attempts to weaken the power of this legislation; however, these efforts have been unsuccessful (Pullen, 1998). The legislation also has been challenged in court as petitioners claim that the Act is unconstitutional because it violates the commerce clause and/or the equal protection clause, and because of its retroactive nature (Mecka, 1998). The Act, however, has withstood constitutional challenges in at least seven different federal jurisdictions (Pullen, 1998).

Despite resistance to the law by some police unions, the IACP have begun to address battering by police officers. They have joined forces with the Office of Community Oriented Policing Services (COPS) and the Violence Against Women Office to write a model police and concept paper on police officer

domestic violence (IACP, 1999a, 1999b). The policy addresses prevention, education, training, program evaluation, and responsibilities of departments, supervisors, and line officers. It also describes response protocols and actions to be
taken to ensure victim safety and protection, as well as post incident administrative and criminal case action. It clearly notes that officers who are found guilty of
domestic violence, either through administrative channels such as internal investigations or through criminal convictions, *must* have their police powers revoked.
Implementation of the Lautenberg Act and policies such as those proposed by
IACP will likely be problematic. It seems reasonable to assume that police officers rarely arrest each other, especially in misdemeanor cases. Nonetheless, it
seems promising that IACP is, at last, calling for police agencies to acknowledge
that sometimes "the batterer wears blue."

It is, however, possible that this firearms provision will have a more immediate impact upon the military, especially in cases of battering that occur off-base
where offenders may have little protection "from their own." A recent study
reports, for example, that "the living room war" is escalating in military families.
Between 1986 and 1993, cases of reported abuse have almost doubled, and the
Army estimates that abuse occurs "in 1 of 3 Army families each year—double the
civilian rate" (Thompson, 1994, p. 35). The study also found that battering is
more common at bases scheduled to shut down. The authors hypothesize that
levels of violence in the Army are probably evident in the other military branches.

Poor and limited data make it impossible to conclude that battering occurs
more frequently in the military; however, it would seem safe to assume that there
is a problem of significant magnitude if the Army itself is addressing the issue.[4]
Certainly several factors including frequent moves, extended absences, and down-
sizing all might contribute to battering. Too often these types of explanations
(social structural examinations that focus on stress) receive an inordinate amount
of visibility. Explanations that examine patriarchal social structures are ignored.
In other words, feminist theory would predict that men in the military are more
apt to abuse their partners because the military emphasizes hierarchal systems of
power, including patriarchy. Militarism and patriarchy go hand in hand as they
recreate and reproduce each other. In fact a recent Pentagon study on domestic
violence reports that "behaviors and attitudes supporting violence in general may
be learned or reinforced by military combat training" (Thompson, 1997, p. 46).

It will be some time before we will be able to ascertain the effect these firearms provisions have upon battering. Perhaps fewer battered women seeking
protection from their batterers will have to plead for help from cops who are
themselves batterers, although the research discussed in the Eigenberg and Kappeler reading suggests that we should not be overly optimistic in this respect. It
also is possible that an unintended consequence will occur in that some victims
may be unwilling to call the police, afraid that their batterers may lose their jobs.
While limiting gun access to those with protective orders also seems like a reasonable action, implementation may prove difficult. Because certain conditions
must be met for the order to qualify, police officers at the scene may not be able
to readily determine whether or not firearms violations have occurred. As a

result, judges should determine whether these conditions have been met and indicate on the face of the order if the defendant is subject to the federal firearms provisions (Hart, 1999). In addition, police, sheriffs, and other law enforcement agencies should establish protocols that discuss search and seizure of weapons under these circumstances (Hart, 1999). Theoretically, these laws should make it more difficult for batterers to obtain firearms and therefore make it safer for battered women. Unfortunately, batterers too often have proved that the only weapons they need are their fists or whatever piece of furniture may be nearby.

Laws on Interstate Battering

Another recent federal legislative reform relates to interstate acts of battering. Provisions of VAWA make it a federal crime to cross state lines or boundaries of Native American reservations with the intent to "injure, harass, or intimidate that person's spouse or intimate partner." Offenders who do so and who intentionally commit a crime of violence that causes bodily injury are subject to federal prosecution (18 U.S.C. Section 2261). Likewise, batterers who take their victims across state lines or reservation boundaries by force, coercion, duress, or fraud and intentionally commit a crime of violence that results in bodily injury also have committed a federal crime (18 U.S.C. Section 2261). Judges may impose fines and/or incarcerate offenders who have violated these laws, depending upon the level of harm suffered. Offenders may be sentenced to life if the victim dies and to a maximum of 20 years if victims experience permanent disfigurement or life-threatening bodily injury. Offenders may be sentenced to a maximum of ten years if serious bodily injury results or if the offender uses a dangerous weapon during the offense.

Offenders who intentionally cross jurisdictional boundaries to violate protective orders also have committed a federal crime, and in this case they need not have caused bodily injury to their victims (18 U.S.C. Section 2262). In fact, offenders who cross state lines or reservation boundaries with the intent to violate a protective order have committed a felony. Likewise, offenders who cross these lines and engage in behavior that would violate the order in the original jurisdiction have committed a felony violation. For example, then, a man who traveled from Northern Virginia to Washington D.C. to verbally harass his wife at her job in the city could be arrested and fined and/or sentenced to a maximum of five years if convicted.

On May 23, 1995 the first conviction under the new interstate domestic violence provision of VAWA was secured in the Southern District of West Virginia. In November 1984, Christopher Baily beat his wife Sonya until she collapsed and then placed her in the trunk of his car and drove for five days through West Virginia and Kentucky before he finally took her to an emergency room for treatment. Sonya Baily suffered permanent brain damage and remains hospitalized in a vegetative state. Her husband was tried, convicted, and sentenced to life in prison for the abuse and kidnapping of his wife (Violence Against Women Office, 1996).

It remains to be seen whether these new laws will have any significant effect in increasing the number of sentences or the amount of time served for violators. It is possible that federal sentences are stiffer than some state penalties; however, it would appear that many of these cases already meet the criteria for existing federal kidnapping laws. It does appear that the greatest potential for increasing penalties may lie in the provisions that make it a federal offense to cross jurisdictional lines to violate a protective order, although it will take some time to determine whether these laws are enforced. As always, the real challenge lies in implementing the legislation. At a minimum though, these laws are symbolically important. They prioritize battering as a federal problem and increase the visibility of these types of cases.

Federal Civil Rights Provision

In addition to making changes in criminal statutes, VAWA also creates a new civil remedy for battered women. This portion of the Act (42 U.S.C. Section 13981) declares that "all persons within the United States shall have the right to be free from crimes of violence" and allows victims to sue their attackers for damages. The remedy was designed to complement existing civil rights laws and victims who experience an act of violence are eligible to file for damages if it was motivated by gender. Violence is defined as any act involving serious risk of injury; the act must be serious enough to qualify as a felony under state or federal law. Criminal charges need not actually be filed, but they are used to establish eligibility. Motivated by gender means that the crime of violence was committed because of gender or on the basis of gender—due, at least in part, to gender animus. Victims bear the burden of proof and must demonstrate beyond a preponderance of the evidence that these felony acts of violence were motivated by gender. The law specifically notes that it is not intended to address random acts of violence unrelated to gender.

It is difficult to determine what level of evidence will be required to evidence gender animus under this legislation (Schmidt am Busch, 1995). It will take some time for the courts to define this concept. However, based on other federal civil rights legislation, it seems reasonable to predict that the courts will examine the totality of the circumstances and make decisions on a case-by-case basis.

Opponents of the law, including Supreme Court Chief Justice William Rehnquist, fought to defeat VAWA while it was still being considered by Congress. They argued that the law would overwhelm the already overburdened federal courts by encouraging frivolous suits (Erwin, 1996) and that the federal courts should be "reserved for issues where important national interests predominate" (Frazee, 1995, p. 2). State judges at an annual conference also initially opposed this portion of VAWA arguing that it would be used as a "'bargaining tool'" in divorces and because "the issue of inter-spousal litigations goes to the very core of family relationships'" (Frazee, 1995, p. 2).

Ironically, instead of using the vast magnitude of the problem as evidence of the need for a separate civil rights bill to protect women from violence, the epidemic nature of the problem was used to argue against the legislation. In an unprecedented action, judges who are supposed to be neutral toward the content of law, publicly campaigned against proposed legislation. Defining the problem as a *private matter* rather than a *public interest*, these judges also simplistically ignored the fact that costs associated with domestic violence do not disappear due to the lack of civil involvement (Frazee, 1995). For example, some of these costs are passed on to the criminal system in the form of arrest, prosecution, and conviction. Other costs are incurred in terms of health care services for battered women. We may never be able to estimate the long term costs of having children exposed to this violence or the costs in lost work and mental health claims suffered by battered women. The approach of the judiciary in this matter was shortsighted and clearly indicated that federal and state judiciaries are reluctant to address this issue.

Opponents also criticized the bill asserting that it would be rendered unconstitutionally vague by the federal courts because it fails to define gender animus. For instance, are crimes against women such as domestic violence and rape evidence of gender animus by definition? In other words, is domestic violence, by definition a crime "motivated by gender" or must a battered woman prove that her batterer beat her because he was motivated by gender animus? If so, what does that mean? Will he have to display sexist epithets while he beats her? What other behaviors would prove gender animus?

Legislative history shows that the tortured definitions in this provision of VAWA, or perhaps more accurately the lack of clear definitions, are a result of the battle over hegemonic assumptions. The bill, as originally introduced, did specifically define domestic violence as a gender-motivated crime of violence, but this language was eliminated in a last minute effort to save the bill from defeat (Frazee, 1995).

Ironically, the American Civil Liberties Union (ACLU)—a group whose very mission is to defend civil rights—opposed the bill, stating it would be too difficult to prove that acts were motivated by gender (Frazee, 1995). This argument ignores that the courts routinely deal with acts motivated *by gender* in all sexual harassment suits and sex discrimination cases. This term is a legal concept that is applied in these types of cases; however, the ACLU argued that it is difficult to distinguish between gender-motivated crimes against women and those that are a result of personal characteristics. In other words, the batterer didn't beat his wife because she was a woman, but because of some other gender neutral reason: that he just didn't like her hair, that she had an annoying voice, or that she woke him up during a nap. This type of rationale ignores the gendered nature of battering. It ignores the very reason the bill was written. Women are battered because they are women, and batterers are able to beat their partners with impunity *because* of their gender. "It might well make sense that a particular husband beats his wife savagely just for burning the toast—but only because we live in a world that takes for granted women's vulnerability to abuse, and the belief that women deserve it" (Frazee, 1995, p. 3).

For the most part, the lower federal courts upheld the civil rights provision of VAWA—nineteen of them found the law to be constitutional (National Organization for Women [NOW]). The Supreme Court, however, found this portion of VAWA to be unconstitutional (United States v. Morrison, 2000). This case involved Christy Brzonkala who filed suit after she was allegedly raped by two students, Antonio Morrison and James Crawford, in 1994 while attending Virginia Polytechnic Institute (Virginia Tech). In early 1995, Brzonkala filed complaints using the university's Sexual Assault Policy. The complaint against Crawford was dismissed based on insufficient evidence. While Morrison was convicted, the charges were reduced upon appeal to the Provost. Ultimately, Morrison's two semester suspension from school was deferred, allowing him to continue to play football although he was required to attend a one hour educational session (NOW). Brzonkala sued Morrison and Crawford, claiming that her civil rights were violated under Section 13981 of the VAWA.[5]

The Supreme Court affirmed lower court rulings and held that this section of VAWA was unconstitutional because it infringed upon state sovereignty. In order to meet constitutional scrutiny, the Court held that violence against women had to substantially affect interstate commerce. The Court concluded that this relationship was not established sufficiently under current case law and that the regulation of criminal conduct is best left to the states. It also held that VAWA was not a violation of the 14th Amendment because equal protection is a constitutional right which applies to state actions and not those of private citizens.

The Court's ruling makes it difficult to envision how Cognress might remedy this section of VAWA to make it withstand constitutional scrutiny. Perhaps state legislation will prove a more fruitful venue for this type of legislation. Thirty-six states joined in a brief supporting this section of VAWA; only Alabama filed a brief requesting the Court to find the statute unconstitutional (Greenhouse, 2000).

While critics have argued that this law benefits few women—that it is only useful if the batterer has substantial financial resources (Erwin, 1996)—there are several reasons to pursue legislation of this type. It is somewhat disingenuous to overstate the class bias in this law. All civil proceedings targeted at individuals unfairly limit respondents to suing defendants with money. For example, all crime victims theoretically can sue for damages as was done in the civil case against O. J. Simpson; however, few perpetrators have enough financial resources to make it worth the effort. Thus, legislation like VAWA is no better or no worse in its limited ability to hold individual batterers financially accountable for their behavior. Civil remedies are important because they empower victims to sue on their own behalf without having to convince governmental officials to pursue cases on their behalf. This type of remedy also bears a lower burden of proof and provides an alternative forum for women who often face an unresponsive criminal justice system. Furthermore, if victims are able to secure substantive damages it will bring public attention to the issue and therefore has important symbolic value. "The act acknowledge[d] that violence against women is a subject for law at its most basic—that which protects us from each other" (Hirshman, 1996, p. 258).

Immigration Provisions

Other federal legislative reforms have made it easier for battered immigrants to secure citizenship. Prior to the 1994 passage of VAWA, immigrant spouses who wished to become permanent citizens or who wanted to apply for permanent resident status because they were married to U.S. citizens could not apply on their own behalf. Instead, the spouse who was the U.S. citizen had to make the application. New VAWA provisions (8 U.S.C. 1154) allow immigrant victims to petition for an exemption as a victim of battering. If approved, they may be allowed to apply for citizenship without relying on their spouses. Obviously, batterers had a tremendous amount of power over victims seeking permanent residency. A batterer could threaten to have his partner deported if she reported his abusive behavior. This threat was even more powerful when there were children involved; a batterer could threaten to deport his partner while keeping the children in the U.S., depriving her of contact with them. It remains to be seen, however, if these types of petitions will be granted with any regularity. It is possible that this exemption will be narrowly implemented.

The second immigration provision was passed as an amendment to the Omnibus Consolidated Appropriations Act of 1997. It amends immigration law (8 U.S.C. Section 1251) and makes domestic violence, stalking, and child abuse grounds for deportation. Individuals convicted of these crimes may be deported, as may persons who violate a protective order by engaging in threats of violence, repeated harassment, or bodily injury toward the person protected by the order. While the threat of deportation for their batterers may empower some victims and thus increase their safety, other victims may refuse to call the police if they are afraid that their batterers will be deported against their wishes. In other words, an immigrant battered woman may need immediate help when she calls the police, but she may not wish to have the batterer deported. There always is the risk that this provision will harm victims in jurisdictions where prosecution and/or orders are pursued against victims engaged in "mutual violence." Thus it is possible that deportation procedures might be used to harm the very victims the law was designed to protect.

SUMMARY

Numerous changes in legislation at both the state and federal level have occurred in the past two decades. Massive change in state legislation now allow for arrest in misdemeanor cases where the police officer is not present to witness the assault therefore dramatically increasing the ability of police to arrest in these cases. The historical reluctance of police officers to arrest, however, has led many states to pass legislation that either encourages or mandates arrest. Police discretion, however, is not easily legislated given the nature of the work environment (Kappeler, Sluder, & Alpert, 1998). Loose supervision and little accountability make it difficult to second-guess the decisions of police officers. Translated, if a police officer responds to a call and fails to make an arrest even in jurisdictions with mandatory arrest policies, there is little that can be done to ensure that the arrest actually occurs. Although some states have initiated mandatory reporting procedures that require officers to document their actions on all domestic violence calls in order to improve police accountability, it is difficult to identify and sanction officers if they fail to act. While extremely egregious cases may surface (e.g., when a police department is sued), changing police practice is a slow and laborious process and one that often resists legislative influence. This does not mean that there is no value in mandatory arrest laws. For example, these laws may increase the individual police officer's risk of legal liability, and some officers may adhere to the law for fear of individual legal responsibility. Furthermore, these laws may help create a police culture and climate that pursues rigorous enforcement of these types of assaults. However, there have been unintended negative consequences associated with mandatory arrest.

While the debate of the efficacy of arrest in misdemeanor assaults continues in academic circles, it appears that legislators and police chiefs have been relatively uninterested in this dialogue. Both chiefs and legislators continue to pursue mandatory and pro-arrest policies and laws, and it does not appear that this trend is losing any momentum. In fact, in most states, it takes considerable diligence to ensure that one is aware of the current state laws pertaining to battering because they change quite rapidly. Rarely does a session of a state legislature pass without the introduction and/or passage of new bills related to some aspect of domestic violence; many, perhaps most, of these bills are related to the criminal justice system response. States also are becoming more innovative and are finding ways to increase the penalties for misdemeanor battering. For example, Oregon has increased misdemeanor battery to a felony if abuse occurs in front of children (Feminist Majority Foundation, June 16, 1998). Unfortunately, there has been little momentum to reform charging practices so that felony battering cases are charged as such.

Revisions in state protective order legislation also are quite common. These newer laws have made protective orders a more powerful tool to combat battering; unfortunately, judges appear to be reluctant to use them to their fullest potential. Federal legislation requiring full faith and credit has the potential to further strengthen the enforcement of orders. However, bureaucratic red tape associated with implementation of full faith and credit may render the federal legislation relatively useless. In states where registration is required and where notification to batterers is made, victims may choose to use stalker legislation as a way to stop harassing behavior.

Federal legislative reform continues as Congress attempts to pass the Violence Against Women Act II. Different versions of the bill exist in the House and the Senate, but both versions include re-authorizing funding for the original VAWA bill for the next five years. It contains monies for grants to criminal justice agencies and increases funds for battered women's shelters and services including the national domestic violence hotline. Some of the other proposed measures include provisions for: granting Section Eight low income housing certificates for battered women who are trying to escape from their batterers; expanding the Family and Medical Leave Act to allow victims time off from work (uncompensated) to address domestic violence and its effects; taking actions to end insurance discrimination against battered women; allowing victims of domestic violence to receive unemployment if they are fired as a result of being battered; funding legal services for battered women who need assistance in civil matters (e.g., divorce, protective orders); and offering training to medical personnel and judges.[6] As of the time this book went to press, it is unclear which of these proposals will pass and become law; however, it appears that the future of VAWA is secure given the tendency to expand existing provisions.

Although the earliest legislative reforms began at the state level, the federal government is becoming increasingly involved and has made several landmark changes in laws with the passage of VAWA. Many of these laws are designed to facilitate law enforcement efforts; however, "the biggest problem with VAWA is that the public is largely unaware of what it says and, perhaps as a consequence, law enforcement officials haven't been paying much attention to it either" (Lardner cited in Websdale & Johnson, 1998, p. 5). Two years after it was passed, there were only 14 prosecutions for violations of new federal provisions (Websdale & Johnson, 1998). It will take some time before we can ascertain whether these new federal laws actually work to empower and safeguard victims. Is it is of critical importance, however, that battering is becoming recognized as a federal issue. While new federal laws on battering are important and help increase the number and type of options for a criminal justice system response, this type of visibility also appears to be translating into much needed funding for victim services. However, all legislation has unintended consequences and additional research is needed to ascertain whether these new laws actually help battered women and increase their safety.

NOTES

[1] Domestic violence laws are not the only misdemeanor legislation to be exempted from the traditional requirement that police officers view the violation. For example, most states exempt shoplifting since it too is a crime that rarely occurs in the presence of the police.

[2] These figures are probably much higher today as this study is quite dated; however, I was unable to locate more recent information with respect to these conditions of orders.

[3] This reform, technically, was not passed as part of VAWA. Both VAWA and this firearms provision are part of the larger 1994 Crime Control Act.

[4] The report of the study discussed in Time magazine does not specifically identify the methodology used in the study. However, the report states that the study found that men and women were about equally likely to use violence, but that women were far more likely to be injured. One can therefore predict that this study uses the Conflict Tactic Scale methodology discussed in a previous chapter. It probably suffers from the limitations of that methodology and makes it difficult, and inconsistent, to "use" this data as evidence of specific increases in violence. I believe the real importance of the study lies in the fact that it was commissioned because the Army apparently is beginning to recognize the problem. As previously discussed, recognizing and defining a problem is the first step toward breaking through the pollution.

[5] Brzonkala also sued Virginia Tech, claiming that the university's actions constituted sex discrimination under Title IX. The university paid Brzonkala $75,000 to settle this portion of the case out of court.

[6] A critical source material to follow legislative reform can be found on the web at: http://thomas.loc.gov. Some of the information in this paragraph was found by checking on the status of H.R. 1248 and 357 as well as S.2110. These cites were accessed on September 9, 1999.

REFERENCES

Adhikari, R., Reinhard, D., & Johnson, J. (1993). The myth of protection orders. *Studies in Symbolic Interaction, 15,* 259–270.

Bachman, R., & Coker, A. (1995). Police intervention in domestic violence. *Violence and Victims, 10,* 98–106.

Balos, B., & Trotzky, K. (1988). Enforcement of the domestic abuse act in Minnesota: A preliminary study. *Law and Inequality, 6,* 83–125.

Belknap, J. (1995). Law enforcement officers' attitudes about the appropriate responses to woman battering. *International Review of Victimology, 4,* 47–62.

Berk, R. (1993). What the scientific evidence shows: On the average, we can do no better than arrest. In R. Gelles & D. Loseke (Eds.), *Current controversies on family violence* (pp. 323–336). Newbury Park, CA: Sage.

Berk, R., Berk, S., Newton, P., & Loseke, D. (1984). Beyesian analysis of the Colorado Springs spouse abuse experiment. *Criminal Law and Criminology, 83,* 317–346.

Binder, A., & Meeker, J. (1988). Experiments as reforms. *Journal of Criminal Justice, 16,* 347–358.

Bourg, S., & Stock, H. (1994). A review of domestic violence arrest statistics in a police department using a pro-arrest policy: Are pro-arrest policies enough? *Journal of Family Violence, 9,* 177–189.

Brown, S. (1984). Police responses to wife beating: Neglect of a crime of violence. *Journal of Criminal Justice, 12,* 277–288.

Buzawa, E. (1982). Police officer response to domestic violence legislation in Michigan. *Journal of Police Science and Administration, 10,* 415–424.

Buzawa, E., & Buzawa, C. (1996). Domestic violence: The criminal justice response (2nd ed.). Thousand Oaks, CA: Sage.

Caringella-MacDonald, S. (1988). Parallels and pitfalls: The aftermath of legal reform for sexual assault, marital rape, and domestic violence victims. *Journal of Interpersonal Violence, 3,* 174–189.

Chaudhuri, M., & Daly, K. (1992). Do restraining orders help? Battered women's experience with male violence and legal process. In E. Buzawa & C. Buzawa (Eds.), *Domestic violence: The changing criminal justice response* (pp. 227–252). Westport, CT: Auburn House.

Coleman, F. (1997). Stalking behavior and the cycle of domestic violence. *Journal of Interpersonal Violence, 12,* 420–432.

Dobash, R. E., & Dobash, R. P. (1979). *Violence against wives: A case against the patriarchy.* New York: Free Press.

Dunford, F. (1990). System-initiated warrants for suspects of misdemeanor domestic assault: A pilot study. *Justice Quarterly, 7,* 631–653.

Dunford, F., Huizinga, D., & Elliott, D. (1990). The role of arrest in domestic assault: The Omaha police experiment. *Criminology, 28,* 183–206.

Eigenberg, H., Scarborough, K., & Kappeler, V. (1996). Contributory factors affecting arrest in domestic and non-domestic assaults. *American Journal of Police, 15*, 55–77.

Elliot, D. (1989). Criminal justice procedures in family violence crimes. In L. Ohlin & M. Tonry (Eds.), *Crime and justice: A review of the research* (pp. 427–480). London: University of Chicago Press.

Erez, E. (1986). Intimacy, violence, and the police. *Human Relations, 39*, 265–281.

Erwin, D. (1996). The Violence Against Women Act: Lip service to underrepresented battered women? In N. Lemon (Ed.), *Domestic violence law: A comprehensive overview of cases and sources* (pp. 260–267). San Francisco: Austin & Winfield.

Fagan, J. (1989). Cessation of family violence: Deterrence and dissuasion. In L. Ohlin & M. Tonry (Eds.), *Crime and justice: A review of the research* (pp. 427–480). London: University of Chicago Press.

Fagan, J. (1996). *The criminalization of domestic violence: Promises and limits.* Washington, DC: National Institute of Justice.

Feder, L. (1996). Police handling of domestic calls: The importance of offender's presence in the arrest decision. *Journal of Criminal Justice, 24*, 481–490.

Feeley, M., & Sarat, A. (1980). *The policy dilemma: Federal crime policy and the Law Enforcement Assistance Administration.* Minneapolis: University of Minnesota Press.

Feminist Majority Foundation (1998, June). Oregon increases penalties for spousal abuse. Retrieved February 20, 1999 from the World Wide Web: http://www.feminist.org/news/newsbyte/april99/0419.html

Fernandez, M., Iwamoto, K., & Muscat, B. (1997). Dependency and severity of abuse: Impact on women's persistence in utilizing the court system as protection against domestic violence. *Women and Criminal Justice, 9*, 39–63.

Ferraro, K. (1989). Policing woman battering. *Social Problems, 36*(1), 643–647.

Ferraro, K., & Pope, L. (1993). Irreconcilable differences: Battered women, police, and the law. In N. Hilton (Ed.), *Legal response to wife assault: Current trends and evaluations* (pp. 96–123). Thousand Oaks, CA: Sage.

Finn, P., & Colson, S. (1990). *Civil protection orders: Legislation, current court practice, and enforcement.* Washington, DC: National Institute of Justice.

Finn, P., & Lee, B. (1987). *Serving crime victims and witnesses.* Washington, DC: National Institute of Justice.

Fischer, K., & Rose, M. (1995). When "enough is enough": Battered women's decision making around court orders of protection. *Crime and Delinquency, 41*, 414–429.

Gartin, P. (1995). Examining differential officer effects in the Minneapolis domestic violence experiment. *American Journal of Police, 14*, 93–110.

Gondolf, E., & Fisher, E. (1988). *Battered women as survivors: An alternative to treating learned helplessness.* New York: Lexington Books.

Gondolf, E., McWilliams, J., Hart, B., & Stuehling, J. (1994). Court response to petitions for civil protection orders. *Journal of Interpersonal Violence, 9*, 503–517.

Grau, J., Fagan, J., & Wexler, S. (1984). Restraining orders for battered women: Issues in access and efficacy. *Women in Politics, 4*, 13–28.

Greenhouse, L. (2000, January 11). Justices cool to law protecting women. *The New York Times*, p. A18.

Harrell, A., Smith, B., & Newmark, L. (1993). *Court processing and the effects of restraining orders for domestic violence victims.* Washington, DC: The Urban Institute.

Harrell, A., & Smith, B. (1996). Effects of restraining orders on domestic violence victims. In E. Buzawa & C. Buzawa (Eds.), *Do arrests and restraining orders work?* (pp. 214–243). Thousand Oaks, CA: Sage.

Hart, B. (No Date). Full faith and credit implementation: Challenges and solutions. Retrieved August 15, 1999 from the World Wide Web: http://www.vaw.umn.edu/FFC/chapter11.html

Hemmens, C., Strom, K., & Schlegel, E. (1998). Gender bias in the courts: A review of the literature. *Sociological Imagination, 35*, 22–42.

Hirschel, J., & Hutchison, I. (1991). Police-preferred arrest policies. In M. Steinman (Ed.), *Women battering: Policy responses* (pp. 49–72). Cincinnati: Anderson.

Hirschel, J., Hutchison, I., & Dean, C. (1992). The failure of arrest to deter spouse abuse. *Journal of Research in Crime and Delinquency, 20*, 7–33.

Hirshman, L. (1996). Making safety a civil right. In N. Lemon (Ed.), *Domestic violence law: A comprehensive overview of cases and sources* (pp. 256–259). San Francisco: Austin & Winfield.

Horton, A., Simonidis, K., & Simonidis, L. (1987). Legal remedies for spousal abuse: Victim characteristics, expectations, and satisfaction. *Journal of Family Violence, 2*, 265–279.

International Association of Chiefs of Police (1999a, April 1). Police Officer Domestic Violence. Retrieved September 4, 1999 from the World Wide Web: http://www.theiacp.org/pubinfo/index.html

International Association of Chiefs of Police (1999b, April 1). Police Officer Domestic Violence: Concepts and Issues Paper. Retrieved September 4, 1999 from the World Wide Web: http://www.theiacp.org/pubinfo/index.html

International Association of Chiefs of Police (No Date). Protecting victims of domestic violence: A law enforcement officer's guide to enforcing orders of protection nationwide. Retrieved September 5, 1999 from the World Wide Web: http://www.theiacp.org/pubinfo/orders.html

Jolin, A. (1983). Domestic violence legislation: An impact assessment. *Journal of Police Science and Administration, 11*, 451–456.

Kappeler, V., Sluder, R., & Alpert, G. (1998). *Forces of deviance* (2nd ed.). Prospect Heights, IL: Waveland Press.

Kappeler, V., Blumberg, M., & Potter, G. (2000). *The mythology of crime and criminal justice* (3rd ed.). Prospect Heights: IL: Waveland Press.

Kinports, K., & Fischer, K. (1993). Orders of protection in domestic violence case: An empirical assessment of the impact of the reform statutes. *Texas Journal of Women and the Law, 2*, 163–276.

Keilitz, S., Davis, C., Efkeman, H., Flango, C., & Hannaford, P. (1998). *Civil protection orders: Victims' views on effectiveness.* Washington, DC: U.S. Department of Justice.

Klein, A. (1996). Re-abuse in a population of court-restrained male batterers: Why restraining orders don't work. In E. Buzawa & C. Buzawa (Eds.), *Do arrests and restraining orders work?* (pp. 192–213). Thousand Oaks, CA: Sage.

Langan, P., & Innes, C. (1986). *Preventing domestic violence against women.* Washington, DC: Department of Justice.

Lawrenz, F., Lembo, J., & Schade, T. (1988). Time series analysis of the effect of a domestic violence directive on the number of arrests per day. *Journal of Criminal Justice, 16*, 493–498.

Lempert, R. (1989). Humility is a virtue: On the publicization of policy-relevant research. *Law and Society Review, 23*, 145–161.

Lerman, L. (1980). Civil protection orders: Obtaining access to court. *Response to Violence in the Family, 3*, 1–28.

Lerman, L., & Livingston, F. (1983, September/October). State legislation on domestic violence. *Responses to Violence in the Family and Sexual Assault, 1–2*, 13–14.

Lyman, M., & Potter, G. (1996). *Drugs in society* (2nd ed.). Cincinnati: Anderson.

Martin, M. (1997). Policy promises: Community policing and domestic violence victim satisfaction. *Policing: An International Journal of Police Strategies and Management, 20,* 519–531.

McGillis, D., & Smith, P. (1983). *Compensating victims of crime: An analysis of programs.* Washington, DC: National Institute of Justice.

Mecka, M. (1998). Seizing the ammunition from domestic violence: Prohibiting the ownership of firearms by abusers. *Rutgers Law Journal, 29,* 607–645.

Miller, N. (1997). *Domestic violence legislation affecting police and prosecutor responsibilities in the
   United States: Inferences from a 50-state review of state statutory codes.* Alexandria, VA: Institute for Law and Justice.

Miller, S. (1989). Unintended side effects of pro-arrest policies and their race and class
   implications for battered women: A cautionary note. *Criminal Justice Policy Review, 3*(3),
   299–316.

Miller, S. (1993). Arrest policies for domestic violence and their implications for battered
   women. In R. Muraskin & T. Alleman (Eds.), *Women and justice* (pp. 334–359). Engle-
   wood Cliffs, NJ: Regents/Prentice Hall.

National Organization for Women. Supreme court spotlight: Brzonkala. Retrieved
   August 27, 2000 from the World Wide Web: http://www.nowldef.org/html/courts/
   brzsumm.htm.

Office for Victims of Crime [a]. Victims of crime act crime victims fund. Retrieved August 14,
   1999 from the World Wide Web: http://www.ojp.usdoj.gov/ovc/factshts/cvfvca/html

Office for Victims of Crime [b]. What is the office for victims of crime? Retrieved August 15,
   1999 from the World Wide Web: http://www.ojp.usdoj.gov/ovc/factshts/cvfvca/html

Parent, D., Auerbach, B., & Carlson, K. (1992). *Compensating crime victims: A summary of policies and practices.* Washington, DC: U.S. Department of Justice.

Pate, A., & Hamilton, E. (1992). Formal and informal deterrents to domestic violence: The
   Dade County spouse assault experiment. *American Sociological Review, 57,* 691–697.

Pullen, E. (1998). Guns, domestic violence, interstate commerce, and the Lautenberg
   Amendment: Simply because congress may conclude that a particular activity substantially affects interstate commerce does not make it so. *South Texas Law Review, 39,*
   1029–1070.

Rasche, C. (1988). Minority women and domestic violence: The unique dilemmas of battered women of color. *Journal of Contemporary Criminal Justice, 4,* 150–171.

Robinson, L. (1995, July 27). A Report to the Assistant Attorney General on Justice Programs: OJP Family Violence Working Group. Retrieved September 4, 1997 from the
   World Wide Web: http://www.ojp.gov/Kits/Family/probst.html

Schechter, S. (1982). *Women and male violence: The visions and struggles of the battered women's
   movement.* Boston: South End Press.

Schmidt am Busch, B. (1995). Domestic Violence and Title III of the Violence Against
   Women Act of 1993: A Feminist Critique. *Hastings Women's Law Journal, 6,* 1–26.

Sherman, L., & Berk, R. (1984). The specific deterrent effects of arrest for domestic
   assault. *American Sociological Review, 49,* 261–272.

Sherman, L., & Cohen, E. (1989). The impact of research on legal policy: The Minneapolis
   domestic violence experiment. *Law and Society Review, 12,* 117–144.

Sherman, L., Smith, D., Schmidt, J., & Rogan, D. (1992). Crime, punishment and stake in
   conformity: Legal and informal control of domestic violence. *American Sociological
   Review, 83,* 137–169.

Sherman, L., Schmidt, J., Rogan, D., Gartin, P., Cohn, E., Collins, D., & Bacich, A. (1992).
   The variable effects of arrest on criminal careers: The Milwaukee domestic violence
   experiment. *Journal of Criminal Law and Criminology, 83,* 137–169.

Stanko, E. (1985). *Intimate intrusions: Women's experiences of male violence.* London: Routledge & Kegan Paul.

Stark, E. (1996). Mandatory arrest of batterers: A reply to its critics. In E. Buzawa & C. Buzawa (Eds.), *Do arrests and restraining orders work?* (pp. 115–149). Thousand Oaks, CA: Sage.

Thompson, M. (1997, October 6). A farewell to arms: How the military plans to enforce a law denying guns to abusive spouses. *Time,* 46.

Thompson, M. (1994, May 23). Armed forced: The living room war. *Time,* 34–37.

Title 8, United States Code, Section 1154

Title 8, United States Code, Section 1251

Title 18,United States Code Section 922

Title 18, United States Code Section 925

Title 18, United States Code Section 2261

Title 18, United States Code Section 2262

Title 18, United States Code Section 2265

Title 42, United States Code Section 13981

Tjaden, P., & Thoennes, N. (1998). *Stalking in America: Findings from the National Violence Against Women Survey.* Washington, DC: National Institute of Justice and Centers for Disease Control and Prevention.

United States v Morrison, 120 S. Ct. 1740 (2000).

Violence Against Women Office (1996, July 22). The Violence Against Women Act: Breaking the Cycle of Violence. Retrieved October 28, 1996 from the World Wide Web: http://www.usdoj.gov/vawo/cycle.html

Violence Against Women Office (1996, August 7). The Violence Against Women Act. Retrieved August 29, 1997 from the World Wide Web: http://www.usdoj.gov/vawo/vawafct.html

Websdale, N. (1995). Rural woman abuse: The voices of Kentucky women. *Violence Against Women, 1,* 309–338.

Websdale, N., & Johnson, B. (1997). The policing of domestic violence in rural and urban areas: The voices of battered women in Kentucky. *Policing and Society, 6,* 297–317.

Websdale, N., & Johnson, B. (1998). Have faith, will travel: Implementing full faith and credit under the 1994 Violence Against Women Act. *Women and Criminal Justice, 9,* 1–45.

Weisz, A., Tolman, R., & Bennett, L. (1998). An ecological study of nonresidential services for battered women within a comprehensive community protocol for domestic violence. *Journal of Family Violence, 13,* 395–415.

Worden, R., & Pollitz, A. (1984). Police arrests in domestic disturbances. *Law and Society Review, 18,* 105–129.

Zeya, S. (No Date). Progress report on full faith and credit enabling legislation and implementation procedures. Retrieved December 10, 1998 from the World Wide Web: http://www.vaw.umn.edu/FFC/chapter1.html

Zorza, J. (1994). Must we stop arresting batterers?: Analysis and policy implications of new police domestic violence studies. *New England Law Review, 28,* 929–939.

Zorza, J. (1996). The criminal law of misdemeanor domestic violence, 1970–1990. In N. Lemon (Ed.), *Domestic violence law: A comprehensive overview of cases and sources* (pp. 517–532). San Francisco: Austin & Winfield.

The Decontextualization of Domestic Violence

Lisa G. Lerman

I. Introduction

In 1983, Lawrence Sherman and Richard Berk made headlines in the *New York Times* with their announcement that police arrests of woman abusers were more effective in deterring subsequent violence than more informal police actions.[1] They based this conclusion on their experiment in Minneapolis, which compared reincidence of violence after six months among 314 abusers who were either arrested, or temporarily separated from their victims by the police, or given some sort of police counseling.[2] The study reported subsequent violence within six months by twenty-four percent of those sent away temporarily, nineteen percent of those counseled by the police, and only ten percent of those arrested. This suggested that the making of an arrest was an effective deterrent.[3]

At the time the Minneapolis Experiment was conducted, a majority of states had adopted statutes that broadened police discretion to make arrests in misdemeanor domestic abuse cases or that mandated the use of arrest.[4] These statutes were part of packages of legislative reforms designed to provide protection and assistance to battered women. Advocates for battered women were pressing state legislatures for adoption of additional measures to strengthen legal remedies and police response. The Minneapolis study offered persuasive empirical data which supported the claims of advocates for abused women that law enforcement against abusers was necessary and appropriate.[5]

The Department of Justice has spent $4 million[6] on replication studies in an effort to test the results of the Minneapolis Experiment. Four million dollars later,[7] the same sociologists turned around and told us that arrest does not have a consistent deterrent effect on wife abusers. The *New York Times* recently quoted Dr. Sherman as saying that "mandatory arrests in domestic violence cases may cause more violence against women in the long run."[8] The *Chicago Tribune*

Journal of Criminal Law & Criminology, Vol. 83, No. 1, pp. 217–240. Copyright 1992 by Northwestern University, School of Law.

reported that Sherman recommends the repeal of all state laws requiring arrest in cases of misdemeanor domestic violence.[9]

This recommendation represents a myopic view of the problem of domestic violence, disregards twenty years of experience of thousands of advocates around the country, and suggests that policy should be made or unmade on the basis of a set of narrow and arguably misguided studies.[10]

While the studies reporting on this issue deal with an important topic and produce some interesting data, they reflect a test tube attitude toward solving a social problem. In this case the items in the test tube are men who batter, and the social scientists want to look at the chemical reaction that results from adding mediation, separation of the parties, a warning, a quick little arrest, or a more time-consuming arrest process.[11]

The social scientists have done a careful job of randomly selecting their "mice"[12] (men) and of isolating the effect of arrest or nonarrest. Perhaps we may extract from these studies some objective data that legislators may use in writing statutes. But before we send this data to the legislators, I would suggest a few more experiments that take account of the context in which the arrests take place, and which factor in as variables the victims' wishes and conduct, other pending legal action, the behavior of officers upon responding, whether and how the cases are prosecuted, and what if any sanctions are imposed. To think about how to design those studies, perhaps we should take a peek outside of the test tube to identify the other variables which might have affected the design of the replication studies and the results obtained. In looking at the impact of arrest as a deterrent, the social scientists have not eliminated the other variables from the experiment, since they are not working in a laboratory but on the street. However, they have ignored the impact of some of these variables in doing their analysis.

II. THE POLICY CONTEXT

How one defines a problem often determines what one perceives to be the solution. In dealing with battering, if the problem is (as some believed in the fifties and sixties) one of female masochism,[13] then the solution is treatment for the victims. If the problem is one of chronic criminal behavior by abusers (a more contemporary view), then an important part of the solution is to enforce criminal law to effectuate deterrence, rehabilitation, incapacitation, or retribution. The researchers who conducted the replication studies do not discuss their own views of the problem or the solution. I begin with a summary of my view, because those beliefs inform my comments on these articles.

Men are violent and abusive toward women because this behavior allows them to establish and to maintain control within the relationships.[14] Many men engage in this behavior because it is effective in maintaining control, and because no one has ever required them to stop. Woman abuse is such a pervasive problem that society, in addition to holding the abuser responsible, must take responsibility for rearranging law, policy, and social services to prevent domestic abuse.

Both civil and criminal legal intervention are useful and important, because they let the individual abuser, the victim, and the community know that woman abuse is a crime and will not be tolerated. Legal intervention can help victims of abuse to become safer and to create conditions in which separation from the abuser is possible. Criminal action gives strong messages that violence is unacceptable, but civil protection orders are very useful also, because of the diverse relief (e.g., child support, temporary custody, return of property, eviction of the abuser, etc.) that is available as part of a civil protection order in most states.[15]

Legal remedies are an essential tool in stopping domestic violence. Some policy-makers have urged that woman abuse be removed from the law enforcement system and relegated to mediation by police or by another public agency. This is a bad idea because the use of mediation ignores the criminality of the abuser's behavior and reinforces his control within the relationship.[16]

One cannot simply initiate one intervention (arrest) in a community and expect to eradicate domestic violence. If the premise of these studies was that making an arrest would stop the violence, the sociologists need only have asked a few advocates whether that was a valid premise. It is the experience of many programs which provide services to battered women that one cannot so much as make a dent in the rate of domestic violence without a coordinated response by the law enforcement, social service and mental health system.[17] To be effective, the entire community of professionals and service providers who come into contact with wife abuse must be educated about the nature of the problem, and they must collaborate to address the complex problems presented by each case.

Failure of coordination will cause the failure of any individual remedy. For example, if a statute requires the police to make arrests but the police department does not adopt a policy implementing the statute, the officers responding to calls may not even be aware of the statute.[18] If a particular department adopts a policy implementing the statute, but the officers do not receive adequate training about the nature of woman abuse, they either may fail to make arrests or make inappropriate arrests.[19] If the police are asked to make arrests but the prosecutor files charges in few of the arrest cases, the police may refuse to act, because they believed that making arrests in cases that will be dropped is a pointless exercise. If the prosecutor adopts a policy of aggressively prosecuting abuse cases but fails to provide victim advocacy services to maintain contact with victims, attend to their safety needs and help them to understand the law enforcement system, then the prosecutor often is doomed to frustration because the victims of abuse are less likely to remain available to testify.[20] If the prosecutor sets up a good system within the office and obtains a high rate of convictions and guilty pleas, but the mental health community does not develop expertise on treatment of abusers and establish close communication with the courts, then most abusers will receive little effective attention. If the probation department fails to monitor abusers who have been convicted of or who plead guilty to charges of spouse abuse, then there will be no deterrent to engaging in post-conviction recidivism.

Requiring that police arrest suspects in domestic violence cases is a useful component of a coordinated response.[21] Absent a requirement that arrests be made, police make very few arrests in domestic abuse cases.[22] If the police have the discretion to decide whether or not to make an arrest in a woman abuse case, they usually exercise that discretion not to make the arrest. Mandatory arrest is therefore one feature of an appropriate criminal justice response, but it is not a sufficient response.[23]

III. MAKING SENSE OF THE DATA

My comments on these data are informed by incomplete understanding of the technical language in the replication papers.[24] Nevertheless, I venture a few observations based on the researchers' own conclusions about their data and a few questions about how the researchers constructed the experiments.[25]

A. Is Arrest an Independent Deterrent?

The replication studies have produced rather inconsistent answers to the question of whether arrest is an effective deterrent of domestic violence. In some cases, different conclusions have been reached about one another's data. In two out of four sites, Milwaukee and Colorado Springs, the researchers found a deterrent effect from making arrests compared with other police responses in cases in which the suspect was "employed, married, high school graduate, and white" (Milwaukee) and in which the suspect was employed by the U.S. military (Colorado Springs). In Milwaukee, arrest was observed to have a criminogenic effect (i.e., the arrest appeared to increase the likelihood of subsequent assault) on a socially "marginal" subcategory of cases. In two other sites, Omaha and Charlotte, the data does not indicate any difference in the likelihood of recidivism between the cases in which the suspects were and were not arrested.

In Milwaukee and Charlotte, researchers identified different factors that predicted whether subsequent violence was likely. In Milwaukee,

> [e]mployed, married, high school graduate and white suspects are all less likely to have any incident of repeat violence reported to the domestic violence hotline if they are arrested than if they are not. Unemployed, unmarried, high school dropouts and black suspects, on average, are reported much more frequently to the domestic violence hotline if they are arrested than if they are not.[26]

In Charlotte, in contrast

> the strongest predictors of recidivism were measures of prior criminal activity, such as possession of a local (felony or misdemeanor) record, possession of a state (felony) record, and number of prior non-traffic arrests within the preceding five years. Further, while prior criminal activity was associated with recidivism, other offender-related variables, such as race, age, marital and employment status, were not. Moreover, knowledge of an offender's prior criminal activity produced only a modest contribution to predicting correctly an offender's probability of recidivating.[27]

However, the Charlotte study found that the likelihood of recidivism was not significantly affected by whether or not the police made an arrest—the only reliable predictors were the offender characteristics presented above. Researchers David Hirschel and Ira Hutchison explain that "[t]he results of the Charlotte experiment are decisive and unambiguous, and indicate that arrest of misdemeanor spouse abusers is neither substantively nor statistically a more effective deterrent to repeat abuse than either of the two other police responses examined in this location." They conclude that "[t]he results of the Charlotte and Omaha studies suggest that there is not adequate support for a mandatory or presumptive arrest policy based on specific deterrence. The hope that arrest alone could contribute to the solution of this serious problem is unfulfilled."[28]

Two of the replication studies, then, found that arrest deterred some people and two of the studies found that arrest did not appear to have a deterrent effect. No site, however, produced data indicating a deterrent effect as strong as that shown by the Minneapolis data. In Minneapolis, the strong deterrent effect was observed in a population that (based on the Milwaukee and Charlotte studies) would indicate a high likelihood of subsequent violence; in the Minneapolis sample, sixty percent of the suspects were unemployed, fifty-nine percent had prior arrests, and eighty percent had committed prior domestic assaults.[29]

B. Arrest out of Context

What conclusions are we to draw from this new wisdom?[30] If arrest does not clearly help to stop violence or reduce calls to the police (depending on which objective one had in mind), should it be abandoned?

These studies provide a limited measure of the specific deterrent effect of arrest when all other forms of intervention are ignored or avoided. If we measured any other aspect of the criminal justice system against this yardstick, it undoubtedly would be found wanting. If the system does not accomplish all of the intended effects, or if it might not, should we abandon it?

As to the "good risks," arrest may be beneficial regardless of the action or inaction of other parts of the law enforcement system. As to "bad risks," it appears that arrest alone might be an aggravating circumstance. Even among the likely recidivists, the data from Milwaukee suggest that arrest does appear to have a short-term (one month) deterrent effect.[31] But to achieve a longer-term deterrent effect, it actually may be necessary to enforce the law in other more lasting ways.

Will arrest produce a demonstrable deterrent effect when combined with prosecution, incarceration, treatment for the abuser, shelter and other services for the victim and her children, and other court orders addressing contact, custody, support, and other issues? This question remains to be examined in another set of experiments.

Even if a law enforcement approach fails to result in specific deterrence in some cases, enforcement of the law (including arrest, prosecution, and the use of other legal remedies for abuse) sends an appropriate message to the community—that domestic violence is not acceptable. Specific deterrence of a particular offender is not the only goal. When an arrest is made, the victim may become more confident of her right not to be abused; her children might begin to understand that violence is not "normal" and is not their mother's fault; other men and women in the community may judge their own situations and conduct differently if they see or hear about arrest or prosecution of a neighbor or co-worker.[32]

C. Police Data vs. Victim Data on Subsequent Incidents

One striking difference between the Minneapolis data and the data produced in the replication studies is that, in tabulating subsequent incidents of violence, the Minneapolis study collected information from victim interviews *and* police reports and arrived at cumulative totals. The more recent studies kept these two sources of information separate but accorded greater weight to the data acquired from the police. For example, in comparing the outcomes obtained at the various sites, Richard Berk and his colleagues used "official data" as the measure of "outcome," explaining that "the 'cleanest' story is told from the treatment assigned and the official data"; the data produced by the victim interviews is characterized as "weaker."[33]

Berk and his colleagues also indicated that the authors of the Milwaukee study, while they collected both official and victim data, "have (to date) focused on the official data, which they felt was far more reliable than the data extracted from the interviews with victims."[34] Indeed, the researchers were not able to talk to all of the victims, nor did the victims consistently call the police when another incident occurred.

In the Colorado Springs study, the researchers noted that "when the Colorado Springs outcome is constructed from the victim reports rather than from the official data, a strong treatment effect surfaces; the odds multiplier for arrest is approximately .65, and the Bayesian ninety-percent confidence region no longer includes 1.0."[35] I think this means that the odds of a subsequent incident of violence being reported after arrest are sixty-five percent of what they are if no arrest is made. This appears to parallel the Minneapolis data. The authors suspected that the victims linked to bad risk suspects were more difficult to re-contact, which would lead to overemphasis of data collected from good risk suspects. Another possibility, however, is that police data is an unreliable source of information about reincidence of violence and that the results produced using such data are ambiguous and misleading. A third possibility is that the victims of bad risk suspects are more likely to request police assistance than are victims of good risk suspects, because of the social stigma attached to calling the police. If this is the case, the apparent deterrent effect among good risk suspects may represent under-reporting.

The Charlotte study does confirm that police data produces a drastically low estimate of the actual percentage of cases in which more violence occurs. The authors noted that, "[b]ased on police data, repeat incidents are the exception rather than the rule." Interviews with victims, however, indicate "alarmingly high levels of repeat incidents of spouse abuse, confirming that the scope of the problem is far greater than police data indicate. . . . 61.5% of women have experienced another abusive incident within six months."[36]

Use of police data is preferred over victim data because the whole sample of victims is assumed to have at least the opportunity to call the police. Victim data is incomplete because some victims cannot be recontacted, while others cannot remember or do not wish to talk about what happened. But the variables that determine whether anyone calls the police when violence occurs are *at least* as unpredictable and as complex as the location and memory of the victims. The data look neater if police reports are used, but do they reflect even a representative sample of the incidence of recidivism?

D. Variations in Police Behavior: Abuser Deterrence and Victim Deterrence

What do we know about how the police behaved during the experiments? In Milwaukee, the police worked from a script, at least with the suspects whom they did not arrest. We are not told what they said, but we can presume that there was some degree of consistency in police communications with the parties. In Omaha, on the other hand, there was little effort to make the police behavior within each treatment uniform. Suppose that, at one site at which no script was given to the officers, the following two scenarios took place:

In one arrest case, the officer came in, looked around and, in the presence of the victim, said the following to the abuser:

> "Why did you hit her?"
> "She's been catting around again."
> "Listen, buddy, I know how you feel. Believe me, I understand. But we are doing this study at the department, and I am going to have to take you in. If it were up to me, I would not do it. Maybe I would even take *her* in. But under our new policy, I'm supposed to bring you in."

In another case, suppose that an officer came in and, after surveying the room, took the victim to a private place to talk, out of the earshot of the abuser, and said:

"Ma'am, I can see you got something you did not deserve. Can you tell us about it?"

During her story, he took notes, nodded, and listened. Then he told her that the abuser would be arrested but might be released in a matter of hours. He then asked whether she would like transportation to a safer location. After helping the victim to work out her plans, the officer returned to the other room and said:

> Sir, you are under arrest for misdemeanor assault. Just because she is your wife doesn't mean you can do this. If you are convicted of these charges, you could spend six months in jail or be fined $10,000 or both. And believe me, quite a few guys are doing time for just what you did to your wife tonight. You will come with us.[37]

In the replication studies, these two interactions would be categorized as the same "treatment." It would not be uncommon for officers in the same department to behave so differently. The divergence of behavior might be limited by the existence of state or municipal laws or departmental policies that encouraged police to treat violence as a crime. It might be limited by the active implementation of those laws or by policies of the police department, the prosecutors' office, or the courts. We are not offered much information about the context in which each of these experiments was conducted. To the extent that police behavior could vary this much, inconclusive results would not be surprising.

Police behavior during response undoubtedly affects both the likelihood of subsequent violence (deterring the abuser) and the likelihood that the victim will call the police for help during the next incident (deterring the victim).[38] If police behavior in a significant number of cases deterred victims from calling the police again, then the variance in behavior might obscure any differences between the assigned interventions.

Victims of abuse may also have been deterred from calling the police in cases assigned to a non-arrest intervention because of disappointment with the police response. If the police warned the abuser and did not make an arrest, the victim may be less likely to call the police for subsequent incidents because she may perceive that they did not help her. (Imagine, for example, that the police "counseled" the couple, and the beating continued following the departure of the police.) If the police made an arrest, the victim may be more likely to call them after the next incident because she may perceive that they were taking action to protect her. This could skew the data on recidivism higher in the arrest group and lower in the warning group, compared with the actual recurrence of violence.[39] The likely skewing raises additional questions about the researchers' reliance on the police data rather than the victim interviews.

Do the descriptions of the experiments reveal anything about the type of skewing that might have occurred? Is it in fact likely that the non-arrest group was discouraged from reporting? Joan Zorza points out that in Charlotte and Omaha the victims were encouraged to leave the home in many cases.[40] This intervention could be read by the victim as signifying that the police believe that she is at least partly responsible for the problem. If the abuser tends to blame the victim for the violence and the victim blames herself, then many victims would be prone to interpret police eviction from the home as signifying that the victim had done wrong.

In many cases the victim is not safe if she stays home, and the only safe solution is for her to go elsewhere. The police can encourage the victim to relocate without communicating blame, but if this "removal of one of the parties" was part of a standard operating procedure, one might wonder what was said, which victims were removed, how they interpreted their eviction, and what impact that conduct could have had on subsequent reporting of violence to the police by those victims.

E. Does Police Intervention "Cause" Separation, or Vice Versa?

In the Milwaukee report, any police response to a domestic violence call is said to have the effect of tending "to split the couple up." Many couples ceased to cohabit between the time of the arrest and the time of the follow-up interview.[41]

The researchers assumed that separation reduces the risk to the victims, presumably by reducing contact hours. They give no basis for concluding that there is a causal connection between the police response and the separation, beyond the reduced number of cohabitants. In light of the frequent escalation of abuse that accompanies the victim's attempt to separate, this assumption is a dubious one.[42]

Perhaps, instead, it is separation that "causes" arrest. Victims of abuse may call the police because they are attempting to escape the violence and the many other types of control exercised over them by their abusers. Perhaps the police are likely to be called at a point at which there is some psychic separation that has not yet resulted in the woman obtaining a separate place to live. Calling the police certainly communicates a message that the behavior is unacceptable. These data may indicate that women who call the police are likely to separate from their abusers. To assume that the separation is "caused" by the arrest is to treat the women as inanimate objects who are acted upon by the abusers and the police but whose own actions are disregarded.

This other imponderable human factor (the victims, largely invisible in these studies) may account for some of the other observed effects of arrest. Consider the "marginal" group in Milwaukee in which arrest seems to increase the likelihood of more violence. If the victim calls the police, arrest of the abuser communicates to the woman that she has a right not to be abused. The arrest may validate her struggle to escape from the abuser. This may lead her to insist on greater personal autonomy—to be able to leave the house without permission, not to be followed around, to be able to go to school or get a job, see friends, or whatever. At the same time the abuser may be angered by the appearance, evidenced by the arrest, that the "system" was on her side. These types of dynamics could explain increased violence.

This hypothesis could explain the results reported by Sherman et al., but it would lead to different conclusions. Rather than recommending that the police cease to make arrests because the arrest is viewed as a "cause" of subsequent violence, this analysis would indicate that the law enforcement system must continue to offer protection and support to the victim and to incarcerate or monitor the abuser after an arrest is made.

F. The Relationship of Arrest and Unemployment to Subsequent Violence

The Milwaukee data indicate that abusers who are unemployed are more likely to become violent in the six months following arrest than they would be if they had not been arrested. The authors do not speculate as to the reasons for this correlation, except for some references to the stake in society (need to go to work) of employed men and their consequent significant response to arrest.

There are other possible explanations of this data. One, mentioned above, is that the victims of employed abusers may be more reluctant to call the police after an arrest is made due to social stigma or other reasons. There may be no deterrent to violence; there may be only a deterrent to calling the police.[43]

Another possibility is that, if the victim is employed and the abuser is not, the abuser may resent the victim's greater level of productivity and social status, and resent being economically dependent on the victim. Such resentment, exacerbated by arrest, could increase the likelihood of assault.

G. What Happened After Arrest?[44]

Most of the researchers seem to prefer to create the impression that they are studying the effect of arrest in a vacuum. They note the fact that the courts do not prosecute many abuse cases, but they then treat this as an immutable status quo and ignore the fact that the effect of arrest may depend entirely on the type of follow-up. They refer to arrest as both "treatment" and "punishment," as if our criminal justice bureaucracy is a toggle switch capable of only two things: arrest or non-arrest.

These studies provide very little information about whether there was any attempt to enforce the law after arrest in the cases included in the study. They also fail to examine whether the other intervention had any impact on the deterrent effect of arrest. The Charlotte study mentions that thirty-five percent of the cases in the sample in which the police made an arrest were prosecuted, but it does not discuss the outcomes in those cases (except to mention that less than one percent of the convicted offenders received jail sentences). The study also fails to mention the reasons why sixty-five percent of the cases did not result in prosecution, or whether the abusers in cases that did result in prosecution were more effectively deterred than were abusers in the cases that were not prosecuted.[45]

To study effectively the deterrent effect of arrest and prosecution, or to compare the impact of arrest alone against the impact of arrest and prosecution, it would be necessary to randomly assign a group of cases to prosecution. At least in Milwaukee, the researchers tried to secure the cooperation of the prosecutor's office and failed. Perhaps this question will be asked during the site selection process when the next study of this sort is planned. There are some prosecutors who are interested in stopping domestic violence.

Another datum we are given regarding additional procedures is that the Colorado Springs study looked at a large number of cases in which arrest was followed by the victim's obtaining an Emergency Protection Order, which was not part of the experiment at the other sites.[46] We are not told what relief the court ordered or in what proportion of cases the court issued a longer-term order. The rate of subsequent violence in Colorado Springs appears to be lower than that in Milwaukee and Omaha.[47] Is this because victims obtained protection orders or because victims received some other services that were not part of the experiment? These studies ask their readers to assume that the outcomes in these cases are linked to arrest alone, even without knowing what other interventions or relief victims may have obtained.

Perhaps taking a "non-marginal" working person and letting him spend a night at the police station may be enough *all by itself* to scare him into behaving better. Perhaps arrest alone does not have that impact on people who have been in such a situation a few times before. If one accords credence to the new results indicating that arrest may not be a significant deterrent for some domestic abus-ers, then the implication of this study is that higher priority must be given to prosecuting these cases, obtaining protection orders for the victims,[48] and ensuring that the abusers are incarcerated or placed in treatment programs for alcohol abuse or for battering, or all of the above.[49]

H. The Attitudes of the Researchers

The articles presenting the results of the replication studies that are pub-lished in this issue disclose little about the authors' views on domestic violence or about their experience in this field. One wonders whether the researchers believe that they are presenting objective reality rather than a point of view.[50]

Who are the people who conducted this research? What do we know about their perspectives about and experience working on domestic violence? From the articles, one can discern that they are twelve men and three women, mostly academics, a few police officers. The non-inclusion of this type of information is standard practice in most professional writing. However, more information would be useful in trying to understand their work. What do they believe about domestic violence? Why did they do this work? One can discern partial answers to some of these questions from the articles, but they are written in traditional anonymous academic style. This "invisible author" approach is especially ill-suited to this field because the personal beliefs of the professional make an enormous difference in how the person perceives the problem of domestic vio-lence and the appropriate responses. Did the researchers receive any advice or assistance from those who work with battered women or with men who batter? If not, why not?

The articles offer little information about the methodology used by these researchers. We do not know who conducted the follow up interviews, whether they were done by men or women, whether they were done in person or on the telephone, whether the abuser was present during the conversation, or what questions the interviewers asked. How can we interpret these results without this type of information?[51]

I ask these questions in part because these studies approach the problem of wife abuse from some considerable distance; the studies are not designed with a good understanding of the perspective of the victim.[52] I offer a few examples that raise concerns about the authors' perspectives.

1. **"Non-Serious" Domestic Violence.** In the Omaha study, the author mentions that "serious (*i.e.,* felony) cases were excluded" from consider-ation. Because this was a randomized experiment, in which some women received less protection than they would have if police had been using their own discretion, it was essential to try to screen out cases in which the risk of harm from the experiment was greatest. Nevertheless, anyone who has worked with battered women who has tried to get assistance from the police or the courts would not have characterized the cases included in the experiment as "non-seri-

ous." Most advocates for battered women regard any violence between intimates as serious. In every case of domestic violence, there is a likelihood that the victim will suffer more violence at the hands of that offender. In most cases, he has continued access to the victim. The attempt to distinguish serious from non-serious domestic violence is useful only to those who wish to exclude some of the cases from the law enforcement system.[53]

One could define some violence as non-serious by looking at the degree of injury inflicted. This analysis is inappropriate because much unmistakably violent behavior causes no injury at all. For example, if a man throws a lamp at the head of a woman but misses and the lamp explodes against the wall, the woman may not be injured at all, but her life may be in serious danger.

If one measures the seriousness of the violence by intent, one finds that the defining characteristic of domestic violence is that it is intended to cause physical harm to a woman or to make her fear that she will suffer harm in the future. It need not involve any touching. The expression of that intent by a man toward a woman with whom he is or has been in an intimate relationship is serious. Is it nonserious if he only wants to scare her, or if he intends to hurt her but not very badly? The answer is apparent in the question.

If those who conducted these experiments shared the perspective that all domestic violence is serious, they might have been reluctant to undertake this research. Suppose one of the calls to the police that was assigned to mediation was followed a week later by a murder? If this had been perceived as a genuine possibility, the experiments might have been conducted differently, or, indeed, not done at all.[54] Was this category of crime selected for this experiment in deterrence because of a perception that it is less serious than other violent crime?

The authors of the Charlotte study assert that it is obvious that "premium jail space will not be used on misdemeanant spouse abusers."[55] The tone of this comment is similar to the comment in the Omaha study about the exclusion of "serious" cases of domestic abuse. Do the authors believe that what we are dealing with here is a little non-serious criminal activity, perhaps down there with littering or shoplifting? In fact, it is common practice by law enforcement officials to classify as a misdemeanor, domestic violence offenses that would be treated as felonies if the act in question had been committed against a stranger. Thus, the misdemeanor/felony distinction is not a meaningful one in the domestic violence context.

2. Failure to Hold the Abuser Responsible for the Violence.   In the Omaha study, one of the "treatment"[56] options was to send "one of the parties" away from the scene.[57] The author says nothing about who was or should have been removed—as if the only significant part of the intervention is to get the parties temporarily physically separated and that who goes where is irrelevant. This neutral reference to separation suggests that the researcher may not recognize the fairness question (why should the victim leave because of the spouse's criminal conduct?) and the safety question (if the victim stays, will she be a sitting duck for the next assault) implicit in any "separation" intervention. Assuming that the author has described the intervention adequately, this "separation" option, built into the experiment, is one which appears to make no systematic effort to communicate to the abuser that his violence is his responsibility. Perhaps some officers would communicate that idea, and others would not. Does the author understand that the essential purpose of enforcing the law in domestic violence cases, as in other criminal cases, is to force the offender to take responsibility for controlling his conduct?

3. The Exclusion of Non-Cohabitants.   The researchers in the Charlotte and Milwaukee studies included only spouse or "spouse-like" relationships, perhaps reflecting a belief that these are the main categories of battering relationships that are worthy of study. This erroneous assumption may be an unfortunate consequence of the absence of terminology that accurately describes the problem of the battering of women who are or have been in intimate relationships with their abusers. Despite inadequate terminology, most people who work in domestic violence learn early in their work that this is not a problem defined by marital status or living arrangement but by intimacy and aggression. These studies include no mention or explanation of the reasons for excluding the significant number of battering cases that involve people who are or have been dating but not cohabiting.

Perhaps the researchers recognized that there is a significant group of battering relationships that involve parties who are or have been dating but not living together.[58] If they had not known that before, then in Charlotte this should have become apparent from the fact that police received 47,687 calls that were coded as domestic violence, and only 18,963 were determined at the scene to involve "spouse-like" situations.

It is possible that the definition of the problem to exclude non-cohabitants reflects a definition in a statute or police policy. If this is the case, it should be explained. Otherwise the research perpetuates this too-narrow definition of domestic violence. This is important because others may draft statutes and policies based on this research, which provide remedies or services to victims who are married to or living with their abusers, and which exclude others. Another thing that is lost by the exclusion of non-cohabitants is the possibility of understanding the relationship between deterrence and the degree of commitment of the parties. The non-cohabiting parties may be younger, their relationships of shorter duration; and it is possible that they would react to police intervention in quite a different way.

4. The Probable Cause Determination.   The researchers in the Charlotte study excluded from the experiment eighty-two percent of the 18,693 spouse-like cases because "there was no probable cause to believe that a crime had been committed."[59] The authors then asserted that "[t]he above analysis clearly indicates that arrest is not an option in the vast majority (82.2%) of the spouse-like cases [to which the police respond]" because of the absence of probable cause.[60] This assumes that police determinations of probable cause are objective and accurate. Because in most cases the police took no action or merely calmed things down, the author concluded that these were situations that involved "minor problems requiring little or no police action."[61]

What is wrong with this picture? For almost twenty years scholars, advocates, and victims of abuse have been documenting that the police tend to perceive, when looking at domestic violence situations, that no crime has been committed unless the victim has been injured so badly that hospitalization is required. The police often classify felony cases as misdemeanors or as non-criminal if the suspect and the victim are intimate.[62] Dispatchers assign these cases low priority, so the response is often very slow, which reduces the likelihood that the abuser will be on the scene when the police arrive. Most important, police often find no probable cause because the police do not believe the victims' allegations, sometimes because the abuser denies them and sometimes for other reasons.[63]

To examine whether there really was no objective basis to find probable cause to arrest in such a high percentage of cases, the researchers would need to interview the victims who called the police and compare the police conclusions about the situation with the victims' stories. It seems unlikely, however, that 19,000 people in Charlotte called the police (almost 9,000 "spouse-like") without a good reason.

In drawing conclusions about their data in an earlier draft of their article, Richard Berk and his co-authors offered the suggestion that if some offenders pose higher risks of recidivating, one could put "further constraints on high risk offenders. . . . For example, bail could be made much higher . . . *suspects* could be strongly encouraged to make use of local shelters for battered women which might also reduce risk of retaliation."[64]

Okay, it is a typo. And probably after the editors read this comment, it will be corrected so that the victims are no longer referred to as the suspects. But one assumes that this article was carefully written, and probably proofread by more than one person before the draft was turned in. And of course anyone could make a mistake. But one must wonder—why this mistake? Why do these authors mix up the victims and the abusers? Would an advocate for battered women have made this error?

5. The Goals of the Researchers.   What do the researchers tell us about their motivations for undertaking this work? Sherman, et al. say little about the purpose of their study. What they do say is that, among the police with whom they were working, "the primary concern was the reduction of calls to police about domestic violence citywide."[65] This made it important for them to look seriously at whether a disproportionate number of calls were coming from a small number of offenders.

Perhaps it is so obvious as not to require mention, but I would have thought the purpose of this study was to determine how to prevent men from abusing women. If the police simply want to reduce the number of domestic calls that they have to respond to, I can think of two simpler methods. (1) Disconnect the phone. (2) Go back to the good old days, and just stop answering these calls.

IV. Conclusion

What are the implications for state legislators and policy makers of this new research on the effectiveness of arrest as a deterrent in domestic violence cases? Dr. Sherman takes the position that in some cases, arresting the offender makes subsequent violence more likely, and therefore, the laws mandating arrest of men who abuse women should be repealed. Sherman acknowledges that prosecution and incarceration of offenders would incapacitate them and might be a deterrent to others. But, he urges, resources are inadequate to undertake prosecution of these cases, because they are so numerous, and even if the resources are available, many prosecutors are not interested.[66]

Dr. Sherman explains this recommendation by asserting that based on the data indicating an escalation effect of arrest among domestic abusers who are unemployed, unmarried, and black, it would be irresponsible to continue to mandate arrests. While this position undoubtedly reflects genuine concern that the police should not take action which might cause harm, this reasoning also provides a justification for withdrawing the criminal justice system from efforts to stop domestic violence. The repeal of the mandatory arrest laws would effect a dramatic cessation of treatment of domestic abuse as a crime, since, in the absence of a mandate, the police tend to exercise discretion not to arrest men who abuse women.

The replication data make a stronger case for more law enforcement than they do for less law enforcement. The data show a high likelihood of repeat assaults—this population of victims is in greater danger than are victims of other violent crime. The data suggest that the risks of subsequent violence is greater if the abuser has a criminal record (Charlotte) or if the abuser is unemployed, unmarried, or black and is arrested (Milwaukee). This offers a possible basis for targeting certain categories of cases for careful and diligent prosecution and for strenuous efforts to jail offenders and to provide services to the victims. No one has yet tested whether a fullscale effort to enforce the law in these cases will produce deterrence, but neither has such an effect been demonstrated for cases involving homicide or drug-dealing. The entire system would grind to a halt if policy initiatives were contingent upon empirical proof of their effectiveness.

In states which have or are considering enactment of mandatory arrest laws, legislators should examine other steps that would help to ensure full enforcement of the law. Legislative options include: funds for domestic violence programs, including shelters, counseling programs; funds to set up domestic violence units in prosecutors' offices; funds to provide training for prosecutors, judges, court personnel and others, on handling of domestic violence cases. State legislatures could enact legislation that would require prosecutors to keep data on their handling of domestic abuse cases and require them to make a written record of reasons for decisions not to prosecute. They could enact legislation that would increase the post-arrest protection offered to victims of abuse during and after prosecution of a charge, by providing for criminal courts to issue specific protective orders as a condition of release and as a condition of probation, and by increasing supervision of abusers while charges are pending and during probation.

In some states it is not possible at present to propose new appropriations. If new resources are not available, the question becomes one of priorities. Prosecutors need to re-evaluate the low priority often assigned to domestic assault. If a principal goal of prosecuting criminals is to protect members of a community from harm, then crimes of violence against persons should be given priority over crimes against property. Violent crimes in which the victim is in continuing danger should be accorded even higher priority than isolated assaults against strangers. A prosecutor might consider reallocating resources presently devoted to prosecution of shoplifters, prostitutes, and burglars to prosecuting men who repeatedly assault women with whom they are or have been in intimate relationships.

The data from the replication studies should lead us to worry about communities in which the police are required to make arrests, and in which the state takes no post-arrest action to protect the victims from further assaults. The escalation effect of arrest on some offenders makes clear that "arrest-only" is not an adequate law enforcement response to domestic violence. But the lesson for legislators, researchers, advocates, prosecutors, judges, and police is that we must focus not only on police conduct in domestic abuse cases, but also on whether and how prosecutors and judges are enforcing the law.

NOTES

[1] Philip Boffey, Domestic Violence: Study Favors Arrest, *New York Times*, April 5, 1983, at C1.

[2] See Lawrence Sherman & Richard Berk, The Minneapolis Domestic Violence Experiment (Police Foundation Reports 1984).

[3] In discussing the legislative implications of this work, the authors emphasized that "[t]his experiment shows the vital importance of state legislatures empowering police to make probable cause arrests in cases of domestic simple assault." Id.

[4] Lisa G. Lerman et al., State Legislation on Domestic Violence, in *Response* (Sept./Oct. 1983) (reporting that thirty-three states had expanded police power to make arrests in domestic abuse cases, and six states had mandated the use of arrest in some domestic abuse cases).

[5] I have the impression that the study tended to focus policy makers on police response as a separate entity and may have led advocates and policy makers to believe that police action *by itself* could offer some sort of solution for abused women. I believe that a great deal more scholarship in the last decade has focused on police response to woman abuse than on prosecution or court action.

[6] Telephone interview with Carol Petrie, National Institute of Justice (Feb. 28, 1991). Petrie estimated that $4 million had been spent on the six replication studies.

[7] I do not mean to malign the Department of Justice for funding research on domestic violence, or even for funding research on the effect of arrest. But, as my comments indicate, I believe that the studies could have been constructed in ways that would have allowed us to learn more from the data. See, e.g., text accompanying notes 44–45 infra.

[8] Daniel Goleman, Do Arrests Increase the Rates of Repeated Domestic Violence? *New York Times*, Nov. 27, 1991, at C8.

[9] Rogers Worthington, Value of Mandatory Arrest for Women Beaters Questioned, *Chicago Tribune*, Nov. 19, 1991, at 5C. The newspaper paraphrases Sherman's comment, and I would be delighted to learn that they had misunderstood him.

[10] I do not wish to communicate disrespect for social science research in general, but only to make the point that looking at one corner of a massive and multifaceted problem through a microscope may not produce any significant new knowledge.

[11] Each study compares the effects of three of these "treatments."

[12] Others have used mouse images to capture situations in which human beings were being treated as experimental animals, see e.g., Art Spiegelman, Maus (1986), or in which human beings have been placed in dehumanizing situations, see e.g., Mon Oncle D'Amerique (Film by Jean Renoir, 1984). Though a mouse would not fit in a test tube, the image is more evocative than that of a paramecium.

[13] See e.g., Snell et al., The Wifebeaters Wife: A Study of Family Interaction, 11 Archives General Psychiatry 107 (1964).

[14] See R. Emerson Dobash & Russell Dobash, Violence Against Wives: A Case Against the Patriarchy (1979).

[15] See National Institute of Justice, Civil Protection Orders: Legislation Current Court Practice and Enforcement (1990); Lisa G. Lerman, A Model State Act: Remedies for Domestic Abuse, 21 Harv. J. On Legis. 61 (1984).

[16] My reasons for this view are explained in Lisa G. Lerman et al., Domestic Abuse and Mediation: Guidelines for Mediators and Policymakers (1990). See also Lisa G. Lerman, Mediation of Wife Abuse Cases: The Adverse Impact of Informal Dispute Resolution on Women, 7 Harv. Women's L. J. 57 (1984).

[17] See e.g., Jeffrey L. Edelson, Coordinated Community Responses, in Woman Battering: Policy Responses 203 (Michael Steinman ed., 1991).

[18] David Hirschel and Ira Hutchison point out that since the Minneapolis Experiment, there has been a fourfold increase in police departments with pro-arrest policies, but that most departments still have not changed their policies to conform with statutes. David Hirschel & Ira Hutchison, Female Spouse Abuse and the Police Response: The Charlotte, North Carolina Experiment, 83 J. Crim. L. & Criminology 73 (1992).

[19] In the District of Columbia, a departmental policy requiring police to file reports and make arrests seemed to have virtually no impact on police conduct. See Saundra Torry, DC Targets Domestic Violence: Law Requires Arrest if Abuse Suspected, Washington Post, Nov. 11, 1991, at C1.

[20] See U.S. Attorney General's Task Force, on Family Violence, U.S. Department of Justice, Final Report 10–26 (1984); Lisa G. Lerman, Prosecution of Spouse Abuse: Innovations in Criminal Justice Response (1981).

[21] Some of the reasons for preferring that arrest be mandated by statute are explained in Sarah Buel, Mandatory Arrest for Domestic Violence, 11 Harv. Women's L. J. 213 (1988).

[22] Sherman & Berk, supra note 2, at 2 (reporting studies that indicated arrest rates in domestic violence cases of ten percent and three percent). A 1989 study in DC found an arrest rate of five percent in domestic violence cases. D.C. Coalition Against Domestic Violence, (Press release) "Study of D.C. Police Response to Domestic Violence Shows Police Do Not Make Arrests, in Violation of their own Guidelines," November 3, 1989.

[23] Changing criminal justice response to a problem is complex. It is not always possible to secure change in every institution at the same time. I recently participated in drafting a mandatory arrest bill for the District of Columbia, as part of the Legal Committee of the D.C. Coalition Against Domestic Violence. In our decision to make police response a primary focus, we considered the chicken/egg question: we were very concerned both about inadequate police response and about the apparent unwillingness of the United States Attorney's Office (which acts as the local prosecutor in D.C.) to

prosecute any but a trivial number of domestic violence cases. Some of us felt that by strengthening police response, we would put pressure on the prosecutor's office to take these cases seriously because when an arrest is made, a decision regarding whether or not to file charges must be made.

24 It does seem that empirical research presented in an interdisciplinary journal to an audience of policy makers ought to be translated into English. These papers are comprehensible in significant part, but they do not reflect much awareness of their non-social science audience.

25 The National Institute of Justice may do some comparative analysis of the data produced by the six replication studies. Telephone interview with Carol Petrie, National Institute of Justice (Feb. 28, 1991). Reports from two of the sites (Atlanta, GA, and Dade County, FL), are not yet available. Id.

26 Lawrence Sherman, et al., The Variable Effects of Arrest on Criminal Careers: The Milwaukee Domestic Violence Experiment, 83 *J. Crim. L. & Criminology* 137, 168 (1992).

27 Hirschel & Hutchison, supra note 18, at 104.

28 Id. at 115, 117.

29 Sherman & Berk, supra note 2, at 5.

30 See infra at 238–40.

31 In analyzing the Milwaukee data, Berk et al. point out that "the two arrest treatments seemed to delay the onset of new violence by a little more than a month compared to the warning treatment." Richard Berk et al., A Bayesian Analysis of the Colorado Springs Spouse Abuse Experiment, 83 *J. Crim. L. & Criminology* 170, 173 (1992).

32 See Hirschel & Hutchison, supra note 18, at 118.

33 See Berk, supra note 31, at 194.

34 Id. at 173.

35 Id. at 197.

36 See Hirschel & Hutchison, supra note 18, at 116.

37 These dialogues are fictitious, but they are extrapolated from many conversations between the author and abused women, police officers, and advocates for abused women about the range of conversations that take place between police officers and abused women.

38 In 1984 Sherman and Berk observed that
There was one factor . . . that seemed to govern the effectiveness of arrest: whether the police showed interest in the victim's side of the story. . . .
If the police do listen, that reduces the occurrence of repeat violence even more. But if the victims think the police did not take the time to listen, then the level of victim-reported violence is much higher. One interpretation of this finding is that by listening to the victim, the police "empower" her with their strength, letting the suspect know that she can influence their behavior.
Sherman & Berk, supra note 2, at 6.

39 This analysis assumes that the victims prefer law enforcement to warning.

40 Joan Zorza, The Criminal Law of Misdemeanor Domestic Violence, 1970–1990, 83 *J. Crim. L. & Criminology* 46, 68 (1992).

41 Sherman et al., explain:
ninety percent of the 1200 police reports and seventy-four percent of the 900 initial victim interviews reported that the couples were cohabiting on the date of the presenting incident. This compares to only forty-one percent of the total follow-up interviews reporting cohabitation since the presenting incident.
Sherman et al., supra note 26, at 152.

[42] See Martha Mahoney, Legal Images of Battered Women: Redefining the Issue of Separation, 90 *Michigan Law Review* 1 (1991).

[43] Some victims might be deterred from calling the police because of threats of harm or death that would follow any additional contact with the police.

[44] See Brian Forst et al., What Happens After Arrest? (1977).

[45] See Hirschel & Hutchison, supra note 18, at 117.

[46] In Milwaukee, cases in which a victim had obtained a restraining order were excluded from the sample.

[47] Berk et al., supra note 31, at Table 3.

[48] After a suspect is arrested, a judge can (as a condition of release or as an independent civil order) issue a very specific injunction designed for the protection of the victim. The effect of arrest might be quite different if such an order is issued, in writing, and a copy given to the police.

[49] Prosecutors can require abusive men to get treatment for their violence problems while charges are pending and can ask a judge to require continued treatment as part of the disposition of the case. Abusive men generally will not go to treatment of their own free will, but they can be compelled to go if they have criminal charges pending against them (as a condition of release on bail), or have a chance at a suspended jail sentence. This type of coercion is not found to interfere in the treatment of abusers as it might with other problems, and it provides ongoing monitoring and attention to the behavior of the abuser. See Donald G. Dutton & Barbara M. S. McGregor, The Symbiosis of Arrest and Treatment for Wife Assault: The Case for Combined Intervention, in Woman Battering: Policy Responses 131 (Michael Steinman ed., 1991). These authors conclude, after examining the effectiveness of specialized treatment for abusers in Canada, that "law and order" and treatment approaches operate symbiotically to reduce further violence. Arrest serves both a didactic and deterrent function, showing the man that wife assault is unacceptable and will be punished by the state. Treatment then provides the opportunity for the man to learn new responses to the interchanges with his wife that formerly generated violent behavior. Id. at 150.

[50] I provide here some information about my own background, to enable the reader to better understand the perspective from which I write. I began working on woman abuse in 1979 when I became the staff attorney on a family violence project at the Center for Women Policy Studies. I had had little exposure to issues of domestic violence before I started work on this project. I brought to this project a feminist perspective, and some previous work on violent pornography to my role as staff attorney. Working under a federal grant from the Law Enforcement Assistance Administration, I studied the usefulness of the various legal interventions in domestic violence situations, reading the literature, participating in professional meetings, and doing site visits, mostly to federally funded demonstration projects. My perspective reflects extensive contact with lawyers and other advocates for abused women.

[51] Dr. Sherman reported to me that in Milwaukee, all of the victim interviewers were women, about half were black, and said that they were recruited from battered women's shelters and from universities. Telephone conversation between Lawrence Sherman and the author, May 7, 1992.

[52] In some of my comments I undoubtedly overgeneralize in my reactions to these articles—this is almost inevitable in a short commentary of this sort.

[53] See, e.g., Charles A. Bethel & Linda R. Singer, Mediation: A New Remedy for Cases of Domestic Violence, 7 *Vt. L. Rev.* 15–25 (1982) (explaining the exclusion of domestic vio-

lence cases involving serious injury from mediation, and then offering as an example of a non-serious injury case one in which the abuser carried a gun and the victim's injuries required a visit to the emergency room but involved no broken bones.) Id. at 22, 24.

[54] When the Minneapolis experiment was funded, many advocates for abused women (I among them) were concerned about the risks posed to victims from random assignment, and the about ethical dilemma and potential liability for the researchers presented by doing this type of experimental work. We were especially concerned about experimenting on a set of cases that involve violent crime and that present a high likelihood that the same suspect will attack the same victim again.

[55] See Hirschel & Hutchison, supra note 18, at 118.

[56] Perhaps it is standard to refer to the thing you are testing in a social science experiment as a "treatment," but it seems misleading in this context, in that the word conveys the impression that the arrest itself is a discrete and independent response, complete and separate from any other aspect of law enforcement. The use of this word reflects the failure of the researchers to view arrest as a step in the law enforcement process.

[57] See Franklyn W. Dunford, The Measurement of Recidivism in Cases of Spouse Assault, 83 J. Crim. L. & Criminology 120 (1992).

[58] Often domestic violence continues after a couple separates, whether the couple has been married or not. See Mahoney, supra note 42. Domestic violence also occurs in dating relationships in which the couple is not cohabiting.

[59] Hirschel & Hutchison, supra note 18, at 94.

[60] Id.

[61] Id.

[62] A graphic example offered by Nancy Loving, infra note 63, from a newspaper article:
It was about 4 o'clock in the afternoon when a call came into the 103rd Precinct station house in Jamaica, Queens, from a woman who said her husband had beaten her, that her face was bleeding and bruised. She thought some of her ribs had been broken. "Can you help me?" she pleaded to the police officer who answered the phone. "My husband's gone now, but he said he would come back and kill me." She was also frightened, she said, that he would start beating the children when she returned.
"It's not a Police Department thing," the officer told her. "It's really a family thing. You'll have to go to Family Court tomorrow. There's nothing that I can do."
New York Times (June 14, 1976).

[63] See United States Commission on Civil Rights, Under the Rule of Thumb: Battered Women and the Administration of Justice 12–22 (1982); See generally Nancy Loving, Responding to Spouse Abuse and Wife Beating: A Guide for Police (1980).

[64] Draft corresponding to Berk et al., supra note 31, at 198–99 (emphasis added).

[65] See Sherman et al., supra note 26, at 155.

[66] Telephone conversations between Dr. Sherman and the author, April 23 and May 8, 1992.

When the Batterer Wears Blue
A National Study of the Institutional Response to Domestic Violence Among Police

Helen M. Eigenberg and Victor E. Kappeler

Before the 1970s, police officers rarely invoked the formal legal process in response to cases of "family violence." Traditionally, officers were trained to avoid arresting perpetrators and were instructed to attempt to defuse or mediate these situations (Berk and Loseke, 1980; Goolkasian, 1986a, 1986b; Loving, 1981; Waits, 1985). Thus, police officers failed to treat battering as a crime, especially when it involved misdemeanor offenses. Instead, it was viewed as a private, family matter. This "classic" police response has been "characterized as one of virtual nonfeasance" with police evading "their responsibility to protect victims of crimes within families" (Buzawa & Buzawa, 1993, p. 338). Because of the historical tendency to ignore the criminal nature of battering and an unwillingness to arrest, particularly in misdemeanor cases, policing has received extensive scrutiny from both advocates and researchers. Perhaps no other segment of the criminal justice system has received as much scrutiny as has policing over the issues of domestic violence.

The police play a critical gatekeeping function in the criminal justice system (Alpert and Dunham, 1997). Since they are the entryway to the system, few criminal laws are enforced unless the police take action. Advocates and researchers alike were interested in examining arrest patterns of police officers. Advocates have long contended that the police institution resists treating battering as a significant crime worthy of its attention. Research seems to support this contention, finding that officers continue to treat battering cases differently than other types of assault. These studies suggest that officers are more apt to arrest in domestic assaults when they believe victims want the batterer arrested and when victims are perceived to be willing to "follow through" with prosecutions (Berk & Loseke, 1980; Buzawa & Austin, 1993; Dolon, Hendricks, & Meagher, 1986; Loving & Fanner cited in Dutton, 1988). Thus despite many improvements, empirical data suggest that police officers are less apt to arrest in domestic than non-domestic assaults (see Eigenberg, Scarborough, & Kappeler, 1996).

While research supports a hesitation on the part of police officers to arrest domestic violence offenders, very little is known about battering when it involves police officers. The paucity of data and inadequate theoretical development make it difficult to ascertain the extent and frequency of the problem, and it is equally difficult to estimate how this police crime might impact institutional responses to battering. The traditional failure of policing to adequately respond to battering, even when committed by the public, would suggest that victims of battering by those in blue—by police officers—will receive little assistance. Furthermore, the literature on deviance and the subcultural aspects of policing suggests that officers are particularly loath to invoke the power of the criminal justice system against "one of their own" (Westley, 1956; Skolnick, 1966; Kappeler, Sluder, & Alpert, 1998). Until recently, domestic violence among police officers has been virtually ignored by the public, police officials, and scholars. Passage of federal legislation, the Lautenberg Act (1996), has brought public visibility to the issue of batterers in blue.

The Lautenberg Act, passed in September 1996, prohibits individuals, including police officers, from owning firearms or ammunition if they have ever been convicted of a misdemeanor act of domestic violence. Shortly after passage of the legislation some police departments as well as local and national organizations began to call for a repeal of the law (Pace, 1997). Opponents of the legislation argue that the law's provisions involve extensive labor to identify officers with convictions and that it will result in the firing of large numbers of officers (Reibstein & Engen, 1996). Many of these may be competent officers who have an older conviction on their record. These organizations argue that the law is too broad and that its retroactive provision is unfair to officers who might have plead guilty to resolve a charge rather than mount an expensive and drawn out legal defense without knowing that it would ultimately cost them their jobs (Pace, 1997). Ironically, then, this argument attempts to summon sympathy for innocent police officers "railroaded" by the criminal justice system—a complaint often noted and rejected in some police circles when made about other "criminals" (see, Skolnick, 1966; Kappeler et al., 1998).

In contrast, some advocates and other proponents of the legislation tended to quote relatively high estimates of the amount of battering by police officers to stress the need for laws that remove batterers from the occupation. They argue that police officers should not be treated differently than other batterers and ask why police should be granted special privileges and be allowed to possess a weapon unlike other members of society? Advocates also argue that police batterers are probably less apt to enforce laws pertaining to domestic violence and that they should, therefore, be removed from the profession. Unfortunately, however, there is a tendency for both sides to rely on speculation and the relatively few studies with little or no mention of their methodological deficiencies.

LITERATURE REVIEW

While there is a growing body of knowledge on police deviance and criminality (Kappeler, Sluder, & Alpert, 1998), very little literature directly addresses domestic violence by police officers. We were only able to identify two empirical studies germane to this issue, and only one of them has been published. The unpublished study by Johnson (1991, cited in Neidig, Russell, & Seng, 1992 and Levinson, 1997), which became the basis for Congressional testimony, purportedly surveyed 728 police officers and 479 spouses of officers in two East Coast departments in the mid-1980s. Johnson reportedly found that 40 percent of the officers surveyed indicated they had behaved violently toward their spouses and/or children in the previous six months. Only 10 percent of the officers' spouses indicated that they had experienced physical violence at the hands of their police-husbands. Abuse, however, was not defined in the study and the context of the violence is not clear—making it impossible to determine what types of acts occurred and whether the violence was an act of aggression or defense.

The published study conducted by Neidig, Russell, and Seng (1992) more clearly defines abuse, but it also fails to ascertain context. The authors surveyed 385 male-police officers, 115 female spouses, and 40 female-police officers attending in-service training and law enforcement conferences in a southwestern state. Using a modified version of the conflict tactics scale, (CTS),[2] respondents were asked whether they had engaged in a variety of behaviors that were classified as serious and minor violence. With respect to minor violence, male officers reported being victimized by their spouses more often than they themselves engaged in violence against their spouses (27 and 25% respectively). In contrast, "wives of male officers" and female officers reported they themselves were more apt to commit minor violence (30% of the wives and 27% of the female officers) than to experience it at the hands of their spouses (25% of the wives and 17% of the female officers). Our analysis of their summary data, however, found these differences statistically non-significant.[3]

In a similar vein, male officers were more apt to report that they had experienced severe violence at the hands of their spouses (6%) than to report that they themselves had committed violence (3%). Wives of officers reported that they were equally likely to commit violence themselves or to be victimized by their officer husbands (3%). In contrast, 20 percent of female officers reported that they had experienced severe violence committed by their spouses, and none reported having committed severe violence. The small sample size makes it impossible, however, to determine whether these differences were significant. In

general, then, the findings suggest that mutual violence exists in police families—that women are as violent as men in these relationships. It is likely, however, that this finding is an aberration of using the CTS.

There are many severe flaws with the CTS. These shortcomings likely produce results that overestimate the amount of violence committed by women
while also underestimating the amount of violence committed by men in intimate relationships. The CTS scale contains no context for the violence it measures. Acts of self-defense and acts of aggression both are counted as acts of
violence and are reflected in the reported estimates of violence. Furthermore, the
CTS estimates only the most serious act of violence and ignores the clustered
nature of violence.

While it is clear that the CTS consistently finds that women commit equal
or higher levels of violence toward their male partners in intimate relationships
(Straus, 1993), there is little indication that the instrument is valid (see Dobash,
Dobash, Wilson, & Daly, 1994). Only studies using the CTS find evidence of sexual symmetry or mutual combat. The National Crime Victimization Survey in
the United States and victimization surveys in both Great Britain and Canada
(Dobash, Dobash, Wilson, & Daly, 1994) indicate that most assaults are committed by men against women, who are their intimate partners. Likewise, studies
based on emergency room records, police reports, prosecution summaries, judicial records, and homicide data all consistently demonstrate that the vast majority of battering victims are women (Tjaden & Thoennes, 1998). Thus, the
findings in the Neidig study which report that men and women are equally and
mutually violent as reported by male officers and their female spouses appear to
be suspect and must be evaluated with great caution.

The Neidig study fails to discuss why one might expect that male officers
experience more violence from their wives than they commit toward their wives.
These findings certainly contradict the image of police officers as very masculine
(even macho) physical men (Hunt, 1990; Harris, 1973; Haarr, 1997) who are
trained to confront violent, armed, and dangerous criminals. The policing literature suggests that male police officers are highly resistant to integrating female
police officers into their ranks (Christopher Commission, 1991; Haarr, 1997) and
that a large part of their opposition is related to stereotypical images of gender
and femininity (Price, 1996; Hunt, 1990). Male police officers report that female
police officers are not aggressive enough for police work (Hindman, 1975; Linden, 1984; Vega and Silverman, 1982); contend that women lack the physical
strength necessary to be effective police officers (Balkin, 1988; Block & Anderson, 1973; Martin, 1980; Remmington, 1983); and assert that women's lack of
physical strength compromises public and police safety (see Koenig, 1978). This
body of literature portrays a dramatically different picture of the nature of
women police. While male police officers consider women, as a group, to be too
small, too weak, and too passive to maintain order even when they are wearing a
gun and sanctioned by the state to use force, male police officers report experiencing women as powerful and physically aggressive at home as evidenced by
data that suggest that women and men are about equally likely to use violence in

police families (Neidig, Russell, & Seng, 1992). In other words, very limited research suggests that male police officers are being physically victimized at home with some degree of frequency by women but, nonetheless, officers are able to maintain a worldview that defines women as members of the "weaker" sex who are incapable of being physically aggressive making them poorly suited for police work.

The Neidig study also fails to discuss another interesting gender difference in their findings. While female officers were about as likely as male officers and their wives to report that they had committed minor violence, female officers were much more likely to report that they experienced serious violence (20% of the female officers, 6% of male officers, and 3% of male officers' wives reported their spouses committed violence against them). Furthermore, none of the female officers reported that they themselves had used serious violence against their spouses (compared to 3% reported by male officers and their spouses). The authors report this finding but fail to discuss why this difference might occur.[4] In fact, after reporting this data, female officers are excluded from all subsequent analysis and discussion. Perhaps female officers are more apt to define certain experiences as serious violence. It is possible that female officers' work experience and training make it more difficult to deny the serious nature of the assaults. It is also possible, however, that male spouses are more apt to commit serious acts of violence against female officers.

The Neidig study concludes by asserting that violence in law enforcement families is disproportionately high based on comparisons that measure violence committed by either the male or female partner in the relationship. It reports that 41 percent of law enforcement families have experienced some form of "relationship violence" compared to 32 percent of military families (Neidig, 1991 cited in Neidig et al., 1992) and 16 percent of the general population (Straus & Gelles, 1990). They contend that the "unique demands of the profession" as well as specific working conditions contribute to the high risk of violence in police officers' homes. Battering, like suicide and divorce, is simply another "hazard" of the profession (p. 37). Implicit in this explanation is the idea that police stress results in more battering.

While it may seem logical to argue that the unique stressors of policing result in more violence in police families, this explanation is problematic for several reasons. First, stress in police work has been examined for over two decades but this body of literature fails to offer much insight into the nature of stress in the profession. While it is generally recognized that police stress exists, there is little, if any, agreement regarding its causes, effects, or extent (Gaines & Van Tubergen, 1989; Kappeler, Blumberg, & Potter, 2000; Mallory & Mays, 1984). Second, this explanation is theoretically void. While there may be some reason to hypothesize that police officers might act out violently at home because of the stress of their jobs, it is less clear why the spouses of officers would engage in violence in response to any supposed job-related stress experienced by spouses. Furthermore, this explanation cannot account for differences by gender. It cannot explain why female officers were more apt to experience severe violence by their partners than were male officers or spouses of male officers. If job-related stress "causes" officers to batter, then one might logically expect that female officers would engage in significantly more frequent and more serious violence toward their intimates since female officers face disproportionately higher levels of job stress due to sexual harassment and sexual discrimination on the force (Martin, 1990; Kraska & Kappeler, 1995; Haarr, 1997).

The most intuitive and perhaps most comforting explanation for police deviance, including battering, is the "rotten apple theory" (Sherman, 1974). Police deviance is viewed as the result of a few aberrant officers—a handful of rogue cops. This type of explanation is quite popular and is often used to explain police deviance ranging from drug use to sexual violence (questioning the adequacy of the theory, Kappeler, et al., 1998; Kraska & Kappeler, 1995). However, scholars have rejected this individualistic conceptualization of police deviance in favor of broader group socialization models (Sherman, 1974, 1982; Stoddard, 1968; Westley, 1953, 1970). From this wider perspective, police deviance is not the product of aberrant officers but rather the product of an entire array of social and cultural forces that shape police behavior.

This model of police deviance also complements feminist theory, which asserts that widespread social values that deem women inferior to men result in social structures that allow for and encourage battering. Instead of seeing battering as mutual violence occurring in response to the breakdown of the family, individual pathologies or stress, feminist scholarship concentrates on the ways in which the institution of marriage itself has been organized, defined, and socially reproduced in ways that facilitate the battering of women. The family reflects the larger social, political, and economic arrangements in a society where male violence against women, especially their wives, is not only tolerated but encouraged and where battering in the family has been viewed as a private matter rather than a crime by society as a whole. It seems improbable that police officers as individuals would be less susceptible to this socialization and therefore less apt to engage in battering than would members of the general public, especially since their occupational core function is the administration of force (Bittner, 1970).

Furthermore, it seems especially unlikely that police officers would view battering among their ranks as serious crime worthy of sanction by the criminal justice system. The literature on police subculture suggests that woman battering, like other forms of police deviance, will be difficult to detect because the subculture promotes solidarity and prohibits officers from exposing deviance to outsiders (Banton, 1964; Manning, 1997; Reuss-Ianni, 1983; Savitz, 1971; Skolnick, 1966, Stoddard, 1968; Westley, 1953, 1956, 1970). The "blue wall of silence" makes it difficult to gather reliable data (Manning, 1997; Skolnick, 1966; and Westley, 1954) and generally is perceived to result in underreporting of all forms of police deviancy. This would seem especially problematic given the changing social views on the acceptability of domestic violence and a less than socially desirable reporting climate. Thus, while the relatively few self-report studies find that there is, indeed, a significant amount of battering committed by police officers, the police deviancy literature suggests that battering will rarely be officially reported when the batterer wears blue.

Historical Context of the Lautenberg Act

The U.S. legal system historically failed to treat women battering as a crime, and this statement is particularly true of misdemeanor assaults. Throughout the 1700s and the 1800s U.S. courts allowed the "physical chastisement" of wives as long as it was within "reasonable" bounds (Stedman, 1917). Courts held that husbands had the power and duty to "discipline" their wives, reasoning that private chastisement caused less public controversy and created less trouble than a public trial. Thus, a long line of legal precedent granted husbands legal immunity for beating their wives. The first U.S. court case to formally recognize this "right" was decided by the Supreme court of Mississippi in 1824, although it illustrates a line of reasoning several centuries old.

> It is true according to the old law, the husband might give his wife moderate correction, it was thought reasonable, to intrust him, with a power, necessary to restrain the indiscretions of one, for whose conduct he was to be made responsible. . . . Family broils and dissensions cannot be investigated before the tribunals of the country, without casting a shade over the character of those who are unfortunately engaged in the controversy. To screen from public reproach those who may be thus unhappily situated, let the husband be permitted to exercise the right moderate chastisement, in cases of great emergency, and use salutary restraints in every case of misbehavior, without being subjected to vexatious prosecutions, resulting in the mutual discredit and shame of all parties concerned. (1824, p. 156)

This decision was overturned seventy years later (*Harris v. State*, 1894), and it took another seventy years before legal reforms undermined a husband's right to beat his wife with virtual impunity. There has been less controversy associated with felony battering. Theoretically, it seems that most individuals and organizations assume the criminal justice system should address felony battering. While enforcement may be problematic, it is difficult to argue, at least in principle, against arrest for severe assaults.

In contrast, it has been more controversial to pursue rigorous law enforcement of misdemeanor cases involving domestic violence. Before the 1980s, most police officers were prohibited from making an arrest in misdemeanor assault cases unless they witnessed the assault. By 1983, 28 states had legislation that allowed the police to make warrantless arrests if police officers had probable cause to believe that a batterer had committed a misdemeanor assault involving domestic violence (Lerman & Livingston, 1983). By 1992, all but two states (West Virginia and Alabama) had made similar changes in state statutes (Zorza, 1992). Some state legislators have gone beyond simply allowing police officers to arrest in these cases and are requiring arrest. In response to the fear of legal liability and to continuing evidence of inadequate policing practices, some states have moved toward requiring arrest in misdemeanor battering cases as a way to eliminate—or more precisely—control police discretion. In a similar vein, some states have initiated mandatory reporting procedures that require officers to document their actions on all domestic violence calls to improve accountability (Zorza, 1992).

While the advantages and disadvantages of mandatory arrest laws (and police policies that effectively require the same action) are often hotly debated among academic circles, it is impossible to fully evaluate both intended and unintended consequences of these reforms. Regardless of one's views on the subject, it is clear that there has been a recent tendency to concentrate on the policing of misdemeanor cases of domestic violence. This historical context is an important factor in the consideration of whether the retroactive nature of the Lautenberg Act is arbitrary and unfair.[5]

The Lautenberg Act was an amendment to the Omnibus Consolidated Appropriations Act of 1997. It modifies the Gun Control Act of 1968. It prohibits possession of firearms and/or ammunition by anyone who has been convicted of domestic violence. While felony convictions, of all kind, have traditionally been used to limit gun ownership, the new law extends this provision to misdemeanor convictions of domestic violence.

The legislation provides that any misdemeanor offense committed by a spouse (current or former), a cohabitating partner (past or present), a person with whom the victim has a child, or a parent or guardian involving the use of physical force or the threatened use of a deadly weapon constitutes an act of domestic violence. The offense need not be legally labeled "domestic violence" by state statute as long as it meets the force or threat criteria. For example, a person may be convicted of trespassing and be ineligible to possess firearms or ammunition regardless of whether the conviction occurred before or after passage of the law. Of course, offenders can have the charge expunged or secure a pardon. Individuals in possession of firearms or ammunition in violation of the Lautenberg Act are instructed by the Bureau of Alcohol, Tobacco and Firearms (BATF) to surrender these items to their attorney, local law enforcement officials, or a licensed gun dealer. Violations of the law are punishable by a fine of $250,000 and/or imprisonment of up to 10 years.

Traditionally, most Federal Acts with firearms provisions have exempted police and military employees (similar to the Violence Against Women Act [VAWA] provision, which allows police officers with a valid protective order to possess a weapon while on duty), and the Lautenberg Act did not specifically set out to break new ground in this respect. Ironically, lawmakers who were "guns-rights" supporters removed the military and police exemption in an attempt to defeat the bill (Thompson, 1997). The tactic backfired, and the bill passed after an all night legislative hearing when Congress was desperate to pass an appropriations bill to avert a government shutdown (*Seattle Times* Staff, 1996). Apparently, the bill was passed before significant opposition could be marshaled.

Shortly after the bill was passed, attempts were made to weaken the legislation. New bills were introduced to exempt police and military personnel and to eliminate the retroactive application of the act (Lautenberg, 1997). However, once the original legislation passed, it became difficult to argue for a repeal. Doing so suggests that police officers and the military should be treated differently—more leniently—than the general public. Nonetheless some local and national police organizations sought to modify the act.

It is difficult to estimate what effect this law will have on the police, although a few high profile cases have come to light. For example, a newly promoted high ranking officer in the Washington D.C. police department recently resigned when it was discovered that he had failed to report a one-year sentence of probation for domestic violence, although officers in the department claim it was common knowledge. In Lakeland, Florida the police chief announced the 1996 Officer of the Year only to learn later that the officer had been subject to a year-long restraining order issued to protect his wife after he had threatened to kill her and himself (Levinson, 1997). Nonetheless, initial indicators suggest that relatively few police officers will be impacted by the new law. For example, only seven police officers in the Los Angeles Police Department were forced to surrender their weapons when the department took actions to comply with the law in July 1997. If a department the size of the LAPD only had seven officers impacted by this legislation, then one can reasonably infer that few officers nationwide will be impacted by the law (see Levinson, 1997).

This study seeks to empirically investigate the impact of the Lautenberg Act to determine whether a significant proportion of U.S. law enforcement agencies are affected by the law and to ascertain whether a significant percentage of the nation's police force will be forced to find alternative employment. Furthermore, it seeks to establish whether law enforcement agencies are aware of the new legislation and to describe what actions, if any, agencies are taking to comply with the provisions of legislation. It also discusses the impact of the law as perceived by law enforcement officials.

METHODOLOGY

A 45-item survey instrument was developed for this study. The survey measured basic departmental demographic information including the population of the jurisdiction, the number of police officers employed, and the political subdivision of the police agency. It also ascertained whether departments had or planned to have a domestic violence unit, whether they had a domestic violence policy, and whether they had adopted community policing. The survey asked for basic information about the number of police officers convicted of domestic violence, the formal response to those convictions by the agency, and the actions taken by individual officers to mitigate the effects of a conviction. Information was solicited about formal organizational measures to ascertain what types of actions departments are using to detect convictions and to determine what actions departments take when convictions are discovered. Additional information was collected that measured respondents' understanding of the federal legislation and its provisions. Finally, police officials were asked to express their perceptions of the Lautenberg Act's impact on the agency and to describe any activities undertaken to influence changes in the legislation.

Sampling Frame

Our sampling frame included state and local law enforcement agencies in the United States serving jurisdictions of 25,000 or more citizens that employ at least 15 sworn officers. This yielded a population of 1,464 law enforcement agencies. An initial mailing of the survey was sent to the entire population of agencies in December of 1997, approximately one year after passage of the Lautenberg Act. This mailing included the survey and a letter of introduction. Because of the secretive and suspicious nature of some police subcultures (Kappeler et al., 1998; Manning, 1997; Skolnick, 1966), the sensitivity of the topic, and the difficult nature of conducting research into police violence against women (Kraska & Kappeler, 1995), the cover letter promised confidentiality. After approximately six weeks, a second wave of surveys was administered. The second wave of surveys included a new cover letter that encouraged agencies to respond to the survey even if they had not experienced incidents of domestic violence among their officers or even if they were not currently taking measures aimed at responding to the federal legislation. After approximately 3 months a total of 816 surveys had been returned for a response rate of 58 percent.

Sample Characteristics

Because of the unique and quite varied nature of state police agencies and their tendency not to have domestic violence units, we excluded state agencies from the analysis.[6] As a result, our sample consisted of 773 respondents. Approximately 80 percent of the responding law enforcement agencies (n = 615) were municipal police departments, while 20 percent (n = 158) were county and sheriff's departments. Thirty-six percent of the agencies were located in small cities (25,000 to 50,000), 30 percent in medium cities (50,001–100,000), and 34 percent in large cities (over 100,000). Eighteen percent of the sample came from the northeast, 24 from the west, 27 from the north central, and 32 from the south.

The number of officers employed by agencies ranged from 16 to 9,870 with the average number of officers being 255. Obviously, these figures varied significantly by jurisdiction and agency size. Departments in small cities averaged 67 officers, while those in medium cities averaged 123 officers and those in large areas 569 officers. These figures are consistent with other national data and suggest that our sample is representative.

ANALYSIS AND FINDINGS DOMESTIC VIOLENCE POLICIES AND UNITS

The vast majority of departments (93%) report that they have a general domestic violence policy. The northeast and north central regions were significantly more apt to have a domestic violence policy (96% for both) than the west (93%) or the south (90%; X^2 = 9.01, p=.03). Interestingly, neither the size of the department, the presence of a domestic violence unit or city size was significantly associated with the existence of a domestic violence policy. The political subdivision of the law enforcement agencies, however, was significantly related with the existence of such a policy. Ninety-five percent of municipal agencies had a policy compared to 87 percent of the county agencies ($X^2 = 14.54$; p=.00) and those departments with domestic violence units were not more likely to have a domestic violence policy. Agencies that reported using community policing were more likely to have domestic violence policies (94 percent) than those that do not (79 percent; $X^2 = 18.08$; p=.00).

Table 1. Comparisons of domestic violence policies and units

	Domestic Violence Policy		Domestic Violence Unit	
	Yes	No	Yes	No
Region				
Northeast	132 (96)	5 (4)**	58 (42)	80 (5)
Northcentral	196 (96)	9 (4)	64 (31)	140(69)
West	216 (90)	25 (10)	97 (41)	142 (59)
South	168 (90)	12 (10)	69 (38)	111 (62)
Political Subdivision				
Municipal	579 (95)	30 (5)*	223 (37)	383 (63)
County	135 (87)	21 (13)	66 (42)	91 (58)
Agency Size				
Small	212 (92)	18 (8)	53 (23)	181 (77)
Medium	58 (28)	147 (72)	92 (35)	174 (65)
Large	81 (35)	150 (65)	144 (55)	119 (45)
City Size				
Small	65 (27)	179 (73)	72 (26)	202 (74)*
Medium	58 (28)	147 (72)	78 (34)	150 (66)
Large	255 (95)	13 (5)	139 (53)	121 (47)
Domestic Violence Unit				
Yes	11 (5)	223 (95)	—	—
No	40 (92)	489 (6)	—	—
Community Policing				
Yes	670 (94)	40 (6)*	230 (32)	486 (68)**
No	42 (79)	11 (21)	9 (17)	44 (83)

*p=.01
**p=.05

Only about a third of the departments (31%) had a domestic violence unit, although an additional 13 percent of the departments reported they planned to institute one in the following year. Agency size (the number of police officers employed) was not significantly associated with the existence of a domestic violence policy. Yet, units are significantly more common in larger cities; 53 percent of the largest jurisdictions, 34 percent of the medium, and 26 percent of the small areas had special units ($X^2 = 43.78$; p=.00). Region or political subdivision was not significantly associated with the presence of a domestic violence unit and municipal and county agencies were equally likely to have domestic violence units.

The overwhelming majority of departments (93%) professed adoption of community policing. Neither region, the size of the department, nor the size of the jurisdiction were significantly related to a departments' inclination to use community policing. Municipalities, however, were significantly more likely than county agencies to employ community policing (94% and 87% respectively; (X^2 = 13.02; p = .00). Departments using community policing also were significantly more apt to have domestic violence policies (94%) than departments without community policing (79%; X^2 = 18.08; p = .00). Likewise, departments using community policing were significantly more likely to have domestic violence units (32%) than departments without community policing (17%; X^2 = 5.28; p = .02).

Knowledge of the Legislation

Three survey items were used to assess respondents' knowledge and awareness of the new legislation. Rather than testing the individual respondent's knowledge of the law, respondents were asked whether certain actions were allowed in their departments.[7] The first item stated that, "Police officers who have been convicted of a misdemeanor domestic violence charge may possess weapons but only while on duty." The second item stated that, "Police officers may possess weapons on duty if convicted of a misdemeanor domestic violence charge as long as this charge occurred over five years ago." The third item stated "Police officers may not possess weapons, even while on duty, if they have been convicted of a misdemeanor assault involving someone they cohabit with or someone with whom they have a child in common." We found that virtually all of the respondents (97%) reported that officers were prohibited from carrying a weapon if they had misdemeanor, domestic violence convictions. Respondents appeared somewhat less sure of some of the details of the law; 9 percent incorrectly reported that officers were allowed to possess guns if the conviction was over 5 years old and 18 percent reported that the law did not apply if the conviction involved cohabitating relationships or relationships where a couple have a child in common. These individual items were combined to form a "knowledge scale" which is used in subsequent analysis. It is a simple additive scale with a range of 0 to 3. The mean for the scale was 2.6, which suggests that most respondents had a good working knowledge of the law.

Few variables were associated with knowledge of the law. Interestingly, respondents in the northeast and west were significantly less informed about the law than those in the north central and south; 40 percent of those in the northeast and 30 percent of those in the west had limited knowledge of the law compared to 29 percent of those in the south and 26 percent of those in the north central regions (N^2 = 7.84; p = .049). Respondents who were less concerned with the law had more knowledge of it (r = -.085; p =.01), suggesting that lack of knowledge coupled with misinformation from media sources may have caused some departments to be fearful of this legislation.

Table 2. Comparisons of knowledge of the legislation		
	Limited	**Good**
Region		
Northeast	54 (40)	82 (60)**
Northcentral	51 (26)	148 (74)
West	52 (30)	122 (70)
South	70 (29)	168 (71)
Political Subdivision		
Municipal	186 (31)	411 (69)
County	41 (27)	111 (73)
Agency Size		
Small	69 (30)	160 (70)
Medium	77 (30)	183 (70)
Large	81 (31)	179 (69)
City Size		
Small	84 (31)	185 (69)
Medium	71 (32)	153 (68)
Large	72 (28)	183 (72)
Domestic Violence Unit		
Yes	161 (31)	357 (69)
No	66 (29)	163 (71)
Domestic Violence Policy		
Yes	204 (30)	487 (70)
No	20 (40)	30 (60)
Community Policing		
Yes	214 (30)	480 (70)
No	12 (23)	41 (77)

$**p = .05$

Departmental Action

Respondents were asked about a variety of organizational responses in several survey items, and they were provided with an open-ended question that asked them to elaborate upon any actions not addressed in the survey. While about two-thirds (60%) of the departments report that they have instituted counseling programs or other preventive measures to assist officers who may have problems with domestic violence, other findings cast doubt on this proactive image of departments. Surprisingly, only about a third (35%) of the departments specifically included questions on their employment application to screen for prior domestic violence convictions. In contrast, virtually all departments (97%) reported that they ran criminal background checks for all potential applicants and checked misdemeanor convictions to ensure that none involve domestic violence (95%). Only a small percentage (16%) of departments, however, ran annual background checks to detect domestic violence convictions after employment and only about a third (31%) of the departments had requested that prosecutors or other court officials notify them in the event that an officer was involved in domestic violence. It appears that police departments have made few organizational changes to detect batterers in blue. Few departments have taken the very basic steps of altering their application forms or modifying their personnel policies. Even fewer departments plan to routinely conduct background checks on an ongoing basis. Instead it appears that many departments believe that an initial background check will suffice; most of these departments probably have been running pre-employment checks for quite some time (Gaines, Kappeler, & Vaughn, 1997).

Three-fourths (75%) of the departments indicated that they distributed memos to notify police officers about the new legislation, and 7 percent of the departments also used a waiver or notification process whereby officers were asked to sign a form stating that they had no domestic violence convictions and that they would inform officials of any convictions in the future. Departments were not very prone to making changes in policy; only about one-third of the departments had modified their personnel policies (37%) or their domestic violence policies (35%) in response to the legislation, although almost two-thirds of the departments had altered their Internal Affairs Department (IAD) process (61%). About two-thirds of departments had conducted some type of training; 65 percent reportedly conducted in-service training, 35 percent supervisory training, and 22 percent field training. In addition, 42 percent of the departments reported that the law was addressed in their basic training classes.

These survey items also were used to create an action scale, which assessed departments' cumulative efforts to address the law. The scale ranges from 0 to 11 and evaluates whether departments have altered their employment applications, completed background checks, planned to implement annual background checks, circulated memos, instituted some type of waiver/form, modified IAD processes, modified policies of any kind (domestic violence, personnel, or other policies), taken preventive actions, or engaged in any other type of actions. The scale had a mean of 5.6, which indicates that while police departments were somewhat active there was still room for improvement.

Several variables were associated with a department's willingness to act. Departments in large jurisdictions or those with more officers were more apt to take action ($r = .20$, $p = .00$; $r = .18$, $p = .00$ respectively). Interestingly, departments with domestic violence policies were significantly more likely to respond actively to implementing the law; 41 percent of the departments without domestic violence policies had taken little to no action compared to 23 percent of those departments with policies ($X^2 = 10.34$, $p = .01$). Likewise, departments with domestic violence units were significantly less apathetic; 26 percent of those departments without a unit had taken little or no action compared to 20 percent of those departments with a domestic violence unit ($X^2 = 7.25$, $p = .03$). In addition, the more training that departments engaged in and the more they knew the law, the more likely they were to take action ($r = .49$, $p = .00$; $r = .12$, $p = .00$ respectively).

Table 3. Comparisons of departmental actions to address legislation		
	Level of Departmental Action		
	Limited	Moderate	Extensive
Region			
Northeast	33 (24)	84 (60)	23 (16)
Northcentra	60 (29)	123 (60)	23 (11)
West	43 (24)	114 (63)	25 (14)
South	50 (21)	144 (59)	49 (20)
Political Subdivision			
Municipal	151 (25)	377 (61)	87 (14)
County	36 (23)	89 (56)	33 (21)
Agency Size			
Small	69 (29)	148 (63)	18 (8)*
Medium	77 (29)	149 (56)	42 (16)
Large	41 (15)	169 (63)	60 (22)
City Size			
Small	170 (61)	53 (19)	54 (19)
Medium	132 (57)	44 (19)	55 (24)
Large	136 (52)	58 (22)	68 (26)
Domestic Violence Unit			
Yes	47 (20)	144 (60)	48 (20)**
No	138 (26)	322 (61)	72 (14)
Domestic Violence Policy			
Yes	164 (23)	433 (61)	117 (16)*
No	21 (41)	27 (53)	3 (6)
Community Policing			
Yes	167 (23)	435 (61)	116 (16)
No	19 (36)	30 (57)	4 (7)
Training			
Limited	154 (35)	258 (59)	27 (6)*
Moderate	17 (11)	117 (75)	21 (14)
Extensive	15 (8)	90 (51)	72 (41)
Knowledge			
Limited	67 (30)	133 (59)	27 (11)*
Good	108 (21)	322 (62)	92 (18)

*p =.01
**p =.05

Magnitude of Effect on Departments

Contrary to the self-report studies, but consistent with the police deviancy literature, a very small number of departments and only a handful of officers were directly affected by the law. Only 9 percent of the departments identified officers convicted of misdemeanor domestic violence offenses. Seven percent of the departments had re-assigned officers to positions that did not require possession of firearms, and 8 percent of the departments had officers who sought counsel as a result of domestic violence convictions. Likewise 8 percent of the departments had officers who had convictions expunged. Only 4 percent of the departments terminated officers because of domestic violence convictions.[8] In total, just over a fifth (22%) of the departments had been affected in some manner (e.g., officers sought counsel, had charges expunged, were convicted, reassigned, or fired); however, this effect was the result of the behavior of only a handful of police officers. Only 141 officers were reported to have had convictions—93 had been reassigned, 131 had sought counsel, 47 had been fired, and 73 had charges expunged. Less than 1 percent (.07%) of the officers represented in the sample (n = 195,823) had domestic violence convictions. Of those with convictions, slightly over half (52%) had their convictions expunged. Only 33 percent of the convictions resulted in termination of employment. One is hard pressed, then, to understand the national concern over this legislation or media reports that provided unrealistically high estimates of the extent of the problem.

Table 4. Comparisons of effect of the legislation on agencies

	Not Effected	Effected
Region		
Northeast	85 (82)	19 (18)
Northcentral	134 (82)	30 (18)
West	99 (30)	34 (70)
South	143 (76)	44 (24)
Political Subdivision		
Municipal	372 (79)	99 (21)
County	91 (76)	28 (24)
Agency Size		
Small	169 (91)	17 (8)*
Medium	173 (83)	35 (17)
Large	121 (62)	75 (38)
City Size		
Small	201 (89)	24 (11)*
Medium	139 (80)	35 (20)
Large	122 (64)	68 (36)
Domestic Violence		
Yes	111 (65)	61 (35)*
No	351 (84	65 (16)
Domestic Violence Policy		
Yes	430 (78)	119 (22)
No	28 (80)	7 (20)
Community Policing		
Yes	428 (78)	121 (22)
No	34 (85)	6 (15)
Training		
Limited	273 (82)	59 (18)*
Moderate	97 (81)	23 (19)
Extensive	93 (68)	44 (32)
Knowledge		
Limited	118 (73)	43 (27)
Good	333 (81)	80 (19)
Action		
Limited	117 (86	19 (14)*
Moderate	285 (79)	75 (21)
Extensive	61 (65)	33 (35)

*p =.01

Predictably, departments serving larger jurisdictions were more affected by the legislation; 36 percent of departments serving large cities had experienced some form of direct effect compared to 20 percent of medium and 11 percent of small departments (X^2 = 38.75; p =.00). Likewise, larger departments were significantly more apt to be affected; 38 percent of the large departments, 17 percent of the medium departments, and 8 percent of the small departments were affected in some manner. Neither region, political subdivision, presence of community policing, nor presence of a domestic violence policy were significantly related to a department's likelihood of being affected. However, departments with domestic violence units were significantly more affected (35%) than those without such units (16%; X^2 = 28.45; p =.00). In addition, departments that conducted more training were significantly more apt to affected; 32 percent of those with quite a bit of training were affected compared to 19 percent of those with moderate training and 18 percent of those with little training (X^2 = 12.31; p =.00). Not surprisingly, departments who took more action were significantly more likely to be affected by the legislation; 35 percent of the departments that took extensive action were affected compared to 21 percent of the departments with moderate levels of action and 14 percent of those with limited to no action (X^2 = 14.96; p =.00). Obviously, if departments took no action to implement the law there was little chance that officers would be identified and dealt with in some manner.

Departmental Impact and Concern

Respondents were asked to describe their perceptions of the impact of the law in an open-ended question. About two-thirds of the respondents (n = 463) completed this item. Since they sometimes offered more than one impact, 481 responses were analyzed. The single most frequent comment was that the law would have little or no impact (noted by 22% of the respondents). On the whole, respondents (60%) were neutral about the impact of the law. Only 7 percent of the respondents saw the law in a positive light, and the remaining 34 percent predicted negative outcomes.[9] Those respondents who were positive about the law were most likely to note that officers with domestic violence convictions had no business in law enforcement and that this would help screen out "bad apples." Less often, but still a common theme, respondents reported they believed that the law would reduce battering by officers. Respondents who viewed the law negatively noted that it was unfair to police officers (especially the retroactive nature of the legislation). Some were concerned that spouses of police officers would not report abuse, fearing that the officers involved would lose their jobs.

In a similar vein, respondents were asked how concerned they were about the new legislation. Half (50%) of the respondents reported that administrators in their departments were seriously concerned, 24 percent somewhat concerned and 26 percent minor or no concern. Few variables were associated with respondent's assessment of the impact of the law or the degree of concern in the department. There was, however, a significant difference in concern by region; 64 percent of the departments in the northeast were seriously concerned compared to 49 percent of those in the north central and south and 44 percent of those in the west (X^2 = 27.28; p =.00).

Table 5. Concern about legislation and working to change its provisions

	Concern about Legislation			Working to Change	
	Minor	Somewhat	Serious	No	Yes
Region					
Northeast	19 (14)	32 (23)	89 (64)*	129 (93)	10 (7)
Northcentral	57 (28)	47 (23)	100 (49)	196 (95)	10 (5)
West	44 (25)	47 (23	78 (44)	177 (97)	5 (3)
South	79 (33)	44 (18)	116 (49)	230 (96)	9 (4)
Political Subdivision					
Municipal	159 (26)	144 (24)	305 (50)	586 (96)	26 (4)
County	41 (26)	36 (23)	78 (50)	148 (95)	8 (5)
Agency Size					
Small	65 (28)	48 (21)	117 (51)	188 (96)	7 (4)*
Medium	73 (27)	63 (24)	130 (49)	151 (90)	17 (10)
Large	62 (23)	69 (26)	136 (51)	327 (89)	39 (11)
City Size					
Small	76 (28	60 (22)	137 (50)	267 (97)	9 (3)
Medium	65 (28)	57 (25)	107 (47	220 (95)	11 (5)
Large	58 (22)	63 (24)	139 (53)	246 (95)	14 (5)
Domestic Unit					
Yes	48 (21)	55 (24)	130 (56)**	233 (95)	11 (5)
No	152 (29)	124 (23)	252 (48)	509 (96)	23 (4)
Domestic Equity					
Yes	180 (25)	169 (24)	357 (51	679 (96)	31 (4)
No	16 (33)	10 (20)	23 (47)	48 (94)	3 (6)
Community Policing					
Yes	184 (26)	164 (23)	360 (51)	682 (96)	31 (4)
No	15 (28)	16 (30)	22 (42)	51 (96)	2 (4)
Training					
Limited	109 (25)	113 (26)	210 (49)	422 (97)	15 (3)
Moderate	45 (29)	30 (19)	80 (52)	148 (96)	6 (4)
Extensive	46 (26)	37 (21)	92 (53)	163 (93)	13 (7)
Knowledge					
Limited	50 (22)	59 (26)	115 (51)	214 (95)	12 (5)
Good	145 (28)	112 (22)	259 (50)	498 (96)	22 (4)
Action					
Limited	45 (24)	49 (26)	91 (49	179 (97)	5 (3)
Moderate	123 (27)	106 (23)	230 (50)	445 (96	19 (4)
Extensive	32 (27)	25 (21)	62 (52)	110 (92)	10 (8)
Effect on Agency					
Not Effected	121 (26)	109 (24)	228 (50)	446 (79)	117 (21)
Effected	23 (19)	36 (29)	65 (52)	17 (65)	9 (35)
Working to Change					
Yes	1 (3)	10 (29)	23 (68)*	—	—
No	198 (27)	168 (23)	359 (50)	—	—

*p =.01
**p =.05

Finally, we asked whether departments were engaged in activities designed to alter the legislation and asked for descriptions of these activities. A very small minority of departments (4%) engaged in this type of action and most of it appeared to be centered around removing the retroactive portion of the law. Only one variable was significantly related to efforts to change the law. Departments that viewed the legislation as a more serious concern were significantly more likely to be working to repeal the law. Six to 8 percent of those who view the legislation as a serious concern were working to change the law as compared to 3 percent of those who believed it was of minor concern (X^2 = 4.59; p =.03).

Multivariate Analyses

Multiple regression was used to examine a few variables in more depth. Regression was used to examine departmental actions taken to respond to the legislation. Regression models employed a fully recursive model using standard multiple regression techniques. Table 6 provides the standardized regression coefficients and shows that some variables were significantly associated with the amount of action taken by a department.

Table 6. Multiple regression analysis of departmental action

Model	B	Std. Error	Beta	t-value	Significance
Constrant	2.030	.443	—	4.583	.000
City Size	.281	.093	.115	3.037	.002
Agency Size	1.725E-04	.000	.045	1.286	.199
Political Subdivision	.119	.183	.023	.651	.515
Domestic Violence Unit	.385	.148	.086	2.611	.009
Domestic Violence Policy	.609	.264	.074	2.303	.022
Community Policing	.355	.254	.045	1.395	.163
Concern with Law	-2.515E-02	.052	-.015	-.482	.630
Level of Training	3.151	.217	.466	14.505	.000
Level of Knowledge	.275	.094	.092	2.933	.003
Working to Change Law	2.120E-02	.310	.002	.068	.945

R	R Squared	Adjusted R	Standard	F-value	Signifiance
.554	.307	.297	1.7177	31.427	.000

Departments serving larger jurisdictions and departments with domestic violence policies or units were more likely to have taken action to comply with the legislation. Likewise, departments that engaged in high levels of training were more likely to take action to detect officers with domestic violence convictions. Community policing, however, did not significantly contribute to explaining departmental action. In all, these variables explain approximate 30 percent of the variance in departmental actions to conform with the requirements of the legislation. It would seem that more innovative agencies, as least as measured by domestic violence units, policies and training, were more likely to be responsive to the Lautenberg Act.

DISCUSSION AND IMPLICATIONS

The passage of the Lautenberg Act received intense but short-lived media attention. Much speculation surrounded the passage of the act, with proponents and opponents making claims about the effect it would have on the police institution. While many predicted that large numbers of agencies and officers would be adversely affected, our research indicates that the law has had a minimal effect on the police institution. In fact, less than one percent of law enforcement officers and less than one-fifth of agencies have been adversely affected by the legislation. Of the relatively few officers detected with domestic violence convictions, most had their convictions expunged and a majority of the remaining officers were merely reassigned to allow them to keep their jobs. The actual number of batterers in blue remains largely unknown.

While the vast majority of law enforcement agencies had a good working knowledge of the legislation and most expressed concern about its provisions, far fewer took more than the most basic actions to comply with its provisions. More often than not, most agencies merely ran background checks for employment purposes and issued memos about the legislation. Both of these practices are routine in most law enforcement agencies. The most proactive agencies were those that had already demonstrated a concern with the issue of domestic violence as evidenced by existing policies, special units, or high levels of training. The police response to this legislation renders the law largely a symbolic statement on domestic violence and policing. The historical reluctance of the police to adequately address domestic violence seems to extend to the institutional response to this legislation—especially when the batterers wear blue.

NOTES

[1] Empirical studies using diverse methodologies support this finding. They include surveys of police officers that ask them to specify how they think they would respond to a variety of different hypothetical scenarios involving domestic assaults; field studies that evaluate police behavior while they perform their duties during domestic calls; content analyses of arrest decisions from actual police reports of domestic assaults; and, studies that actually compare domestic and non-domestic acts.

[2] It is difficult to determine just how the scale was modified. The authors do not describe the modifications in any detail. Instead they cite a prior paper which is not easily accessible (Neidig, 1984).

[3] The study fails to report significance tests. We used the reported percentages to conduct Chi-Square tests.

[4] There was no comparison group involving spouses of female officers, presumably because of the small sample size for female officers (n = 40).

[5] It also is important to acknowledge that the Lautenberg Act was passed in the shadow of other important federal legislation: the Violence Against Women Act (VAWA). VAWA was passed as part of the 1994 Crime Bill and was the first piece of federal legislation created specifically to address violence against women including: child sexual assault, domestic violence, sexual assault, and stalking. The act was supposed to

"respond both to the underlying attitude that this violence is somehow less serious than other crime and to the resulting failure of our criminal justice system to address such violence" (Staff of Senate Committee on the Judiciary, cited in Klein, 1995, p. 254). VAWA required states and Indian tribal law enforcement officials to honor protective orders even if they were issued in other counties, other states, or even other countries. VAWA created new laws pertaining to interstate battering, making it a federal crime to cross state lines to commit battering or to violate a protective order under certain circumstances. It established a new civil rights law and allowed victims of gender-motivated violence, including battering, to seek civil damages. It created a new exemption to immigration regulations which makes it somewhat easier for a victim of battering to apply for citizenship. VAWA also prohibited individuals against whom a valid protective order was issued from possessing firearms or ammunition, although law enforcement officials and members of the military were exempt from the provision and were allowed to possess firearms while on duty.

[6] All bivariate and multivariate analyses were conducted with state respondents included and excluded. There were no significant differences in the analysis.

[7] This resulted in a measure of departmental compliance and individual respondent's knowledge of the law.

[8] These percentages sum 100 because it is possible to have one officer counted in multiple categories. For example, an officer might have been convicted and reassigned; convicted and had the charge expunged, etc.

[9] Total equals 101 percent due to rounding.

REFERENCES

Alpert, G. P., & Dunham, R. G. (1997). *Policing urban America* (3rd ed.). Prospect Heights, IL: Waveland Press.

Balkin, J. (1988). Why policemen don't like policewomen. *Journal of Police Science and Administration, 16*(1), 29–38.

Banton, M. (1964). *The police in the community.* London, England: Travistock.

Berk, S., & Loseke, D. (1980). Handling family violence: Situational determinants of police arrest in domestic disturbances. *Law and Society Review, 15*(2), 317–346.

Bittner, E. (1970). *The functions of police in modern society.* Chevy Chase, MD: National Clearinghouse for Mental Health.

Block, P., & Anderson, D. (1974). *Policewomen on patrol.* Washington, DC: The Police Foundation.

Buzawa, E., & Austin, T. (1993). Determining police response to domestic violence victims: The role of victim preferences. *American Behavioral Scientist, 36*(5), 610–623.

Buzawa, E., & Buzawa, C. (1993). The scientific evidence is not conclusive: Arrest is no panacea. In R. Gelles & D. Loseke (Eds.), *Current controversies on family violence* (pp. 337–356). Newbury Park, CA: Sage.

Christopher, W. (1991). Summary: Report of the Independent Commission on the Los Angeles Police Department. *Criminal Law and Criminology, 46,* 46–72.

Dobash, R. E., Dobash, R. P., Wilson, M., & Daly, M. (1992). The myth of sexual symmetry in marital violence. *Social Problems, 39,* 71–91.

Dolon, R., Hendricks, J., & Meagher, M. (1986). Police practices and attitudes toward domestic violence. *Journal of Police Science and Administration, 14*(3), 187–192.

Dutton, D. (1988). *The domestic assault of women: Psychological and criminal justice perspectives.* Boston: Allyn and Bacon.

Eigenberg, H., Kappeler, V., & Scarborough, K. (1996). Contributory factors affecting arrest in domestic and non-domestic assaults. *American Journal of Police*, 15(4), 5, 5–77.

Gaines, L. K., & Kappeler, V. (1992). The police selection process: What works. In G. Cordner & D. Hale, (Eds.), *What works in policing* (pp. 107–123). Cincinnati, OH: Anderson.

Gaines, L. K., & Van Tubergen, N. (1989). Job stress in police work: An exploratory analysis into structural causes. *American Journal of Criminal Justice*, 13(3), 197–214.

Goolkasian, G. (1986a). Confronting domestic violence: A guide for criminal justice agencies. National Institute of Justice. *Research in Brief*. Washington, DC: U.S. Department of Justice.

Goolkasian, G. (1986b). Confronting domestic violence: The role of criminal court judges. National Institute of Justice. *Research in Brief*. Washington, DC: U.S. Department of Justice.

Haarr, R. N. (1997). Patterns of interaction in a police patrol bureau: Race and gender barriers to integration. *Justice Quarterly*, 14(1), 53–85.

Harris, R. (1973). *The police academy: An insider's view*. New York: John Wiley.

Hindman, R. E. (1975). A survey related to use of female law enforcement officers. *Police Chief*, 42(4), 58–60.

Hunt, J. (1990). The logic of sexism among police. *Women & Criminal Justice*, 1(2), 330.

Kappeler, V. E., Blumberg, M., & Potter, G. W. (2000). *The mythology of crime and criminal justice* (3rd ed.). Prospect Heights, IL: Waveland Press.

Kappeler, V. E., Sluder, R., & Alpert, G. (1998). *Forces of deviance: Understanding the dark side of the force* (2nd ed.). Prospect Heights, IL: Waveland Press.

Kraska, P. B., & Kappeler, V. E. (1988). Police on-duty drug use: A theoretical and descriptive examination. *American Journal of Police*, 7(1), 1–28.

Kraska, P. B., & Kappeler, V. E. (1995). To serve and pursue: Exploring police sexual violence against women. *Justice Quarterly*, 12(1), 85–111.

Lautenberg, F. R. (1997, April 3). Domestic violence gun ban. *The Washington Post*.

Levinson, A. (1997, December 11). Federal gun ban hard to enforce. *Associated Press*.

Lerman, L., & Livingston, F. (1983). State legislation on domestic violence. *Responses to violence in the family and sexual assault*. September/October, 1–2, 13–14.

Linden, R. (1983). Women in policing—A study of lower mainland Royal Canadian Mounted Police detachments. *Canadian Police College Journal*, 7, 217–229.

Loving, N. (1981). *Spouse abuse: A curriculum guide for police trainers*. Washington, DC: Police Executive Research Forum.

Malloy, T., & Mays, G. (1984). The police stress hypothesis: A critical evaluation. *Criminal Justice and Behavior*, 11(2), 197–224.

Manning, P. K. (1997). *Police Work: The social organization of policing* (2nd ed.). Prospect Heights, IL: Waveland Press.

Martin, S. (1990) *Women on the move? A report on the status of women in policing*. Washington, DC: Police Foundation.

Morash, M., & Haarr, R. (1995). Gender, workplace problems and stress in policewomen. *Justice Quarterly*, 12(1), 113–140.

Neidig, P., Russell, H., & Seng, A. (1992). Interpersonal aggression in law enforcement families: A preliminary investigation. *Police Studies*, 15(1), 30–38.

Pace, D. (1997, January 8). GOP blocks retroactive gun ban. *Associated Press*.

Price, B. R. (1996). Female police officers in the United States. In M. Pagon (Ed.), *Policing in Central and Eastern Europe: Comparing firsthand knowledge with experience from the west* (pp. 33–51). Slovenia: College of Police and Security Studies.

Reibstein, L., & Engen, J. (1996, December 23). One Strike and You're Out. *Time.*

Remmington, P. (1983). Women in police: integration or separation? *Qualitative Sociology,* 6(2), 118–135.

Reuss-Ianni, E. (1983). *Two cultures of policing.* New Brunswick, NJ: Transaction Books.

Savitz, L. (1971). The dimensions of police loyalty. In H. Hann, (Ed.), *Police in urban society.* Beverly Hills, CA: Sage.

Seattle Times Staff (1996, December 30). Close-up: Police with domestic-violence history lose guns. *Seattle Times.*

Sherman, L. W. (1974). *Police corruption: A sociological perspective.* New York: Anchor Books.

Sherman, L. W. (1978). *Scandal and reform: Controlling police corruption.* Berkeley, CA: University of California Press.

Skolnick, J. H. (1966). *Justice without trial: Law enforcement in a democratic society.* New York: John Wiley and Sons.

Stoddard, E. R. (1968). The informal code of police deviancy: A group approach to blue-collar crime. *Journal of Criminal Law, Criminology and Police Science,* 59(2), 201–213.

Straus, M. (1993). Physical assaults by wives—A major social problem. In R. J. Gelles & D. J. Loseke (Eds.), *Current controversies on family violence* (pp. 67–87). Newbury Park, CA: Sage.

Straus, M., & Gelles, R. (1990). *Physical violence in American families.* New Brunswick, NJ: Transaction Books.

Tjaden, P., & Thoennes, N. (1998). *Prevalence, incidence, and consequences of violence against women: Findings from the national violence against women survey.* Washington, DC: National Institute of Justice.

Vega, M., & Silverman, I. J. (1982). Female police officers as viewed by their male counterparts. *Police Studies,* 5, 31–39.

Waits, K. (1985). The criminal justice system's response to battering: Understanding the problem, forging the solutions. *Washington Law Review,* 60, 267–329.

Westley, W. A. (1953). Violence and the police. *American Journal of Sociology,* 59, 34–41.

Westley, W. A. (1956). Secrecy and the police. *Social Forces,* 34(3), 254–257.

Westley, W. A. (1970). *Violence and the police: A sociological study of law, custom and morality.* Cambridge, MA: MIT Press.

Worden, R., & Pollitz, A. (1984). Police arrests in domestic disturbances: A further look. *Law and Society Review,* 18(1), 105–119.

Zorza, J. (1992). The criminal law of misdemeanor domestic violence, 1970–1990. *Journal of Criminal Law & Criminology,* 46, 46–76.

CASES CITED

2 Miss. (Walker) 156 (1824).

Hartis v. State, 71 Miss. 462 (1894).

CHAPTER FIVE

CRIMINAL JUSTICE SYSTEM RESPONSE

The tendency to deal with battering primarily in terms of a criminal justice response suggests that advocates have made some progress in changing the hegemonic definition of battering from a private, family matter to a public, criminal one. For example, police officers historically were discouraged from making arrests in "domestic disputes" (Berk & Loseke, 1980; Buzawa & Buzawa, 1996; Goolkasian, 1986; Hirschel et al., 1992; Loving, 1981; Waits, 1985) that were virtually ignored by police (Sherman, 1980) as well as prosecutors (Fagan, 1996; Okun, 1986) and the courts (Lerman, 1986). As the social construction of the problem has changed, there has been an increased willingness to view it as a crime worthy of attention by the criminal justice system.

Until recently, the police received the most attention by those attempting to increase the criminal justice system's response to battering. Efforts concentrated on the police because they play a critical gatekeeping role; a case cannot enter the system for response until there is an arrest. While the police have often born the brunt of criticism by advocates working to change the criminal justice response, there is no evidence that prosecutors or judges were any more inclined to view battering cases as serious criminal offenses, and correctional responses basically have been ignored. Increased arrests as a result of reform efforts have resulted in cases reaching farther into the system, allowing for an evaluation of prosecutorial, judicial, and correctional responses. This chapter examines the various components of the criminal justice system—the police, courts, and corrections—and their responses to battering.

POLICE RESPONSE TO BATTERING

As discussed previously, much of the attention devoted to policing and battering has examined whether or not arrest deters battering. It is interesting that so much academic debate has been structured around this issue. For example, our approach might be quite different if we spent as much time addressing whether police officers treat battering differently than other types of assaults.

As the accompanying article by Eigenberg, Scarborough, and Kappeler indicates, there is empirical evidence that police officers are less willing to arrest in battering cases when compared to other types of assaults. The article reviews the literature and concludes that most studies on police response to battering provide evidence of differential treatment. The majority of these studies find that officers are more likely to arrest in domestic assaults if the victim insists on it or if the offender acts badly toward the police. It also appears that officers are more apt to arrest in domestic assaults when there are additional witnesses. This body of research consistently finds that neither injuries nor weapons are significantly related to officers' decisions to arrest in domestic assaults. Studies that directly compare officers' willingness to arrest in domestic assaults to non-domestic assaults report mixed results. The study by Eigenberg and her colleagues as well as one other (Fyfe, Klinger, & Flavin, 1997) found that officers treat domestic assaults differently. However, two other studies found that police officers arrest in battering situations at a similar rate to stranger assaults (Klinger, 1995; Feder, 1998). Additional research is needed to clarify these contradictory results and it seems quite likely that the institutional culture of a particular police department will impact the results.

There are several possible reasons why police officers may treat battering cases differently. First, as discussed previously, the behavior of policing agents mirrors the values of the larger social culture, which historically has failed to view battering as a serious social problem. Second, these calls have been classified as a form of social work. Despite the fact that the vast majority of a police officer's time is spent in service work, officers and their occupational culture highlight the crime fighting and law enforcement nature of the work (Gaines, Kappeler, & Vaughn, 1999; Kappeler, Blumberg & Potter, 2000; Manning, 1999; Reiss, 1971; Wilson, 1968; Van Maanen, 1974). Third, police officers seem to dislike these calls.

Some officers have disdain for battering calls because there is no formal organizational incentives that reward performance in this area (Buzawa & Buzawa, 1996). Officers often are evaluated on felony arrest rates and subsequent clearances; battering cases rarely contribute to that type of measurement. Written tests for promotion concentrate on law enforcement related activities and rarely address battering (Buzawa & Buzawa, 1996). In addition, these cases can be very time consuming if an officer is thorough. For example, the on-scene investigation and the arrest alone take time. If officers also assist the victim with referrals and/or transport her to a shelter or hospital, the call takes considerably longer. The perception often is that police officers should dispose of these personal disputes so they can get back to "fighting crime." Unfortunately, the organizational structure of many, perhaps most, police departments fails to reward police officers for fighting this type of crime. Finally, police officers deplore battering calls because they believe these calls are extraordinarily dangerous.

Danger to Police Officers in Battering Cases

It is ironic that we traditionally have paid more attention to the threat that battering poses to the safety of police officers than to the threat that batterers pose to their victims. Historically, the police were trained to protect themselves but not to safeguard battered women. In general, police officers were trained about the potential risk of hysterical women "turning" on officers just as they pulled the batterer off the victim. Police fatalities were used to reinforce this notion and to caution officers that these calls were deadly.

This type of social construction is especially paradoxical since the data fail to substantiate these claims. As Garner and Clemmer (1986) demonstrate, this interpretation is erroneous and offers a highly distorted picture of the risk to police officers in battering cases. Overgeneralization of the findings and poor operationalization of the variables led to critical misrepresentations. The category that was used to assert that domestic calls were dangerous was named "disturbance calls" and included data from a broad definition of violence. This category included bar fights, gang calls, general public disturbances short of a riot, "man with a gun calls" (where an individual is flashing a gun and not much other detail is available), and woman battering cases. When the domestic violence calls are placed into a separate category, it is clear that these calls are not a serious threat to officers' lives when compared to other types of calls. In fact, officers were more likely to die "*accidentally* as a result of their own action or the actions of other police officers" (Garner & Clemmer, 1986, p. 7) than they were to die in domestic violence calls. While homicide is only one way to measure the dangerousness of these calls, other research also indicates that domestic violence calls result in relatively few injuries to police officers when compared to other types of police calls (Hirschel, Dean, & Lumb, 1994). Furthermore, and in contrast to the vindictive wife image, police officers are usually assaulted or killed by male batterers not female victims (Hirschel, Dean, & Lumb, 1994).

Nonetheless, it has been very difficult to de-bunk the stereotype that battering calls are particularly dangerous for the police. Ironically, police officers empowered by law to use deadly force are cautioned about *their* safety, while the safety of the victim is virtually ignored. As Buzawa and Buzawa note (1996):

> When officers respond to a domestic violence call, they often have been instructed to emphasize the adoption of a defensive–reactive strategy, protecting their own safety at the expense of effectively reacting. Under such circumstances, it is not surprising that innovations in police responses or a more activist approach were discouraged. (p. 42)

Researchers have suggested modifications to police training to reduce or eliminate the emphasis on danger to the police (Hirschel, Dean, & Lumb, 1994).

The limited time devoted to training on the dangers of battering might be better used to develop officers' crisis intervention skills and to educate officers about the legal requirements in battering cases, which change frequently. Better training could result in more effective police officers who are less apt to engage in activities that might expose either the department or the individual to lawsuits.

Legal Liability

While it is possible that advocates who worked to change the social construction of battering were successful in getting police officers to see it as a crime, it seems more likely that police agencies have responded to the threat of legal liability. Since the 1960s, there has been a dramatic increase in both the number of civil cases filed and the number of cases successfully litigated against police departments (Kappeler & Kappeler, 1992; Kappeler, 1997). Furthermore, litigation is quite expensive—not only because of large jury awards and out of court settlements, but also due to attorneys fees associated with any legal action (Kappeler, 1997, p. 9). Litigation offers an avenue of redress to victims who have been harmed by the actions of a police department, and it can deter officers from violating policy. However, litigation also has the power to secure change; as the old adage goes, money talks. "Suits against the police that prove inadequate administrative controls, deficient policies, or customs and practices that are improper or illegal, can force the department to correct its specific deficiencies and review all policies, practices and customs" (Alpert & Dunham, 1997, p. 244).

As discussed previously, many state legislators and police chiefs have instituted mandatory or presumptive arrest policies. One important reason for this shift is related to legal liability. These types of policies and laws leave less discretion to individual police officers and may help insulate departments against liability. If the department can demonstrate that officers were informed about the policy and/or law and trained appropriately, it may help protect against organizational liability. Likewise, if the department can demonstrate that the officer was acting in contradiction to departmental policy or state law, then the department may be able to shift the liability to the individual officer. As of 1997, 16 states require local agencies to have policies and procedures specific to domestic violence (Miller, 1997).

Battered women have made some progress suing police departments for their failure to protect. Several cases, in particular, appear to have had an important impact on police policies and practices nationwide in the late 1970s and mid 1980s. Two of these cases were highly publicized class action suits filed in federal court in Oakland (California) and New York City (*Bruno v Codd*, 1977; *Scott v Hart*, 1976). These suits, however, only requested injunctive relief. Instead of seeking damages, the plaintiffs sought to have the courts mandate these police departments to do what the law required: to enforce assault statutes in order to protect battered women. Both departments settled out of court and agreed to extensive changes in police operations and policies in order to facilitate the arrest of batterers; however, because these type of suits do not result in any type of monetary settlement for the clients, most victims cannot afford to pursue these types of cases even though they may be effective in changing the behavior of police departments.

Another important case was a highly publicized lawsuit decided in 1984. In a landmark case, *Thurman v Torrington*, a federal district court found that a police policy that advocated non-arrest in a case of domestic violence was unconstitutional. The victim, Tracy Thurman, had her neck broken and was repeatedly stabbed in the presence of a police officer. She ultimately received about two million dollars in compensatory damages when she successfully argued that, despite her many calls for assistance, her constitutional right to equal protection had been violated when law enforcement officials refused to arrest her husband because she was married to him. The size of the damage award and the vast amount of media publicity led many police departments to fear that the Thurman case would be the first of many more to come (Buzawa & Buzawa, 1996; Sherman, Cohn, & Hamilton, 1986).

The Thurman case also was important because it was the first time a battered woman had successfully used Title 42 U.S. Section 1983 to sue a police department. This piece of legislation is part of the Civil Rights Act of 1871 and provides civil remedies in cases where governmental officials violate federally protected constitutional rights (Kappeler, 1997; Zorza, 1996). The statute holds that anyone acting under color of law, generally interpreted to mean any governmental employee, can be held liable for violating a constitutional or federally protected right. It was designed to offer monetary compensation to African-American victims who were deprived of their civil rights after the Civil War, frequently at the hands of white, Southern sheriffs. For almost 100 years, the statute was virtually ignored until other groups began to use it. For example, much of prison litigation uses Section 1983 and it also is used to hold police officials accountable in cases of excessive use of force.

There are several advantages to filing Section 1983 cases (Kappeler, 1997). The case is tried in federal court where women may have a better opportunity to escape the local politics. For example, the jury may be drawn from a larger geographical area than the area in which the police department is located. Furthermore, the statute requires that the defendant pay for the attorney's fees of the plaintiff if they win any portion of their case. Thus, if battered women are successful and can demonstrate police liability, the city or county must pay the legal fees as part of the settlement. In addition, this statute provides for compensatory and punitive damages that have fewer limits than those imposed by most state tort legislation.

In 1989, however, the Supreme Court ruling on a child abuse case made it substantially more difficult for battered women to sue police officials (Zorza, 1996). In *DeShaney v Winnebago County Department of Social Services* the Court held that the mother in the case was not entitled to damages when the father of the child was allowed to maintain custody despite repeated complaints of abuse. Ultimately, the father beat the child so severely that he was left with permanent and profound brain damage. The mother of the child filed suit under Section 1983 claiming that when social services refused to act they violated her son's rights to due process under the 14th Amendment. The Supreme Court rejected the argument. Chief Justice Rehnquist authored the majority opinion and held that the purpose of the due process clause "is to protect people from the state, not from each other's private violence" (Zorza, 1996, p. 545). The Court held that the due process clause limits the state's power to act. It does not establish a minimum standard that the state must provide for safety and security, even when the victim expresses a desire for protection and when the state knows of the danger (Zorza, 1996, p. 547).

The Court has ruled that there are exceptions to the DeShaney ruling. Victims in custodial relationships or victims who are exposed to increased danger by the state may be able to establish grounds for a successful liability claim. However, both of these exceptions have been tailored very narrowly and appear to exclude most cases of domestic violence (Zorza, 1996). In a case decided just six days after DeShaney, *Canton v Harris*, the Court ruled that police departments may be held liable when victims are injured as a result of inadequate police training. The Court ruled that it was acceptable to hold a city liable for failing to train police officers to recognize when a person in custody needed medical attention. The Court held that the failure to train amounted to deliberate indifference and thereby resulted in a due process violation. Thus, it appears that battered women might successfully establish a 1983 case based on due process violation if they can demonstrate that a particular police department's training was so inadequate that it demonstrated deliberate indifference to the victims of domestic violence (Zorza, 1996).

In addition to the exceptions to the ruling in DeShaney, the Court made it clear that its decision did not affect equal protection claims. In other words, battered women may have a valid Section 1983 case if they can prove that they are being treated differently because of their gender. These cases, however, are difficult to win for several reasons (Zorza, 1996). First, since women do not qualify as a suspect class, government agencies are given more leniency to treat women differently as a class.[1] Second, the courts are inconsistent when looking for a comparison group to use when women argue violations of equal protection. Women have argued that their constitutional right to equal protection has been violated when police treat battered women differently than victims of stranger assault. In other words, the argument is that the police fail to arrest batterers as a group because they are prejudiced against battered women — using victims (men and women) of stranger assault as the comparison group. However, in some jurisdictions, the courts have held that battered women must show that they have been treated differently from men who are battered in order to demonstrate unequal treatment of constitutional magnitude. Shifting the comparison group, then, makes it virtually impossible to demonstrate that differential treatment has occurred because too few men are battered by women to allow for comparative data.

It is possible that VAWA will create new avenues of litigation under Section 1983, which allows for suits when a constitutional or federally protected right is violated. As discussed earlier, the civil rights legislation created by VAWA (42 U.S.C. Section 13981) prohibits violence that is motivated by gender. Persons who are subject to suit include individuals other than intimate partners. Persons, by statute, include individuals who are acting under color of any statute, ordinance, regulation, custom, or usage of any state. In essence, then, the federal government has created a new civil right, and it is possible that police officers may be sued for violation of women's civil rights if women can demonstrate that police officers exposed women to violence based on the department's gender animus toward the victim.

While Section 1983 precedent is evolving rapidly, the courts have been inconsistent. Furthermore, it is difficult to determine whether VAWA will affect Section 1983 cases on battering. However, Section 1983 cases are not the only vehicle that can be used to establish liability. Victims may also sue the police based upon state tort law.

Tort laws vary tremendously from state to state. In general, torts are civil suits that address private actions that harm individuals. Generally speaking, there are two types of torts: intentional and negligent.

Intentional torts can be filed when the police intentionally do something that results in harm to an individual (Kappeler, 1997). In general, these cases usually involve wrongful death, false arrest, false imprisonment, and assault and battery (Gaines, Kappeler, & Vaughn, 1999, p. 397). These cases are difficult to prove because the plaintiff has to demonstrate that the police intentionally took action that resulted in the harm. For example, mistakenly arresting a batterer is not grounds for a successful false arrest case, even if the officer fails to have probable cause for arrest, unless the police officer consciously meant to make an unlawful arrest. Since one must prove intent, cases of this nature are rare, and they usually fail. Nonetheless, police officers reportedly are reluctant to make arrests in domestic violence cases because they fear legal liability associated with false arrest (Lerman, 1981). However, police officers are more likely to be sued for negligence—for failing to protect victims than for false arrest.

Negligence torts do not require that the petitioner prove intent. While they differ from state to state, they require that four general criteria be met: (1) duty on the part of the defendant, (2) failure to perform the duty, (3) proximate cause, and (4) actual damage (Kappeler, 1997). Thus, one can successfully sue a police officer if s/he had a duty to act and failed to act, if that failure to act resulted in real damages such as injuries, and if the victim can demonstrate that the failure to act by the officer was the cause of the damage. These cases may be stronger if a protective order exists because the court may rule that a special relationship exists. The court has, in essence, alerted the police to a higher level of danger when a protective order is granted; a higher level of response is required.

In general, victims will fare better if they sue the city or state (a governmental agency). Practically speaking, it is difficult to recover enough money to make it worthwhile to sue the average governmental employee—the "pockets" aren't "deep" enough. In order to establish municipal liability, victims have to demonstrate that the employee was acting in accordance with policy or custom. As a result, local police officials must take great caution when writing departmental policy and must ensure that it is in compliance with state and federal law. For example, departmental policy that advises officers to mediate domestic violence cases may be ill advised for many reasons, but the department significantly increases its chances of liability if state law mandates arrest. In this case, it would be relatively easy to argue that the city was negligent in writing a policy that discouraged police officers from making arrests despite state law that required arrest whenever probable cause existed. The liability would be even greater if the police department trained its officers to act in accordance with this misinformed policy since the courts often examine training to establish custom and policy. Training procedures can protect departments from liability since police departments usually are not held financially accountable for the actions of renegade officers. Administrators are best protected from legal liability when they write strong policies that give police officers guidance in arrest decisions and when officers are well trained on these policies.

In order to protect their departments, Barrineau makes some broad recommendations to police executives (1987, p. 83–85). First, know the law. While we assume that police officers (and administrators) know the law, this may not be the case (see Belknap, 1990; Eigenberg & Moriarty, 1991). As simplistic as it sounds, this is not easy, especially in an area like domestic violence where statutes may be changing with great frequency and regularity. (Recall the discussion about the Lautenberg Act in chapter 4 and reading 12.) If a department allows a patrol officer with a misdemeanor conviction for domestic violence to remain armed and a victim is harmed as a result of that officer's actions, the odds of liability would be high (International Association of Chiefs of Police, [IACP] 1999a, 1999b).

Second, quality training is essential. It will be used in any suit as a measure of policy and custom. Training must continually be evaluated to reflect current legislation and must be consistent with state law and local policy and/or custom. For example, simply providing training will be insufficient if it is poorly designed and delivered and if it neglects important content areas.

Third, supervision is critical because if officials knew or *should* have known about the behavior in question, liability will shift to the police department. If deliberate indifference or gross abuse is established, liability will ensue. The fairly consistent movement toward pro-active enforcement efforts continues to place additional responsibilities on law enforcement officers. Supervision will be needed to ensure that adequate implementation occurs.

Fourth, documentation is crucial. Documentation is used to establish custom and policy. As Barrineau notes: "One thing is certain—*when a goof occurs, someone will hang* (guilty or not); and it is equally as certain that the *one with the least documentation will be the one to hang*" (1987, p. 84). The lesson for individual officers is to keep documentation that will pass the lawsuit up the chain of command. The lesson for police agencies is to require officers to document their actions, allowing better supervision of employees and enhancing accountability on the part of individual officers. As of 1997, police officers are required to file incident reports on domestic violence calls in 33 states (Miller, 1997). Officers should be aware that these reports will certainly be used in any lawsuits and that they are an important source of documentation.

Fifth, honest evaluations help identify problem areas before a lawsuit occurs. Officers with a history of dealing poorly with battering cases should be held accountable in the evaluation process and should be fired if they cannot improve inadequate performances. Departments that refuse to do so risk exposing the department to institutional liability if they do not address officers with known problems.

Sixth, manage resources by identifying those that require funds and those that require managerial responses. Domestic violence probably requires more of the latter than the former. In most cases, the most significant expense is training so that officers implement laws adequately.

Seventh, prioritize areas of potential liability. Certainly domestic violence should be on any chief's top ten list given the increasing potential for liability in this area and the number of legislative changes.

Eighth, develop and implement a master plan. Here again, domestic violence should be central to all master plans to ensure that all aspects of the organization adequately deal with issues that might affect liability. For example, if a department is sued and the plaintiff argues that the department's treatment of her amounted to deliberate indifference, the department will be better positioned to argue that they have been responsible if they can point to systematic attention to battering across the master plan. For example, a plaintiff might use personnel policies to argue that the department failed to ensure that new recruits had no prior domestic violence convictions and might point to dispatch policies that ignore battering all together. These types of omissions may be used as part of an in-depth examination that may highlight numerous ways in which a department ignores or minimizes battering—thereby demonstrating deliberate indifference.

Training

Before the 1960s, police training on battering was rare. Officers were instructed to defuse the situation and make referrals to social service agencies in the community (Bard, 1970; Berk & Loseke, 1980; Goolkasian, 1986; Loving, 1981; Waits, 1985). In the 1960s and 1970s, law enforcement officers were instructed to use crisis intervention skills to "mediate" and to avoid arrest whenever possible (IACP, 1967). A national review of basic training in the late 1970s (see Buzawa & Buzawa, 1996) found that police training on battering was usually briefly mentioned during a four to eight hour lecture on "disturbed" persons, which addressed hostage situations, suicides, mentally disturbed individuals, substance abusers, and child abuse. "Arrests were actively discouraged as a waste of time except when disrespect or threats by an offender or victim indicated that the officer might lose control of the situation. Arrest, therefore, was primarily used to assert authority rather than to respond to a criminal action" (Buzawa & Buzawa, 1996, p.80). Recruits were instructed that these calls were unproductive and intervention was ineffective. Generally speaking, officers received more training about the supposed danger to themselves than they did about the dynamic of battering and the appropriate legal response (Bell, 1985).

Most improvements in training on domestic violence generally have been limited to new recruits in the academy. On average, new recruits spend eight to ten weeks in basic training where they are oriented to the job and socialized into the police culture. These programs spend inordinate amounts of time on physical fitness and firearms training. For example, the number of hours devoted to domestic violence training generally ranges from 2 to 30, with 10 being the average (Miller, 1997). These figures are remarkably low when one considers that the average recruit receives from 300 to 700 hours of training. It is difficult to provide even a rudimentary overview of the law in less than an afternoon, much less a review of the complicated issues of victimization. To address these concerns, some states are legislating training requirements. In 1997, 29 states require domestic violence training for new recruits, and 21 of those states outline the minimum standards for content (Miller, 1997).

In addition to basic training, officers often go through field training. Rookies are assigned to work with a veteran officer. Attitudes and knowledge gained from the academy are often modified or distorted as seasoned officers reinforce the notion that the academy fails to teach officers "how things really work." Since officers with more experience are also those who are most likely to have been trained according to older standards advocating mediation and stressing danger to police officers, this contact with new recruits often undermines even the best academy training (Buzawa & Buzawa, 1996). Unfortunately, domestic violence is rarely included in any formal way as part of field training.

In-service training designed for veteran officers to provide them with new skills or to update their knowledge in particular areas generally is quite limited. (Gaines, Kappeler, & Vaughn, 1999). In-service training can be delivered in several ways including: (1) roll call training where officers are given short lessons during roll calls that accompany shift changes; (2) radio training where very short periods (one to five minutes) of training are offered over the police radio; (3) departmental sessions where officers are released from duty for a day or so and trained on site; (4) specialized training where officers are sent to unique academies or programs for specific training on select topics (Gaines, Kappeler, & Vaughn, 1999, p. 143). The first two methods are relatively ineffective in dealing with a complex topic like battering, and the latter two options are very expensive for departments to implement. They must release officers from their normal duties and replace them with other officers who often are on overtime. It appears, however, that in-service training on battering is becoming somewhat more common. Eleven states require in-service training on domestic violence and two more require it of officers who did not receive it in the academy (Miller, 1997). The federal government also is providing some funding for these types of programs through the Violence Against Women Act.

There is also a critical need for training for supervisors and administrators, including police chiefs. The best written law or policy will not be effective if it is undermined or poorly implemented by those responsible for administering it. At least one study reports that chiefs in one state had very negative attitudes toward domestic violence, resulting in low enrollments in voluntary domestic violence training, an absence of written policies on battering, and low arrest rates for battering (Buzawa, 1988). One chief even stated that "he could not recall a 'genuine' call for domestic violence in his numerous years as an administrator" (p. 175). I have had similar experiences in working with statewide training for police chiefs. While many were interested in learning and trying to be effective leaders, many were quite reluctant and even hostile. One chief "joked" and asked whether I would be teaching him tips on how to commit domestic violence.

The IACP recently has recommended that comprehensive training be conducted for all department employees to ensure that everyone has a working knowledge of the dynamics of domestic violence (1999b). It advises that all new recruits; patrol, field training, internal affairs officers; dispatchers/communication officers; and administrative command (including supervisors) receive comprehensive domestic violence training on the following topics: general issues (including cultural, racial, gender, and same sex issues); domestic violence dynamics and potential barriers to assistance/intervention; stalking; warning signs of abuse by officers; response protocol; command notification and reporting procedures; general investigation and evidence collection; primary or dominant aggressor determination; officer safety; victim rights and safety; confidentiality issues; ethical considerations; criminal and civil liability; lethality assessment and safety planning; working with advocates; weapons removal and seizure; cross-jurisdictional policies and protocols; intra/interstate enforcement of protective orders; and federal legislation including stalking, domestic violence and gun control laws (1999a). IACP also recommends additional training for administrative and command personnel to include: department legal considerations and liability; media and public relations; criminal versus administrative investigations; and conducting lethality/dangerousness assessments (1999a). IACP calls for departments to "make a significant commitment of time to training on all the topics listed in the policy" and notes that the "optimal time for baseline training is estimated at 40 hours" (1999b, p. 3). From these statements, it is not clear whether they are recommending 40 hours minimum for new recruits or for all the listed employees. It is possible that they are deliberately vague, as it would seem impossible to conduct meaningful training for all employees on all of these topics without at least 40 hours. At the same time, such a huge commitment of departmental resources would likely be met with much dissent from police departments nationwide. Regardless, it is significant that IACP is beginning to be an advocate for additional and more comprehensive training on domestic violence.

It also is important that attention is being devoted to an often ignored contingency: police dispatchers. Most police departments have routine call-screening processes used by dispatchers to assign priorities for incoming calls for service. Traditionally, misdemeanor assaults received low priority and were answered only when officers had free time (Buzawa & Buzawa, 1996; Manning, 1988; Oppenlander, 1982). Battered women who called for service may have been referred to social service agencies or even told that the police did not deal with "marital conflicts." Furthermore, dispatchers often are not sworn officers and were poorly trained. As Buzawa and Buzawa note:

> All too often, the consequence was that untrained or inexperienced individuals were screening calls. They might not have been sensitized to the requirements of an effective response to domestic violence or may have been concerned more with the impact of another disliked call on overburdened patrol officers. (1996, p. 49)

The lack of training that resulted in this treatment of battering cases clearly increased the danger to battered women. It is impossible to ascertain how many domestic homicides might have been prevented by a prompt police response. Furthermore, a delayed police response allowed batterers to beat their victims and gave them time to leave the scene of the crime so that they could escape arrest when the police finally did arrive (Ford, 1983). Interestingly, this police practice has received little attention. It would appear that policies need to be revised and dispatchers need to be better trained in order to ensure that the police have an opportunity to respond. The best mandatory arrest policy will not have much impact if the police are never directed to answer these calls for service.

There is little doubt that police practices have been heavily scrutinized in the past few decades. While officers in the past were motivated to resolve battering cases as fast as possible, there is an increasing awareness that these cases are complicated situations that require significant attention. In addition to arrest, there are a variety of actions police officers should take upon their arrival at a battering call (Goolkasian, 1986; IACP, No Date). Officers should assume control of the immediate situation to ensure the safety of everyone involved. They should ascertain whether medical attention is needed and arrange for transportation to the emergency room if necessary. They should secure and protect the crime scene and gather any evidence. Officers should determine whether a protective order exists and if it has been violated. They should seek voluntary surrender of firearms or seize them under circumstances where it is legal to do so. Officers also should advise victims of their legal options and provide them with telephone numbers for local shelters, hotlines, victim advocates, and any other community agencies that might assist them. Officers should conduct safety planning with the victim. In fact, in some jurisdictions, referrals and safety plans are on brochures or business cards that may be left with the victim.[2] Officers also can arrange transportation to a shelter if victims wish to go and/or actually take them there if necessary. Officers should order batterers to leave the premises if the victims are entitled to residence (e.g. if the lease is only in their name). If batterers refuse to leave, they should be arrested for trespassing. Or, if victims choose to leave, officers should stay to ensure that battered women can leave safely.

Unfortunately, many police officers refuse to engage in these types of services, which seem like "social work" rather than "law enforcement." For example, officers often refuse to transport victims, citing the risk of legal liability that might result if the officer had a traffic accident in route. They may claim that making referrals or staying at the scene take too much time away from "crime fighting," and research suggests that officers rarely provide information about shelter (Belknap & McCall, 1994; Brown, 1984; Oppenlander, 1982). Some state legislatures have responded to these concerns by specifically authorizing the police to transport victims and/or mandating that they make social service referrals. However, these types of actions will also require a change in the organizational culture. Police officers and the organization itself will have to value these actions and reward officers for taking these non-traditional responses.

WOMAN BATTERING AND THE COURTS

In contrast to the police, the courts and correctional systems historically have received very little attention in terms of their responses to battering. In part, this apathy exists because the doctrine of sovereign immunity prohibits lawsuits against prosecutors and judges, so they have not been "forced" to change. As changes in legislation and police departmental policies increase the number of cases that are working their way through the system, we are learning more about the ways in which prosecutors and judges influence the criminal justice system's response to battering.

Prosecutorial Response

Prosecution begins when a complaint is filed. Complaints may be brought by police officers following an arrest or by victims who may file an affidavit alleging that a crime has occurred. There is some indication that complaints brought by the police are treated more seriously (Buzawa & Buzawa, 1996). Prosecutors play a critical role in the adjudication process; they determine if charges will be filed, what type of charges will be filed, and what type of plea bargains might be considered. Historically, battering cases have been a low priority for most prosecutors (Cahn & Lerman, 1991; Fagan, 1996). For example, only 5% of the 136 batterers arrested during the Minneapolis experiment were prosecuted (Sherman & Berk, 1984). The rate of prosecution remains low—from 5 to 20% for misdemeanor cases (Fagan, 1989; Davis & Smith, 1995; Ford, 1993; McLeod, 1983; Rauman, 1984; Schmidt & Steury, 1989). "Domestic violence prosecution rates are consistently shown to be lower than rates for misdemeanors such as shoplifting and simple assaults, despite the often serious nature of domestic assaults and the known identity of the perpetrator" (Martin, 1994, p. 214). There are two possible explanations for these low rates: (1) a disproportionately high percentage of victims in these cases request that charges be dropped or refuse to cooperate in the prosecution of the case or (2) prosecutors treat these cases differently and have little motivation to prosecute.

The research discussed in the article by Belknap and her colleagues indicates that women's decisions to cooperate with prosecutors are motivated by a wide range of factors, and there are substantial barriers for them to negotiate.

Attrition rates in cases where victims initiate prosecution range between 60 to 80 percent (Field & Field, 1973; Ford, 1983; Lerman, 1981; Vera Institute, 1977). These high rates can be explained by several factors (Buzawa & Buzawa, 1996). First, prosecutors may directly and indirectly encourage victims to drop the charges; they tend to make victims feel personally responsible for the outcome. Prosecutors may deviate from routine procedures and require "cooling off" periods before they will file these cases (Quarm & Schwartz, 1985; Ferraro & Boychuck, 1992). Second, as Belknap and her colleagues report, victims may experience additional harm because of prosecution. They often experience retaliation or are threatened with the same (Quarm & Schwartz, 1985). Victims may experience economic harm if batterers lose their job. Victims may lose household income or child support. Victims also may experience out of pocket expenses if they take off work and secure childcare while they attend a trial. Third, victims' attitudes may change over time, and they may no longer want their batterers punished. He may have charmed his way back into her good graces, or she may have left him and does not want to re-visit the issue. Fourth, victims may blame themselves in a society that emphasizes that battered women are at fault. Fifth, victims have very complex motives; prosecutors often fail to be responsive to victims and their needs (Erez & Belknap, 1998). Finally, victims may become frustrated when serious, violent assaults are classified and prosecuted as misdemeanors. Victims may feel that the prosecutor fails to see their victimization as serious and that it is not worth the risk to cooperate (Hart, 1993; Langan & Innes, 1986).

Prosecutors contribute to low rates of conviction. Prosecutors may fail to file charges for a wide variety of reasons. Ironically, mandatory arrest policies may produce too many cases for prosecutors to handle, since they rarely have received any additional funding or staff (Balos & Trotzky, 1988; Davis, Smith, & Nickles, 1998). Other structural factors influence prosecution decisions as well. Most of these cases are prosecuted at the misdemeanor level. As a group, these cases are viewed as low priority. Prosecutors, in general, prefer cases that have high conviction rates (Rauma, 1984) as well as those that are disposed of easily and efficiently (Ellis, 1984). Neither of these situations is true of battering cases. Time limitations brought about by excessive caseloads aggravated by the mandatory requirements for prosecution of drug offenses (in many jurisdictions) play a role in prosecutorial decision making (Buzawa & Buzawa, 1996; Cahn & Lerman, 1991). Personal values can affect prosecution. Prosecutors influenced by patriarchal values (Fagan, 1996) continue to view these cases as private, family matters (Cahn & Lerman, 1991; Edwards, 1989). Furthermore, prosecutors may become discouraged and lack motivation to pursue cases when disinterested judges fail to respond with meaningful sanctions (Fagan, 1996).

The most salient reason for failure to prosecute appears to relate to victim motivation. Prosecutors are disinclined to prosecute because they *believe* that battered women will drop the charges (Ellis, 1984; Ford & Regoli, 1993; Miethe, 1987; Woods, 1981). This stereotype was codified by the National Association of District Attorneys (1980) when they advised that prosecutors should consider whether victims would cooperate and whether they would refuse to live apart from their batterer. As a result, it should be no surprise that the U.S. Commission on Civil Rights reported that prosecutors "applied more stringent filing requirements and charging policies to domestic assaults than to other assaults" (Goolkasian, 1986, p. 60).

Prosecutors who fail to bring charges against batterers may discourage police officers from conducting careful investigations or making arrests. Officers may feel that there is no point in doing so if prosecutors do not follow through (Ellis, 1984). Failure to prosecute cases also undermines any deterrent effect arrest might have (Fagan, 1996). Batterers learn that there are no *real* consequences for using violence against women, regardless of what happens at the arrest stage. Battered women learn that the system ultimately places them in greater jeopardy when prosecutors fail to follow through. Battered women are not stupid; they will refuse to press charges or request that charges be dropped if the system fails to protect them. If batterers are arrested but there is no prosecution or punishment, battered women probably are at higher risk of subsequent victimization (Ford & Regoli, 1993). If the criminal justice system abandons women after the arrest process, battered women will not cooperate with the system because they will be afraid of retaliation from batterers.

Mandatory Prosecution and "No Drop Policies"

It is becoming more common for jurisdictions to implement mandatory prosecution policies (Rebovich, 1996). At least four states (Utah, Wisconsin, Florida, and Minnesota) have legislated such action (Mills, 1998). The federal government also encourages mandatory prosecution by providing funds to states that adopt these types of policies (Mills, 1998). In some cases, mandatory prosecution policies are described as "no drop" policies because prosecutors refuse to dismiss battering cases, regardless of the victims' wishes. In some jurisdictions, exceptions to no-drop policies may be made if the victim meets with a counselor or if the victim can cite "extraordinary circumstances" that would warrant a departure from policy (Cahn & Lerman, 1991).

Mandatory prosecution polices offer several advantages (Cahn & Lerman, 1991; Davis & Smith, 1995; Goolkasian, 1986). They eliminate or at least reduce prosecutorial bias. They also benefit the community as whole, by conveying that this behavior is unacceptable and criminal. Most importantly, these policies, at least in theory, reduce the likelihood that batterers will coerce victims (either with violence or threats of the same) to drop the charges because prosecutors, not battered women, are the actors responsible for pursuing the case. Theoretically, this action provides a cushion for the victim. If she is not in charge of the process, there may be less potential for retaliation. Prosecutors can subpoena victims who can, theoretically, insulate themselves by informing batterers that they have no choice but to testify because they have been ordered to do so (Cahn & Lerman, 1991). Prosecutors also may use experts to testify about the dynamics of battering and explain how a typical battered woman might react to criminal justice intervention. In other words, the victim's reluctance on the stand can be used to assist the prosecution if they use expert testimony to explain that battered women are afraid of retaliation.

There are problems, however, with no-drop policies. First, batterers may not believe that victims lack the power to get the charges dismissed. Batterers may think that victims are lying or that prosecutors are bluffing. Batterers may not care whether victims actually have the power to influence charging decisions. A batterer may be frustrated and angry, and he may take it out on the battered woman regardless of her ability to influence the outcome of the case. Second, battered women may be disempowered by this approach. As Goolkasian (1986) notes,

> Victims have a right and are able to decide whether or not they want criminal justice intervention, when given full information. There are several reasons why a battered woman might choose not to prosecute: for example, she prefers civil remedies, she faces life-threatening danger and must flee the area, she fears race-biased sentencing, or she would lose critical financial support. (p. 63)

Furthermore, some battered women may use battering charges as a way to bargain for security. As Ford & Regoli (1993) note:

> Prosecution is a victim power resource when used in negotiation for security. The bargain may involve simple promises of leaving her alone. Or it may involve agreements for structural arrangements likely to bring longer-term security (e.g., counseling, favorable terms for divorce, support payments, child visitation rights, etc.). Dropping charges fulfills the victim's part of the agreement. (p. 142)

Refusing to drop charges when victims request it, in effect, disempowers women. Just as batterers fail to consider the victims' wishes, the criminal justice system fails to consider the needs of victims. The system replaces the batterer, and battered women still have no control over processes that affect their lives. In addition, policies that fail to accommodate the wishes of the victim may alienate women and keep them from calling the police or seeking other intervention in the future.

Prosecutors can pursue a case without any cooperation from the victim because assault is a crime against the state, not the individual women per se. It is still possible to get a successful conviction (Cahn & Lerman, 1991). Prosecutors often have substantial physical evidence to proceed, especially if police officers are trained to collect evidence of this nature. For example, in misdemeanor battering cases it is particularly important for police officers to photograph injuries. Testimony about hitting, shoving, slapping is much more powerful when there are pictures that graphically depict swollen, bruised, and battered bodies. It also is important that pictures be taken shortly after the incident and again a few days later. Especially in misdemeanor cases, a large part of the injuries may be bruises that appear minor or insignificant shortly after the crime but which develop into major discoloration and offer evidence of substantial battering after time passes. For example, if a woman is beaten with a baseball bat, she may show virtually no injuries the day of the assault. Several days later, though, her entire torso may be black and blue, yellow and green because of massive bruising. These types of photos are very powerful and allow prosecutors to present strong cases even when victims refuse to testify or when they do so reluctantly. Videotape of a victim of domestic violence can also be used in court if victims are unavailable for trial (Cahn & Lerman, 1991).

Prosecutors may have other witnesses testify about the abuse instead of relying exclusively on the testimony of battered women (Lerman, 1981). For example, neighbors and children may corroborate the abuse, and police officers should be trained to record all statements by witnesses. Officers should impound all evidence such as torn or bloody clothes and any weapons—all of which can be introduced at trial. Certainly 911 tapes, police reports, and medical records provide evidence of abuse. Prosecutors who are motivated to treat these cases seriously often have ample evidence for a conviction even if victims refuse to testify.

Other Prosecutorial Options

In addition to prosecution of assault charges, there are a variety of other ways that prosecutors affect the court's response to woman battering. Prosecutors play an important role in the enforcement of protective orders. If an offender has violated a protective order by assaulting a woman, charges should be filed for both the violation of the order and the new act of violence.[3] If prosecutors fail to ensure that orders are enforced rigorously, both batterers and victims will quickly learn that protective orders are not "worth the paper they are written on."

Prosecutors also may increase the likelihood of a successful prosecution if they abolish the practice of forcing victims to file formal complaints. In many jurisdictions, prosecutors will not pursue a case unless the victim files a complaint (U.S. Attorney General's Task Force on Family Violence, 1984). The rationale has been that if victims are unwilling to file complaints, they will be unwilling to cooperate in prosecution making a conviction unlikely. There is no legal requirement for a complaint to be on file. Making battered women sign complaints increases vulnerability to future violence from their batterers. Prosecutors should abolish this practice. For the same reasons, battered women should not be required to appear or testify at pre-trial hearings (U.S. Attorney General's Task Force, 1984, p. 27).

Prosecutors also can require defendants in battering cases to appear in court at arraignment even if it is customary to let defendants waive this procedure in other similar cases. Doing so communicates that this is a serious crime and sets the tone for future contacts. If the defendant is to be released prior to trial (and most are) on bail or on their own recognizance, prosecutors should secure conditions of release that prohibit contact with and/or commission of additional acts of violence. While protective orders may be issued at this time, prosecutors can place their own conditions on pre-trial release; prosecutors should request these types of conditions as a normal part of the bail or ROR process and pursue revocation procedures if conditions are violated (U.S. Attorney General's Task Force, 1984, p. 27).

In some cases, prosecution is suspended or deferred pending completion of a treatment program or some other type of counseling (Ford & Regoli, 1993). Charges are then dismissed if the defendant meets the conditions set forth by the prosecution. Pretrial diversion is most likely to occur for misdemeanor cases and often secures the same result (treatment) as a successful conviction without the expense of prosecution and a trial (Lerman, 1981). However, there are some disadvantages. It is possible that offenders perceive this as getting off lightly and batterers may take the treatment more seriously when it is administered as part of a sentence and as a condition of probation (Goolkasian, 1986, p. 75). Another disadvantage of pretrial diversion is that it takes longer to respond to a failure in treatment. For example, if the batterer drops out of treatment and batters the victim again, charges (old and possibly new) have to be filed, and there is no immediate sanction. In contrast, if the treatment had been part of a sentence, sanctions could be administered promptly without waiting for a trial. Furthermore, diversion cases rarely are monitored adequately; therefore, offenders seldom are prosecuted for failure to comply with the conditions specified. Instead, these cases generally re-enter the system only when a new assault occurs (Cahn & Lerman, 1991). Finally, any prosecutor who wants to ensure that the perpetrator will not have easy and legal access to a firearm may want to avoid the routine practice of pretrial diversion in favor of pursuing actual convictions because *convicted* offenders are no longer eligible to own firearms.

In large jurisdictions, the use of specialized domestic violence units is an important reform that has made prosecution more efficient and effective (Davis, Smith, & Nickles, 1998; Fagan, 1996; Goolkasian, 1986). These units create an atmosphere and organizational climate that make domestic violence cases a high priority; these cases do not have to compete with other types of cases for scarce resources (Fagan, 1996). In smaller jurisdictions, similar results may occur by assigning a specific prosecutor to concentrate only on battering cases. If these types of structural changes are not possible, prosecutorial guidelines and protocols are useful ways to structure discretion. These types of practices will never abolish prosecutorial discretion; it is too embedded in the system. It does, however, facilitate a systematic response that prevents batterers from manipulating the system to escape accountability. It also helps ensure that prosecutors do not plea-bargain these cases in ways that suggest that woman battering is less serious than other types of assault.

Thus, prosecutors can, and should, take actions to facilitate pro-active pursuit of battering cases. Too often, they have been allowed to "cop out" and contend that there is nothing they can do when victims will not cooperate. It would appear that training would facilitate prosecutorial reform although training rarely has been mandated. For example, in 1997 only 4 states required prosecutorial training on domestic violence (Miller, 1997).

Judicial Response

Unfortunately, the most pro-active prosecutor will be unable to ensure that batterers are held accountable unless judges also convict. Judges play a critical role in the criminal justice system's response to battering; however, historically, judges rarely saw batterers in their courtroom especially in misdemeanor cases (Goolkasian, 1986b). When cases were prosecuted, they often were dismissed by judges who shared many of the same attitudes and faced similar structural constraints of prosecutors (Buzawa & Buzawa, 1996). In the rare cases where convictions were secured, sentences generally were quite lenient and few offenders received jail time (Sherman, 1993). Furthermore, sentences for battering cases often were more lenient than those rendered when the offense involved strangers (Goolkasian, 1986b; see Hemmens, Strom, & Schlegel, 1998).

As more and more cases reach the court today, some judges no longer attribute the violent behavior to "relationship problems" between couples who are in need of "marriage counseling." Instead, judges have been confronted with a "complex problem of persistent intimidation and physical injury" (Finn & Colson, 1990, p. 4). There has been an increased tendency to provide judges with training. The State Justice Institute, the National Judicial College, the National Council of Juvenile and Family Court Judges, and the American Bar Association Judicial Administration Division are examples of organizations that are designing training and actively promoting attendance by the judiciary (Dutton, 1996). Nonetheless, there is some evidence that judges still blame victims and refuse to view battering as a crime (see Hemmens, Strom, & Schlegel, 1998).

In some jurisdictions, judges have created model protocols or sentencing guidelines to ensure greater conformity and accountability in sentencing. Sentencing guidelines and/or protocols help structure judicial discretion and prevent batterers from escaping sanctions through judge shopping. However, because the vast majority of the cases before the courts are misdemeanor assault charges, maximum sentences are quite limited. Judges have several options in these cases.

Judges might fine the defendant (within limits specified by law); however, this type of sanction may harm the financially dependent woman. This traditional response has not been very effective. Batterers conclude that paying a relatively small amount of money is the only penalty for beating a woman.

Judges have the option to incarcerate offenders, but this is most common in felony cases. In misdemeanor cases, offenders can be sentenced to a maximum of one year in jail (or even less in some jurisdictions depending on the specific charge). However, judges historically have been reluctant to use jail time especially in first offenses involving misdemeanor violations (Goolkasian, 1986a, p. 85). Ignoring that this is merely the first time that the case made it this far (and almost never the *first* instance of abuse), judges rarely sentence batterers to jail. Given the current overcrowded state of our jail systems, many judges are reluctant to use this resource for batterers. Instead, judges often adopt a compromise of sort.

Batterers in many jurisdictions are required to participate in treatment pro-grams (Goolkasian, 1986a, 1986b; Healey & Smith, 1998; Healey, Smith, & O'Sul-livan, 1998). Judges might accomplish this sentence in a variety of ways: they might suspend the charges; they may enter a finding of guilty and suspend a jail sentence; they might impose the program as a condition of probation; or they might impose it as a condition of a protective order. Thus, while the exact means of forcing batterers into treatment may vary depending upon the circumstances of the case and according to state law, the effect is the same. The batterer is not incarcerated as long as he participates in the court ordered treatment program and refrains from harming the victim.

There is a tremendous amount of diversity in batterers' treatment programs, which makes generalization difficult. Most court ordered programs involve group counseling and educational programs, although there is no universal agreement about what types of programs are best suited for batterers (Gondolf, 1997). In the worst case scenario, some opportunistic therapists have jumped on the band wagon seeing this as a lucrative business opportunity since batterers are often required to pay for these programs. Even poor men usually find a way to pay for programs when it is a way to avoid jail (sometimes taking food from the family table). In some jurisdictions, batterers must participate in programs that are certified by the court; others require counselors to participate in mandatory training in an attempt to maintain some control over the content and/or integ-rity of these programs.

As an example of what happens when there is no oversight, O. J. Simpson's court-ordered treatment following his 1989 assault on Nicole apparently amounted to telephone counseling with a private counselor. There appears to be a growing trend towards legislative control to prevent these types of situations. As of 1997, 26 states and the District of Columbia have passed some form of legis-lative standards, although they vary a great deal (Austin & Dankwort, 1999). In some states they are mandatory, and in others they are voluntary and proscrip-tive. Interestingly, most standards (81%) identified victim safety as an essential focus for batterer treatment programs, and the majority of the standards (70%) specifically articulated that patriarchy was a primary causal factor associated with battering. The overwhelming majority of standards (92%) noted that treat-ment programs for batterers were one facet of a multifaceted, coordinated, com-munity response. Advocates have thus had considerable success in ensuring that treatment programs for batterers are conceptualized consistently with domain assumptions of a feminist perspective.

However, many salient concerns remain. There is no consensus over which program approaches are most effective. Should programs concentrate on drug use and anger control management? Should they focus on power or control? Which is more effective? There also are concerns about the high rate of dropout and noncompliance in these programs. The effectiveness of these programs is often debated, and success rates in many programs seem to be overly optimistic about the reformation of batterers. Programs are often not available in rural and minority communities. There is a need to be able to assess dangerousness of batterers with better reliability to ensure the safety of battered women. If he "falls off the wagon," does she pay for it with her life?

It does, however, appear that batterer's treatment programs are useful. First, they allow at least some men to get a grip on their problems and change their behavior. Second, in some cases, it may be an important part of the process for many women. Some women hang on to the hope that he can or will change if he would just get some help. When batterers fail to change in treatment, some battered women are empowered to leave; they recognize that he is not going to change and that it is not safe for them to stay. Third, judges seem more willing to sentence men when they have violated judicial orders. Men who fail to attend treatment, engage in additional violence, or violate other court orders may find themselves in jail. In the past, too frequently, the court did not treat these repeated violations as serious behavior and judges have not held batterers accountable for these violations. The use of treatment programs has helped to bridge that gap. However, judges must still ensure that all orders are consistently enforced and that there are consequences for any violations. In other words, treatment programs will be most effective when used as part of a coordinated response (Healey & Smith, 1998). Otherwise, batterers will manipulate the system, and the victim will, again, be in jeopardy.

Judges, however, also may ensure that batterers attend treatment as part of a sentence rather than as part of an attempt to divert batterers. This goal is best achieved through the use of probation. If offenders receive probation, there is a formal finding of guilt and offenders are prohibited from owning firearms. As discussed earlier, it is much easier to revoke probation than to return to court if the original charges were suspended. Judges have wide latitude in setting conditions of probation so that many goals may be achieved (Goolkasian, 1986a, 1986b).[4] Offenders should be prevented from harassing, threatening, or assaulting the victim in any way. Offenders should be required to participate in counseling, and restitution to the victim should be mandated. Offenders may also be required to refrain from the use of drugs and alcohol and be required to participate in substance abuse programs, if there is evidence that the abuse is related to this use. In general, judges should impose comprehensive conditions on probation, and violations should be taken seriously. Enforcement of conditions of probation, however, will require that correctional officials be actively involved in addressing battering.

Battering and Correctional Responses

Virtually every text or anthology published on battering omits corrections. This neglect ignores some very important aspects of a total systemic response. For example, probation officers impact the treatment of battering cases when officers prepare pre-sentence investigations (Goolkasian, 1986b). Probation officers may affect the sentence in the case by their recommendation or by the tone of the report. For example, does it acknowledge and address domestic violence or is that behavior minimized? Probation officers also play a critical role in monitoring compliance with the conditions of probation and participating in the revocation of probation when conditions are violated (Goolkasian, 1986b).

To facilitate enforcement of conditions, offenders should be required to sign a release of information form that allows counselors to release privileged information to the probation officer about the offenders' progress in treatment (Goolkasian, 1986a, p. 93). Probation officers also should notify the offender, preferably in writing, that they will be in contact with the victim and that victims will be encouraged to report any acts of violence or violations of orders. Officers should request revocation when violations occur. (Victims should be notified immediately of revocation hearings because there may be increased risk of violence.) Protocols and policies are quite helpful in guiding probation officers. They minimize discretion and thereby help reduce any bias by officers in enforcement, but they also help outline procedures that make the system more effective.

Unfortunately, we know little about probation officers and their role in battering cases. Since most cases involve misdemeanor offenses, these cases are low priority in most jurisdictions. Probation officers have the difficult job of enforcing orders with limited resources in a system that can barely cope with its felony caseload. One can predict that probation officers will fail to devote their already overextended time to enforcing cases that have been traditionally viewed as unimportant unless supervisors prioritize these cases and reward officers who devote the necessary attention to them. Probation officers who fail to enforce conditions will lead batterers to conclude that there are no real repercussions for their violent behavior, only some inconvenience.

Parole officers have received even less attention in the literature than probation officers, in part, because of the overwhelming concentration of misdemeanor cases. As a result, few cases are processed at the felony level where parole is a factor. Parole officers, like probation officers, are responsible for monitoring compliance and initiating revocation hearings after batterers are released from prison.

Other correctional officials also play an important role in terms of victim notification procedures. Unfortunately, there have been several high profile cases where batterers have been released from jail or prison and have killed their partners who were unaware of the release. To help prevent some of these tragedies, victims should be notified before an offender is released from jail or prison through bail, work release, furlough, parole, or release to a halfway house. Victims who are aware that their offenders are "on the loose" can take actions to ensure their safety. Kentucky was the first state in the United States to allow for 24-hour information and victim notification. This program, VINE (Victim Information Notification Everyday) was first implemented in Jefferson County (Louisville) after the tragic death of Mary Byron (VINE Brochure, No Date, 1999). In 1995, her ex-boyfriend shot her to death after posting bail, one week after he was arrested and charged with kidnapping her (Trone, 1999). Victims may call an 800 number and get information about the status of any convicted offender, day or night. The date of release is provided for inmates in custody as well as the name, address, and phone number for the current institution. The date of the next parole hearing (if applicable) and the tentative release date (based on expiration of the sentence; VINE Brochure, No Date, 1999) are also provided. Since VINE's inception, more than 33 states have created similar programs (Trone, 1999). Although other victims can access VINE, the program has defined battered women as its primary service group (Trone, 1999).

In addition to notifying victims of release, correctional officials can take actions to address battering while they have custody of the offender. For example, most prisons and some jails provide drug and alcohol treatment programs. Correctional officials should provide programs designed to address battering and/or other crimes of violence committed against women. A comprehensive program that examines violence, its role in interpersonal relationships, and subsequent criminal behavior would be one such approach. They might replicate treatment programs that focus on anger management, or they might offer an educational/counseling-based program. Given the large amount of interpersonal violence in society, it is quite ironic that most prisons ignore this type of programming all together.

We need to pay more attention to correctional responses to battering. While efforts to change the criminal justice system have targeted the police, and to some extent prosecutors and judges, correctional systems generally have been ignored. A growing body of evidence suggests that the entire criminal justice system must work as a system if there is any hope of reducing the amount of battering.

SUMMARY

An examination of the criminal justice system response indicates that there has been progress in terms of changing the cultural hegemony, and battering is more apt to be viewed as a crime than in the past. The types of reform also illustrate some of the tension associated with the effort to transform the social construction of battering. For example, there has been more attention given to whether or not arrest alone deters battering than to whether or not police officers treat battering cases differently from other assaults. Likewise, police officers continue to emphasize the supposed danger they face in battering cases while ignoring the danger posed to victims. The police become the victims and battered women the enemy.

Reform in the courts also illustrates the tension surrounding the social construction of battered women and their role in the criminal justice system. The tendency to drop charges if victims failed to cooperate indicated that the system required individual battered women to assume responsibility for the prosecution of these types of criminals. In an attempt to rectify this situation, the courts have pursued reforms that may endanger victims. For example, it is not clear whether mandatory prosecution policies make battered women safer. Do these policies evidence a commitment to moving responsibility for prosecution from battered women to the system? Are most prosecutors really willing to place a high priority on prosecuting misdemeanor battering cases even when the victims refuse to cooperate? Will the judiciary continue to emphasize treatment over punishment, and what effect does this have on battered women and their willingness to cooperate in prosecution? It is interesting that the criminal justice system seems reluctant to use a jail bed for batterers but has no qualms about using this precious resource for drug offenders. Thus batterers continue to receive treatment, but drug users are punished in the hopes that it will deter them from future substance use. These types of inconsistencies suggest that the criminal justice system is still reluctant to fully recognize that battering is a crime and to treat it as such.

NOTES

[1] The government is allowed to make some distinctions between men and women if they can demonstrate that they have an important objective and that the state is substantially related to the advancement of its objective. In contrast, other types of discrimination face a higher standard in that the government has to have a compelling interest in making any distinctions (by race or ethnicity for example). This test is referred to as the strict scrutiny test. It is unclear how women of color fit in this legal analysis because the classification system dichotomizes race and gender. In general, however, it appears that women of color are treated as women if they file on the grounds of gender discrimination and as minorities if they file on grounds of racial discrimination. Obviously, the distinction between the experiences of women of color rarely divide themselves so clearly.

[2] This type of information, however, should never just be left at the scene. Victims may be in danger if they are unaware of this literature in the house and if batterers find it first.

[3] While there is some concern over double jeopardy, most experts agree that there is no risk if the charges are filed correctly.

[4] Mediation, however, should be approached cautiously (Goolkasian,1986b; Hamberger & Hastings, 1993) as it assumes that both parties have equal power to negotiate.

REFERENCES

Alpert, G., & Dunham, R. (1997). *Policing urban America* (3rd ed.). Prospect Heights, IL: Waveland Press.

Austin, J., & Dankwort, J. (1999). Standards for batterer programs: A review and analysis. *Journal of Interpersonal Violence, 14,* 152–168.

Balos, B., & Trotsky, I. (1988). Enforcement of the domestic abuse act in Minnesota: A preliminary study. *Law and Inequality, 6,* 83–125.

Bard, M. (1970). *Training police as specialists in family crisis intervention.* Washington, DC: U.S. Government Printing Office.

Barrineau, H. (1987). *Civil liability in criminal justice.* Cincinnati: Anderson.

Belknap, J. (1990). Police training in domestic violence: Perceptions of training and knowledge of the law. *American Journal of Criminal Justice, 14,* 248–267.

Belknap, J., & McCall, K. (1994). Woman battering and police referrals. *Journal of Criminal Justice, 22,* 223–236.

Bell, D. (1985). A multiyear study of Ohio urban, suburban, and rural police dispositions of domestic disputes. *Victimology, 10,* 301–310.

Berk, S., & Loseke, D. (1980). "Handling" family violence: Situational determinants of police arrest in domestic disturbances. *Law and Society Review 15*(2), 317–346.

Brown, S. (1984). Police responses to wife beating: Neglect of a crime of violence. *Journal of Criminal Justice, 12*, 277–288.

Bruno v Codd, 396 N.Y.S. 2nd 974, NY, Sup Ct (1977).

Buzawa, E. (1988). Explaining variations in police response to domestic violence: A case study in Detroit and New England. In G. Hotaling, D. Finkelhor, J. Kirkpatrick, & M. Straus (Eds.), *Coping with family violence* (pp. 169–182). Beverly Hills, CA: Sage.

Buzawa, E., & Buzawa, C. (1996). *Domestic violence: The criminal justice response* (2nd ed.). Thousand Oaks, CA: Sage.

Cahn, N., & Lerman, L. (1991). Prosecuting woman abuse. In M. Steinman (Ed.), *Woman battering: Policy responses* (pp. 95–112). Cincinnati: Anderson.

Canton v Harris, 109 S. Ct. 1197 (1989).

Davis, R., & Smith, B. (1995). Domestic violence reforms: Empty promises of fulfilled expectations. *Crime and Delinquency, 41*, 541–552.

Davis, R., Smith, B., & Nickles, L. (1988). Prosecuting domestic violence cases with reluctant victims: Assessing two novel approaches in Milwaukee. In *Legal interventions in family violence: Research findings and policy implications* (pp. 71–72). Washington, DC: National Institute of Justice & American Bar Association.

Davis, R., Smith, B., & Nickles, L. (1998). The deterrent effect of prosecuting domestic violence misdemeanors. *Crime and Delinquency, 44*, 434–442.

DeShaney v Winnebago County Department of Social Services, 109 S. Ct. 998 (1989).

Dutton, M. (1996). *The validity and use of evidence concerning battering and its effects in criminal trials: A report to Congress under the Violence Against Women Act.* Washington, DC: U.S. Department of Justice, National Institute of Justice & U.S. Department of Health and Human Services.

Edwards, S. (1989). *Policing domestic violence: Women, law and the state.* London: Sage.

Eigenberg, H., & Moriarty, L. (1991). Domestic violence and local law enforcement in Texas: Examining police officer's awareness of state legislation. *Journal of Interpersonal Violence, 6*(1), 102–109.

Elliot, D. (1989). Criminal justice procedures in family violence crimes. In L. Ohlin & M. Tonry (Eds.), *Family violence* (pp. 427–480). Chicago: University of Chicago Press.

Ellis, J. (1984). Prosecutorial discretion to charge in cases of spousal assault: A dialogue. *Journal of Criminal Law and Criminology, 75*, 56–102.

Erez, E., & Belknap, J. (1998). In their own words: Battered women's assessment of the criminal processing system's responses. *Violence and Victims, 13*, 251–268.

Fagan, J. (1989). Cessation of family violence: Deterrence and dissuasion. In L. Ohlin & M. Tonry (Eds.), *Crime and justice: A review of the research* (pp. 427–480). London: University of Chicago Press.

Fagan, J. (1996). *The criminalization of domestic violence: Promises and limits.* Washington, DC: National Institute of Justice.

Fagan, J., Friedman, E., Wexler, S., & Lewis, V. (1984). *National family violence evaluation final report.* San Francisco: Ursa Institute.

Feder, L. (1998). Police handling of domestic and non-domestic assault calls: Is there a case for discrimination. *Crime and Delinquency, 44*, 335–349.

Feder, L. (1997). Domestic violence and police response in a pro-arrest jurisdiction. *Women and Criminal Justice, 8*, 79–98.

Ferraro, K., & Boychuck, T. (1992). The courts response to interpersonal violence: A comparison of intimate and nonintimate assault. In E. Buzawa & C. Buzawa (Eds.),

Domestic violence: The changing criminal justice response (pp. 209–225). Westport, CT: Auburn House.

Field, M., & Field, H. (1973). Marital violence and the criminal process: Neither justice nor peace. *Social Service Review, 47*, 221–240.

Finn, P., & Colson, S. (1990). *Civil protection orders: Legislation, current court practice, and enforcement.* Washington, DC: National Institute of Justice.

Ford, D. (1983). Wife battery and criminal justice: A study of victim decision-making. *Family Relations, 32*, 463–475.

Ford, D. (1993). *The Indianapolis domestic violence prosecution experiment.* Indianapolis: Indiana University.

Ford, D., & Regoli, M. (1992). The preventative impacts of policies for prosecuting wife batterers. In E. Buzawa & C. Buzawa (Eds.), *Domestic violence: The changing criminal justice system* (pp. 181–201). Westport, CT: Auburn House.

Ford, D., & Regoli, M. (1993). The criminal prosecution of wife assaulters: Process, problems, and effects. In Z. Hilton (Ed.), *Legal responses to wife assault: Current trends and evaluation* (pp. 127–164). Newbury Park, CA: Sage.

Frazee, D. (1995, Fall). Court TV we'd like to see: A plain English guide to the Violence Against Women Act. Retrieved August 29, 1997 from the World Wide Web: http://www.womensnet.apc.org/onissues/f95vama.html

Fyfe, J., Klinger, D., & Flavin, J. (1997). Differential police treatment of male-on-female spousal violence. *Criminology, 35*, 455–473.

Gaines, L., Kappeler, V., & Vaughn, J. (1999). *Policing in America* (3rd ed.). Cincinnati: Anderson.

Garner, J., & Clemmer, E. (1986). *Danger to police in domestic disturbances—A new look.* Washington, DC: National Institute of Justice.

Gondolf, E. (1997). Batterer programs: What we need to know. *Journal of Interpersonal Violence, 12*, 83–98.

Goolkasian, G. (November, 1986a). *Confronting domestic violence: A guide for criminal justice agencies.* Washington, DC: National Institute of Justice.

Goolkasian, G. (1986b). *Confronting domestic violence: The role of criminal court judges.* Washington, DC: National Institute of Justice.

Hamberger, L., & Hastings, J. (1993). Court-mandated treatment of men who assault their partner: Issues, controversies, and outcomes. In N. Hilton (Ed.), *Legal responses to wife assault: Current trends and evaluation* (pp. 188–232). Newbury Park, CA: Sage.

Hart, B. (1993). Battered women and the criminal justice system. *American Behavioral Scientist, 83*, 73–119.

Healey, K., & Smith, C. (1998). *Batterer programs: What criminal justice agencies need to know.* Washington, DC: National Institute of Justice.

Healey, K., Smith, C., & O'Sullivan, C. (1998). *Batterer intervention: Program approaches and criminal justice strategies.* Washington, DC: National Institute of Justice.

Hemmens, C., Strom, K., & Schlegel, E. (1998). Gender bias in the courts: A review of the literature. *Sociological Imagination, 35*, 22–42.

Hirschel, J., Dean, C., & Lumb, R. (1994). The relative contribution of domestic violence to assault and injury of police officers. *Justice Quarterly, 11*, 99–117.

Hirschel, J., Hutchinson, I., Dean, C., & Mills, A. (1992). Review essay on the law enforcement response to spouse abuse: Past, present, and future. *Justice Quarterly, 9*, 247–283.

International Association of Chiefs of Police (1967). *Training key 16: Handling domestic disturbance calls.* Gaithersburg, MD: IACP.

International Association of Chiefs of Police (1999a, April 1). Police Officer Domestic Violence. Retrieved September 4, 1999 from the World Wide Web: http://www.theiacp.org/pubinfo/index.html

International Association of Chiefs of Police (1999b, April 1). Police Officer Domestic Violence: Concepts and Issues Paper. Retrieved September 4, 1999 from the World Wide Web: http://www.theiacp.org/pubinfo/index.html

International Association of Chiefs of Police (No Date). Helpful Interventions. Retrieved September 5, 1999 from the World Wide Web: http://www.theiacp.org/pubinfo/ordersinterventions.html

Kappeler, V. (1997). *Critical issues in police civil liability* (2nd ed.). Prospect Heights, IL: Waveland Press.

Kappeler, V., Blumberg, M., & Potter, G. (2000). *The mythology of crime and criminal justice* (3rd ed.). Prospect Heights, IL: Waveland Press.

Kappeler, S., & Kappeler, V. (1992). A research note on Section 1983 claims against the police: Cases before the federal district courts in 1990. *American Journal of Police, 11*, 65–73.

Klinger, D. (1995). Policing spousal assault. *Journal of Research in Crime and Delinquency, 32*, 308–324.

Langan, P., & Innes, C. (1986). *Preventing domestic violence against women.* Washington, DC: Bureau of Justice Statistics.

Lerman, L. (1981). *Prosecution of spouse abuse: Innovations in criminal justice response.* Washington, DC: Police Executive Research Forum.

Lerman, L. (1986). Protection of wife beaters: Institutional obstacles and innovations. In M. Lystad (Ed.), *Violent in the home: Interdisciplinary perspectives* (pp. 250–295). New York: Brunner/Mazel.

Loving, N. (1981). *Spouse abuse: A curriculum guide for police trainers.* Washington, DC: Police Executive Research Forum.

Manning, P. (1999). The police: Mandate, strategies, and appearances. In V. Kappeler (Ed.), *Police and society: Touchstone readings* (2nd ed., pp. 94–122). Prospect Heights, IL: Waveland Press.

Manning, P. (1988). *Symbolic interaction: Signifying calls and police response.* Cambridge: MIT Press.

Martin, M. (1994). Mandatory arrest for domestic violence: The court's response. *Criminal Justice Review, 19*, 212–227.

McLeod, M. (1983). Victim noncooperation in the prosecution of domestic assault. *Criminology, 21*, 395–416.

Miethe, T. (1987). Stereotypical conceptions and criminal processing: The case of the victim-offender relationship. *Justice Quarterly, 4*, 571–593.

Miller, N. (1997). *Domestic violence legislation affecting police and prosecutor responsibilities in the United States: Inferences from a 50-state review of state statutory codes.* Alexandria, VA: Institute for Law and Justice.

Mills, L. (1998). Mandatory arrest and prosecution policies for domestic violence: A critical literature review and the case for more research to test victim empowerment approaches. *Criminal Justice and Behavior, 25*, 306–318.

Murphy, C., Musser, P., & Matton, K. (1998). Coordinated community intervention for domestic abusers: Intervention system involvement and criminal recidivism. *Journal of Family Violence, 13*, 263–284.

Niederhoffer, A. (1967). *Behind the shield: The police in urban society.* New York: Doubleday.

Okun, L. (1986). *Woman abuse: Facts replacing myths.* Albany: State University of New York.

Oppenlander, N. (1992). Coping or copping out. *Criminology, 20*, 449–465.

Pence, E. (1999). Some thoughts on philosophy. In M. Shepard & E. Pence (Eds.), *Coordination community response to domestic violence: Lessons from Duluth and beyond* (pp. 25–40). Thousand Oaks, CA: Sage.

Pence, E., & McDonnell, C. (1999). Developing policies and protocols. In M. Shepard & E. Pence (Eds.), *Coordination community response to domestic violence: Lessons from Duluth and beyond* (pp. 25–40). Thousand Oaks, CA: Sage.

Pence, E., & Shepard, M. (1988). Integrating feminist theory and practice: The challenge of the battered women's movement. In K. Yllo & M. Bograd (Eds.), *Feminist perspectives on wife abuse* (pp. 282–298). Beverly Hills, CA: Sage.

Quarm, D., & Schwartz, M. (1985). Domestic violence in criminal court: An examination of new legislation in Ohio. In C. Scheber & C. Fineman (Eds.), *Criminal justice politics and women: The aftermath of legally mandated change* (pp. 29–46). New York: Haworth Press.

Rauma, D. (1984). Going for the gold: Prosecutorial decision making in cases of wife assault. *Social Science Research, 13,* 321–351.

Rebovich, D. (1996). Prosecution response to domestic violence: Results of a survey of large jurisdictions. In E. Buzawa & C. Buzawa (Eds.), *Do arrests and restraining orders work?* (pp. 178–191). Thousand Oaks, CA: Sage.

Reiss, A. (1971). *The police and the public.* New Haven, CT: Yale University Press.

Roberts, A. (1996a). Court responses to battered women. In A. Roberts (Ed.), *Helping battered women: New perspectives and remedies* (pp. 96–101). New York: Oxford University Press.

Roberts, A. (1996b). Police responses to battered women: Past, present and future. In A. Roberts (Ed.), *Helping battered women: New perspectives and remedies* (pp. 85–95). New York: Oxford University Press.

Schmidt, J., & Steury, E. (1989). Prosecutorial discretion in filing charges in domestic violence cases. *Criminology, 27,* 487–510.

Scott v Hart, No., C-76-2396 (N.D. Cal. 1976).

Sherman, L. (1980). Causes of police behavior: The current state of quantitative research. *Journal of Research in Crime and Delinquency, 49,* 69–100.

Sherman, L. (1993). *Policing domestic violence: Experiments and dilemmas.* New York: Free Press.

Sherman, L., & Berk, R. (1984). The specific deterrent effects of arrest for domestic assault. *American Sociological Review, 49,* 261–272.

Sherman, L., Cohn, E., & Hamilton, E. (1986). *Police policy on domestic violence: A national survey.* Washington, DC: Crime Control Institute.

Steinman, M. (1991). Coordinated criminal justice interventions and recidivism among batterers. In M. Steinman (Ed.), *Women battering: Policy responses* (pp. 221–236). Cincinnati: Anderson.

Thurman v Torrington, Connecticut, 595 F. Supp. 1521 (D. Connecticut 1984).

Tolman, R., & Weiscz, A. (1995). Coordinated community intervention for domestic violence: The effects of arrest and prosecution on recidivism of woman abuse perpetrators. *Crime and Delinquency, 41,* 481–495.

Trone, J. (1999). *When victims have a right to know: Automating notification with VINE.* New York: VERA Institute of Justice.

U.S. Attorney General's Task Force on Family Violence (1984). *Final report.* Washington, DC: Government Printing Office.

Van Maanen, J. (1974). Working the street: A developmental view of police behavior. In H. Jacob (Ed.), *The potential for reform of criminal justice* (pp. 83–130). Beverly Hills: Sage.

Vera Institute of Justice (1977). *Felony arrests: Their prosecution and disposition in New York City's courts.* New York: Vera Institute of Justice.

VINE Brochure (No Date). Victim Information and Notification Everyday. Retrieved August 30, 1999 from the World Wide Web: http://www.state.ky.us/agencies/gov/domviol/vinebrch.htm

Waits, K. (1985). The criminal justice system's response to battering: Understanding the problem, forging the solutions. *Washington Law Review, 60,* 267–329.

Wilson, J. (1968). *Varieties of police behavior: The management of law and order in eight communities.* Cambridge, MA: Harvard University Press.

Woods, L. (1981). Litigation on behalf of battered women. *Women's Rights Law Reporter, 7,* 39–45.

Zorza, J. (1996). Suing the police after DeShaney. In N. Lemon (Ed.), *Domestic violence law: A comprehensive overview of cases and sources* (pp. 547–560). San Francisco: Austin & Winfield.

Contributory Factors Affecting Arrest in Domestic and Non-Domestic Assaults

Helen M. Eigenberg, Kathryn E. Scarborough, and Victor E. Kappeler

Traditionally, police officers have viewed domestic "disputes" as private, family matters. In the 1960s and 1970s, officers were trained not to arrest the perpetrators of domestic violence. Instead, officers were trained to defuse the situation. Some police agencies even developed domestic dispute teams that coupled police and social service workers to mediate these disputes (Berk and Loseke, 1980; Goolkasian, 1986 Loving, 1981; Waits, 1985).

A variety of factors in the early 1980s led police departments to reevaluate their policies involving domestic violence, and departments nationwide began to implement pro/mandatory arrest policies. One of the factors which precipitated this change was an increased risk of legal liability for failure to arrest in domestic violence cases. This risk was illustrated by the two million dollar settlement in the highly publicized case involving Tracey Thurman (*Thurman v. City of Torrington*, 1984; Jerin, 1989). In addition, several other developments seemed to "get the attention" of police officials nationwide: the Minneapolis Police Foundation study's conclusion that arrest, in and of itself, had a deterrent effect on future battering, the study's subsequent publicity, and a general tendency toward increased public awareness (Buzawa and Buzawa, 1993; Eigenberg and Moriarty, 1991; Sherman et al., 1986).

Furthermore, numerous advocacy groups created in the mid-1960s and early 1970s had time to mature and began making headway with state legislators in

American Journal of Police, Vol. XV, No. 4, pp. 27–54, 1996.

many locations across the United States.[1] As a result of these factors, state laws and police department policies were altered in the mid-1980s to facilitate arrest in domestic violence cases.

There is considerable debate over the desirability of these changes (Berk, 1993; Bowman, 1992; Buzawa and Buzawa, 1993; Frisch, 1992; Lerman, 1992; Manning, 1993). Some researchers point to the Minneapolis replication studies and argue for a repeal of mandatory arrest policies since the growing body of evidence suggests that arrest fails to deter battering. They also contend that treatment for batterers may be more appropriate than arrest and the costs associated with arrest may result in a decline of financial support for victim services (Buzawa and Buzawa, 1990,1993; Schmidt and Sherman, 1993; Sherman et al, 1992). Other researchers are critical of the replication studies and point out that these findings, like those from Minneapolis, must be evaluated cautiously (Berk, 1993; Binder and Meeker, 1988; Bowman, 1992; Frisch, 1992; Lerman, 1992; Miller, 1989). These studies focus on only seven cities and are full of nuances which take time to digest and which make generalizations very difficult. At the most simplistic level, however, it does not appear that the replication studies have found any startling evidence that arresting offenders in domestic assaults makes things worse.

While the debate rages on about the appropriateness of arrest, there is virtually unanimous agreement that the police have, historically, failed to treat domestic violence seriously (Buzawa and Buzawa, 1990, 1993; Pagelow, 1987; Pleck, 1987; Schechter, 1982; Stark, 1993). Victims have long contended that the police tend to do "little or nothing helpful when (and if) they responded to calls" (Pagelow, 1987, pp. 4–5) and that they have been reluctant to make arrests. As Buzawa and Buzawa (1993) note:

> There can be little argument with the basic premise that until relatively recently, virtually all U.S. jurisdictions systematically minimized the role of arrest in handling domestic violence cases. In fact, the "classic" police response to domestic violence could be characterized as one of virtual nonfeasance, the development of procedures by which the police evaded their responsibility to protect victims of crimes within families. (p. 338)

Despite the widespread acceptance of this premise, there are relatively few studies that have compared police officers' responses in domestic assaults to other types of assaults to determine whether domestic cases are treated more leniently.

LITERATURE REVIEW

Only a few studies have actually compared arrest rates in domestic and non-domestic assault cases to confirm the popularly held assumption that police officers are less apt to make arrests in cases of domestic assault. Ironically, and in contrast to the popular assertion in the literature, the only studies directly comparing domestic to non-domestic assaults find no evidence of discriminatory enforcement; they report that officers are equally or more apt to arrest in domestic assaults (Black, 1971; Oppenlander, 1982; Smith and Klein, 1984). These findings, however, must be interpreted cautiously. There is a paucity of research in the area and the data sets are dated (gathered in 1966 and 1977). The over-reliance on bivariate analyses also makes it difficult to decipher how factors simultaneously affect officers' arrest decisions and fail to provide a complete picture of the complex process of arrest.[2]

The overwhelming majority of the studies on police response have concentrated on identifying factors which predict arrest in domestic assaults. However, they have no comparison group so disparate treatment can only be inferred (Berk and Loseke, 1980; Buzawa and Austin, 1993; Dolan et al., 1986; Ferraro, 1989; Ford cited in Dutton, 1988; Friday et al., 1991; Holmes, 1993; Loving and Farmer cited in Dutton, 1988; Waaland and Keeley, 1985; Worden and Pollitz, 1984). These studies suggest that officers are more apt to arrest in domestic assaults if the victim prefers it (Berk and Loseke, 1980; Buzawa and Austin, 1993; Dolan et al., 1986; Loving and Farmer cited in Dutton, 1988; Worden and Pollitz, 1984) or if the offender acts badly toward police officers (Dolan et al., 1986; Loving and Farmer cited in Dutton, 1988; Waaland and Keeley, 1985; Worden and Pollitz, 1984). It also appears that officers are more apt to arrest in domestic assaults when there are additional witnesses (Buzawa and Austin, 1993; Holmes, 1993), although one study reports that the officers are less apt to arrest if witnesses are present (Worden and Pollitz, 1984). Finally, there are contradictory findings about the effects of weapons and injuries. While some studies using bivariate analyses (Buzawa and Austin, 1993; Dolan et al., 1986; Ferraro, 1989; Loving and Farmer cited in Dutton, 1988; Waaland and Keeley, 1985) find that the presence of injuries and weapons increases the probability of arrest, studies using multivariate analyses (Berk and Loseke, 1980; Holmes, 1993; Worden and Pollitz, 1984) find no such relationship.

The research on police response to domestic violence can be divided into four general categories:

1. surveys of police officers which ask them to specify how they think they would respond to a variety of different hypothetical scenarios involving domestic assaults;

2. field studies which evaluate police behavior while they perform their duties during domestic calls;

3. content analyses of arrest decisions reconstructed from actual police reports of domestic assaults; and

4. studies which actually compare domestic and non-domestic assaults. The following section reviews each of these types of research.

Survey Research

Several authors have examined officers' purported reactions to hypothetical situations of domestic assault. Most of this research concentrates on whether a variety of situational factors including legal and extralegal variables influence officers' self-reported willingness to arrest.

Loving and Farmer (cited in Dutton, 1988) surveyed 130 officers in 16 police agencies. They do not report an arrest rate for domestic violence assaults but instead focus on identifying factors that police officers believe affect their decisions to arrest. Officers indicated a willingness to arrest when (in decreasing order of importance): the offense was a felony, there was serious injury to the victim, the incident involved a weapon, violence was used against the officers, there was a likelihood of future violence, there was a history of legal action against the offender, there had been a prior injury to a victim, prior damage had been done to property, and the offender had been using drugs and/or alcohol. Police reported they were not inclined to arrest when the victim refused to press charges, if the victim indicated a tendency to drop charges, or if there was a lack of serious injuries.

A similar study conducted by Waaland and Keeley (1985) involved a survey of 36 officers in Oregon. Officers appeared to be reluctant to make arrests in domestic assaults as 58 percent of the officers said they would not make an arrest even when victims were depicted as moderately injured (e.g. multiple bruises or black eyes), despite the fact that all vignettes provided ample grounds for arrest under the state statute. Officers indicated that they believed that abusive husbands were responsible for the abuse, and they said they would be more inclined to make an arrest if the offender acted poorly toward the police officers. Officers reported that the offender's history of domestic violence did not affect their decisions to arrest, but that they would be less apt to view the situation seriously if the victim had precipitated the violence or had been using alcohol. Officers reported that they would be more inclined to arrest if the victim was seriously injured than if there were minor injuries, although only about one-half of the officers endorsed arrest under either circumstance.

Ford (cited in Dutton, 1988) also administered a hypothetical vignette to 439 police officers in Indiana. While this scenario also provided ample probable cause for making an arrest, police officers were relatively reluctant to report that they would make an arrest. Only 20 percent of the officers indicated more than a 50/50 chance of arrest despite the existence of a state policy mandating arrest under the circumstances described in the survey. Officers who believed that the couple was intact and that the woman had not made an effort to leave the relationship were less apt to indicate they would arrest, and officers who were more apt to suggest arrest did so because of their belief that the violence would continue.

In another study, Dolan et al., (1986) surveyed 125 police officers in three municipal agencies in the Midwest. They did not ask officers how frequently they made arrests in domestic assaults, but they did identify factors influencing their decisions to arrest. Officers reported more willingness to arrest (in ascending order) when: the officer's safety was threatened, a felony was committed, a weapon was used, the victim was seriously injured, future violence was likely, there was a history of frequent calls from the household, the batterer was under the influence of alcohol or drugs, the offenders failed to respect the police officer's authority, the victim had previously been injured, there had been prior legal action (i.e. a restraining order), and the victim had requested arrest. Officers also reported factors that affected their decision not to make an arrest. In descending order of importance, officers listed the following factors: victims' refusal to press charges, victims' tendency to drop charges, lack of serious injury, commission of a misdemeanor, jail overcrowding, intoxicated participants, availability of other civil alternatives, frequency of calls for police assistance, availability of social services, victims' first contact with the police, absence of weapon, and added paperwork burden.

Friday et al., (1991) surveyed 51 police officers in a Midwestern community. Officers were not asked how often they would make an arrest, but were asked to describe their actions in the last domestic assault case they had attended. Police officers suggested several reasons why they had failed to make an arrest. The vast majority of officers (80 percent) reported that there was no evidence of physical abuse, about one-quarter (26 percent) reported that the victim did not want them to arrest, and about one-fifth (18 percent) suggested that there appeared to be no need as the situation seemed to be under control. About one-third of the officers reported that when they made an arrest they did so because the offender's actions challenged the authority of the officers.

The surveys of police officers, as a whole, suggest that officers are somewhat reluctant to make arrests in domestic assaults. Officers report that they would arrest in between 20 and 50 percent of the cases, even though all vignettes provided ample evidence of probable cause. Officers also report that many factors influence their willingness to make an arrest. They are most inclined to do so if the case is a felony involving serious injuries and/or weapons; there is a history of domestic violence; or the offender is using drugs/alcohol or somehow challenges officers at the scene. Officers indicate that they are least apt to make an arrest when the victim refuses to press charges, officers believe that the victim will drop the charges, there are no visible injuries, or the victim is using drugs/alcohol. These findings have been used to argue that there is evidence of differential treatment. The findings are consistent with the assertion that battered women have historically confronted police officers who are unwilling to arrest and that these women have had to be assertive to overcome officer's biases about victims and their willingness to "follow through." These studies, however, have not compared officers' hypothetical responses to domestic assaults to other types of assaults. Perhaps this same set of variables predict arrest, regardless of the nature of the assault. Without direct comparisons it is impossible to determine if these findings, in fact, are evidence of differential treatment.

FIELD STUDIES

Obviously, when one surveys police officers we only have an account of what they say they will do. Thus, field studies are somewhat more reliable because they generally involve the observation of police work and documentation of actual police behavior in domestic assault cases. Worden and Pollitz (1984) undertook such an examination of 167 incidents of domestic violence recorded by trained observers who accompanied police on calls in 24 police departments located in three metropolitan communities in three different states.[3] Observers found that officers rarely made arrests in domestic assaults, using this option in only about 9 percent of the cases. The authors also tested a more sophisticated model using regression analyses to identify those factors which affected officers' decisions. They found that offenders were more apt to be arrested when the victim agreed to sign a complaint or if the offender was present at the scene, had been drinking, or was disrespectful to the police.[4] Arrest was not significantly affected by the location of the assault (private versus public), victim injuries, time of call, race of the offender, or who called the police for assistance.

Extending this avenue of inquiry, Ferraro (1989) also examined police officers' actions in domestic violence cases in 1984 following legislative changes in Arizona state law and subsequent to the adoption of a presumptive arrest policy in Phoenix. A team of six field observers rode with officers for 44 nights which produced 69 incidents of domestic violence for analyses. Here again, the arrest rate was quite low (18 percent). While officers considered severe injuries or the use of a weapon as sufficient grounds to establish probable cause, minor injury, property damage and the presence of child witnesses were considered insufficient to establish probable cause. Officers also indicated that they believed battered women would drop charges and that women choose to stay in battering relationships.

These two field studies point out some interesting distinctions when compared to surveys of police officers. First, observations of officers find lower arrest rates for domestic assault than do surveys asking officers about their purported behavior. Second, while officers frequently say they focus on the presence of injuries and weapons, this relationship was not particularly strong. In one of the field studies (Worden and Pollitz, 1984) injuries did not significantly affect arrest decisions when controlling for the effects of other independent variables, and in the other study (Ferraro, 1989) only serious injury appeared to be related to arrest. Again, without comparative studies it is impossible to determine whether these variables are impacting uniquely on arrest decisions in domestic assaults.

CONTENT ANALYSES

While field studies may give us a more accurate description of actual police behavior, content analyses of police reports also offer insight into officers' behavior. Police reports are sometimes criticized as *"ex post facto* reconstructions of incidents intended to 'justify actions already taken'" (Worden and Pollitz, 1984, p. 106), although they provide insight into the ways that police officers socially construct domestic assaults. Furthermore, we were unable to locate any study which directly compared officers' actions in the field to police reports of domestic assaults to determine the reliability of these reports. In the absence of evidence suggesting widespread distortion between reports and behavior, studies of police reports provide an accessible and financially feasible means of examining some aspects of police behavior.

Berk and Loseke (1980) examined 262 police reports from Santa Barbara County, California, and found that officers made arrests in 39 percent of the domestic assault cases. Regression analyses indicated that arrest was significantly more likely when: the victim agreed to sign a complaint; both the victim and offender were present when the officer arrived; and the offender had been drinking. Property damage, injuries, marital status: time of offense, and race of the offender were not significantly associated with arrest. Interestingly, arrest was significantly less apt to occur when the victim called the police for assistance. However, this finding may be related to a specification error in the model. The authors did not measure or control for the presence of witnesses. Thus, it is possible that victims tend to call the police themselves when there are no other witnesses, and the apparent relationship between the victim's call for help and the offender's arrest is a by-product of failing to control for the effect of witnesses.

Friday et al., (1991) examined 166 police reports of domestic assaults in a Midwestern community. Data are rather limited, but the authors reported that about one-half of all cases resulted in arrest and officers were significantly more apt to arrest in cases where injuries had resulted. They also reported that previous arrests, prior calls to the police for domestic violence, and race or age of either the victim or offender were not associated with officers' decisions to arrest.

Buzawa and Austin (1993) examined 165 police reports over a four month period in Detroit and report that arrest occurred in about 30 percent of the cases. Officers were significantly more apt to arrest when other witnesses or bystanders were present, children witnessed the violence, serious injury was inflicted on the victim, or the victim preferred prosecution. Officers also were significantly more apt to arrest offenders who were living with their victims, although marital status itself was not significantly associated with arrest decisions. When guns and/or knives were present, officers were more apt to make an arrest compared to cases involving other weapons or one's body (hands, feet, etc.), although these relationships were not significant.

Two hundred police records of domestic assaults were collected from seven police agencies in Massachusetts. Holmes (1993) found that officers made arrests in only 7.5 percent of the cases. Officers were more apt to arrest when a protective order was violated, witnesses were present, the assault took place in public, and the offender was African American. Officers also were significantly more apt to arrest when victims called the police quickly after the incident and when a higher number of officers responded to the call. The use of a weapon, injury to the victim, repeated incidents, victim preference, and involvement of children were not significantly associated with arrest. Holmes also completed two logistical regression models, but only a few variables remained statistically significant in the multivariate analyses. In the first model, arrest resulted when a restraining order was in place and when there was a tendency for the department to endorse a practice of non-arrest.[5] In the second model, only the length of time the victim took to report the offense significantly affected officers' decisions to arrest.

By and large, the content analyses of police reports offer some support for the premise that victims of domestic assault experience differential treatment. Officers are more apt to arrest in domestic assaults when there are additional witnesses to the act (Buzawa and Austin, 1993; Holmes, 1993), weapons are present (Friday et al., 1991), and the victim prefers arrest (Berk and Loseke, 1980; Buzawa and Austin, 1993). Thus, the analyses of police reports suggest that victims in domestic assaults must be willing to "prove" their victimization. If they can back it up with other witnesses and/or weapons, or if they plead for arrest, then perhaps the perpetrator will be arrested. It also is possible, however, that police officers use these same criteria in non-domestic assaults. Here again, it is impossible to determine whether differential treatment exists without a comparison group.

COMPARISONS OF DOMESTIC AND NON-DOMESTIC ASSAULT CASES

We were able to locate only three studies which directly compared domestic to non-domestic assaults. The earliest study offers a limited amount of information and is a small part of a larger study on the social organization of arrest. Black (1971) analyzed 176 incidents recorded by trained observers. He found that officers were about equally likely to arrest family members (46 percent) as they were non-family members (48 percent).[6]

Oppenlander (1982) used the same data set as Worden and Pollitz (1984) to compare police response in domestic and non-domestic assaults. She analyzed 596 cases of assault reported by trained observers in field studies in three metropolitan cities. She found that dispatchers were significantly more apt to classify domestic violence cases as arguments rather than assaults and that police were significantly slower to arrive on the scene of domestic violence cases. Victims were significantly more apt to be injured in domestic assaults and more apt to be arguing with the suspect when the police arrived. In addition, victims in domestic assaults were significantly more apt to request arrest, to sign a complaint, and to be asked to sign a complaint by the attending officer. Contrary to popular assertions, Oppenlander found that police officers were more likely to make an arrest in domestic assaults than other assaults. Officers made an arrest in 22 percent of the domestic assaults, but only 13 percent of the other assaults resulted in arrest; however, this difference does not appear to be significant.[7]

Smith and Klein (1984) also used the data set involving the three metropolitan cites (as did Oppenlander, 1982 and Worden and Pollitz, 1984), although this study compared officers' responses in domestic assaults to other types of interpersonal disputes. They found that arrest was less likely in domestic violence disputes than other types of interpersonal disputes, although the difference was not significant. Officers were significantly less apt to arrest offenders for domestic violence in middle and higher income neighborhoods and equally likely to arrest offenders for either domestic violence or non-domestic violent disputes in lower incomes areas.

Thus, none of the comparison studies find that officers are less apt to arrest in domestic than in non-domestic assaults. In two of the studies (Black, 1971; Smith and Klein, 1984), officers were about equally apt to arrest in domestic versus non-domestic assaults. In Oppenlander's (1982) study, officers were more apt to arrest in domestic (22 percent) than nondomestic assaults (13 percent). These findings, however, must be evaluated cautiously. There is a paucity of research in the area and the data sets are quite dated. There is a pressing need for additional research and more sophisticated analyses in this area.

The current study seeks to address some of the void in the current literature. It examines police reports in a small Midwestern police department to determine whether domestic assaults are treated differently than non-domestic assaults, to explore whether a variety of variables affect officers' decisions to arrest in both types of assaults, and to determine whether these variables impact similarly on domestic assaults and non-domestic assaults.

METHODS

Research Setting

The department in this study is located in a city with a population of over 60,000. Although the city has a mixed economy, it is primarily known as a university town. Several higher educational institutions are located here including a large state university, a four-year college and several community/vocational colleges.

The department itself has about 120 full-time sworn police officers. During the five year period of the study, the department had a low turnover (4.5 percent) most of which resulted from retirements. Officers are predominantly male (84 percent) and white (88 percent). They were on average 38 years old and had worked for the department for about ten years. Slightly over three-quarters (79 percent) of the department were employed at the line-staff level, and 71 percent of the officers had completed four-year college degrees. The high proportion of college graduates in part reflects an innovative administrative ideology as the department requires officers to have a minimum of 60 hours of college credit.

The police department operates under a classical organizational structure. The department is organized into two major divisions: operations and administration. It operates with three fixed shifts and limits specialization to a few areas. There is no specialized domestic violence unit and most officers are routinely rotated from patrol through areas of specialization and back to patrol. Thus, the majority of officers in the department would have been involved in patrol duties during the five year study period, and many of them would have had investigative experience. While education is stressed in the department, police officers did not have any specific training on domestic violence during the study period aside from any minimal training that might have occurred in basic academy training. In addition, state law at the time did not suggest a preference for arrest in domestic assaults and the department had no policy on domestic violence.

Sampling Procedures

A total of 92,000 police reports were subjected to a systematic random sample. Every tenth police report for assault generated from 1982 through 1987 was sampled from the police department. Reports were then examined and excluded from the analyses if they failed to involve an assault or if they could not be analyzed because of their condition. The final sample in the study consists of 515 police reports: 180 cases of domestic assault and 335 cases of non-domestic assault. Thus, 35 percent of the cases in the sample represent domestic assaults and 65 percent are non-domestic assaults.

Operationalization of Variables

Eight variables were available in this data set. First, to allow comparisons, cases were identified as domestic versus non-domestic assaults. They were coded as domestic assaults when the intimates involved in the case had a prior or current intimate relationship which included marriage, cohabitation and dating. There were no cases involving same sex partners (homosexual battering), nor were there any reports of battering that involved male victims. If there was no indication of a prior or current intimate relationship then the case was coded as a non-domestic assault.

The dependent variable—police action—includes three possible police responses: no arrest, issued warrant, and made an arrest. For the purposes of analyses, this scheme was dichotomized into categories of taking action to pursue arrest (seeking a warrant for arrest or making a warrantless arrest) or taking action which did not result in an arrest. For case of discussion, this variable is discussed in the remainder of the paper as arrest or non-arrest.

The remaining six variables represent independent variables which were used to predict arrest. These include injuries, weapons, witnesses, victim's request, suspect's presence at scene, and suspect's actions. Injuries were coded based on three categories: none present or visible; minor and not requiring medical attention; and serious which required medical treatment. Weapons were dichotomized into categories of yes and no. Use of one's body was not classified as a weapon. Thus, feet and fists, for example, do not constitute weapons. Witnesses were coded into three groups: complainant only; complainant and one additional witness; and complainant and two or more additional witnesses. Victim preference was coded according to three options: requested no action or only that a report be taken; requested removal; or requested arrest. If suspects were present at the scene this was coded "yes" and if they were absent it was coded "no." If suspects were present, their actions were coded as normal, verbally abusive, and violent or criminal.

Limitations of Data

Certain limitations affect this analysis. First, officers may fail to file a report for a variety of reasons and thereby preclude analysis of their behavior from a study such as the current one. Second, like all secondary data analysis, we only have access to those variables present in the data set. Third, police reports, by nature, suffer from reductionism as officers seek to cull information for the purposes of documentation. Unfortunately, police reports rarely are tailored to meet the needs of social scientists, and therefore important information is sometimes unavailable.

Analyses

After descriptive analyses, several bivariate tests were conducted. First, we examined officers' actions to determine whether they were significantly more apt to arrest in domestic than non-domestic assaults. Second, we compared arrest rates in domestic and non-domestic assaults to determine whether arrest was affected by a variety of victim, offender and offense characteristics. Third, we compared domestic and non-domestic assaults to identify whether they have similar characteristics. All bivariate analyses used Chi-square tests to evaluate the significance of the differences.

Finally, the sample was separated into domestic and non-domestic assaults, and logistic regression was used to determine whether the same variables affected officers' decisions to arrest in domestic versus non-domestic assaults when controlling for the effect of other independent variables. Logistic regression was used because the dependent variable is a dichotomous, nominal variable. Conceptually, it is similar to multiple regression in that it is used to make predictions about the probability that an event will occur, and most experts argue that it is appropriate to use logistic analysis when the dependent variable is not at least ordinal level data (Hair et al., 1987).

FINDINGS

While non-domestic assaults were over-represented in the study (65 percent), there were sufficient cases of domestic assault to offer comparisons (35 percent). Likewise, while arrest was employed less frequently than other options (79 percent of the time), there were sufficient numbers of arrests in the data to allow for analyses (21 percent). The sample as a whole suggests that most victims of assault experienced no visible injuries (46 percent) and weapons were relatively rare (30 percent). Half of the cases only had the complainant as a witness and the remaining half had additional witnesses. Victims requested no action in about half (54 percent) of the cases. Suspects infrequently remained at the scene when officers arrived (34 percent) and they acted 'Normally" the vast majority of the time (69 percent) when they were there.

CONTINGENCY ANALYSES

Table 1 displays the results of the Chi-square tests and shows that officers are significantly less apt to arrest in domestic assaults than in non-domestic assaults. While officers made arrests or sought a warrant for arrest in 24 percent of the non-domestic assaults, they arrested in only 17 percent of the domestic cases. Suspects were present at the scene in only about one-third of the cases in the study; however, offenders were about equally apt to be present when officers arrived in domestic and non-domestic cases (37 percent and 32 percent, respectively). Thus, offenders of domestic assaults were not significantly less available for arrest than offenders in non-domestic assaults.

Table 1. Bivariate analyses of variables that distinguish domestic from non-domestic assaults

Variables which examine differential treatment	Domestic assault Cases[a]		Non-domestic assault Cases[a]	
	No.	%	No.	%
Police action*				
Arrest	29	17	76	24
Other response	144	83	236	76
Suspects present at scene				
No	111	63	209	68
Yes	65	37	100	32
Suspect's conduct at scene*				
Normal	50	78	60	63
Verbally abusive/violent	14	22	35	37
Injuries*				
Non-visible	73	42	147	48
Minor	75	43	93	31
Serious	26	15	63	21
Weapons*				
No	130	76	206	67
Yes	41	24	101	33
Witness*				
Complainant only	121	68	132	40
Multiple witnesses	58	32	196	60
Victim preference*				
Arrest requested	72	42	95	33
Arrest not requested	99	58	193	67

[a] The number of cases may vary slightly throughout the table because of missing data

*Denotes that the Chi-square was significant at the 0.05 level or below

The data also suggest some interesting differences between domestic and non-domestic assaults. These findings are presented in Tables 1 and 2.[8] Three variables represent characteristics of the crime: injuries, weapon use and presence of witnesses. Victims of domestic assaults are more apt to experience minor injuries, but officers' decisions to arrest were not significantly related to injuries. Officers were about as apt to arrest in domestic assaults when there were injuries (57 percent) as they were to arrest in non-domestic assaults (51 percent). Thus, injuries do not appear to affect arrest decisions at this level of analysis.

Similarly, while domestic assaults were significantly less apt to involve weapons (24 percent) than were non-domestic assaults (33 percent), the pres-

Table 2. Bivariate analyses of variables that affect arrests in domestic versus non-domestic assaults

Variables which examine differential treatment	Arrests in domestic assaults[a]		Arrests in non-domesic assaults[a]	
	No.	%	No.	%
Suspect present at scene				
No	12	42	19	27
Yes	17	59	51	73
Suspect's conduct at scene*				
Normal	20	71	34	50
Verbally abusive/violent	8	29	34	50
Injuries*				
None visible	12	43	33	49
Injuries present	16	57	34	51
Weapons*				
None	16	57	43	61
Present	12	43	28	39
Witness*				
Complainant	13	45	19	25
Multiple witnesses	16	55	56	75
Victim preference*				
Arrest requested	17	63	26	51
Arrest not requested	10	37	25	49

[a] The number of cases may vary slightly throughout the table because of missing data

*Denotes that the Chi-square was significant at the 0.05 level or below

ence of weapons was not significantly associated with officers' arrest rates (43 percent in domestic and 39 percent in non-domestic assaults). Thus, while weapons may be less apt to be present in domestic assaults, the bivariate findings suggest that weapons are not associated with officers' arrest decisions.

The presence of witnesses, though, was significant in several ways. Victims were significantly more apt to be the sole witness in domestic (68 percent) rather than non-domestic assaults (40 percent); however, cases with single complainants were significantly more apt to result in arrest in domestic assault cases (45 percent compared to 25 percent of non-domestic assaults). Domestic assaults appear to be more hidden in nature and less often result in witnesses although officers apparently recognize this problem, at least to some degree, since they are significantly more apt to make arrests in domestic assaults in the absence of additional witnesses.

Victim characteristics in this study are limited to one variable: victims' preference for arrest. Ironically, the data contradict the stereotype of the reluctant victim in domestic assaults. Domestic violence victims were significantly more apt to request arrest. Almost half (42 percent) of the victims requested arrest in the domestic assaults compared to about one-third (33 percent) of the victims in non-domestic cases. While arrests were more common in domestic (63 percent) than non-domestic assaults (51 percent), officers' arrest decisions were not affected by victim preference at the bivariate level of analysis.

Finally, we have limited data on offender characteristics. As previously discussed, only about one-third of the offenders were present when the officers arrived at the scene. In those cases, offenders were significantly more apt to act "normal" in domestic (78 percent) than in non-domestic assaults (63 percent), although it apparently did not pay off as well as they might have hoped. Arrests were significantly more apt to occur in domestic than in non-domestic assaults when the offender was at the scene, even though the offender seemed to be acting appropriately toward the officer at the scene of the crime.

In sum, then, the bivariate analysis finds that domestic assaults are less apt to result in arrest than non-domestic assaults and that the difference in arrest rates cannot be explained by the availability of the suspect at the scene. It also suggests that domestic assaults have some different characteristics than do non-domestic assaults; they are significantly more apt to be characterized by minor injuries, fewer weapons and fewer complainants. Domestic assaults also are significantly more apt to have victims who request arrest and offenders who act normal at the scene. Officers, however, were significantly more apt to arrest in domestic assaults than in non-domestic cases when the offender was present at the scene, despite the fact that offenders were significantly more apt to act normal in domestic assaults and even though domestic assaults were significantly less apt to have additional witnesses to corroborate their victimization. Thus, by and large, the bivariate analyses suggest that domestic and non-domestic assaults are characterized by differences in the nature of the assault, but that the evidence of disparate treatment in arrest is limited. The multivariate analysis further explores this issue.

Logistic Regression

Table 3 displays the results of the logistic analyses which examines whether similar variables predict arrest in domestic and non-domestic assaults when controlling for the effects of a series of independent variables.[9] The beta values offer some indication of magnitude of effect and are interpreted similar to an unstandardized regression coefficient (Menard, 1995).

In domestic assaults, arrest is significantly affected by the suspect's presence at the scene, weapon use, the availability of additional witnesses, and the victim's preference for arrest. Only injuries were not significantly related to arrest decisions. Officers are more apt to arrest in domestic assaults if there is a suspect at the scene, weapons are used, there are additional corroborating witnesses, or the victim requests arrest.

In non-domestic assaults, arrest also is significantly related to the suspect's presence at the scene, the availability of additional witnesses, and the victim's

Table 3. Logistic regression of independent variables on type of assault

Independent variable	Domestic assaults		Non-domestic assaults	
	β	SE	β	SE
Suspect present at scene	1.09*	(0.48)	2.08*	(0.38)
Industries present	–0.32	(0.49)	0.05	(0.39)
Weapons present	1.29*	(0.50)	0.59	(0.38)
Number of witnesses	0.99*	(0.49)	1.33*	(0.43)
Victim preference for arrest	1.16*	(0.49)	0.74*	(0.38)
Constant	3.34		3.70	
Overall correct classification	85.35		84.55	
Pseudo R^2	14%		16%	

*Demotes significance at the 0.05 level or below

preference for arrest. In this equation, however, neither weapons nor injuries were significantly related to arrest decisions. Officers are more apt to arrest in non-domestic assaults when the suspect is at the scene, there are corroborating witnesses, or when the victim requests arrest.

Thus, the analyses suggest that at least some variables operate differently in domestic and non-domestic assaults. The presence of weapons is a significant predictor for arrests in domestic assaults but not in non-domestic assaults. The victim's preference for arrest also is a stronger predictor of arrest in domestic than in non-domestic assaults. The presence of the suspect at the scene and the number of witnesses are much stronger predictors of arrest in non-domestic than domestic assaults. Thus, the logistic analyses suggests that victims in domestic assaults have to convince police officers that they are earnest and that the assault is serious. In contrast, it appears that officers concentrate on availability of offenders and the presence of witnesses in non-domestic assaults, and victim preference is considered far less important in these cases. Thus, at least some findings in the study at both the bivariate and multivariate level support the hypothesis that domestic assaults are treated differently than their non-domestic counterparts. The significance of these findings are discussed below.

DISCUSSION

Most importantly, this study is the first empirical evidence to suggest that police officers are less apt to arrest in domestic violence cases when directly comparing officers' responses in domestic and non-domestic assaults. In contrast to previous research which found that domestic assaults were equally or more apt to result in arrests than were non-domestic assaults (Black, 1971; Oppenlander, 1982; Smith and Klein, 1984), our study certainly supports the premise of disparate treatment for domestic assaults.

Furthermore, several other findings from the current study also support the notion that police treat domestic violence cases differently. For example, prior studies suggest that officers say they consider injuries when making decisions about arrests in domestic assaults (Dolan et al., 1986; Loving and Farmer, cited in Dutton, 1988; Waaland and Keeley, 1985), and this finding is confirmed both by observations of police behavior (Ferraro, 1989) and by content analyses of police reports (Buzawa and Austin, 1993). However, the multivariate analyses of domestic assaults using both field studies and content analyses report that injuries are not related to officers' decisions to arrest (Berk and Loseke, 1980; Holmes, 1993; Worden and Pollitz, 1984). Our findings are very similar to the latter body of research. We found that injuries were about equally apt to be present in cases of arrest for domestic and non-domestic assault, although victims were more apt to experience minor injuries in domestic assaults. Thus, it appears that while victims of domestic violence cases are more frequently victims of minor violence, the level of injuries in and of itself has relatively little to do with arrest in either domestic or non-domestic assaults.

Interestingly, the previous studies have not included weapon use in their designs as often as they have included injuries. Hence, it appears that the studies tend to focus more on the experiences of the victims than the behavior of the perpetrator. There is some evidence that officers say they are more apt to arrest when weapons are present in domestic violence cases, and this finding has been confirmed in a field study observing police behavior (Ferraro, 1989) and a content analysis of police reports (Friday et al., 1991). Here again, though the only multivariate study which examined this variable finds that weapons have a nonsignificant effect on arrest decisions in domestic assaults, our findings contradict this interpretation.

At the bivariate level, we found that officers were about equally apt to arrest in domestic as in non-domestic assaults when weapons were present. However, the multivariate analysis suggests that weapons affected officers' arrest decisions in cases of domestic violence but not in other assault cases when the effects of other independent variables are controlled. Thus, it also appears that officers may be more willing to view domestic assaults as "real" only when "real" weapons are used.

It is quite perplexing to find that injuries have no effect on arrest decisions and that the impact of weapons is limited. By statutory definition, injuries and weapons are part of the criteria used to determine whether an action amounts to a legal violation. One would expect that offenders who administer severe injuries or who use weapons would be more apt to be arrested in either domestic or non-domestic assaults.

Future research needs to attend to these variables in more depth. We need to explore the subtler nuances of these variables. For example, do officers view injuries that produce cuts and bruises differently depending on the level of med-ical treatment required or based on how the injury was produced? Do they treat a deep cut caused by a knife differently, as more lethal and/or more worthy of arrest, than a cut caused by a fist? Do they search for evidence of injuries that may not be readily apparent? Do they ask victims, out of the presence of the per-petrators, about any injuries that might be hidden by clothing or that may take a few hours to appear (e.g. bruises)? Do they acknowledge that puffy eyes may well be black by morning and that a blow to the temple poses a threat of fatal cerebral hemorrhage whether produced by a club or a fist? In short, we need to re-examine how officers define injuries and weapons and we need to attend to our own operationalization of these variables to ensure a better understanding of the complex relationships among these variables.

We also need additional research on the effect witnesses have on arrest decisions. While two of the prior studies on witnesses (Buzawa and Austin, 1993; Holmes, 1993) find that officers are more apt to arrest in domestic assaults when there are additional witnesses to corroborate the assault, a third study (Worden and Pollitz, 1984) reports that officers are less apt to make arrests in domestic assaults when witnesses are present. Two of these studies involve mul-tivariate analyses (Holmes, 1993; Worden and Pollitz, 1984) and two focus on content analyses of police reports (Buzawa and Austin, 1993; Holmes, 1993). The current study finds that officers are more apt to arrest when there are corrobo-rating witnesses regardless of the nature of the assault, but that the effect of wit-nesses is more powerful in non-domestic assaults.

It seems reasonable to assume that officers prefer to arrest when there are additional bystanders because, realistically, a case is stronger if there are corrob-orating witnesses. It also is possible that officers are more apt to arrest and to write up reports in cases where there are multiple witnesses to "cover their ass," since their actions could be challenged by numerous individuals instead of one witness if any further attention is given to the case. It is unclear, however, why witnesses seem more important in non-domestic than domestic assault cases. Perhaps officers are more apt to be concerned about strangers causing trouble in non-domestic assaults and calling attention to the officers' behavior. Or, perhaps the witnesses in domestic assaults are more suspect because they are more apt to be relatives and/or children.

We had limited information on the offenders' conduct so it is difficult to make comparisons to prior research. We found that offenders in domestic assaults were more apt to act appropriately at the scene than were offenders in non-domestic cases, but that it apparently did them little good since their conduct did not reduce the likelihood of arrest. However, because too few offenders were at the scene we would have lost too many cases if this variable had been included in the logistic regression; therefore, it was deleted. This is a definite limitation of the cur-rent work and makes it impossible to speculate on how the remaining dependent variables might have been affected if we had been able to include this information.

Our results provide the strongest support for the previous finding that offic-ers are more apt to arrest in domestic violence cases when the victim asks for this action (or in all probability demands it). Police officers clearly say they are more apt to arrest if the victim is cooperative (Dolan et al., 1986; Loving and Farmer, cited in Dutton, 1988), and this finding was observed in a field study of officers behavior (Worden and Pollitz, 1984) and in two of the content analyses of police reports (Berk and Loseke, 1980; Buzawa and Austin, 1993). Furthermore, two of the three multivariate studies (Berk and Loseke, 1980; Worden and Pollitz, 1984) find that this variable is the most important predictor in the models. Our findings confirm these results.

In this study, victims are significantly more apt to request arrest in domestic than non-domestic assaults and the multivariate analyses find that victim preference is a stronger predictor of arrests in domestic assault cases. In other words, it appears that victims can facilitate arrests in non-domestic assaults by asking for this action, but that victims in domestic assaults must prove their victimization and then plead or demand for arrest to get action. Our findings appear to confirm the previous assertion that victims in domestic assaults must insist on arrest in too many cases and that officers may not be inclined to arrest if they believe that victims are insincere.

Obviously, there are many limitations in the current study. The sample is small and the data set is limited. However, it is one of a handful of comparative studies, thereby contributing to our knowledge in an area where research is scarce. Furthermore, many of our findings are consistent with prior research. We find that officers are less inclined to arrest in domestic than non-domestic assaults, and that different variables predict whether an arrest will occur in both types of assaults. Victims of domestic assaults apparently have to work harder to prove their victimization before batterers are arrested and they require more evidence to validate their claims.

Future research should continue to explore the issue of disparate treatment in domestic assaults, but we must ensure that more of these studies have comparative samples. Most research has assumed officers react differently in domestic assaults and then look for evidence of prejudicial treatment. This approach is inappropriate. Without direct comparisons across types of assault categories, we can only assume that any given factor is operating uniquely with respect to domestic assault; however, this cannot be demonstrated empirically.

In the meantime, the best available evidence suggests that there is a continued need to design training programs, laws and policies that ensure equitable treatment of domestic violence victims by police officers. Unfortunately, it appears that it is still necessary to stress to victims that they must be clear and directive if they have much hope of getting the batterer arrested. We also must continue to train police officers that victim preference should not be more important in domestic assaults than in non-domestic assaults. In addition, we must question academicians who support a return to mediation and counseling when the existing evidence suggests that the playing field is still not level.

In other words, it seems premature to move away from proactive arrest policies without first ascertaining that arrest in domestic assaults has had the opportunity to work at least as well (or as badly) as arrest in non-domestic assault cases. Until we can empirically demonstrate a lack of police bias toward domestic assaults, such an argument does to victims of domestic violence what police decision making has already done: it requires these victims to prove that they are worthy of legal protection.

Notes

[1] See Schechter (1982) for a good review of the early days of the women's advocacy movement.

[2] Most of the studies reviewed in this paper provide no information about contextual factors that might have impacted on their findings. For example, they generally fail to discuss whether there were policy statements or state law which endorsed arrest or what types of responses were stressed in any training that might have existed.

[3] This study is actually a replication of an earlier study conducted by Berk and Loseke (1980). In that study, however, the authors examined police reports while in the Worden and Pollitz study the authors used similar methodology and variables in a field study to examine officers' actions. The Berk and Loseke study will be examined in the third section.

[4] The authors ran two separate regression equations—one which was similar to Berk and Loseke to examine whether their results were replicable and a second equation which added variables absent in Berk and Loseke's study. Marital status was significant in the first equation as officers were less apt to arrest when offenders and victims were married. This relationship is not significant in the second model. It is somewhat difficult to determine what effects are occurring, as some variables in the first model are eliminated from the second model and there are variables in the second model that are absent from the first model.

[5] The author never really discusses the apparent contradiction between a departmental custom of non-arrest resulting in a tendency to facilitate arrest.

[6] These figures are computed from Table 3 in Black's 1971 publication.

[7] This finding is difficult to interpret from the tables and text of the paper. Table 3 lists several responses: settle argument, tell someone to leave, referrals, threaten arrest, arrest, and none of the above. None of the above is reported as significant though it is not clear to what this category refers. It would appear that it means to take no action since there seem to be a paucity of alternatives left, but the interpretation is unclear.

[8] Several variables had to be collapsed for the Chi-square analyses to prevent violations in the assumptions of the test (specifically those associated with small cell frequencies). Thus, suspects' actions were collapsed into two categories: normal actions and provocative action which included offenders who were verbally abusive and violent. Victim preference was collapsed from request for no action, request for removal, and request for arrest, to two categories: requesting arrest or having other preferences. The witness variables also were reduced from complainant only, complainant and one victim, and complainant and multiple witnesses, to complainant as sole witness and other witnesses present.

[9] The independent variables that were previously collapsed for the bivariate analysis were used in their original form in the logistic regression. All of these variables can be considered ordinal variables and there was no reason to reduce any power of the analysis by reducing the level of measurement of these variables.

REFERENCES

Berk, R. (1993). "What the scientific evidence shows: on the average, we can do no better than arrest," in Gelles, R. and Loseke, D. (Eds.), *Current Controversies on Family Violence.* Newbury Park, CA: Sage, pp. 323–36.

Berk, S. and Loseke, D. (1980). "Handling family violence: situational determinants of police arrest in domestic disturbances." *Law and Society Review,* Vol. 15, No. 2, pp. 317–46.

Binder, A. and Meeker, J. (1988). "Experiments as reforms." *Journal of Criminal Justice,* Vol. 16, pp. 347–58.

Black, D. (1971). "The social organization of arrest." *Standford Law Review,* Vol. 23, pp. 1087–111.

Bowman, C. (1992). "The arrest experiments: a feminist critique." *The Journal of Criminal Law and Criminology,* Vol. 83, No. 1, pp. 201–8.

Buzawa, E. and Austin, T. (1993). "Determining police response to domestic violence victims: the role of victim preferences." *American Behavioral Scientist,* Vol. 36, No. 5, pp. 610–23.

Buzawa, E. and Buzawa, C. (1990). *Domestic Violence: The Criminal Justice Response.* Newbury Park, CA: Sage.

Buzawa, E. and Buzawa, C. (1993). "The scientific evidence is not conclusive: arrest is no panacea," in Gelles, R. and Loseke, D. (Eds.), *Current Controversies on Family Violence.* Newbury Park, CA: Sage, pp. 337–56.

Dolan, R., Hendricks, J. and Meagher, M. (1986). "Police practices and attitudes toward domestic violence." *Journal of Police Science and Administration,* Vol. 14, No. 3, pp. 187–92.

Dutton, D. (1988). *The Domestic Assault of Women: Psychological and Criminal Justice Perspectives.* Boston, MA: Allyn & Bacon.

Eigenberg, H. and Moriarty, L. (1991). "Domestic violence and local law enforcement in Texas: examining police officer's awareness of state legislation." *Journal of Interpersonal Violence,* Vol. 6, No. 1, pp. 102–9.

Ferraro, K. (1989). "Policing woman battering." *Social Problems,* Vol. 36, No. 1, pp. 643–7.

Friday, P., Metzgar, S., and Walters, D. (1991). "Policing domestic violence: perceptions, experience, and reality." *Criminal Justice Review,* Vol. 16, No. 2, pp. 198–213.

Frisch, L. (1992). "Research that succeeds, policies that fail." *The Journal of Criminal Law and Criminology,* Vol. 83, No. 1, pp. 209–16.

Goolkasian, G. (1986). "Confronting domestic violence: a guide for criminal justice agencies." *National Institute of Justice,* Research in Brief. Washington, DC: U.S. Department of Justice.

Hair, J. F., Anderson, R. E., Tatham, R. L., and Black, W. C. (1987). *Multivariate Data Analysis with Readings.* New York: Macmillan.

Holmes, W. (1993). "Police arrests for domestic violence." *American Journal of Police,* Vol. 12, No. 4, pp. 101–25.

Jerin, R. (1989). "Police liability for failure to protect battered women." *American Journal of Police,* Vol. 8, No. 1, pp. 71–87.

Lerman, L. (1992). "The decontextualization of domestic violence." *The Journal of Criminal Law and Criminology,* Vol. 83, No. 1, pp. 217–40.

Loving, N. (1981). *Spouse Abuse: A Curriculum Guide for Police Trainers.* Washington, DC: Police Executive Research Forum.

Manning, P. (1993). "The preventive conceit: The black box in market context." *American Behavioral Scientist,* Vol. 36, No. 5, pp. 639–50.

Menard, S. (1995). *Applied Logistic Regression Analysis*. Thousand Oaks, CA: Sage.

Miller, S. (1989). "Unintended side effects of pro-arrest policies and their race and class implications for battered women: a cautionary note." *Criminal Justice Policy Review*, Vol. 3, No. 3, pp. 299–316.

Oppenlander, N. (1982). "Coping or copping out." *Criminology*, Vol. 20, Nos. 3–4, pp. 449–65.

Pagelow, M. (1987). "Application of research on spouse abuse." Unpublished manuscript. Paper presented at the Third National Family Violence Research Conference.

Pleck, E. (1987). *Domestic Tyranny: The Making of American Social Policy against Family Violence from Colonial Times to the Present*. New York: Oxford.

Schechter, S. (1982). *Women and Male Violence: The Visions and Struggles of the Battered Women's Movement*. Boston, MA: South End Press.

Schmidt, J. and Sherman, L. (1993). "Does arrest deter domestic violence?" *American Behavioral Scientist*, Vol. 36, No. 5, pp. 601–9.

Sherman, L., Cohen, E., and Hamilton, E. (1986). "Police policy on domestic violence: a national survey." *Crime Control Reports*, January, pp. 1–11.

Sherman, L., Schmidt, J., and Rogan, D. (1992). *Policing Domestic Violence: Experiments and Dilemmas*. New York: Free Press.

Smith, D. and Klein, J. (1984). "Police control of interpersonal disputes." *Social Problems*, Vol. 31, No. 4, pp. 468–81.

Stark, E. (1993). "Mandatory arrest of batterers: a reply to its critics." *American Behavioral Scientist*, Vol. 36, No. 5, pp. 651–80.

Thurman v. City of Torrington, 595 F. Supp. 1521 (D. Conn., 1984).

Waaland, P. and Keeley, S. (1985). "Police decision making in wife abuse: the impact of legal and extralegal factors." *Law and Human Behavior*, Vol. 9, No. 4, pp. 355–66.

Waits, K. (1985). "The criminal justice system's response to battering: understanding the problem, forging the solutions." *Washington Law Review*, Vol. 60, pp. 267–329.

Worden, R. and Pollitz, A. (1984). "Police arrests in domestic disturbances: a further look." *Law and Society Review*, Vol. 18, No. 1, pp. 105–19.

To Go or Not To Go?

Preliminary Findings on Battered Women's Decisions Regarding Court Cases

Joanne Belknap, Ruth E. Fleury, Heather C. Melton,
Cris M. Sullivan, and Amy Leisenring

Research on the court processing of woman battering has largely been ignored. This oversight is troubling on a number of counts. First, if police experience a court system that "doesn't care" about woman battering, it is unlikely that they will be invested in collecting adequate evidence and the other behaviors necessary for convictions of batterers (see Belknap, 1996, p. 190). Second, with the implementation of pro-arrest policies, the courts are being flooded with domestic violence cases at an unprecedented rate (see Buzawa and Buzawa, 1990; Cohn and Sherman, 1987; Goolkasian, 1986). Third, given the goal of the criminal processing system to deter crime and punish offenders, it is necessary to have court workers (e.g., prosecutors and district attorneys) invested in obtaining guilty verdicts. Fourth, the little research that exists on the court responses to woman battering suggests that judges and prosecutors, like the police, often fail to take woman battering seriously (see Hart, 1993). However, the only experimental study to date on prosecutors' responses to domestic violence cases found that batterers were less likely to recidivate when prosecutors proceeded through the initial hearing (Ford and Regoli, 1992).

Personnel in both the police and courts often have accused battered women of being "uncooperative" or "reluctant" victims/witnesses. For example, just about everyone in the general population has heard of or experienced "frustrating" examples of battered women who "choose" to stay with or even defend their batterers. This lack of "cooperation," also referred to as victim "reluctance," and requires a closer examination. *Many battered women are not reluctant to "'cooperate" with those who want to help them, but instead, are unable to locate anyone with any power who wants to help them* (see, for example, Browne, 1987; Cahn, 1992; Gondolf and Fisher, 1988; Jones, 1994; Sullivan, 1991; Walker, 1989; Websdale, 1995). Moreover, many batterers, not surprisingly, actively strategize to keep women from pressing charges or proceeding with court cases. For example, one study found that many women who drop charges in domestic violence cases are "escorted" by their batterers to the courts to drop the charges, and cite fear as their major reason for dropping charges against their batterers (Quarm and Schwartz, 1985). Nonetheless, both the criminal processing system and the public continue to blame victims/witnesses who are reluctant or too afraid to testify against their assailants, and this blame-the-victim approach likely serves to justify further abuse in the batterers' (and others') eyes.

There is little available research on battered women's motives for cooperating with decision-makers in the criminal processing system. In one of the few studies on victim/witness reluctance, Cannavale and Falcon (1976a, 1976b) interviewed 922 witnesses randomly selected from closed felony and misdemeanor cases in the District of Columbia. The offenses included, but were not limited to, woman battering. They found that "fear of reprisal" was the reason victims most often gave for their reluctance to cooperate with the prosecution. Fear of reprisal was reported by approximately equal percentages of "cooperators" and "noncooperators" and of victims and non-victims; however, more women than men expressed fear of reprisal (31% vs. 26%), and more residents than nonresidents expressed this fear (30% vs. 17%). These findings suggest that proximity of the victim to the offender, in terms of both physical distance and intimacy, is related to fear of reprisal. Cannavale and Falcon's findings were not specific to woman battering cases, although evidence from other studies suggests that fear of reprisal is related to women's reluctance to cooperate in these cases (Buzawa and Austin, 1993; Martin, 1994; McLeod, 1983; Singer, 1988).

Other research indicates that while prosecutors are often successful without victim/witness participation, charges against defendants are far more likely to be dismissed if victims fail to testify when they are acquainted with the defendants (Davis, 1983). While this study did not examine woman battering specifically, the findings have obvious implications for woman battering cases. Many criminal processing system personnel count on victims' testimony to make a case. Thus, we need to know more about how victims make decisions regarding participation and barriers that prevent them from cooperating fully. The current study was designed to address these important issues.

METHOD

The research reported in this chapter is part of a larger, longitudinal study designed to explore battered women's experiences with the police and courts over time. Data collection took place in three sites: Denver, Colorado; Boulder County, Colorado; and Lansing, Michigan. Battered women were sent flyers and postcards asking them to participate in the study shortly after their court cases closed. If the women were interested, they could call the project office or mail in a stamped postcard to find out more about the study, and if still interested, sign up to participate. Interviews lasted approximately two hours and were conducted face-to-face using highly trained interviewers.

The data reported in this chapter are based on initial interviews with the first 107 women who elected to take part in the study. The goals of the study are to (a) understand how battered women's personal and situational characteristics are related to court outcomes and (b) determine how court outcomes are related to women's re-victimization and their subsequent decisions involving the police and courts. The findings presented here describe the reasons women gave for attending or failing to participate in the court case against their batterer.

FINDINGS

The sample ranged in age from 18 to 60 years old, with a mean age of 32. Approximately two-thirds of the sample was white, one-fifth was African American, and one-seventh was Latina/Chicana. Four-fifths of the sample reported being employed in the past 6 months, and the same percentage had at least a high school diploma or G.E.D. Twelve percent reported being married, 17 percent were separated, 9 percent were divorced, 13 percent were girlfriend/boyfriend, and 43 percent were ex-boyfriend/ex-girlfriend at the time of the initial interview. Almost three-quarters of the women had children, and the mean number of children was 1.6. About three-fifths of the sample (61%) went to court at least once. Of these women, 45 percent reported that the case was canceled or rescheduled at least once.

As can be seen in Table 1, the women in this sample reported a significant amount of abuse in the six months before the arrest that initiated the court case against their batterer. During this time frame, 82% of the women had been threatened with violence by their assailants, and 47% reported being threatened with murder. The most frequently experienced type of physical abuse was being grabbed (89%), and the least likely abuse was being stabbed with a knife (5%). The overwhelming majority of the women had been pushed or shoved (84%). Over half of them had an object thrown at them (59%), had been slapped (51%) or had been beaten up (51%). Slightly less than half of them had experienced an attempted hit with an object from their batterer (48%). Likewise, slightly less than half of them had been hit with a fist, (48%), physically restrained (45%), strangled/choked (44%), had their hair pulled (42%), had their arm or leg twisted (41%), or had experienced broken glasses or torn clothing (41%). About a third of them had been kicked (36%) or hit with an object (35%). About one-fifth of them had been threatened with a knife (22%), raped (19%), or threatened with a gun. They were least apt to have been bitten (13%), burned (6%), or stabbed (5%).

In addition to the types of abuse listed in table 1, we also examined respondents' experiences with their abusers *stalking* them, both prior to the arrest and in between the arrest and court case. The majority of the respondents experienced

Table 1. Threats/violence experienced in the 6 months before the arrest (N=107)

Variable	%	(n)
Threats Experienced at Least Once		
Threatened in general	82.2%	(88)
Threatened w/murder	46.7%	(50)
Violence Experienced at Least Once[a]		
Grabbed	88.8%	(95)
Pushed or shoved	84.1%	(90)
Object thrown at	58.9%	(63)
Slapped	52.3%	(56)
Beat up	50.5%	(54)
Hit with a fist	47.7%	(51)
Tried to hit with an object	47.7%	(51)
Tied up or physically restrained	44.9%	(48)
Strangled/choked	43.9%	(47)
Pulled hair	42.1%	(45)
Arm or leg twisted	41.1%	(44)
Broke glasses or tore clothing	41.1%	(44)
Kicked	36.4%	(39)
Hit with an object	34.6%	(37)
Threatened with a knife	21.5%	(23)
Raped	18.7%	(20)
Threatened with a gun	16.8%	(18)
Bitten	13.0%	(14)
Burned	5.6%	(6)
Stabbed	4.7%	(5)

[a]Respondents could report "yes" to any number (including none or all) of these.

some of the stalking variables at least once in the six months preceding the arrest. For example, 80% of the respondents reported experiencing being "checked up on" at least once and almost half of the women reported it occurred often. Of the respondents who had new partners in that time period, 71% reported their new partners were threatened or harmed by their former partners/batterers. Sixty-three percent of the women reported their batterers made unwanted calls to home or work, 59% followed or watched her, 57% made unwanted visits to home, work, or school and 53% left unwanted messages at her home or work. While the following stalking behaviors were not as prevalent as the above, 41% of the women had their mail stolen or read, 35% of the batterers broke into her home or car, and 27% sent unwanted gifts, photos, and letters. Finally, approximately half (49%) of the respondents reported experiencing some form of stalking between the arrest and the final court date; 8% reported experiencing stalking behavior everyday. Clearly, these findings emphasize the necessity of studying stalking as a significant form of intimate partner abuse, even in intimate partner relationships where the victim and offender are not "broken up."

Despite experiencing significant levels of violence and much stalking, almost two-thirds (61%) of the sample went to court at least once. As table 2 demonstrates, the two most frequently cited reasons for going to court were associated with a sense of obligation as well as a desire for protection. Almost all of the women who went (91%) felt that they ought to go and most (89%) wanted to stop the abusers from causing pain. The next most frequently reported reasons were to get help for the batterer (74%), because she was subpoenaed (72%), to teach the batterer a lesson (69%), and because they were afraid of the defendants (62%). About half of the women reported going to court because they thought they were legally required to do so (52%) or to get their abusers sent to jail (51%). Women rarely reported that they went to court to get the charges dropped (29%) or because of pressure from family and friends (20%).

Table 2. Reasons women went to court and the barriers they faced (N=65)[a]

Variable	%	(n)
Reasons for Going to Court		
Felt like she ought to go	90.8%	(59)
To get assailant to stop hurting her	89.2%	(58)
To get assailant help	73.8%	(48)
Went because of a subpoena	72.3%	(47)
To teach assailant a lesson	69.2%	(45)
Fear of the assailant	61.5%	(40)
Thought legally she had no choice	52.3%	(34)
To send assailant to jail	50.8%	(33)
Wanted charges dropped	29.2%	(19)
Pressure from family/friends	20.0%	(13)
Barriers to Going to Court		
Fear of the batterer	47.7%	(31)
Problems with getting time off work	27.7%	(18)
Wanted to work things out with assailant	24.6%	(16)
Pressure from his family/friends	24.6%	(16)
Prior bad experiences with court	21.5%	(14)
Problems getting childcare[b]	10.7%	(7)
Pressure from her family/friends	10.7%	(7)
Problems getting transportation	10.7%	(7)
Fear of being arrested herself	9.2%	(6)

[a]Respondents could report "yes" to any number (including none or all) of these. These questions were only asked of those women who went to court.
[b]This percentage doubled when we controlled for whether the women had dependent children.

Table 2 also presents the barriers women overcame in order to go to court. By far the most commonly reported barrier, cited by almost half of the participants, was *fear of the batterer.* Three other barriers to going to court reported by approximately one-quarter of the respondents were problems with getting time off work, wanting to work things out with the abuser, and pressure from the abuser's family/friends. One-fifth of the women reported prior bad experiences with the courts as a barrier. Four reasons were reported by approximately one-tenth of the women: (1) problems getting child care, (2) pressure from the victim's friends/family, (3) problems getting transportation to court, and (4) the victim's own fear of being arrested.

A minority of women failed to attend court; 39% of the sample reported they never went. *However, it is an important finding that one out of five women who did not go to court reported that the reason they did not go was because they had not been informed of the court date.*

The most frequently cited reason for not going to court, for those women who knew their court dates, was that they did not want to go (69%; see table 3). Two-fifths of this sample of women reported four reasons for not going to court: (1) they didn't think that prosecution would help, (2) they wanted to work things out with their abusers, (3) they wanted the charges dropped, and (4) they didn't want the abuser to go to jail. An additional four reasons for not going to court were reported by about one-quarter of the sample of women who knew their court dates but did not go: (1) the victim had prior bad experiences with the court, (2) the victim was dependent on the abuser for money/housing, (3) the victim was afraid of the abuser, and (4) the victim felt pressure from the abuser's family or friends not to go. Two reasons were reported by about one-fifth of the women as reasons they did not go to court: (1) they couldn't get time off work, and (2) they didn't know they could go. Less than 1 in 10 women reported that they failed to court because they lacked child care (9%), did not know where to go (6%), felt pressure from their own family and friends not to go (6%), and had trouble getting transportation to court (3%).

Table 3. Reasons women reported for not going to court

Variable	N	%	(n)
Knew About Hearing/Trial in Advance	40		
Yes		80.0%	(32)
No		20.0%	(8)
Reasons for Not Going to Court if Knew About It[a]	32		
Did not want to go		68.8%	(22)
Didn't think that prosecution would help		43.8%	(14)
Wanted to work things out with the assailant		43.8%	(14)
Wanted charges dropped		40.6%	(13)
Didn't want assailant to go to jail		37.5%	(12)
Had prior bad experience with court		28.1%	(9)
Dependent on assailant for money/housing		25.0%	(8)
Fear of the assailant		25.0%	(8)
Felt pressure from his family/friends		25.0%	(8)
Couldn't get time off work		21.9%	(7)
Didn't know she could go		18.8%	(6)
Had trouble getting childcare		9.4%	(3)
Didn't know where to go		6.3%	(2)
Felt pressure from her family/friends		6.3%	(2)
Had trouble getting transportation		3.1%	(1)

[a]Respondents could report "yes" to any number (including none or all) of these. This question was only asked of those women who did not go to court, but knew about it in advance.

CONCLUSIONS

These findings affirm the need for further research on the court processing of intimate partner battering cases. The detailed, woman-centered data also speak to the need for asking women how they made the decisions they made regarding court attendance. The data suggest that women's reasons for participating in the court cases involving their abusers are far more complicated and go beyond the notion of "reluctance" or "uncooperative." For example, of those battered women who went to court, over three-fifths reported going *because* they were afraid of their batterers, *yet* the most frequently listed barrier women overcame to attend court was fear of their abuser. For those women who knew about the court date but did not attend, one-quarter reported their failure to appear was related to fear of their batterers. Thus, fear of the batterer is multifaceted and plays varying roles in battered women's decisions about court attendance. Moreover, while about three-fifths of the women went to court at least once, of those who did not go, one-fifth did not go because they did not know about the hearing or trial, suggesting poor court functioning more than victim reluctance/non-cooperation.

Fewer than one-third of the women who went to court did so because they wanted the charges dropped. In fact, there was more support for many of the variables measuring victim cooperation: almost 90 percent of the women reported going to court to get their abusers to stop hurting them, about 70 percent reported going to court to teach their abusers a lesson, and about half reported court attendance to get their batterers sent to jail (although this is rarely what happened).

Another means of measuring battered women's cooperation is by asking about the barriers that made it difficult to attend court, even for those women who did so. The women in this study reported facing numerous barriers to court attendance, including not being informed of the court date, pressure from family and friends (both hers and the batterer's), prior bad court experiences, child care and transportation problems, and trouble getting time off work for the court case. Yet, despite these barriers, three-fifths of the women abused by their partners went to court.

Future research needs to carefully assess why women make the choices they do regarding participating in the court process, including but not limited to examining structural barriers and the physical danger they face from their assailants. Continued efforts are also needed to minimize the need for women to participate in the prosecution of their batterers. More and more communities are implementing "evidence based" prosecution of woman batterers, with more emphasis on collecting photographs, 911 transcripts, medical records, and other physical evidence that would reduce the need for victim testimony. The findings presented in this chapter suggest that many battered women have to use nothing short of heroic means to hurdle the roadblocks they face to attend court when their abusers have been charged. They also fear for their safety and the safety of their children. We as a society must do more to protect survivors from intimate partner violence and to hold batterers accountable for their behavior.

REFERENCES

Belknap, J. (1996). *The invisible woman: Gender, crime, and justice.* Belmont, CA: Wadsworth.

Browne, A. (1987). *When battered women kill.* New York: Free Press.

Buzawa, E. S., & Austin, T. (1993). Determining police response to domestic violence victims. *American Behavioral Scientist, 36*(5), 610–623.

Buzawa, E. S., & Buzawa, C. G. (1990). *Domestic Violence: The criminal justice system response.* Newbury Park, CA: Sage.

Cahn, N. R. (1992). Innovative approaches to the prosecution of domestic crimes. In E. S. Buzawa and C. G. Buzawa (Eds.), *The Changing Criminal Justice Response* (pp. 161–180. Westport, CT: Auburn House.

Cannavale, F. J., & Falcon, W. D. (1976a). *Improving witness cooperation: Summary report of the District of Columbia witness survey and a handbook for witness management.* National Institute of Law Enforcement and Criminal Justice Law Enforcement Assistance Administration, U.S. Department of Justice. D.C. Heath and Company.

Cannavale, F. J., & Falcon, W. D. (1976b). *Witness cooperation with a handbook of witness management.* Toronto: Lexington Books.

Cohn, E. G., & Sherman, L. W. (1987). Police policy on domestic violence, 1986: A national survey. *Crime Control Institute, Crime Control Reports,* No. 5.

Davis, R. C. (1983). Victim/witness noncooperation: A second look at a persistent phenomenon. *Journal of Criminal Justice, 11,* 287–299.

Ford, D. A., & Regoli, M. J. (1992). The preventive impacts of policies for prosecuting wife batterers. In E. S. Buzawa & C. G. Buzawa, *Domestic violence: The changing criminal justice response* (pp. 181–207). Westport, CT: Auburn House.

Gondolf, E. W., with Fisher, E. R. (1988). *Battered women as survivors: An alternative to treating learned helplessness.* New York: Lexington Books.

Goolkasian, G. A. (1986). Confronting domestic violence: The role of criminal court judges. National Institute of Justice, Research in Brief, Washington DC, November.

Hart, B. (1993). Battered women and the criminal justice system. *American Behavioral Scientist, 83,* 73–119.

Jones, A. (1994). *Next time, she'll be dead: Battering and how to stop it.* Boston: Beacon Press.

Martin, M. E. (1994). Mandatory arrest for domestic violence: The courts' response. *Criminal Justice Review, 19*(2), 212–227.

McLeod, M. (1983). Victim noncooperation in the prosecution of domestic assault. *Criminology, 21*(3), 395–416.

Quarm, D., & Schwartz, M. (1985). Domestic violence in criminal court: An examination of new legislation in Ohio. In C. Schweber & C. Feinman (Eds.), *Criminal justice politics and women: The aftermath of legally mandated change* (pp. 29–46). New York: Haworth Press.

Singer, S. I. (1988) The fear of reprisal and the failure of victims to report a personal crime. *Journal of Quantitative Criminology, 4*(3), 289–302.

Sullivan, C. M. (1991). Battered women as active helpseekers. *Violence Update, 1*(12), 1, 8, 10–11.

Walker, L. E. (1989). *Terrifying love: why battered women kill and how society responds.* New York: Harper Perennial.

Websdale, N. (1995). Rural woman abuse: The voices of Kentucky women. *Violence Against Women, 1*(4), 309–338.

CHAPTER SIX

SUMMARY AND RECOMMENDATIONS

W hile the criminal justice system and other agents of social control rarely have addressed battering because it was viewed as a private, family matter, it is becoming more difficult to maintain this hegemonic view. Advocates continue to challenge society to see battering in a different light and to hold batterers accountable for their behavior. The hegemonic battle over the definition of the situation is far from complete, but society is somewhat less willing to blame victims and more willing to look for ways to deal with the problem on a social, structural level. As Pence and Shepard note (1999):

> Every state has expanded the obligation and authority of police to arrest abusive partners. Every state has passed some version of a protection order that allows the court to exclude abusive partners from their homes. The National Council of Family and Juvenile Court Judges has published an extensive model state code recommending that state lawmakers adopt a comprehensive legislative approach to the reform of the antiquated legal system. The American Medical Association and the American Bar Association, two of the most powerful professional lobbies in Washington D.C., have both adopted far-reaching positions on domestic violence. Public opinion, though far from fully enlightened, has dramatically changed as court watch groups, community-based legal advocacy projects, and battered women's shelters have put the spotlight on practitioners, their failures to respond to domestic violence, and the way abusers escape social sanction. Men who beat their partners can no longer expect to use violence and remain immune from social sanction, nor can practitioners who fail to respond to the violence be assured of anonymity. (citations omitted from quote, p. 5)

Battered women are not as alone as they were 25 or 30 years ago, and there is more public recognition that "something" needs to be done. What that something is or should be is still far from being resolved.

The debate over the role of the criminal justice system is contentious. There are those who continue to argue that the criminal justice system is an ineffective way to address woman battering. Some base this argument on "new science" such as the Minneapolis replication studies, and others rightfully note that many "reforms" do nothing to make battered women safer. In some cases, the reforms make matters worse. However, this debate ignores the reality that battered women look to the criminal justice system for help. "At the concrete, everyday level for survival, many women require police assistance" (Ferraro & Polk, 1993, p. 99). Thus, "the question of whether we should use the courts to protect women [is] in a sense rhetorical, as women were already inextricably hooked into the legal system" (Pence & Shepard, 1999, p. 10). Advocates sometimes are required to ignore the needs or desires of individual women for the good of the greater goal. Pence (1999) likens this dilemma to civil rights advocates in the 1960s.

> When the first children walked into previously all-white schools, those children did not get a better education. We have all seen news stories of those tense days [as] African-American children walked through crowds of screaming, threatening white adults. They entered empty classrooms. *The victory was for those who followed.* (emphasis added, p. 33)

Refusing to act, is, itself, an action. Therefore, we must continue to search for solutions to this serious social problem. Sometimes our actions may benefit those who follow, but often reforms are initiated and implemented without consideration for victims and their safety. Too often change takes place in a compartmentalized, fractured context. For example, a police department may initiate a pro-arrest policy without cooperation from prosecutors who may be hesitant to file charges or judges who are reluctant to convict. There are, however, some notable exceptions. A number of communities are using systemic, coordinated responses to hold batterers accountable, while also attending to the safety of victims.

SYSTEMIC COORDINATED COMMUNITY RESPONSES

Generally, victims of domestic violence interact with a broad variety of agencies: the criminal justice system, health care providers, social service agencies, shelter organizations, mental health workers, counselors, religious groups, and voluntary non-profit organizations. While networking and cooperative relationships usually exist between individuals, rarely do these organizations communicate in any formal, organized manner about domestic violence services. There is, however, a growing recognition that this situation must change. Many communities are embracing interdisciplinary, inter-agency, coordinated responses. One of the earliest programs to pursue this type of approach was developed in Duluth, Minnesota.

The Domestic Abuse Intervention Project (DIAP)

From its beginning in the early 1980s, the Duluth program challenged the way both the criminal justice system and social services systems responded to woman battering (Pence & Shepard, 1988). Several Minnesota foundations funded DIAP to create a model of interagency response to battering. Funding provided a full year of planning, which was vital to the success of the design. Project organizers were three women who had extensive experience as advocates for battered women. During the first four or five months, staff met informally with individual actors in the criminal justice system to assess what types of action were needed, what kind of resistance might emerge, and how proposed reforms might impact the safety of battered women (Pence, 1999). Four specific objectives were identified:

1. to bring cases into the court for resolution and to reduce the screening out of cases by police, prosecutors, judges, and other court personnel

2. to impose and enforce legal sanctions and to provide rehabilitation services to the assailant to deter him from committing further acts of violence

3. to provide safe emergency housing, education, and legal advocacy for women who are assaulted

4. to prevent assailants from either getting lost in or manipulating the judicial system by coordinating interagency information flow and monitoring each agency's adherence to agreed-upon policies and procedures (Pence & Shepard, 1988, p. 286).

The project was designed to use official agencies of social control to ensure that batterers remained accountable for their violence, but organizers never lost sight of the primary purpose of protecting victims.

A number of activities ensured that these objectives were met (Pence & Shepard, 1988; Shepard & Pence, 1999). The police department implemented mandatory arrest policy in 1982. Police officers were required to file reports on all assault calls, and shelter advocates were allowed to review these reports weekly to provide follow-up advocacy in cases where arrests had not occurred. If offenders were arrested, jail officials contacted the shelter so they could provide information and assistance to victims. Shelter advocates were dispatched to meet with victims within two hours to discuss legal options and to give social service referrals while the batterer remained in custody (generally overnight). Prosecutors adopted guidelines that discouraged the dismissal of charges, but victims were not required to participate against their wishes. County judges considered input from victims by ordering pre-sentence investigations and by following guidelines adopted by the judges. The court generally agreed to stay all imposed jail sentences for first-time misdemeanors without aggravating circumstances if the batterer participated in a six-month treatment program and chemical dependency treatment in cases where it was warranted.

DIAP also stressed the use of protective orders and employed them even in cases where both parties were residing together. In most states, there are no longer legal stipulations that require a couple to be separated in order to receive a protective order, but many judges have not been willing to issue orders under such circumstances. They apparently feel that orders are useless if victims are willing to continue to reside with their abusers. In contrast, the Duluth system allowed batterers to return home, if the partner so desired, but with a protective order in place. This empowered the battered woman legally and made it easier for her to take actions if he violated the order. It also allowed some men to be sent to counseling through the protective order process, without a conviction. If the judge established that a preponderance of the evidence suggested that battering existed, the batterer could be ordered into treatment via the protective order process.

Whether batterers entered the treatment program through a civil process of protective order or as a result of a criminal conviction, the treatment program was the same. Batterers were required to attend a 26-week program. The program used a "psycho educational model," which stressed "client accountability, a clear and consistent treatment goal, use of confrontational techniques, a structured group format, and a directive counselor role" (Pence & Shepard, 1988, p. 288). This approach used time out procedures and anger control management. Batterers were confronted with the ways in which they used control and domination in the relationship. In other words, treatment programs merged feminist and psychological perspectives to create a treatment program designed to address both perspectives.

Evaluations of the program found significant improvements (see Pence & Shepard, 1988; Shepard & Pence, 1999). Arrests rose from 22 in 1980 to 175 in 1983. Likewise, convictions rose from 20% in 1980 to 87% in 1983 (Pence & Shepard, 1988, p. 286). Almost three-fourths of the victims (70%) reported no physical abuse when a one year follow-up evaluation was conducted. While 60% reported experiencing psychological abuse, 60% of the women also reported they felt safer when the batterer was in group therapy and 80% reported that the combined systemic response had been helpful (Pence & Shepard, 1988, p. 292). Even more remarkably, Duluth had not experienced a single "domestic homicide" a decade after these reforms were implemented (Hoffman, 1992). Perhaps no other program has so clearly demonstrated that systemic reform works. *If the system, as a whole, works to hold batterers accountable for their behavior while also placing victim safety at the forefront of all reform efforts, the system can help reduce harm to women and battered women will use it.*

DIAP invented many of the strategies now used nationally to reform the criminal justice system and other social service agency responses to woman battering. After over 20 years of experience, they clearly are national leaders in community intervention projects. They have provided many important insights for other communities interested in attempting a more coordinated approach (see Pence & McDonnell, 1999). A few of these lessons are reviewed here.

DIAP recommends that policies be developed that control the screening of cases at all levels and mandate appropriate responses while linking actors/agencies together (Pence & McDonnell, 1999). These actions help control discretion and assure that accountability will result. In addition, policies should concentrate on changing behavior by altering the way that practitioners process a case. To do this, DIAP emphasizes the "text." They argue that every practitioner in the system encounters a myriad of forms that are designed to meet a multitude of needs. Practitioners tend to document only that which is required and, in turn, learn to value that which requires documentation. DIAP made significant changes by altering the forms. For example, police officers interview victims using a checklist that includes questions about the suspect's history of prior violence. Officers are required to document the involvement of any children and to file a complete report outlining the details of the call.

Police reports are given priority in the word processing department. When completed they are forwarded to: (a) a central information network, (b) the shelter advocate assigned to the case, (c) the probation officer and judge at pretrial court, (d) the court administrator, (e) the detective bureau (to see if charges can be upgraded), (f) the suspect's probation officer (if there is a previous conviction), and (g) a central domestic violence file. When a suspect is booked, threatening remarks are recorded on the jail incident form and submitted to the court during arraignment proceedings. A comprehensive file is prepared that includes the current and prior arrest reports, risk assessment forms completed by the advocate, photos of injuries, copies of protection orders, information on any known prior victims, and criminal history. Prosecutors, judges, probation officers, and individuals in charge of counseling programs all have access to the file and use it for making decisions. In sum, then, there is a coordinated approach to gathering and disseminating information. By changing the text, DIAP communicated that battering is a serious issue. If it requires documentation, it must be important.

DIAP also notes that communication between agencies is critical to the success of any reform. DIAP contends that more honest and open communication occurs in separate and private meetings with key individuals in an agency where there is less of a tendency for administrators to react defensively (Gamache & Asmus, 1999). Initial meetings should concentrate on securing a general commitment to an interagency approach. These should be followed by dialogue with line staff to gain an in-depth understanding of the actual day-to-day practices of actors. Issues that require systemic response should be clarified prior to calling larger meetings with representatives from the agency and certainly before any interagency meetings.

In addition, DIAP recommends that agencies "assess current practices relative to the primary goals of intervention" (Pence & McDonnell, 1999, p. 46). Continual monitoring was a central component of the process from the beginning, and DIAP changed over time in response to different needs and/or in response to evaluative data. In 1995, DIAP employed a newly designed safety and accountability audit. This audit offers communities a blueprint to determine what policies and procedures need to be altered to improve systemic response (Pence & McDonnell, 1999). An interagency team including staff from various criminal justice system offices and victim advocates interviewed employees in each agency and randomly examined case records to determine compliance with policy. Even after 18 years of successful collaboration and reform, 60 recommendations for additional changes were made (Gamache & Asmus, 1999, p. 85). The lesson is clear, systemic reform requires vigilant monitoring to ensure that changes are implemented as planned and to see that they have the intended outcome. Interagency coordination is not a one shot deal.

While DIAP relies heavily on interagency cooperation and coordination, the model is different from many of the coordinating councils discussed in the literature. Most councils fail to start with a clearly defined goal. For example, a recent publication by the National Institute of Justice and the American Medical Association reports the results of a national conference designed to enhance coordinating councils and interagency coordination (Witwer & Crawford, 1995). While victim safety is noted in some portions of the report, the section describing the purpose of a council fails to mention it as a specific goal. There is concern that "coordination not be seen as an end in itself, but as a means to achieve an overall goal" (Gamache & Asmus, 1999, p. 77). In other words, some councils may be so concerned with coordinating interagency responses that they lose sight of why it is important to cooperate in the first place. "When reform efforts focus on coordinating the system rather than on building safety considerations into the infrastructure, the system could actually become more harmful to victims than the previously unexamined system" (Pence & McDonnell, 1999, p. 41). DIAP always considered victim safety to be their primary goal. Most coordinating councils do not have external monitoring agencies committed to victim advocacy and supervision of the process; they rarely form new policy (Gamache & Asmus, 1999).

Unfortunately, many of the lessons of Duluth are overlooked when cities try to replicate the model without attending to the process. Minnesota has a long history of strong grassroots feminism and advocacy for victims. Officials in Duluth, for the most part, came on board voluntarily, and extensive planning meetings were held to devise the model. A great deal of processing occurred as battered women, advocates, police officials, prosecutors, judges, mental health workers, and social service providers all came to the table to talk to and listen to one another. It is unlikely that the model itself will work well if community leaders fail to assess local problems and adjust the model to fit local needs. It is difficult to do interagency work if people don't spend time engaged in dialogue or if they are not invested in the process. All this takes time, energy, commitment, and leadership in addition to a good model.

While the DIAP program is not an instant fix or a panacea, it is an excellent blueprint for communities seeking to engage in a coordinated community response. It has been exported to several cities known for their success in reforming the system and improving the criminal justice system response. Some examples include Denver, Minneapolis, Nashville, Quincy (MA), San Francisco, and San Diego. The DIAP model clearly demonstrates that the criminal justice system can make a difference—it can increase the safety of battered women by holding batterers accountable for their behavior. In other words, it has demonstrated that the criminal justice system can be reformed in ways that are useful to battered women, if these reforms are motivated by the goal of victim safety. It also demonstrates that there is a need to be ever vigilant, to monitor these reforms, to ensure that practices are implemented as designed and to evaluate the success of intended outcomes. Communities that are inclined to replicate Duluth should take time before implementing each and every action to ask whether their actions make battered women safer.

WHAT COMMUNITIES CAN DO TO END BATTERING

Even in communities where coordinated, interagency responses are non-existent, there are actions that the community can take to address battering. The article in this section by the Violence Against Women Office (VAWO) describes a community checklist of actions that can be taken by religious communities; colleges and universities; law enforcement officials; health care professionals; sports organizations; media groups; and workplaces. More and more organizations and institutions in society are recognizing that battering is an important social problem they need to address. The following section will briefly review some of the issues associated with these community agencies and will suggest new avenues of research.

Battering and the Religious Community

There is growing awareness that the religious community can play an important role in addressing battering in society. Many women view the church and their clergy as a major source of support, advice, and counseling. Some research reports that women are more likely to contact the clergy than any other helping professionals (except the police; Bowker & Mauer, 1986), but they may be disappointed in the response they receive. At least one study indicates that ministers may not respond in a very supportive manner. Alsdurf (1985) surveyed 5,700 clergy and found that about one-fourth of them believed that a wife should be subordinate to her husband and that God would either stop the abuse or provide her with the strength to bear it. About half of the ministers felt the abuse should not be used as a justification for divorce and about one-fifth of them indicated that no amount of abuse justified divorce. One has to wonder how many battered women have been seriously hurt and/or killed when their ministers have sent them home telling them that marriage is a lifetime commitment in the eyes of God and that they should pray that it will stop. No doubt, battered women already have tried that option. Too often, the clergy and organized religions have been part of the problem, rather than part of the solution (Dobash & Dobash, 1979; Martin, 1978; Walker, 1979).

There is a need to understand how battered women negotiate the conflict that sometimes results between religious values that dictate they stay in a relationship and their need to leave in order to protect themselves. We need to devise strategies to assist them and to recognize that religious organizations are not a monolithic group. Different strategies will likely be needed for different religions and denominations. The VAWO article offers several suggestions for the religious community. They generally require that clergy become better educated about the dynamics of battering. Clergy need to be trained to assist battered women and to provide referrals to other social service agencies in the community.

Colleges and Universities

It is interesting that colleges in this country, generally, have been uninvolved in the social movement to address battering. While campuses are increasingly becoming more sensitive to the issue of date rape, there is no similar growing awareness when it comes to physical battering. While some research suggests that the rate of battering is lower among college students in dating relationships than it is in for younger daters (teens) or for women who are cohabitating or married (Makepeace, 1989; Stets & Henderson, 1991; Yllo & Straus, 1981), the limited research in this area makes that assumption very tenuous. For example, one study reports that 32% of college women report dating violence (White & Koss, 1991).

There is a need for additional research on battering in dating relationships as most research has concentrated on adult women in cohabitating and married relationships. It is likely that some of this inattention is related to the "why does she stay" issue discussed in chapter 2. If we, as a society, have problems understanding why married women with children do not simply leave their batterers at the first sign of abuse, this problem is magnified tenfold when it comes to dating relationships. The economic issues discussed in chapter 2 are less common in dating relationships, so why doesn't she just break up with him? There are undoubtedly many complex answers to that question. Too many young women are taught that they must "get" a man, and their self-esteem is often related to their ability to secure a "good catch." Just as adult women in marriages sometimes feel that any man is better than no man, younger women may feel similarly. Any date to the homecoming dance may be better than no date at all. It also is likely that young men in these relationships have their own techniques for ensuring that she does not break up with him, such as threatening to tell friends and family members that she is having sex with him (whether it is true or not).

One would expect high rates of battering on most campuses given the concentration of women in the high risk age group. As the VAWO article indicates, there is much that colleges and universities can do. They can take actions to make their campuses safer, help increase awareness, coordinate resources, pursue administrative responses, and encourage reporting. Unfortunately, most universities will fail to be pro-active on their own initiative. Most parents do not want to send their children to school if they believe that violence is common so there is no incentive for universities to highlight violence against women in general and battering specifically. If experience is any indication, advocates will probably have to be vocal and insist that universities act before any real attention will be given to the issue.

Law Enforcement and the Criminal Justice System

The VAWO article provides an overview of suggestions that law enforcement and the criminal justice system can take to address battering. Many of these ideas have been discussed elsewhere in this book. There is, however, an interesting omission in the VAWO recommendations, one that is evident in the literature as a whole. While community policing dominates discussions of policing, virtually none of this body of literature addresses battering.

"Community policing is currently the dominant paradigm of police practice" (Martin, 1997, p. 524) and the "buzz phrase" of the 1990s (Gaines, Kappeler, & Vaughn, 1999, p. 168). The 1994 Crime Bill intensified the move toward community policing when it required communities to adopt community policing initiatives in order to receive federal funding. While there is no consensus about the definition of community policing, one general theme is that the police need to work more closely with the community to solve problems; they are to be proactive rather than re-active and they should concentrate on problem solving (Corder, 1995; Eck & Spelman, 1987; Gaines, Kappeler, & Vaughn, 1999; Grine, 1994; Martin, 1997). Thus, one would predict that domestic violence would be a central issue when discussing community policing models. The reality is quite the opposite. Battering is still viewed by most police administrators and academicians as a "special problem" outside the confines of what is "real police work."[1]

Battering and the Medical Field

Research clearly indicates that battering is a significant problem for the health care system. One study reports that battering results in 21,000 hospital visits, 99,800 days of hospitalization, and 39,900 physician visits annually (McLeer & Anwar, 1987). In addition to the direct costs associated with treatment for bruises, broken bones, cuts, and the like, battered women also are more apt to experience arthritis, hypertension, heart disease, miscarriage, premature birth, low birth weight infants, and death than are non-battered women (AMA, 1992; Bullock et al., 1989; Campbell et al., 1993).

Historically, the medical field has responded to battering much like the criminal justice system—identifying and assisting battered women was considered outside the purview of medicine. The role of health care professionals was to treat the victim's body, not to counsel her about abuse. Despite the fact that the criminal justice system is often seen as the major point of contact with battered women, it is likely that more health professionals come into contact with battered women than do police officers. Some battered women never have contact with the criminal justice system, although many victims seek medical treatment at some time or another. Several studies report that between 22 to 35% of all women who visit emergency rooms (ERs) are injured by current or former partners (American Medical Association [AMA], 1991; Appleton, 1980; Goldberg & Tomlanovich, 1984; McLeer & Anwar, 1987, 1989; Randall, 1990; Stark, Flitcraft, & Frazier, 1979). A recent report found that 37% of female victims in ERs are battered women (Rand & Strom, 1997). They also found that the estimated number of individuals treated in ERs for injuries by an intimate partner is four times higher than estimates from the National Crime Victimization Survey would suggest.

Some efforts are being made to train nurses, emergency room physicians, primary care doctors, and other medical personnel to recognize battering. There is a growing realization that the health care system needs to respond better. For example, the U.S. Department of Health, Centers for Disease Control, American Nurses Association, American College of Obstetricians and Gynecologists, and the American Medical Association have all issued statements calling for more attention to this issue (Wilson, 1994). Consistent with the VAWO suggestions, these organizations advise medical personnel to screen for abuse. In particular they advise health care professionals to use direct questions when they have reason to suspect battering (e.g., Did someone hit you?). They also need to document the violence, (American Medical Association, 1992; Buel, 1998; Jenkins & Hutchinson, 1996; Sassetti, 1993; Schornstein, 1997). Good documentation of the abuse, including statements from the victim attributing the injury to the batterer, is of vital importance. Medical records are generally admissible in court and often are the only corroborating evidence of abuse (Buel, 1998). Medical personnel also should offer support to the battered woman, provide information about resources, and make referrals to local shelters and agencies.

Unfortunately, most of the literature on health care and battering suggests that health care professionals do not take these types of actions in response to battering (Browne, 1992; Ferris & Tudiver, 1992; Friedman et al., 1992; Gin et al., 1991; Goldberg & Tomlanovich, 1984; Hamberger, Saunders, & Hovey, 1992; Helton, McFarlane, & Anderson, 1987; Kurz, 1987; McLeer & Anwar, 1989; Stark et al., 1979). Battered women report that health care professionals are not supportive, especially when compared to other sources of contact (Bowker & Maurer, 1987; Brendtro & Bowker, 1989; Gerbert et al., 1996; Hoff, 1990). In fact, some research reports that medical personnel actually discourage disclosure by selectively attending to the "medical facts," while ignoring the context surrounding the injury. For example, a physician might note that the patient has a split lip while ignoring that the victim disclosed that her husband slapped her across the face (Anspach, 1987, 1988; Kleinman, 1988; Warshaw, 1993). While time constraints on physicians and nurses are significant, it would seem to be cost effective to take the time to address battering. Furthermore, if the aim of treatment is prevention, battering must be addressed. Failing to address the root cause of the problem is the equivalent of a physician sending a patient to treatment for lung cancer without a discussion about smoking.

Ironically, at the same time that the medical field is being encouraged to identify and document battering, there is a movement among insurance companies to use this information to deny health, life, and disability insurance contending that battered women are high risk patients with pre-existing medical conditions (Zorza, 1994). As discussed previously, legislation is currently before Congress (VAWA II) to prohibit these types of actions. The irony is that battered women who are not "diagnosed" as such may be at greater risk for harm, therefore costing the system more, yet eligible for treatment because health insurance has not been denied.

There is a need for additional research in the health care field. The identification of battering as a health issue is in its infancy. Most of the research on battering and health care has concentrated on ER populations. Little is known about victims who visit physicians in private practice. There also is a need to expand the scope of inquiry to other health care professions. For example, medical social workers, emergency medical technicians, nurses, and home health workers are professionals who are likely to have frequent contact with batterers. Dentists may have contact with battered women who often need dental work after being hit in the face. The School of Dentistry at the University of Minnesota has created a pilot training videotape and curriculum for dentists and their staff to teach them how to assist victims effectively (Office of Victims of Crime, 1998).

In addition to diagnosis and treatment, there are opportunities for the health care system to be pro-active in helping to address battering. One innovative example is The National Domestic Violence Project. It provides free plastic surgery for women who have permanent scars from abuse if they have been out of the relationship for a year and if they are willing to participate in counseling. Victims may call a toll free number (800-842-4546) to get a referral to a physician in their area (Feminist Majority Foundation [FMF], 1996a).

Sports and Battering

While O. J. Simpson may be the most famous athlete accused of battering, the following list is a sampling of other athletes who have been accused of violence against women: Courtney Alexander, Dante Bichette, Tim Barnett, Barry Bonds, Jaime Brandon, Jose Canseco, Duane Causwell, Michael Cooper, Wil Cordero, Bobby Cox, John Daly, Mark Fitzpatrick, Mark Gastineau, Vance Johnson, Sugar Ray Leonard, Moses Malone, Warren Moon, Marcus Moore, Robert Parrish, Gerald Perry, Christian Peters, Lawrence Phillips, Scottie Pippen, Olden Polynice, Darryl Strawberry, Mike Tyson, Kenny Walker, and Otis Wilson (Craft, No Date; Dabbs, 1998; Jefferson, 1997; Levy, 1996; Messner & Sabo, 1994; Nack & Munson, 1995). A recent example involves Rae Carruth, football player for the Carolina Panthers (Macenka, 1999). Carruth allegedly contracted with three other men to shoot his intimate partner, Cherica Adams. Adams, who was pregnant, delivered the baby 10 weeks premature before she died after being hospitalized for approximately one month.

There is a great deal of controversy regarding the relationship between organized sports and violence against women, including battering. While it is possible that sports figures merely receive more attention for committing these acts, at least some experts contend that athletes, especially football players, are more apt to commit violence. Two sources are most often cited to support this hypothesis. A feature story in the *Washington Post* reported that from January 1989 to mid-November 1994 there were 141 current or ex-football players (56 professional and 85 collegiate) charged with some form of violence against women

(Brubaker, 1994). These findings are supported by researchers at Northeastern University who studied reported cases of sexual assault at Division I universities. They found that student athletes made up only 3.3% of the total male student body, but that they accounted for 19% of the assaults (cited in Nack & Munson, 1995). There are several possible explanations that support the link between sports and violence against women. First, players who use violence on the field may use violence in other situations including interpersonal relationships. The rhetoric of the sport has included responses to questions about losing a football game as inappropriate as "I'm going to go home . . . and beat my wife" (cited in Harvard Law Review, 1996, p. 1). Second, men and boys construct a masculine identity through competitive sports; it provides a "legitimate" outlet for violence and aggression (Dunning, 1986; Hargreaves, 1986; Messner, 1990, 1992; Miller, 1997). The vernacular use of the expression "locker room talk" indicates that we, as a society, acknowledge the hyper masculine nature of this environment as a place where men can boast of their sexual conquests. In fact, misogynist attitudes are often central to sports; men are cautioned not to throw like girls and are called sissies and other derogatory names if they fail to compete aggressively. This attitude was evident when one Los Angeles high school football coach painted vaginas on the tackling dummies to motivate his players' performance (Dabbs, 1998, p. 171). Third, athletes may have more opportunity to commit crimes against women. At least one professional football player has argued that these athletes attend more functions, are around more drinking, and have greater access to women (Dabbs, 1998). Finally, athletes may receive preferential treatment from disciplinary boards and the criminal justice system that reinforces the notion that they are different and entitled to special treatment.

Currently, only the National Football League (NFL) has a formal written policy that allows for disciplinary actions against players who commit battering or sexual assault. While the NFL will discipline athletes who use drugs or gamble, they appear to be reluctant to take action when players engage in violence against women (Miller, 1997). For example, Arizona Cardinals' player Lorenzo Lynch was jailed for assaulting his girlfriend. An assistant coach came to the jail to prepare Lynch for the game, stating "we want to get our best players on the field" (cited in Dabbs, 1998, p. 185).

Some experts contend that there is little incentive for organized sports to take pro-active responses (Dabbs, 1998). There is no evidence that violence against women impacts the game itself or that the public will refuse to support teams who allow batterers and rapists to play for them. However, there is evidence that suggests men who watch violent sports such as football may, themselves, become more violent (Nelson, 1994; White, Katz, & Scarborough, 1992). If so, organized sports would appear to have an obligation to address the problem. Furthermore, as the VAWO article in this section notes, sports figures and organizations have a tremendous ability to influence Americans given the status and visibility of sports figures. Even if athletes do not engage in any more violence than other men in society, there is a compelling need for sports organizations to take actions to deal with battering and other forms of violence against women.

Media

It is well accepted in mainstream criminology that the media provide distort-ing images of crime that magnify the risk of stranger violence (Bortner, 1984; Surette, 1992; Cavender & Bond-Maupin, 1993; Kappeler, Blumberg, & Potter, 2000). The social construction of crime in the media reassures all of us that there is nothing wrong with our society and that crime is committed by a few "rotten apples" (Tunnell, 1992, p. 299). Media coverage treats each incident as a separate, unique event. There is a tendency to ignore the larger social issues by focusing on the details of a specific incident. For example, the link between violent sports (such as football) and battering was rarely explored in the Simpson case despite the hours and hours of reporting and the need to present new "angles" to the cover-age. Cases with famous perpetrators often receive intense scrutiny but fade quickly from our collective memory. This type of coverage avoids examining the pervasive nature of battering as a social problem, the links between social institutions such as sports and battering, and the need for social structural responses to the problem.

Although there has been little scholarly study of the media and woman bat-tering (Berns, 1999), there is some indication that coverage tends to minimize violence against women. If the topic is addressed, it perpetuates stereotype (Meyers, 1997). For example, a study on reality programs such as *Cops* found that battered women are often portrayed as uncooperative victims and as masochists who derive some pleasure or gratification from their victimization (Carmody, 1998). In addition, these programs frequently present incidents involving mutual violence (about a third of the time) and emphasize the role of alcohol use. They also emphasize victims with minor, non-life threatening injuries that reinforces the perception that battering is nothing more than "lovers' quarrels." Similar findings are reported in a study on women's magazines. Berns (1999) reports that while the sheer number of articles published has increased from the 1970s to the 1990s, the content has not. These magazines portray battering as a private prob-lem and place responsibility on the victims to deal with it, most often through therapy or counseling. "There is no advice on how *society* can change to help the victim. Rather, the victim must overcome these obstacles" (Berns, 1999, p. 91).

In the past 20 to 30 in years, the media has helped to break the silence sur-rounding woman battering. Battering is represented in soap operas, movies, talk shows, magazines, "reality" programs, and news sources; however, many of these images reinforce stereotypes and increase feelings of powerlessness and fear among female viewers (Reid & Finchilescu, 1995). The VAWO article makes suggestions for responsible reporting, but the task will not be an easy one. While there is debate over whether the media creates impressions or whether they merely reflect the larger social structure, one thing is clear. The media has a tre-mendous amount of power to affect the social construction of any issue. Current media presentations appear to do little to challenge us to think more deeply or to pay attention to the social structural influences that contribute to battering.

Battering and the Workplace

The connection between battering and the workplace was significantly magnified with the passage of the 1996 Personal Responsibility and Work Opportunity Reconciliation Act. This Act abolished AFDC (Aid to Families with Dependent Children) and replaced it with the Temporary Assistance to Needy Families (TANF) program (Davies, 1996). Under AFDC, federal law required that families receive assistance if they met certain criteria; however, TANF now provides the state with block grants and the states are free to decide who is eligible for assistance. TANF does, however, place certain restrictions upon the states, including prohibiting funding for families who have had assistance for five years. States may exempt up to 20% of their caseload, and battering is one example of hardship that may make a recipient eligible for an exemption. Overall, funding by the federal government was reduced; therefore, it is likely that fewer families will receive funds and there is no guarantee that battered women will receive exemptions.

Welfare "reform" is of great concern to advocates for battered women because research suggests that a significant proportion of battered women are on welfare. Studies suggest that about half of welfare recipients have been battered at some point in their lives, and about 20 to 30% of them report recent abuse (Allard et al., cited in Lyon, 1999; Browne & Bassuk, 1997; Curcio, 1997; Lloyd, 1997; Raphael, cited in Lyon, 1999). Research, however, is less clear about the nature of the relationship between welfare and battering. For example, do battered women stay on welfare because their batterers keep them from working, or do battered women use welfare as a stopgap measure to provide financial assistance when they leave until they can secure employment? The studies on welfare suggest that both factors may be at work, but this complex relationship needs further investigation (Lyon, 1999). Research is critical so that welfare policies are not implemented in ways that trap battered women in abusive relationships with no hope of economic survival if they leave.

Domestic violence is increasingly becoming an issue of concern for employers. One study reports that almost 50% of all incidents of workplace violence experienced by women were committed by intimates (Warchol, 1998). Homicide is the leading cause of occupational death for women (Walstedt cited in Brownell, 1996). Battering also affects the workplace in a myriad of ways. Both victims and batterers may exhibit lateness, absenteeism, lost productivity, and substance abuse (Brownell, 1996). In addition, co-workers are affected when battering "spills over" from the home into the workplace. Batterers may find the workplace threatening because it may represent financial independence. Women who have left their batterers may be particularly vulnerable; work may be the only place he can find her.

The VAWO article demonstrates that employers can take a variety of actions to prevent, protect, and intervene (also see Brownell, 1996). Prevention strategies include educational programs and poster campaigns to raise consciousness about the issue. Protective strategies involve security protocols to make the workplace a safer place. For example, companies can devise policies to deal with victims who have protective orders. In addition, policies may need to be developed that allow victims to take time off for court appearances or to seek shelter without fear of losing their jobs. Intervention efforts can include offering short-term counseling and crisis intervention on site through employee assistance programs or through referrals to local agencies.

There is still much work to be done in this area. The public sector and nonprofit agencies, as well as corporations and unions, need to acknowledge how battering affects the workplace and begin to take action. It is not only principled to do so, it is fiscally responsible. Several large U.S. corporations have taken the lead on this issue. For example, Polaroid has developed comprehensive policies and protocols for management and workers guided by the principle that victims should be protected in the workplace and should not be re-victimized by losing their jobs (see Buel, 1998; Hardeman cited in Brownell, 1996). Supervisors and managers undergo extensive training, and supervisors are granted flexibility to help victims in ways that best fit the given situation. AETNA insurance also has taken a pro-active role implementing a planned security program and providing counseling through their employee assistance program.

The federal government, recently, also has begun to address battering in the workplace. In 1998 President Clinton directed the U.S. Office of Personnel Management (OPM) to prepare a handbook on domestic violence for all federal employees. It provides information that can be used to validate that an individual is in an abusive relationship and provides information about safety planning and community resources. It also discusses the ways in which victims can get assistance in the workplace, including notifying victims that they are eligible for a leave of absence (without pay) under the Family and Medical Leave Act. The manual also discusses how supervisors and co-workers can be supportive of victims, and it provides a plan for workplace education and awareness (OPM, 1999).

Corporations play an important role in terms of fundraising. As discussed previously, shelters historically have had limited to no state and federal funding. While the funding situation is improving somewhat in recent years, it still remains woefully inadequate. As a result, too few shelters exist nationwide and battered women frequently find that space is unavailable (Frisch & MacKenzie, 1991); women in rural areas often lack access altogether (Websdale, 1998). This same situation is true of other social services such as hotlines and counseling groups. For too long, shelters have functioned from a "bake sale" mentality, raising funds through charity auctions. While these funds clearly help, they are no substitute for corporate donations. Polaroid's CEO, Gary DiCamello, for example, was able to secure corporate sponsorship for every shelter in Massachusetts by involving about 60 other CEOs in the state (Buel, 1998; Hardeman cited in Brownell, 1996). In addition to donations, Polaroid also agreed to provide job training to 100 battered women a year (Buel, 1998). Liz Claiborne sponsors an annual charity shopping day and donates 10% of its profits to local agencies that assist battered women (Ettinger cited in Brownell, 1996). There is a pressing need for powerful and wealthy corporations to "take on" battering as one of their fundraising priorities. Ford, for example, has been very involved in the battle against breast cancer with its "Race for the Cure" activities. Imagine how many shelters could be funded if they were to provide a similar level of support for battered women.

Mental Health Community and Battering

The list of agencies and organizations discussed in the VAWO article is by no means exhaustive. For example, there is a need for the mental health community to become more involved. Social workers, psychologists, and counselors historically have been unaware of the extent of battering and have failed to recognize and treat both victims and perpetrators who are patients (Gondolf, 1992; Hansen, Harway, & Cervantes, 1991). These professionals have the power to assist both victims and perpetrators. It is important that they understand the dynamics of battering in order to avoid blaming victims or placing them in situations that may be dangerous (i.e., asking them to talk about battering in a counseling situation with the batterer present). It also is important that they understand the manipulative style evidenced by most perpetrators and inform themselves of appropriate treatment modalities.

Individual Action

In addition to getting involved at the community level, individual actions make a difference. At a minimum, friends can assist battered women by handing out safety plans and referral numbers for local social service agencies and shelters (Buel, 1988). A copy of a safety plan is attached at the end of this section. It helps victims think about what actions to take if they need to leave; it is a plan to help them stay alive.

If you know someone who is being abused, there are several things you can do.[2] Listen without judging and give her ample time to talk. Don't try to fix things for her or push her into actions she is not comfortable with taking. Reinforce your concern for her safety and the safety of any children; do not let her minimize the seriousness of the violence. Emphasize that there are social service agencies that can help her when she is ready to leave. Give her the national domestic violence hotline number (1-800-787-7233) or information about local services. Show her how to find information and support services on the Internet.[3] Be supportive of her and continue your relationship with her even if she does not leave; you may be her only support system. Tell her over and over again that she does not deserve to be abused and that it is not her fault. As Buel notes:

> When we asked hundreds of abuse victims in support groups what would be the most helpful message we could give when they were still with the batterer, they asked us to be patient and say at every opportunity: "You do not deserve to be abused." (1998, p. 109)

Affirmations such as these may be particularly powerful when they come from respected professionals or close friends and relatives. It also is something that costs nothing and that each of us can easily do.

There are many actions that require few resources other than commitment. For example, call the police if you hear or see battering occurring. Vote for politicians who support social, economic, and political equality of women as well as those who vote for programs that help battered women. Get information (brochures, posters, bumper stickers) from your local shelter (or make them) and post them in places where battered women may see them (especially in restrooms). Ask your physician, dentist, veterinarian, beautician, day care center, grocery store, and clergy to post information. Develop a web page for your local shelter or post links on your own page. Wear a purple ribbon in October (or all year long) to remind people that it is Domestic Violence Awareness month. Ask your minister or rabbi to give a sermon on battering. Join an organization or volunteer at your local shelter. As a former volunteer coordinator, I assure you that they can always use help even if you think you don't have any special skills to offer. Donate your used clothes and furniture to the local shelter. Donate money if you can. Write the president of your university and ask him/her why there are no programs on campus for battered women. Write an op-ed piece for the campus newspaper on battering and services (or the lack thereof) on campus. Eliminate violence from your life—refuse to spank your children, hit your partner, or engage in horseplay with loved ones. Refuse to watch violent movies and television shows. Eliminate violent language from your vocabulary (e.g., I'm so mad I could just slap you.) Speak out against battering and challenge people when you hear stereotypical remarks made about battered women. Speak out against sexism and gender role stereotypes; they reinforce belief systems that support woman battering. Let your boys cry, and raise your girls to be strong and independent.

All of us have the potential to be advocates for social change. Each of us can make a difference. On the surface, some actions may seem small and insignificant. However, a central argument of this book has been that battering is related to the social inequality of women in society and the conceptualization of the family as a private institution where wives are submissive to their husbands. As a result, any action taken to challenge hegemonic ideals about the family, gender, and the role of women in society is one small step toward eliminating battering as a major social problem. Peek through the pollution and take others with you to that mountaintop. Once you have viewed the smog, it is very difficult to live with it or to ignore it.

NOTES

[1] A recent article by Martin (1997) is a notable exception. It looks at the ways in which victim satisfaction in domestic violence cases is a relevant indicator of the success of any community policing program.

[2] Be careful that actions are not taken that could harm victims further. For example, leaving literature about shelters at a victim's house could endanger her safety. Make sure that any actions are acceptable with the victim and that you always stop to ask whether you could be endangering her safety.

[3] Also help her learn about Internet safety. If an abuser knows how to read the victim's computer's history or cache file, he can tell what sites she has visited recently. For

information on how to clear this information, visit: http://www.abanet.org/domviol/
internet.html. In addition, if the abuser has access to a victim's email account, he can
read incoming and outgoing mail. If he sends harassing email messages, they should be
saved as evidence.

REFERENCES

Alsdurf, J. (1985). Wife abuse and the church: The response of pastors. *Response, 8*(1), 9–11.

American Medical Association, Council on Scientific Affairs (1991). *Violence against women*
[Report Number Three]. Chicago: Author.

American Medical Association. (1992). Physicians and domestic violence: Ethical considerations. *Journal of the American Medical Association, 267,* 3190–3193.

Anspach, R. (1987). Prognostic conflict in life-and-death decisions. *Journal of Health and
Social Behavior, 28,* 215–231.

Anspach, R. (1988). The sociology of medical discourse: The language of case presentation. *Journal of Health and Social Behavior, 29,* 357–375.

Appleton, W. (1980). The battered women syndrome. *Annals of Emergency Medicine, 9,* 84–91.

Berk, R., Newton, P., & Berk, S. (1986). What a difference a day makes: An empirical study
of the impact of shelters for battered women. *Journal of Marriage and Family, 48,* 481–490.

Berns, N. (1999). "My problem and how I solved it": Domestic violence in women's magazines. *The Sociological Quarterly, 40,* 85–108.

Brendtro, M., & Bowker, L. (1989). Battered women: How can nurses help? *Issues in Mental
Health Nursing, 10,* 169–180.

Bowker, L., & Mauer, L. (1986). The effectiveness of counseling services utilized by battered women. *Women and Therapy, 5,* 65–82.

Bowker, L., & Mauer, L. (1987). The medical treatment of battered wives. *Women and
Health, 12,* 25–45.

Bortner, M. (1984). Media images and public attitudes toward crime and justice. In R.
Surrette (Ed.), *Justice and the media* (pp. 15–30). Springfield, IL: Charles C. Thomas.

Browne, A. (1992). Violence against women: Relevance for medical practitioners. *Journal of
the American Medical Association, 267,* 3184–3189.

Browne, A., & Bassuk, S. (1997). Intimate violence in the lives of homeless and poor
housed women: Prevalence and patterns in an ethnically diverse sample. *American
Journal of Orthopsychiatry, 67,* 261–278.

Brownell, P. (1996). Domestic violence in the workplace: An emergent issue. *Crisis Intervention, 3,* 129–141.

Brubaker, B. (1994, November 13). Violence in football extends off the field. *Washington
Post,* pp. A1, A24

Bullock, L., McFarlane, J., Bateman, L., & Miller, V. (1989). The prevalence and characteristics of battered women in a primary care setting. *The Nurse Practitioner, 14,* 47–52.

Campbell, J., McKenna, L., Torres, S., Sheridan, D., & Landenburger, K. (1993). Nursing
care of abused women. In J. Campbell & J. Humphreys (Eds.), *Nursing care of survivors
of family violence* (pp. 248–289). St. Louis: Mosby.

Carmody, D. (1998). Mixed messages: Images of domestic violence on "reality" television.
In M. Fishman & G. Cavender (Eds.), *Entertaining crime: Television reality programs* (pp.
159–174). Hawthorne, NY: Aldine De Gruyter.

Cavender, G., & Bond-Maupin, L. (1993). Fear and loathing on reality televisions: An
analysis of *America's Most Wanted* and *Unsolved Mysteries. Sociological Inquiry, 63,* 305–317.

Cordner, G. (1995). Community policing: Elements and effects. *Police Forum,* 5(3), 1–7.

Craft, N. (No date). Welcome to the ACLU Sports Hall of Shame! Retrieved September 19, 1996 from the World Wide Web: http://www.igc.apc.org/nemesis/ACLU/Sports-HallofShame/

Curcio, C. (1997). *The Passaic County study of AFDC recipients in a welfare to work program.* Passaic, NJ: Passaic County Board of Social Services.

Dabbs, E. (1998). Intentional fouls: Athletes and violence against women. *Columbia Journal of Law and Social Problems,* 31, 167–199.

Davies, J. (November 4, 1999). The new welfare law: Implications for battered women—Introduction to the law. Retrieved December 21, 1999 from the World Wide Web: http://www.vaw.umn.edu/FinalDocuments/welpoll.htm

Dobash, R., & Dobash, R. (1979). *Violence against wives: A case against the patriarchy.* New York: Free Press.

Dunning, E. (1986). Sport as a male preserve: Notes on the social sources of masculine identity and its transformations. *Theory, Culture, and Society,* 3, 79–90.

Eck, J., & Spelman, W. (1987). Who ya gonna call? The police as problem-busters. *Crime and Delinquence,* 33, 31–52.

Family Violence Prevention Fund (No Date). How to talk with women you think may be abused. Retrieved January 16, 2000 from the World Wide Web: http://www.fvpf.org/action/talk.html

Feminist Majority Foundation (1996a, June 4). Program helps women leave behind scars of abuse. Retrieved August 31, 1997 from the World Wide Web: http://www.feminist.org/news/newsbyte/june96/0604/html

Feminist Majority Foundation (1996b, July 12). Cities form strategies to combat domestic violence. Retrieved January 8, 1997 from the World Wide Web: http://www.feminist.org/news/newsbyte/july96/0712/html

Feminist Majority Foundation (1998a, February 13). Emergency cell phones dispensed to domestic violence victims. Retrieved September 5, 1999 from the World Wide Web: http://www.feminist.org/news/newsbyte/february98/0213/html

Feminist Majority Foundation (1998b, October 7). Abused women suffer physical, mental health problems. Retrieved February 20, 1999 from the World Wide Web: http://www.feminist.org/news/newsbyte/november98/0917/html

Feminist Majority Foundation (1998c, November 17). Free cell phones for domestic violence victims. Retrieved February 20, 1999 from the World Wide Web: http://www.feminist.org/news/newsbyte/november98/0917/html

Feminist Majority Foundation (1999, February 9). New protection for domestic violence survivors. Retrieved February 20, 1999 from the World Wide Web: http://www.feminist.org/news/newsbyte/february99/0209/html

Ferraro, K. & Pope, L. (1993). Irreconcilable differences: Battered women, police, and the law. In N. Hilton (Ed.), *Legal responses to wife assault: Current trends and evaluation* (pp. 96–123). Newbury Park, CA: Sage.

Ferris, L., & Tudiver, F. (1992). Family physicians' approach to wife abuse: A study of Ontario, Canada practices. *Family Medicine,* 24, 276–282.

Friedman, L., Samet, J., Roberts, M., Hudlin, M., & Hans, P. (1992). Inquiry about victimization experiences: A survey of patient preferences and physician practices. *Archives of Internal Medicine,* 152, 1186–1190.

Frisch, M., & MacKenzie, C. (1991). A comparison of formerly and chronically battered women on cognitive and situational dimensions. *Psychotherapy,* 28, 339–344.

Gaines, L., Kappeler, V., & Vaughn, J. (1999). *Policing in America* (3rd ed.). Cincinnati: Anderson.

Gamache, D., & Asmus, M. (1999). Enhancing networking among service providers: Elements of successful coordination strategies. In M. Shepard & E. Pence (Eds.), *Coordination community response to domestic violence: Lessons from Duluth and beyond* (pp. 25–40). Thousand Oaks, CA: Sage.

Gerbert, B., Johnston, K., Caspers, N., Bleecker, T., Woods, A., & Rosenbaum, A. (1996). Experiences of battered women in health care settings: A qualitative study. *Women and Health, 24,* 1–17.

Gin, N., Rucker, L., Frayne, S., Cygan, R., & Hubbell, F. (1991). Prevalence of domestic violence among patients in three ambulatory care internal medicine clinics. *Journal of General Internal Medicine, 6,* 317–322.

Goldberg, W., & Tomlanovich, M. (1984). Domestic violence victims in the emergency department: New findings. *Journal of Medicine and Philosophy, 12,* 205–217.

Gondolf, E. (1992). Discussion of violence in psychiatric evaluations. *Journal of Interpersonal Violence, 7,* 334–349.

Grine, R. (1994). Angels in marble: Problems in stimulating community involvement in community policing. *Crime and Delinquency, 40,* 437–468.

Hamberger, L., Saunders, D., & Hovey, M. (1992). Prevalence of domestic violence in community practice and rate of physician inquiry. *Family Medicine, 24,* 283–287.

Hansen, M., Harway, M., & Cervantes, N. (1991). Therapists' perceptions of severity in cases of family violence. *Victims and Violence, 6,* 225–235.

Hargreaves, J. (1982). *Sport, culture and ideology.* London: Routledge & Kegan Paul.

Harvard Law Review (1996). Out of bounds: Professional sports leagues and domestic violence. *Harvard Law Review, 109,* 1048–1065.

Helton, A., McFarlane, J., & Anderson, E. (1987). Battered and pregnant: A prevalence study. *American Journal of Public Health, 77,* 1337–1339.

Helton, A., & Snodgrass, F. (1987). Battering during pregnancy: Intervention strategies. *Birth, 14,* 142–147.

Hillard, P. (1985). Physical abuse in pregnancy. *Obstetrics and Gynecology, 66,* 185–190.

Hoff, L. (1990). *Battered women as survivors.* New York: Routledge.

Hoffman, J. (1992, February 16). When men hit women. *New York Times Magazine,* 1–3, 27, 64–66.

Levy, P. (1996, January 9). Studies find more violence by athletes. *Minneapolis Star Tribune,* p. A1.

Jefferson, A. (1997). The NFL and domestic violence: The commissioner's power to punish domestic abusers. *Seton Hall Journal of Sport Law, 7,* 343–370.

Jenkins, R., & Hutchinson, J. (1998). The public health model for violence prevention: A partnership in medicine and education. *Journal of Negro Education, 65,* 255–266.

Kappeler, V., Blumberg, M., & Potter, G. (2000). *The mythology of crime and criminal justice* (3rd ed.). Prospect Heights, IL: Waveland.

Kleinman, A. (1988). *The illness narratives: Suffering, healing, and the human condition.* New York: Basic.

Koss, M., Gidycz, C., & Wisniewski, N. (1987). The scope of rape: Incidence and prevalence of sexual aggression and victimization in a national sample of higher education students. *Journal of Consulting and Clinical Psychology, 55,* 162–170.

Kurtz, D. (1992). Battering and the criminal justice system: A feminist view. In E. Buzawa & C. Buzawa (Eds.), *Domestic violence: The changing criminal justice system response* (pp. 21–40). Westport, CT: Auburn House.

Kurz, D. (1987). Emergency department responses to battered women: Resistance to medicalization. *Social Problems, 34,* 69–81.

Littel, K., Malefyt, J., & Walker, A. (1998). *Addressing the justice system response to violence against women.* Washington, DC: STOP Violence Against Women Grants Office.

Lloyd, S. (1997). The effects of domestic violence on women's employment. *Law and Policy, 19,* 139–167.

Lyon, E. (1999). Poverty, welfare and battered women: What does the research tell us? Retrieved December 21, 1999 from the World Wide Web: http://www.vaw.umn.edu/FinalDocuments/welres.html

Macenka, J. (1999, December 6). Carruth posts bond; Panthers say he can't return. Retrieved December 6, 1999 from the World Wide Web: http://sports.yahoo.com/nfl/news/ap/19991206/ap-carruth-sho.html

Makepeace, J. (1989). Dating, living together, and courtship violence. In M. Pirog-Good & J. Stets (Eds.), *Violence in dating relationships* (pp. 94–107). New York: Praeger.

Malefyt, J., & Walker, A. (1998). *Assessing the justice system response to violence against women.* Washington, DC: STOP Violence Against Women Grants Office.

Martin, D. (1978). Battered women: Society's problem. In J. Chapman & M. Gates (Eds.), *The victimization of women* (pp. 111–141). Beverly Hills: Sage.

McDonald, P. (1989). Transition houses and the problem of family violence. In B. Pressman, G. Cameron, & M. Rothery (Eds.), *Interviewing with assaulted women: Current theory research and practice* (pp. 111–123). Hillsdale, NJ: Erlbaum.

McFarlane, J., Parker, B., Soeken, L., & Bullock, L. (1992). Assessing for abuse during pregnancy: Severity and frequency of injuries and associated entry into prenatal care. *Journal of the American Medical Association, 267,* 3176–3179.

McLeer, S., & Anwar, R. (1987). The role of the emergency physician in the prevention of domestic violence. *Annals of Emergency Medicine, 16,* 1155–1161.

McLeer, S., & Anwar, R. (1989). A study of battered women presenting in an emergency department. *American Journal of Public Health, 79,* 65–66.

Messner, M. A. (1992). *Power at play: Sports and the problem of masculinity.* Boston: Beacon Press.

Messner, M. A., & Sabo, D. F. (1990). *Sport, men and the gender order: Critical feminist perspectives.* Champaign, IL: Human Kinetics.

Messner, M. A., & Sabo, D. (1994). *Sex, violence & power in sports.* Freedom, CA: The Crossing Press.

Meyers, M. (1997). *News coverage of violence against women: Engendering blame.* Thousand Oaks, CA: Sage.

Miller, L. (1997). Study: Male athletes may be more likely to commit violent crimes against women. Retrieved November 12, 1999 from the World Wide Web: http://www.massmed.org/physicians/pubs/vs/sept97/public.html

Nack, W., & Munson, L. (1995, July 31). Sports' Dirty Secret. *Sports Illustrated,* pp. 62, 64–65.

Nelson, M. (1994). *The stronger women get, the more men love football.* New York: Avon.

Office of Personnel Management (March 1999). Responding to domestic violence: Where federal employees can find help. Retrieved December 21, 1999 from the World Wide Web: http://www.opm.gov/workplac/html/omestic.htm

Office for Victims of Crime (1998). *OVC fact sheet.* Washington, DC: U.S. Department of Justice.

Parker, B., McFarlane, J., Soeken, K., Torres, S., & Campbell, D. (1993). Physical and emotional abuse in pregnancy: A comparison of adult and teenage women. *Nursing Research, 42,* 173–178.

Pence, E. (1999). Some thoughts on philosophy. In M. Shepard & E. Pence (Eds.), *Coordination community response to domestic violence: Lessons from Duluth and beyond* (pp. 25–40). Thousand Oaks, CA: Sage.

Pence, E., & McDonnell, C. (1999). Developing policies and protocols. In M. Shepard & E. Pence (Eds.), *Coordination community response to domestic violence: Lessons from Duluth and beyond* (pp. 25–40). Thousand Oaks, CA: Sage.

Pence, E., & Shepard, M. (1988). Integrating feminist theory and practice: The challenge of the battered women's movement. In K. Yllo & M. Bograd (Eds.), *Feminist perspectives on wife abuse* (pp. 282–298). Beverly Hills, CA: Sage.

Pence, E., & Shepard, M. (1999). An introduction: Developing a coordinated community response. In M. Shepard & E. Pence (Eds.), *Coordinating community responses to domestic violence: Lessons from Duluth and beyond* (pp. 3–24). Thousand Oaks, CA: Sage.

Rand, M., & Strom, K. (1997). *Violence-related injuries treated in hospital emergency departments.* Washington, DC: Bureau of Justice Statistics.

Randall, T. (1990). Domestic violence intervention calls for more than treating injuries. *Journal of the American Medical Association, 264,* 939–940.

Roberts, A., & Roberts, B. (1990). A comprehensive model for crisis intervention with battered women and their children. In A. Roberts (Ed.), *Intervention handbook: Assessment, treatment and research* (pp. 106–123). Belmont, CA: Wadsworth.

Roche, S., & Sadoske, P. (1996). Social action for battered women. In A. Roberts (Ed.), *Helping battered women: New perspectives and remedies* (pp. 13–30). New York: Oxford.

Schornstein, S. (1997). *Domestic violence and health care.* Thousand Oaks, CA: Sage.

Shepard, M., & Pence, E. (Eds.). (1999). *Coordinating community responses to domestic violence: Lessons from Duluth and beyond.* Thousand Oaks, CA: Sage.

Stark, E., Flitcraft, A., & Frazier, W. (1979). Medicine and patriarchal violence: The social construction of a private event. *International Journal of Health Services, 6,* 461–492.

Stets, J., & Henderson, D. (1991). Contextual factors surrounding conflict resolution while dating: Results from a national study. *Family Relations, 40,* 29–36.

Tunnell, K. (1992). Film at eleven: Recent developments in the commodification of crime. *Sociological Spectrum, 12,* 293–313.

Walker, L. (1979). *The battered woman.* New York: Harper & Row.

Warchol, G. (1998). *Workplace violence, 1992–96.* Washington, DC: Bureau of Justice Statistics.

Warshaw, C. (1993). Limitations of the medical model in the care of battered women. In P. Bart & E. Moran (Eds.), *Violence against women: The bloody footprints* (pp. 134–146). Newbury Park, CA: Sage.

Websdale, N. (1995). An ethnographic assessment of the policing of domestic violence in rural Eastern Kentucky. *Social Justice, 22,* 102–122.

Websdale, N. (1998). *Rural woman battering and the justice system: An ethnography.* Thousand Oaks, CA: Sage.

White, G., Katz, J., & Scarborough, K. (1992). The impact of professional football games upon violent assaults on women. *Violence and Victims, 7,* 157–171.

White, J., & Koss, M. (1991). Courtship violence: Incidence in a national sample of higher education students. *Violence and Victims, 6,* 247–256.

Wilson, J. (1994). Guidelines for the care of abused women: The least we can do. *Home Healthcare Nurse, 12,* 47–53.

Witwer, M., & Crawford, C. (1995). *A coordinated approach to reducing family violence: Conference highlights.* Washington, DC: National Institute of Justice & American Medical Association.

Yllo, K., & Straus, M. (1981). Interpersonal violence among married and cohabiting couples. *Family Relations, 30,* 339–347.

Zorza, J. (1994). Woman battering: High costs and the state of the law. *Clearinghouse Review, 28,* 383–395.

A Community Checklist
Important Steps To End Violence Against Women
"... what can we do about it?"

Advisory Council on Violence Against Women

On July 13, 1995 we created the Advisory Council on Violence Against Women to help promote greater awareness of the problem of violence against women and its victims, to help devise solutions to the problem, and to advise the federal government on implementing the 1994 Violence Against Women Act. From police to doctors to clergy, the Advisory Council's 47 members draw on the many different professions that can help fight violence against women and assist victims.

Members of the Advisory Council have created working groups that focus on different segments of the community and what they might do to address the problem of violence against women. At the third meeting of the Advisory Council, held on July 18, 1996, each subgroup created a checklist of important steps communities can take to end violence against women. We are grateful for their input and for the commitment of each member to this issue.

This checklist identifies actions that can be taken by the religious community, colleges and universities, law enforcement, health care professionals, the sports industry, through the media, and in the workplace. We also recognize that there are many other facets of the community that can have a significant effect in this effort. The initial distribution of this booklet is taking place during October 1996 in recognition of National Domestic Violence Awareness Month.

This is not intended to be an exhaustive list but is meant to offer some straightforward, practical suggestions that we believe can make a difference in communities across the country. By coming together as a community, exchang-

http://www.usdoj.gov/vawo/checklist.htm

ing ideas, and coordinating efforts, we can begin to end this violence which
destroys so many American lives.

Janet Reno
Donna E. Shalala

Religious Community

The religious community provides a safe haven for women and families in need. In addi-
tion, it exhorts society to share compassion and comfort with those afflicted by the tragedy of
domestic violence. Leaders of the religious community have identified actions to share with the
nation to create a unified response to violence against women.

- Become a Safe Place. Make your church, temple, mosque or synagogue a
  safe place where victims of domestic violence can come for help. Display
  brochures and posters which include the telephone number of the domestic violence and sexual assault programs in your area. Publicize the
  National Domestic Violence Hotline number, 1-800-799-SAFE(7233) or 1-
  800-787-3224(TDD).

- Educate the Congregation. Provide ways for members of the congregation
  to learn as much as they can about domestic and sexual violence. Routinely include information in monthly newsletters, on bulletin boards,
  and in marriage preparation classes. Sponsor educational seminars on violence against women in your congregation.

- Speak Out. Speak out about domestic violence and sexual assault from
  the pulpit. As a faith leader, you can have a powerful impact on peoples'
  attitudes and beliefs.

- Lead by Example. Volunteer. Volunteer to serve on the board of directors
  at the local domestic violence/sexual assault program or attend a training
  to become a crisis volunteer.

- Offer Space. Offer meeting space for educational seminars or weekly support groups or serve as a supervised visitation site when parents need to
  visit safely their children.

- Partner with Existing Resources. Include your local domestic violence or
  sexual assault program in donations and community service projects.
  Adopt a shelter for which your church, temple, mosque or synagogue provides material support, or provide similar support to families as they
  rebuild their lives following a shelter stay.

- Prepare to be a Resource. Do the theological and scriptural homework
  necessary to better understand and respond to family violence and
  receive training from professionals in the fields of sexual and domestic
  violence.

- Intervene. If you suspect violence is occurring in a relationship, speak to
  each member of the couple separately. Help the victim plan for safety. Let

both individuals know of the community resources available to assist them. Do not attempt couples counseling.

- Support Professional Training. Encourage and support training and education for clergy and lay leaders, hospital chaplains, and seminary students to increase awareness about sexual and domestic violence.

- Address Internal Issues. Encourage continued efforts by religious institutions to address allegations of abuse by religious leaders to insure that religious leaders are a safe resource for victims and their children.

[Adapted in part from the Nebraska Domestic Violence and Sexual Assault Coalition and the Center for the Prevention of Sexual and Domestic Violence, Seattle, WA. Used with permission.]

COLLEGES & UNIVERSITIES

Colleges and universities offer important opportunities to educate young men and women about violence against women. Experiences on campuses will be carried forth to everyday life and will influence future actions. Therefore, every effort to inform students may mean one less victim abused or one less crime committed. Leaders in higher education have identified the following strategies to assist educators across the country in reaching out to students and communities and to make campuses safe places for women.

- Make Campus a Safe Place. Evaluate the safety and security of the campus environment and the quality and availability of resources to insure safety. For example, establish campus escort services through campus security and student government programs.

- Increase Awareness. Educate your students, faculty, and staff about the problem of sexual assault and dating violence on college campuses. Provide adequate training on the signs that often accompany abuse, on victims' legal rights and on available resources.

- Target Special Groups. Identify target groups (e.g. new students, fraternities and sororities, athletes, etc.) on your campus and develop specialized training and resources for them.

- Coordinate Resources. Identify resources addressing violence against women on your campus and bring together local community and university service providers.

- Encourage Reporting of Violence. Through orientation and awareness programs on campus, encourage students, faculty and staff to report incidents of violence. Develop effective linkages between campus and community law enforcement personnel.

- Provide Services to the Campus Community. Support a coordinated community response to violence against women; ensure that services are comprehensive and appropriate for the entire campus community.

- Develop an Administration Response to Violence on Campus. Establish protocols to manage complaints of violence on your campus with care for the victim as the first priority. Your protocol should include a clearly defined process for providing assistance to victims and holding the perpetrators accountable.

- Review and Revise the Student Code of Conduct and Policies. Review your campus policies and disciplinary sanctions to assess that violence against women is treated as seriously as other crimes, with equally severe punishments.

- Provide A Voice for Women on Campus. Provide support for students and faculty to establish victim advocacy groups on campus.

- Get the Message Out to the Campus Community. Speak out against domestic violence and sexual assault in your position of leadership on campus. Communicate expectations about appropriate conduct, include them in student policy statements. Post information about available resources in dining halls, health facilities, dormitories, locker rooms, and other places students are likely to see it.

LAW ENFORCEMENT

Across the country, law enforcement is developing innovative and effective strategies to prevent and prosecute violence against women more effectively. Law enforcement leaders have identified several of these strategies that, if used consistently, may go a long way toward reducing incidents of violence against women.

- Create a Community Roundtable. Convene a community roundtable bringing together police, prosecutors, judges, child protection agencies, survivors, religious leaders, health professionals, business leaders, educators, defense attorneys and victim advocate groups, and meet regularly. Create specific plans for needed change, and develop policies among law enforcement, prosecutors, and others that will result in coordinated, consistent responses to domestic violence.

- Record Domestic Violence. To help understand and respond to the dimensions of violence against women, develop and require the use of a uniform domestic violence reporting form. It should include an investigative checklist for use in all domestic violence incidents or responses.

- Continue to Educate. Create informational brochures on domestic violence and sexual assault, which include safety plans and a list of referral services, for distribution in all court houses, police stations, and prosecutors' offices AND in non-legal settings such as grocery stores, libraries, laundromats, schools, and health centers.

- Provide Clear Guidance on Responding to Domestic Violence. Write new or adapt existing protocol policies for police, courts, and prosecutors regarding domestic violence and sexual assault incidents, and train all employees to follow them. Policies should specify that domestic violence and sexual assault cases must be treated with the highest priority, regardless of the severity of the offense charged or injuries inflicted.

- Ensure Law Enforcement is Well-Informed. Designate at least one staff member to serve as your agency's domestic violence and sexual assault contact, with responsibility for keeping current on legal developments, training resources, availability of services and grant funds. Wherever possible, create a unit of employees with special expertise to handle domestic violence and sexual assault cases in prosecutor's offices, police departments, and probation/parole agencies, and ensure that these employees are well trained regarding their responsibilities.

- Reach Out to Front Lines. Identify and meet with staff and residents from local battered women's shelters and rape crisis centers to discuss their perceptions of current needs from the law enforcement community. Solicit suggestions for improving the law enforcement response to these crimes.

- Improve Enforcement by Implementing a Registry of Restraining Orders and a Uniform Order for Protection. Implement a statewide registry of restraining orders designed to provide accurate, up-to-date, and easily accessible information on current and prior restraining orders for use by law enforcement and judicial personnel. Develop a uniform statewide protection order for more effective and efficient enforcement.

- Support and Pursue Legislative Initiatives. Develop and support legislative initiatives to address issues regarding domestic violence and sexual assault including: a) stalking, b) death review teams, c) sentencing guidelines, d) indefinite restraining orders, and e) batterers intervention programs.

- Conduct Training. Conduct on-going multi-disciplinary domestic violence and sexual assault training for police, prosecutors, judges, advocates, defenders, service providers, child protection workers, educators and others. Training should include the victim's perspective and an emphasis on safety planning.

- Structure Courts to Respond to Domestic Violence/Create Specialized Domestic Violence Courts. Develop specialized courts that deal exclusively with domestic violence cases in a coordinated, comprehensive manner, where community and court resources can be utilized together to address domestic violence effectively. At a minimum, all court personnel involved with domestic violence cases, including judges, prosecutors, public defenders, probation officers, and corrections and parole officers should receive relevant and practical domestic violence training and have an understanding of the dynamics of domestic violence.

HEALTH CARE PROFESSIONALS

Health care professionals are in the critical position of providing services to victims of violence as the first contact point for many of these victims. It is crucial that health care professionals recognize their potential to intervene appropriately. Immediate recognition of the problem and the provision of medical care and referrals to appropriate resources within the community can make all the difference. Leaders in the field have identified the following strategies to make interventions by health care professionals more effective.

- Incorporate Training into Curricula. Support the incorporation of domestic violence and sexual assault training in medical, nursing, and allied health care professional education curricula.

- Make Resources Available to Patients. Make resource materials available in waiting rooms and restrooms. Include the National Domestic Violence Hotline number 1-800-799-SAFE(7233) or 1-800-787-3224(TDD).

- Support Incorporation of Protocols into Accreditation Process. Support efforts to ensure that domestic violence and sexual assault protocols are addressed through the National Commission for Quality Assurance and the Joint Commission on Accreditation of Hospitals.

- Encourage Continuing Education on Violence against Women Issues. Encourage your state licensing boards and various specialty groups to encourage physicians and nurses to allocate continuing medical education (CME) hours to violence against women-related issues for re-licensure requirements.

- Involve Medical Organizations and Societies in Increasing Awareness. Collaborate with health care professional organizations and societies in your area to increase medical school and health care professional involvement in addressing violence against women.

- Feature Violence Against Women on Meeting Agendas. Arrange presentations and symposiums on violence against women at various health care specialty annual, regional and local meetings.

- Highlight Commitment to Violence Against Women Issues. Give awards, citations, and certificates to exceptional organizations and individuals for their continued commitment to addressing violence against women.

- Develop a Standard Intake Form. Develop a standardized intake assessment form for health care professionals who interact with victims of domestic or sexual violence. This assessment form would ensure that certain information regarding these incidents is identified and proper resources are utilized.

- Ensure Employee Assistance Programs are Responsive to Victims of Domestic Violence. Determine whether your health care facility's employee assistance program (EAP) includes domestic violence services or referrals. If it does not, speak with your human resources director or the appropriate manager about the possibility of expanding the program to address the needs of employees facing violence in their homes. All EAP personnel should receive domestic violence training and have an understanding of the dynamics of domestic violence.

- Volunteer. Provide a health care series on a volunteer basis to community organizations that serve victims of domestic and sexual violence.

SPORTS

Today, more than ever, our sports players and organizations have an enormous capacity to influence the minds and behaviors of Americans, both young and old. The reason is simple. For many Americans, professional, college and olympic athletes are today's heroes. We must utilize this outlet to send a positive message to all Americans about preventing domestic violence and sexual assault. Following are a number of ways communities can work with the local sports industry to help stop the violence.

- Bring Sports Leagues Together in a Common Cause. Encourage local sports teams to come together in a joint effort to combat violence against women through joint awareness campaigns and public appearances.
- Create Strict Disciplinary Policies. Encourage the creation of disciplinary policies for players on domestic violence and violence against women similar to drug policies. These policies should include stiff sanctions and penalties for committing domestic violence and sexual assault.
- Push for PSAs During Broadcast of Sporting Events. Write or call sports leagues in support PSAs about violence against women during the broadcast of major sporting events, including NCAA games.
- Promote the Distribution of Educational Materials. Promote the distribution of educational materials from local shelters and programs to players by offering the materials to the teams.
- Involve Local Sports Heroes in Community Activities. Involve local sports heroes in rallies and events which bring attention to the problem of violence against women.
- Reach Out to Potential Sponsors. If there are businesses in the area that are known for making or selling sporting equipment or clothing, approach them for sponsorship of community awareness activities.

MEDIA

The media industry represents much more than television and film stars. It is the most influential source of information for millions of Americans. Before we can change people's attitudes about violence against women and prevent violent behavior, we must not only change the way violence is portrayed in the media, but also educate members of the media who report on domestic violence and sexual assault crime. Leaders in the media industry have identified ways in which communities can work with their local media to encourage responsible reporting of violence against women.

- Use the Power of Communication. Contact local television, radio, and newspapers urging thoughtful and accurate coverage of violence against women, and the provision of educational messages about the problem when possible.

- Urge Action Through the Local Paper. Through community organizations, distribute model op-ed piece and letters to the editor and urge community action for placement of these pieces.

- Link Media with Experts. Provide media outlets with a list of well-known experts available for interviews, as well as a packet of materials with information on a variety of related subject areas, such as local shelters and programs.

- Organize Public Events. Plan a public event, such as a community education forum on violence against women, and solicit local media coverage.

- Encourage Employee Awareness. Encourage the development of domestic violence awareness programs for employees of media outlets.

- Build a Bridge between Media and Law Enforcement. Urge police chiefs and commissioners to go on air locally to discuss domestic violence and violence against women.

- Provide a Forum for Community Leaders. Encourage community leaders to speak to media about issues of violence against women.

- Publicize Local Resources During Reporting. Encourage local media to include the National Domestic Violence Hotline number, 1-800-799-SAFE (7233) or 1-800-787-3224 (TDD), during reporting on incidents of domestic violence.

THE WORKPLACE

Men and women spend more and more of their daily lives in the workplace. Domestic violence is a workplace issue which affects the safety, health, and productivity of America's workers. Business and labor leaders have identified several strategies that can be used to create safer and more supportive workplaces.

- Start with the Top and Get Corporate Leadership on Board. Encourage CEOs or the management team to establish a workplace which is intolerant of domestic violence and aids a victim in obtaining assistance and protection.

- Establish Employee Policies that Meet the Needs of Victims of Domestic Violence. Work with your management and unions to develop and negotiate paid leave and benefit policies which recognize and are responsive to the particular needs of your employees who are victims of domestic violence.

- Ensure Employee Assistance Programs are Responsive to Victims of Domestic Violence. Determine whether your company's employee assistance program (EAP) includes domestic violence services or referrals. If it does not, speak with your human resources director or the appropriate manager about the possibility of expanding the program to address the needs of employees facing violence in their homes. All EAP personnel should receive domestic violence training and have an understanding of the dynamics of domestic violence.

- Provide Management with the Tools to Respond to Domestic Violence. Establish a training program for all supervisors and managers at your workplace to give them guidance on how to respond when an employee is a victim or perpetrator of domestic violence.

- Educate Employees About Domestic Violence. Sponsor a workshop or series of workshops at your workplace on domestic violence. Invite a domestic violence survivor to speak about her experiences and to discuss the impact of violence on her life and her work.

- Share Materials About Domestic Violence. Distribute educational materials about domestic violence to all employees in your workplace and display posters and brochures in public places which explain the issue. Send the message that there is no excuse for domestic violence. Make victim safety information available in private places such as restrooms or in paycheck envelopes. All information should include the National Domestic Violence Hotline number, 1-800-799-SAFE(7233) or 1-800-787-3224(TDD).

- Increase Safety At the Workplace. Find out whether security guards at your workplace have been trained to handle the special safety needs of battered women, who may be stalked at work. If they have not, speak with the appropriate manager to arrange training and help security personnel develop safety procedures.

- Coordinate with Local Law Enforcement. Arrange a meeting between security personnel at your workplace and local law enforcement agencies to facilitate appropriate information sharing and the development of collaborative working relationships.

- Join in Local Community Efforts to Combat Domestic Violence. Conduct a drive in your workplace to collect items for local domestic violence shelters. Be sure to contact the programs first to find out what they want, but common needs for shelters are toys, clothing, furniture, office equipment, office supplies and food. Alternatively, make a contribution of company products.

- Donate Time and Resources. Adopt a local domestic violence shelter by collecting money from coworkers for a joint donation or getting a group of coworkers to make a commitment of volunteer hours. For example, raise money to pay for a new roof for a shelter; organize groups of volunteers to paint a shelter, do yard work around the shelter, assist with a special event, or provide other specialized skills.

Write Out a Safety Plan

Writing out a safety plan helps you to evaluate the risks and benefits of different options and identify ways to reduce risks. The checklist that follows can help you in your planning by pointing out issues you may need to address. There's no right or wrong way to develop a safety plan. Use what applies. Add to it. Change it to reflect your particular situation. Make it your own, then review it regularly and make changes as needed. You don't have to figure it all out on your own. Ask your Employee Assistance Program counselor at work or a domestic violence advocate for help.

Remember that abusive partners tend to escalate violence when their partners try to separate. With this in mind, make special efforts to keep your written safety plan away from your partner. If you're unable to find a safe place to keep a written safety plan—where your partner will not find it—ask a friend to keep a copy for you. If you're working with your local domestic violence program, you can ask them to keep a copy of your plan for you. Whether it's safe to write down your plan or not, it's still important to make one. Ideally, you will have your safety options committed to memory.

http://www.opm.gov/workplac/html/domestic

Personalized Safety Plan
BEING READY FOR A CRISIS

Planning to leave

- If I decide to leave, I will _____. (Practice how to get out safely. What doors, windows, elevators, stairwells or fire escapes would you use?)
- I can keep my purse and car keys ready and put them _____ in order to leave quickly.
- I will leave money and an extra set of keys with _____ so I can leave quickly.
- I will keep copies of important documents or keys at _____.
- If I have to leave my home, I will go _____.
- If I cannot go to the above location, I can go_____.
- The domestic violence hotline number is _____. I can call it if I need shelter.
- If it's not safe to talk openly, I will use _____ as the code word/signal to my children that we are going to go, or to my family or friends that we are coming.
- I can leave extra clothes with _____.

I can use my judgment

- When I expect my partner and I are going to argue, I will try to move to a space that is lowest risk, such as _____. (Try to avoid arguments in the bathroom, garage, kitchen, near weapons, or in rooms without an outside exit.)
- I will use my judgment and intuition. If the situation is very serious, I can give my partner what he wants to try and calm him down. I have to protect myself until I/we are out of danger.
- I can also teach some of these strategies to some/all of my children, as appropriate.
- I will keep important numbers and change for phone calls with me at all times. I know that my partner can learn who I've been talking to by looking at phone bills, so I can see if friends will let me use their phones and/or their phone credit cards.
- I will check with _____ and _____ to see who would be able to let me stay with them or lend me money, if I need it.
- I can increase my independence by opening a bank account and getting credit cards in my own name; taking classes or getting job skills; getting copies of all the important papers and documents I might need and keeping them with _____.
- Other things I can do to increase my independence include:_____
  _____.

- I can rehearse my escape plan and, if appropriate, practice it with my children.
- If I have a joint bank account with my partner, I can make arrangements to ensure I will have access to money.

I can get help

- I can tell _____ about the violence and request that they call the police if they hear noises coming from my house.
- I can teach my children how to use the telephone to contact the police and the fire department. I will make sure they know the address.
- If I have a programmable phone, I can program emergency numbers and teach my children how to use the auto dial.
- I will use _____ as my code word with my children or my friends so they will call for help.

After I Leave

- I can enhance the locks on my doors and windows.
- I can replace wooden doors with steel/metal doors.
- I can install security systems including additional locks, window bars, poles to wedge against doors, an electronic system, etc.
- I can purchase rope ladders to be used for escape from second floor windows.
- I can install smoke detectors and put fire extinguishers on each floor in my home.
- I will teach my children how to use the phone to make a collect call to me if they are concerned about their safety.
- I can tell people who take care of my children which people have permission to pick them up and make sure they know how to recognize those people.
- I will give the people who take care of my children copies of custody and protective orders, and emergency numbers.

At Work and in Public

- I can inform security, my supervisor and/or the Employee Assistance Program about my situation. Phone numbers to have at work are _____.
- I can ask _____to screen my calls at work or have my phone number changed.
- When leaving work, I can _____.
- When traveling to and from work, if there's trouble, I can _____.
- I can ask for a flexible schedule.
- I can ask for a parking space closer to the building.

- I can ask to move my workspace to a safer location.
- I can ask security to escort me to and from my car.
- I can change my patterns to avoid places where my partner might find me, such as _____, (stores, banks, laundromats).
- I can tell _____ and _____ that I am no longer with my partner and ask them to call the police if they believe my children or I are in danger.
- I can explore the option of telecommuting with my supervisor and human resources office.

With an Order of Protection

- I will keep my protection order _____, where I know it will be safe.
- I will give copies of my protection order to police departments in the community in which I live and those where I visit friends and family.
- I will give copies to my employer, my religious advisor, my closest friend, my children's school and day care center, and _____.
- If my partner destroys my protection order or if I lose it, I can get another copy from the court that issued it.
- If my partner violates the order, I can call the police and report a violation, contact my attorney, call my advocate, and/or advise the court of the violation.
- I can call a domestic violence program if I have questions about how to enforce an order or if I have problems getting it enforced.

Items to Take When Leaving

- Identification for myself
- Children's birth certificates
- My birth certificate
- Social Security cards
- School/vaccination records
- Money, checkbook, bank books, cash cards
- Credit cards
- Medication/prescription cards
- Keys—house, car, office
- Driver's license/car registration
- Insurance papers
- Public Assistance ID/Medicaid Cards
- Passports, work permits
- Divorce or separation papers

- Lease, rental agreement, or house deed
- Car/mortgage payment book
- Children's toys, security blankets, stuffed animals
- Sentimental items, photos
- My Personalized Safety Plan

My Emotional Health

- If I am feeling down, lonely, or confused, I can call _____ or the domestic violence hotline _____.
- I can take care of my physical health by getting a checkup with my doctor, gynecologist, and dentist. If I don't have a doctor, I will call the local clinic or _____ to get one.
- If I have left my partner and am considering returning, I will call _____ or spend time with _____ before I make a decision.
- I will remind myself daily of my best qualities. They are:_____ _____
- I can attend support groups, workshops, or classes at the local domestic violence program or _____ in order to build a support system, learn skills or get information.
- I will look at how and when I drink alcohol. If I am going to drink, I will do it in a place where people are committed to my safety.
- I can explore information available on the Web sites listed in the back of this guide.
- Other things I can do to feel stronger are: _____

Remember, there are many obstacles to achieving safety or to ending a relationship with a violent partner, and the choices women confront are not risk-free.

Decisions that are beneficial in the long-run, such as leaving the abuser or obtaining a protective order, can actually increase immediate danger for the woman and her children. Safety planning is the process of evaluating the risks and benefits of different options and identifying ways to reduce risks.

INDEX